for my dearest dear:
we lived with loads of loving . . .
good years together

you found me for life
I found you forever more
living life as one

CONTENTS

PROLOGUE

In *Wandering the World with George*, I tell the story of my travels with my husband, George Hennings, an environmentalist and a science professor at Kean University in New Jersey from 1960 to 1987. This book is my account of our forty-eight years of travel—my memories of those years together. In some respects it is also a "sort of" biography of my husband, because travel was a major part of his life after our marriage in 1968 and even before.

I started my memoir during the COVID-19 pandemic of 2020, when I could not travel and was sheltering at home. George had passed in 2016, so I was truly home alone. One morning early in the pandemic, I awoke with a thought-provoking idea: If I could no longer get on a plane or ship, I could travel in my mind, mentally returning to places we had visited.

From then on, each morning, I would wake up and focus on one trip or place that George and I had enjoyed together. I would think about the high points and the low points. I would run pictures through my mind and remember a wonderful time we had shared on the road or on the sea.

For nearly fifty years, we had traveled the world by ship, plane, car, and bus. We had walked the streets of some of the greatest and most beautiful cities on earth—Beijing, Istanbul, Dubai, Cairo, Sydney, Paris, Rio, Cape Town, London, Saint Petersburg, Bangkok, Oslo, Singapore, Shanghai, Mumbai, and so many more.

Together, we had visited Machu Picchu, the Great Wall of China, Easter Island, Borobudur, Angkor Wat, the Great Pyramid of Giza, the Taj Mahal, Notre Dame, St. Peter's Basilica, and numerous other UNESCO World Heritage Sites. We had transited the Panama, the Suez, and the Corinth canals.

Side by side, we had stood before the geysers and waterfalls of Iceland, trod the moonscape of Namibia, seen Victoria water lilies in their natural habitat on the Amazon, taken a safari in Kenya, sailed the icy waters of Antarctica, walked among the penguins on the Falklands, and gone swimming in the warm waters of Bali and Bora Bora.

As I began to revisit our travels, I made a decision that literally changed my life for the next year. I decided I would turn my memories into this book—*Wandering the World with George*.

The focus of my memoir would be on the natural wonders we had seen. It would be on the wonders humankind has created and that George and I had been fortunate enough to visit. The focus, too, would be on the interesting and compassionate peoples we had met on our travels. I would write especially about the extraordinary things we had done, our impressions of what we had seen, and the happiest and saddest moments of our trips.

I decided that I would also share general travel hints, including suggestions about how to stay safe, and some musings about life lessons learned through traveling the world.

This would be the story I would tell. Indeed, *Wandering the World with George* would be a *story*, our story—the tale of our forty-eight-year love affair with the world, with travel, and with each other.

And so, at a time when visiting the world's marvels in person was not an option, I began to write my travel memoir.

To anyone thinking of walking the paths we walked or sailing the seas we sailed, I quote the words of Jawaharlal Nehru, former prime minister of India: "We live in a wonderful world that is full of beauty, charm and adventure. There is no end to the adventures we can have if only we seek them with our eyes open."

Happy travels!

Midnight aboard the M S Sagafjord at the North Cape, June 1978.

Part

1

OPENING WINDOWS WIDE
1968-2003

Chapter One
STARTING OUR STORY

The moon was full above the watering hole. It sent a luminous glow over the red soil that surrounded the pool and made the night feel ethereal to George and me as we sat on the screened verandah of our bungalow in Tsavo East National Park, Kenya. We said not a word to one another as we watched a family of elephants lumber toward the watering hole and then slowly wade into it. There were majestic adults in the group and youngsters who followed closely behind their mothers. We sat for over an hour as the ceiling fan whirred overhead and the elephants trumpeted back and forth. The year was 2009, and George and I were on a world cruise that had docked the day before in Mombasa.

Life cannot get better than this. It was in search of such magical moments that George and I traveled the world for almost fifty years.

When the elephants finally plodded out of the water and disappeared into the darkness of night, we went inside our bungalow. We snuggled in our bed under the mosquito netting that covered it and reminisced about similar moments we had experienced on a prior safari in Kenya.

In June 1979, George and I had taken a land tour with a group of students from Kean University where we both were teaching. We remembered sitting around a campfire, listening to hyenas crying in the distance while a park ranger told us stories about the animals and peoples of Kenya. We remembered being escorted to our tented cabin by a spear-carrying Maasai warrior. And we remembered lying in bed that same night and hearing cape buffalo outside, scratching at the earth.

We recalled a visit during that trip to the camp of wildlife researcher Cynthia Moss, where we listened to her talk about relationships within elephant family groups. As we sat on the ground at her feet, the elephant family she had been studying for years paraded into camp. The researcher pointed out the matriarch, her offspring, her sisters, and their children. She identified them by names she had given them and explained how she used physical characteristics such as notches in their ears to distinguish one from the other. She spoke of elephants as if they were people, with personalities that made each distinctive. It was obvious she loved "her" elephants.

And my dear George ate up every moment of that. He was a biology professor who loved the natural world and gloried in experiences such as this. He was an environmentalist through and through.

George married me in 1968, June 15 to be exact. It was the first marriage for both of us. I was thirty-three and he would turn forty-six the next day. We had met in Bruce Hall at Kean University in 1965 when I arrived as an associate professor of education and he was a professor of science. We both had done some traveling before we teamed up. I had traveled mostly in Europe. George had made two trips that he often talked about.

George's first trip before he married me was probably the most significant of his life. It was 1941. George was a junior at a New Jersey state college back then. But in 1941 the attack on Pearl Harbor changed the world. George was called to serve in early March of the next year and, with his college buddy Fred Arnold, was sent for special training to army bases in the eastern part of the United States. He received training in radar technology, and after a brief stint at Fort Dix, in New Jersey, shipped out to England on the *RMS Queen Elizabeth*. He often spoke of this as his first cruise.

George loved to tell stories of his crossing on the *Queen*. He proudly told of his cabin "on the promenade deck," pausing to add, "which I shared with fourteen other guys." He would explain how he grabbed a top bunk so that no one could upchuck on him. He explained, too, how the troops were fed continuously. The GIs would stand in line in the stairwells and wend their way down to the dining room. George would never eat marmalade nor stewed tomatoes after that. He said he had had enough of those on the *Queen* to last a lifetime.

More seriously, he would recall how he and Fred, who made the crossing with him, would stand at the stern of the ship and watch the wake. The wake provided evidence of their jig-jag path across the ocean, made without a convoy of war ships to protect them. The *Queen* carried 15,000 men and was so fast she could outrun German U-boats. I guess this was not a very restful "cruise," but it was probably George's most memorable one.

When the war was over, George was stationed in Germany for a while. He told two travel-related stories about that time in service.

Somehow, he finagled a position as driver to an officer. The officer would requisition a jeep on weekends and go to Paris, with George at the wheel. George told me how in Paris he drove down the Champs-Élysées and around the Arc de Triomphe, his jeep the only vehicle on the avenue. What a memory to have, and no wonder he loved to talk about it!

But George's favorite story—which he told over and over again to anyone who would listen—was about something that happened while he and four of his buddies were on an army assignment somewhere in Germany after the war had ended. One of the GIs had bartered for eggs; they also had some government-issued canned bacon, some bread, and a frying pan. They had made a fire on the side of the road where they had camped overnight, and had started to fry bacon and eggs for breakfast when they saw three older men in long, gray woolen overcoats walking down the road. The men stopped, looked longingly at the food, and asked to eat any scraps left over from the meal.

One of the older men spoke a bit of English. He explained that they were Hungarians who had been conscripted into the German army. After the armistice, the Americans had stamped their papers "discharged" and sent them on their way home. The Hungarians knew the way to go, for this was their *second* walk home from Germany to Hungary. At the end of World War I, the Americans had similarly discharged them, and they had walked all the way back to Hungary. The memory of these hungry men and the thought that war is so futile stayed with George his entire life. A postscript to George's story: Of course, the GIs shared their breakfast with the Hungarians.

When George got home after the war, he finished his education at Montclair State College under the GI Bill. He became a high school biology teacher and taught a few years in New Jersey and New York. He returned to Montclair during this time to earn a master's degree in science education and then picked up a doctorate in education from Columbia University, attending part-time even as he taught.

Having earned his doctorate, George moved in 1960 to Kean University as a biology professor. With his summers free of teaching responsibilities, he decided he wanted to see the United States, especially the national parks. He threw a sleeping bag and other camping gear into the back of his station wagon and off he went—west—by himself. He drove to the Pacific Coast, stopping on the way to visit the Grand Canyon, Bryce Canyon, the Painted Desert, and Hoover Dam. He stayed with a cousin in California before heading east. Yosemite, Yellowstone, Devil's Tower, the Badlands, Mount Rushmore—he did them all. Once in a while, he stopped at a motel to clean up, but he did this trip "on the cheap." George was not one to need the most expensive, nor the most elaborate. He was a humble man with simple needs.

Besides biology, George was certified to teach geology, chemistry, and physics. What he loved most about his road trip was seeing the landforms of our country as he crossed the plains and the mountains. The Grand Canyon was his favorite. There he saw the beds of Precambrian rock, uncovered by the Colorado River, that provide a record in stone of the geologic history of the region. Often, as we traveled together, George would tell me to look at the outcropping rock beds, especially those that had been broken or bent by earthquake forces. In my travels, I still pick up rock samples to bring home as souvenirs, and I look at the rock outcroppings as George taught me to do.

Chapter Two
BEGINNING OUR TRAVELS TOGETHER

After we married, George and I did not take a honeymoon. We were too busy having our house built. But sometime in early 1969, George received a brochure from the National Science Teachers Association. It described a convention of the association to be held that summer in Hawaii. At the close of the convention, the NSTA was sponsoring a trip to several of the Hawaiian Islands. George wondered aloud, "Are you interested?"

I answered him with questions: "Why should we fly just to Hawaii? Why not keep going around the world?" We had the whole summer. I had never been to Asia, nor had he. It would be our honeymoon—just a year late.

We made our honeymoon plans. We would sign onto the NSTA's tour of Hawaii, pick up a Japan Tourist Bureau tour in Japan, fly to Hong Kong, and make stops in Bangkok, New Delhi, Istanbul, and Lisbon before flying the Atlantic to New York. Our journey would take forty days. Here are the highs and lows of our first round-the-world trip—a trip that took place over fifty years ago.

HAWAII

As amateur geologists, we loved Hawaii: actively spewing volcanoes, lava fields, a lava tube, fantastic flora, and accommodations that were superb. It was nothing like the camping that George had done on his own or his sharing a cabin with fourteen other GIs.

Our last evening in Hawaii stands out among my memories of our first visit to the islands. That evening we were not dining with the tour group, so George and I splurged; we dined in the top-of-the-line restaurant in our hotel. I am not sure on which of the islands we were, but in my mind I have a clear picture of the dining room set high on a cliff above the Pacific Ocean. Waves were crashing on the shore below. The view from our window table was absolutely glorious. George and I sat for a long time after the meal, watching the sun drop into the sea and stars slowly fill the sky.

As we enjoyed our coffee, we struck up a conversation with a group of Japanese businessmen at an adjacent table. They asked us about our trip, and we told them we had toured the main islands of Hawaii and were going on to Japan and from there around the world.

They asked us where we were stopping in Japan, and we mentioned Kyoto as one of the cities we would be visiting in the coming weeks. This piqued their interest, as they lived in Kyoto and would be returning home in a few days.

It was then that one of the men extended an amazing invitation: He offered to show us the sights of his city. We explained that we were booked on a tour and that, on our one free day, we had already made plans to visit with the president of Kyoto University. We told him we were professors and that this was one of two visits with university leaders that colleagues at Kean University had arranged for us.

"Wonderful," he said, proffering his business card so we would have his phone number. "I will pick you up and drive you to the university." He told us we would need help getting in, for the university was in lockdown with students in protest mode over some local issue.

We could hardly believe this man's generosity. Our after-dinner conversation had been so enjoyable—a highlight, actually, of our stay in

Hawaii. Now we would have the opportunity to meet again when we were in Japan.

The next morning, George and I flew back to Honolulu to catch our flight to Tokyo. In those days, Pan American World Airways offered round-the-world service. The route was called Pan Am Flight 001 when flying westward. We had to wait at the airport for a short time, but after that, boarding went smoothly and we were soon in the air.

Our plane was about an hour out of Honolulu when the pilot announced that we were turning back. There was a problem with the landing equipment: We would have been getting into Tokyo in the dark, and the instrument that was essential for a night landing was defective. I could feel George tense up. My George loved to travel, but he hated flying. He got even more tense as the pilot began to dump fuel. We could see gasoline flying by the windows and could smell it in the cabin.

Fortunately, our plane landed safely in Honolulu. We had to stay in the boarding area for a couple of hours, but once we reboarded, all systems were go. Needless to say, George breathed a sigh of relief when the wheels of our plane hit the tarmac and we taxied to the arrival gate in Tokyo.

WITH EDUCATORS: JAPAN

In Tokyo, we met our Japan Tourist Bureau guide and "did" the city with him and our tour group. We also had plans for our one free day in Tokyo. A colleague at Kean University, who had visited with the president of a private college on the outskirts of the city, had arranged for us to meet and chat with that gentleman about problems facing higher education in both our countries.

The morning of our visit, we went to the main railway station in Tokyo, one of the largest in the world, and boarded a train to the college town. It was at the height of the commuting hour. Navigating the station and finding the platform where we were to board our train was an adventure, to say the least. All signs were in Japanese and everyone was rushing to get to work.

We had asked the hotel concierge to write out directions in English—directions to the station and then to the platform from which our train would depart. I will never forget that morning. We held hands so we would not lose one another in the mob of rushing commuters. We sighed with relief when we settled into our seats and the train pulled out of the station. To be sure we got off at the right station, the hotel concierge had told us the number of stops before our stop at the college town. Everything worked. Wow! We were proud of ourselves.

The walk from the station to the college was short. The president came out to welcome us and to invite us into his office. There, we sat on tatami mats and enjoyed a cup of tea with him. He spoke English so we could converse easily.

This day provided extraordinary memories. It was a wonderfully rewarding experience for us and probably for the college president, who had not welcomed many educators from America. Looking back, I recall that we spent most of our time talking about our colleague at Kean, Joe Darden of the Health Education Department, who had set up our meeting. It turned out that Dr. Darden and this college president were close friends.

The next day, the Japan Tourist Bureau guide took us on a different train trip—the bullet train down to Kyoto. Before we left the hotel, he warned that when the train pulled into the station, it stayed for only a very few minutes. When we saw it coming down the tracks, we were to have our bags in hand. Once the train stopped, we were to run for the nearest door. On the station platform, we did as we had been told: We ran—with the guide prodding us from behind.

When we reached Kyoto, our hotel concierge helped us call the new friend we had met in Hawaii. He promised to pick us up in the morning, accompanied by an associate who wanted practice speaking English. He also explained that, because of the protests, the university president had moved his office to an off-campus site. Our new friend would sneak us in, taking a circuitous route through a park to avoid detection by the protesters.

Again, the president of the school spoke English, we sat on tatami mats, and we were served tea in the formal Japanese style. The room was beautifully furnished, with a lovely ceiling-to-floor scroll at one end and a bouquet of fresh flowers on the floor beneath it. The furniture was heavy, dark, and carved. We offered greetings from Dr. Eugene Wilkins, then president of Kean, and presented a pen from him bearing our college's logo.

Our new friend was waiting for us when we left the president's office. He drove us to a shop he owned and told me to pick one item as a gift. I chose a clutch purse; it was simple in design and subdued in color. The gentleman told me I had "the taste of a Japanese lady." Those were his exact words, which I remember especially on occasions when I carry my purse.

Our Japanese friend had other associates waiting for us at a nearby teahouse, all of whom wanted practice speaking our language. Our tea and conversation with these gentlemen and our meeting with the president of Kyoto University were highlights of our stay in Japan. Seeing palaces, temples, and even botanical gardens is wonderful. Talking with people in a natural setting is even more wonderful. In this case, too, we learned how generous and welcoming people can be.

WE REPRESENT AMERICA

We stopped in Hong Kong and Bangkok before we arrived for a two-day stop in New Delhi. The first day of our New Delhi visit was July 20, 1969.

George and I were up early for our day trip to Agra. We were so eager to see the Taj Mahal that we were the first in the hotel breakfast room. When the waiters saw us coming, they lined up at the door, and as we entered, each bowed and congratulated us. "Why on earth are they doing this?" I wondered aloud.

One waiter explained. Americans had just landed on the moon! We represented America; therefore, we were to be congratulated. George and I were amazed at their show of respect for us. That day, we were Americans basking in the reflected glory of our country.

After our early breakfast, an agent from the tour company we were using for the India portion of our trip picked us up at our hotel. He escorted us to our seats on a train bound for Agra. Once aboard, I read aloud the sections of our guidebooks that focused on the Taj. Our anticipation increased as I read about the white marble structure framed by four stately minarets. The guidebook described the onion-shaped dome under which lie the tombs of Shah Jahan and his wife Mumtaz Mahal. It told about the impressive main gateway through which we would pass, the reflecting pool we would see, and the Arabic calligraphy at the entrance to the tomb itself. In just a short time we would be there.

It was hot and humid when we got off the train in Agra and boarded a non-air-conditioned bus to ride to the Taj. We had been promised cold drinks on the ride, and we certainly needed them by the time we arrived at the mausoleum. We were parched.

I felt George poking me as we looked out from the bus window. Down the road came a donkey cart, filled with Coke bottles covered with dirty burlap. Some of that dirty burlap covered the bottle caps, and we would be drinking directly from a bottle. We looked at each other in perfect agreement. We were no longer thirsty.

This, of course, was before the days of inexpensive bottled water. In those days, we carried iodine tablets that we would put in our water. The rule was to wait a half hour before drinking, and of course, the water tasted awful. It was a long time until lunch when we could drink iodine-tinged water.

The most striking memory we brought home from our day trip, however, was not of the Coke and the donkey cart nor even of the sublime beauty and perfection of the memorial that Shah Jahan had commissioned in 1631 to honor his wife. It was of our very late arrival at the Delhi station that evening. We looked out from our train seats and saw a sea of people lying and sitting on the station platform, jammed closely together. Obviously, the platform was their bedroom for the night.

A British family was sharing our compartment, and the young daughter cried, "Mama, I don't want to get off."

I have to say that I shared her feelings until I saw our Indian escort standing on the platform waiting for us. When we got off, George grabbed tightly to my left arm and, with my right, I hugged the arm of our escort. He had done this many times before, and he expertly guided us through the mass of people and out into the street where he had a car waiting. A beggar navigating on a single crutch followed closely on our heels.

This was the first time we had seen such poverty. It made us realize how easy our lives were compared to many others who live in third-world countries. We complain about little things, rather than being thankful for what we have.

A CONTRASTING MEMORY

We flew out of New Delhi, still on Pan Am Flight 001, and arrived in Istanbul after a refueling stop in Lebanon. In the Beirut airport, we saw armed soldiers guarding the runways. We had heard that there had been violence in Beirut, and had not chanced booking an overnight there. In retrospect, I guess we were too cautious, for compared to conditions today in some places we have visited, Lebanon was not that dangerous.

After our experience in the Indian rail station, Istanbul looked like an exotic paradise. We were booked into the Hilton Hotel up on a hill overlooking the Bosphorus. I was exhausted from our travels and had only enough energy to go to the hotel dining room for supper. I ordered a hamburger. No other hamburger had ever tasted so fabulously good to me! In my mind, I still have a picture of my sitting there by the window, looking out over the Bosphorus with the moon casting a silvery glow on the water, and eating that ordinary but delicious hamburger.

Now, George would have none of that. If he were in Istanbul, he insisted, he was going to eat Turkish-style. Not at all tired and still in adventure mode, he dressed up and ventured down the road to find a Turkish restaurant. He came back a happy traveler, for he had found a cozy restaurant and enjoyed some distinctive flavors of Turkey.

He also came back with ideas as to what to do the next day: We should cross over the Galata Bridge into the old district of Sultanahmet to explore the Hagia Sophia (known now as Aya Sofya), the Blue Mosque, the Grand Bazaar, and the Topkapi Palace. His waiter had told him these were the big four sites of Istanbul. According to his waiter, the Blue Mosque was a "must see." We had to view the stained-glass windows of the mosque and the thousands of hand-painted blue tiles that adorn it.

Right down the street from our hotel, however, was a carpet shop. In the window, George had seen a small prayer rug in shades of orange that he thought would fit wonderfully in our foyer at home. Up early the next morning, we bought our Turkish prayer rug before doing anything else. George solved the problem of getting it home. He folded the rug over a hanger, wrapped his raincoat over the hanger, and carried both over his arm as he boarded each plane on our route back to New Jersey. With the more relaxed rules regarding carry-on luggage back then, he was easily able to get our carpet home.

Chapter Three
CRUISING THE CARIBBEAN

A year later at Christmastime in 1970, we discovered cruising. The ship was the *SS Europa* of the German Lloyd Line. George and I had a small outside cabin down in the bowels of the ship. We teased each other that our feet were actually below the waterline. George reminded me that on his first cruise sponsored by Uncle Sam, his cabin had been on the promenade deck.

The *Europa* sailed from New York City. Traveling outbound, George and I saw the New York City skyline on the port side, the Statue of Liberty on the starboard. That view at sail-away is always awesome, and on the return brings shivers up the spine. The scene is the most fantastic in the world, especially to an American.

PORT-AU-PRINCE, HAITI

Perhaps the picture that stayed with us the longest from our first cruise was of the activity in the harbor of the capital of Haiti, Port-au-Prince. Cruise ships no longer go into Port-au-Prince; it is considered too dangerous.

In 1970, the harbor scene where we anchored was the epitome of what we thought was the *real* Caribbean. Small local boats circled our ship; they were carrying young men selling wood carvings. Bargaining between buyers on board our ship and sellers down below was noisy and fast. When a sale was finalized, the resourceful entrepreneurs had rigged a pulley system so they could hoist the purchase up to the promenade deck and buyers could lower money down. Some passengers would just throw coins down to the men, who would dive into the water to retrieve them. This would never be allowed today. It would be considered polluting the waters, and having the little boats that close to our big ship would be considered an accident waiting to happen.

We rode a tender boat to shore. On the pier was a crowd of children, each offering his or her services as our guide. We chose a youngster and gave him the prestigious position of our escort for the morning. Our ten-year-old guide led us to the Iron Market, a huge handicraft emporium where we haggled for carved figures of a man and a woman. He also took us to an upscale art gallery where we bought a signed primitive that hangs in our house to this day. In many of our stops on our flying world tour in 1969, we had made purchases in addition to our Turkish prayer rug. We had come home ladened down. So here we were, continuing our custom of bringing home substantive memories of our travels.

Soon after our 1970 trip, Haiti was deemed off-limits to cruise ships, so we were glad to have had this unusual stop. We brought home not only material memories but also images in our minds of the streets of Haiti and of our young guide who chased off other boys who were looking for work.

CHARLOTTE AMALIE — THEN AND NOW

Almost every cruise to the Eastern Caribbean includes a stop in Charlotte Amalie on the island of St. Thomas in the U.S. Virgin Islands. Today Charlotte Amalie is a shopper's mecca, but back in 1970 the capital city was much quieter, with ships docking downtown at the end of Main Street rather than in Havensight Mall, a bus ride away from town. Back then, St. Thomas had everything we had thought to find in the Caribbean: sun, sea, sand, and shopping! We were enthralled.

The morning of our first day ever in St. Thomas, we climbed aboard the typical island transport, an open-air bus that took us over the mountain ridge to Magens Bay. The view from the ridge down across the bay was so beautiful: the sun glistening on the waters of the bay, houses nestled on the green hillsides that rim it, little boats bobbing below, and the beach itself spread out in a wide arc.

After 1970, George and I made the trek over the ridge to the bay many times, but the first time was the most special. Used to the pounding surf of the Jersey Shore, we felt as if we had dropped onto another planet. Here the surf was gentle. Here the water was warm.

Back in town in the afternoon, we hit the shops. Main Street was different back then, uncrowded and with more upscale boutiques. Of course, there were the liquor shops and the jewelry shops and the T-shirt shops. Amid all the touristy places, we found a clothing store where George bought a colorful jacket with a floral design of blue blossoms on a white background. We decided it was a perfect jacket for him to wear on formal nights on cruises. Since we had fallen in love with cruising, we knew that he would have many opportunities in future years to wear it. And he did. The jacket was ideal for cruises to the Caribbean, South America, and eventually the islands of Polynesia. I always loved to see George dressed up in his flowery evening jacket.

We wandered down Main Street and into Colombian Emeralds, a shop you can find even today on many of the islands of the Caribbean. Could I resist buying? No way. I picked out a pair of dangling gold earrings with a single pearl at the bottom of each. These earrings remain a favorite and still go cruising with me. They were really quite costly—$250. But they are fourteen-karat gold and the pearls are large and of good quality. Whenever I wear them, I picture myself standing at the counter of Colombian Emeralds, debating whether to buy them. When I wondered aloud whether we should spend that kind of money on earrings, George turned to me and asked, "Do you want them?" Hearing me say "Yes," he replied, "Well, let's buy them!"

I think I got the better deal. I had bought expensive earrings, he a cotton floral jacket.

19

IN NEPTUNE'S DOMAIN

George, the ecologist/biologist/naturalist, appreciated everything and anything related to living organisms. For that reason, on our first Caribbean cruise, we took an excursion to view the fauna and flora that live in the sea—in Neptune's domain. According to mythology, it is King Neptune who rules the seven seas.

Think of a submarine-like vessel with a top surface that remains above the sea, but with most of its structure submerged. This kind of semi-submersible vessel has side windows through which passengers can look out upon Neptune's domain. A ladder extends from the top down into the interior. Passengers use that ladder to climb inside the submarine; seats line the windows so that viewing is easy and comfortable. When George and I got to Bonaire in the Netherlands Antilles near Aruba, we signed up for this kind of excursion.

We had to walk a distance to get from our ship to our semi-submersible. Once on board and out into the reef area, however, we knew we had chosen the perfect excursion. Until then, we had only seen the animals of the sea in aquariums. This was the *real* thing. The young men who ran the boat scattered food into the water, which attracted lots of fish, diverse in color and size. The fish swam by, often in large schools. Supplied with labeled pictures, we were able to identify the fish we were seeing. Of course, we also saw corals and seaweeds. After our first Caribbean trip when we discovered semi-submersibles, we often repeated the below-the-surface-of-the-sea adventure. This was definitely a George kind of excursion.

BEACH BREAKS

Since we took numbers of Caribbean cruises during Christmas and spring breaks throughout the years we taught at Kean, we had the opportunity to visit all the areas and islands of the Caribbean:

eastern, western, and southern. Aruba is a popular island on the southern route. George and I went to Aruba more times than I can remember.

On our first Caribbean trip, we discovered that the Holiday Inn on the calm-water side of the island welcomed day visitors. It was easy to catch a cab to take us there. The Holiday Inn even let tourists use their restroom facilities and walk through the lobby to get to the beach. The hotel had probably learned that tourists pay their way by buying souvenirs in the gift shop. This was true of us, too, for on our first Holiday Inn beach break, I bought two pairs of small hoop earrings. They are still among my favorites.

But what we loved most about our mornings at the Aruba Holiday Inn was strolling the beach and swimming in the warm, calm waters. We loved it so much that, year after year when we went to Aruba, we would spend the morning at the beach before returning to town to walk the streets and visit the shops. I wonder if it is still possible today to go for a day on the sand at the Holiday Inn. I understand from friends that there are many new hotels and condos in that area now; these hotels on the beach may also accept day guests.

Similarly, George and I enjoyed swimming at Harbour Lights Beach in Barbados because the water is so calm. Located in a peaceful cove, Harbour Lights is on the other side of Bridgetown from the dock and just a short hop away by taxi. There, we would rent beach chairs and an umbrella. Although it is more difficult to get into the ocean due to sharp shells at the waterline, we also liked swimming at the famed Seven Mile Beach on Grand Cayman.

From St. Maarten where our ship often docked, we sometimes grabbed a cab over to Orient Bay Beach—a beauty of a beach on the French side of the island. An endless expanse of fine white sand with little waves lapping gently on the shore, Orient caters to those who like nude bathing. I must admit that I still retain a picture in my mind of a middle-aged couple, sauntering nonchalantly hand in hand along the beach clad only in their sun-baked skin. And I remember a much older gentleman wading in the surf, adorned simply in a black money bag that he wore around his waist.

LIFE ABOARD SHIP — THEN AND NOW

Often when we returned from one of our cruises, folks asked us how we had spent our time on sea days. Being in a small cabin in the middle of the ocean sounded boring to them. To be succinct, the opposite was and is true.

Dining is obviously an important part of a cruise. Our first cruise with the German Lloyd Line was at a time when formality was the norm. There were formal nights when we would wear evening attire, a gown for me and an evening jacket, a bow tie, and a formal dress shirt for George. Often, George would wear the white jacket he had bought for our wedding. My wedding gown had a straight skirt and a simple design; that was one of my formal outfits. We found it fun to dress up in the same clothes in which we had been so recently married. On casual nights, men still had to wear jackets and ties to the main dining room; the women wore very nice, stylish outfits.

The service was beyond compare. The dining stewards wore white gloves as they served dinner, course by course. We generally asked for a table for six or eight diners, and were lucky with the folks with whom we shared a table at night. That was how we met our dear friends Phil and Eileen, Mel and Kelley, and many others over the years. At dinner time, we would talk about what we had done during the day on shore, so we learned more about the places where we had stopped. Conversation was lively. Only once in all our years of cruising were we unhappy with our dining companions. We just suffered, but in retrospect, we should have asked the maitre d' for a reassignment.

And now about the food. On our first few cruises, a tower of caviar on ice sat near the entrance to the main dining room, where the food was bountiful and nicely presented. Some evenings, we dined upstairs in the cafeteria on the lido deck or in the specialty restaurant. In those days there was just one specialty restaurant for which one paid a surcharge. Today most ships offer several and the surcharge can be hefty. Don't forget afternoon tea with scones, tea sandwiches, and a variety of finger cakes. Oh yes, and don't forget the Midnight Buffet, which back then was really at midnight and offered towers of shrimp, cakes, and sandwiches.

Our first cruise. Note George's flowered jacket.

Today things have changed. Meals are not so lavish, and service is not so formal. In the evening, dress in the main dining rooms is much more casual, although shorts are generally not allowed and jeans are frowned upon. Passengers can snack on a slim buffet at night that starts about 10:30 and can drop in for afternoon tea, morning coffee, and even hot soup on deck when something special is going on.

And then there's the entertainment. For years after our first cruise on *Europa*, George and I would talk about the "Butterfly Lady." She was the entertainer night after night in the lounge. There was no theater on *Europa*, just the lounge where people gathered in the evening to talk with friends and dance to live music. At about nine, the entertainment began. The Butterfly Lady would come wafting in, spreading wings attached to her back, dancing to the music. That was her entire act.

Today evening entertainment on board is far more elaborate. Held in a tiered theater, the main entertainment consists of floor shows as well as individual, professional acts and a movie from time to time. The acts include vocalists, instrumentalists, comedians, puppeteers, magicians. Most cruisers attend the show each night, so seating can be tight and it pays to get to the theater early.

In addition, ensembles perform in smaller venues around the ship: dueling pianos in a piano bar, classical music in a quiet nook, a rock band in a central location, a dance band in a lounge.

Chapter Four
DRIVING EUROPE WITH GEORGE

George had great faith in himself as a highway driver. He had learned to drive in the late 1930s when cars were shifted manually, so a stick-shift car was no obstacle for him. Before coming to Kean University, he had worked for a few years as a demonstration teacher at Ball State University in Indiana. He often told me how, at Christmastime, he would hop into his old Chevrolet and drive home to spend the holidays with his parents in Jersey. His story always included how on one trip, he had had to fight his way home across Indiana, Ohio, and Pennsylvania in a blinding snowstorm. For some part of the trip, he followed a snowplow that cleared a path for him.

His story was not an exaggeration of his skill. After we were married, he twice got us home to Warren from Union, New Jersey, in a snowstorm. The first time, returning from a day at Kean, we found the roads barely passable, thick with snow. To get home via Route 22, we had to climb two hills. I sat petrified as George kept the car climbing, passing one stalled car after another. He just kept going, driving in the left lane with a firm, steady foot on the accelerator.

The second time, we had gone down to Kean to attend an evening concert. When we came out of the theater, heavy snow was falling and the ground was covered. By then, we were making the commute via Route 78. Well, we had to climb a hill to get up into Warren on that route, too. Again, George just kept his foot on the pedal, pulling into the left lane to pass car after stalled car. I prayed that no vehicle was coming in the opposite direction. My sister was with us, in the back seat, petrified, too. George was cool and calm, sure of his ability to control our Buick.

DRIVING SWITZERLAND, LIECHTENSTEIN, GERMANY, AND ITALY

Because I had seen how cool and calm George was under the pressure of harsh driving conditions, I was confident that he could drive European roads in a manual-shift car. Together, we started planning a holiday on the continent, and in the summer of 1970, we set out on our first road trip. It would take us through Switzerland, Italy, Liechtenstein, and Germany.

I am not certain into which Swiss city we flew or where we picked up our rental car, but it probably was Zurich. The first memory I have of the trip is our walking across the covered bridge in Lucerne and going to see the Lion of Lucerne, a rock relief of a dying lion. A bench stood in front of the carving then. I recall that George and I sat on it and studied the detail of the carving and the plaque explaining that the sculpture commemorates the Swiss Guards massacred during the French Revolution.

My second memory is of our boat ride across Lake Lucerne the next day. A small excursion boat took us across the lake, which is nestled among mountains and about which many little villages cluster. These two days were a fabulous introduction for George into the natural beauty of Switzerland. I had been to Lucerne before, but this was George's first time in Switzerland and the Alps, and he was rendered almost speechless by what he was seeing. "Simply fantastic," was all he could say—just those two words, over and over.

From Lucerne, George drove me to Interlaken, a Swiss town set between two lakes. A river runs parallel to the main street, which is lined with hotels. From our window in one of those hotels, we could look up at the mountains towering above.

As most tourists do, we had gone to Interlaken to ride the railroad up the Jungfrau, one of the tallest alpine peaks. That railroad is said to be the highest in Europe, and it is truly remarkable. The train took us through a tunnel carved through the rock. Emerging from it, we saw before us magnificent mountain scenery with glistening glaciers, deep glacial valleys, and ridges and peaks soaring above. There is an ice cave at the railway terminus. We walked through it to find another exceptional view of glorious mountains spread out before us.

Back in Interlaken, we stopped at a clock shop on the corner of a side street. After more than fifty years, I can still picture the shop sitting on that corner! We went in and found a wall clock topped with a small Atlas holding the world on his shoulders. It had two heavy brass weights and fine carving around the sides. We knew immediately that this clock had our name on it.

I did wonder how we would get the heavy weights home, given airline limitations. George solved the problem, again. He carried the weights onto the airplane in his jacket pockets. Because there were no security checks back then, this was a good solution. Incidentally, after our "Swiss" clock had hung on our wall for years, it needed cleaning. We took it to a repair shop. The clock expert told us that our "Swiss" clock had been made in Holland.

We were still in Switzerland when our rental car began to sputter. I cannot remember what was wrong with the car, but I still can see my husband standing in a service station and talking to the mechanic. George had studied German, but not French. He knew a few French expressions, however. Using those expressions, his high-school level German, and hand gestures with some English thrown in, George explained to the mechanic what was wrong with the car. We sat in the garage for about an hour, at which point the mechanic drove our car out of the repair area. It was fixed and ready to go.

Our route took us down the coastal road of Italy. The road was perched on the edge of sea cliffs, guardrails were non-existent, and other cars were passing even on blind curves. George was not especially fond of heights, but he did it. He got me to the town we had chosen for our night's stay, a bit shaken but in one piece.

At that point, we had begun to stay in some private bed-and-breakfast-type accommodations, *zimmer freis*, as they may be called on parts of the continent. We would ride through a town, watching for signs offering overnight accommodations. George would park outside a B and B that looked OK, and I would go in to see if a room was available and the place neat and clean. This worked well and the price was right for us, much cheaper than a hotel. George generally could park the car in a driveway or in front of the premises, so it was convenient, as well.

We went south down the boot of Italy as far as Pisa, where we spent the night and walked out to see the Leaning Tower and the lovely cathedral. The next day we turned east to get to Venice. We found a hotel in a town just outside the city. The rates were lower than in the city and a train connected the town to Venice. The next morning, we hopped on the train that took us to the central rail station in Venice. From there we climbed on a water taxi to St. Mark's Square. We found the square flooded with water from recent heavy rains. We had to walk on wooden planks that were spread around the square and even in St. Mark's Cathedral. That will always be my picture of Venice—flooded and planked.

That day we walked and walked and walked, following the canals into back areas and crossing bridges as we wandered from plaza to plaza. We walked across the Rialto Bridge, twisting our way back to the central area where we visited the Doge's Palace and saw the Bridge of Sighs. And yes, we took a gondola ride.

After we left Venice, George drove us north. We eventually got to Liechtenstein, high up in the Alps. Somewhere I had learned of a motel that sat at the very top of a mountain in Vaduz, the capital city. George drove our car up the mountain road and we settled in the motel for the night. We breakfasted in the motel dining room overlooking the city and the royal castle. It was a gloriously clear day; we could see far into the distance, peer down into the valley below, and look up at tall mountains.

George decided to try his rudimentary German on the waiter. He asked for something like "Hauser vaser" to dilute his morning coffee. Somehow what he ordered sounded more like ice water than hot water, for ice water is what the waiter brought. I still can see George's expression when the ice water arrived. George gave up on German that morning and reordered in English.

Thinking back to a trip like this, I find it interesting which things I remember, for after all, this was about fifty years ago, and I did not keep a log. Usually, the events I recall are those that have some humorous or scary aspect or were otherwise exceptional. For example, I remember that George was impressed when we stopped in Switzerland at a hotel near the Rhine Falls. The dining room overlooked the falls. But the thing that struck George was the fact that our waiter spoke to us in English, to the diners at the next table in French, and to those at more distant tables in German and Italian. George drew my attention to this, and so I remembered.

DRIVING ENGLAND

George did such a great job driving on the scary roads of Italy and the mountain roads of Switzerland, Austria, and Liechtenstein that, in the summer of 1972, we flew to England for our second European road trip. Our car was delivered to us in the street outside our London hotel. The courier explained how the vehicle worked, we signed the papers accepting delivery of the car, and we were off. Now remember, we were in central London during the early morning rush hour and Londoners drive on the left side of the road. That is where our road trip began. I had plotted our route out of the city the night before, so I navigated. George drove. I kept reminding him, "Keep left. Keep left."

Leaving the city, George found that the hardest part was managing the roundabouts. We both kept concentrating on staying left. Sometimes we would go around a circle several times before daring to make the cutoff onto the side road we were looking for. Another hard part was remembering what side of the road to drive on after we had pulled off to view the scenery.

In England, we generally stayed in bed and breakfasts. Only once did we have a problem finding a place to stay. That was in Cambridge, where a university event was going on. We were turned away from a couple of places, and I was getting nervous. We finally settled for so-so accommodations with a shared bathroom down the hall. At least we had a place to hang our hat for two nights as we explored the buildings and gardens of this old university town.

Because we were university people, we loved walking through the courtyards of the different colleges within Cambridge. On another road trip, we enjoyed Oxford, as well. In Oxford, we especially appreciated the lovely botanical gardens, the oldest in England.

Of the places we visited on the road, the city of York stands out still in my mind. Located in a stone row house, our bed and breakfast there was run by a woman and her son. When we checked in, the proprietress served us tea in her lounge—a thoughtful touch given that we had been on the road for hours. She sat down to chat and even mapped out the sights we should see.

York is an old walled city built on top of a Viking town. First on our self-guided tour was a walk on the wall. We climbed the steep stairs to the top and strolled around. Eventually we climbed down to the narrow city streets to wander among the shops. We sat for a time in a pew in the mighty Minster—the cathedral—to catch our breath and rest from our hours of walking. Recovered, we bought tickets to the underground museum and rode a tram-like vehicle from exhibit to exhibit that depicted life during Viking days. The next day we paid a visit to the train museum to look at vintage engines and rail cars. On display was a railroad car used by the English royal family. Of course, we spent time in the woolen shops where I bought a lovely scarf and a wool plaid skirt.

To "see" a city like York requires several days and much walking—obviously. We were fortunate, for we were educators with summers free to travel. We were still young when we just took it for granted that we could walk for hours at a time. Thinking back, I realize now that I never thought then about George's being thirteen years older than me; I was the one who ran out of steam first. George had great energy and was happiest when he was on the go. He was like a windup toy; once he got started, he could keep going and going.

The Lake District of England also stands out, especially our visit to Beatrix Potter's home. We found a bed and breakfast across the lake from the Potter house and on a sunny morning crossed the lake by boat. This gave us the opportunity to enjoy the scenery for which the Lake District is known.

Seeing the Potter house for me was a sheer delight. At her house were displays of original manuscripts and drawings that are such an integral part of Potter's children's stories. What was most delightful was seeing and hearing the children who had also come for a visit. They squealed when they pointed out their favorite characters: Peter Rabbit and Mr. McGregor, Flopsy, Mopsy, and Cottontail. I have to say that this day was ideal for me. I taught courses in children's literature at Kean University, and I saw some of my favorite Potter characters, too. For my husband, the lake scenery was what made the day exceptional.

George drove us north toward Lake Windermere, the largest lake in England. The scenery was serenely lovely, and we often stopped by the side of the road to drink in the beauty. Getting back into our car, we had to remember again to "keep to the left." It was so easy to forget!

In Windermere, we got really fortunate. Our bed and breakfast was a gray stone house with a large bay window on the second floor. The room with that bay window was ours for the night. After supper, we sat in the window and looked out upon the local people going about their normal activities. To some folks that might not have been special, but to us it was.

Perhaps the most vivid memories I have from our English road trips are of Stonehenge and Salisbury. I had read about the cathedral and the market city of Salisbury and had learned of an old inn located on the green and within walking distance of the cathedral. We checked in early at the New Inn, some parts of which date back to the 12th century. We had decided we deserved at least one night spent in a real English inn, with a pub restaurant where we could have supper, English-style.

Having secured a room for the evening, we drove to Stonehenge, which is close by. Stonehenge is the best known standing-stone circle structure in Britain. In the early 1970s, we could walk among the stones and read the informative plaques located there. Today, visitors to the site are not allowed into the circle and must view it from the outside perimeter. I remember that the sun was shining on our afternoon there. I remember, too, that the stones were casting shadows on the ground. If I recall correctly, the way the sun slants through the openings between the stones suggests the purpose of the stone circles—a seasonal calendar of some sort.

We spent an hour just walking amidst the stones and then we drove back to Salisbury, ate an early pub dinner in the New Inn, and walked across the green to the cathedral. Salisbury Cathedral has the tallest spire of any of the many English cathedrals. It is stunning.

What made the early evening even more wonderful was the organ being played as we entered the cathedral. We sat close together in one of the pews, just relaxing and absorbing the beauty of the place—a calm haven after a full day. We had read that somewhere in the cathedral is a copy of the Magna Carta, but by that time we were worn out and did not have the energy to look for it.

George drove me around England three times in all. We returned in 1975 and 1983. During each of those road trips, we spent time in London, seeing a little more on each return visit. We revisited favorite venues such as Poet's Corner in Westminster Abbey and the British Museum with its Elgin Marbles taken from the Greek Parthenon. Once we rode a boat down the Thames to Greenwich to visit the observatory and to straddle the Prime Meridian. Another time we went out to see Hampton Court, and still another time we visited Windsor Castle and Eton. Often, we shopped in Harrods and Selfridges and searched the second-hand stalls on Sundays in Petticoat Lane. We generally took in a show or two in the West End. I remember that we even snagged tickets to *Annie* to hear one of our favorite songs, "Tomorrow."

The days we spent in London and the days we spent traveling the English countryside were always jam-packed. And we always came back with memories both visual and substantive: a brass bell from Petticoat Lane that still hangs in our foyer, a Grant plaid kilt for me from Harrods, a deerstalker hat and several tweed jackets from Dunn&Co. for George. The deerstalker is just like the one that the fictional detective Sherlock Holmes wears in the television series. When George would wear his hat and one of his tweed jackets down to his office at Kean, students would turn around and look. Some even called out, "There goes Sherlock Holmes." George would simply smile and wave.

Chapter Five

FLYING TO FARAWAY PLACES

George and I looked out from our two-engine plane to see thick, green jungle spreading in every direction. We were flying low over the island of Borneo on our way to Sarawak. We peered down on treetops where the foliage was so dense we could not see the ground.

It was 1974 when George and I took that surreal small plane ride over jungle terrain. We were on an air/land tour of Southeast Asia with stops in Sarawak and Brunei on the island of Borneo; Sumatra, Java, and Bali in Indonesia; Manila in the Philippines; and Bangkok in Thailand. We had flown in from the states via Tokyo, with a short stay there as well as in Kyoto. Our desire was to see "faraway places with strange-soundin' names." And that is what we did.

We chose to travel on an escorted, fly-from-one-city-to-the-next kind of tour because we thought that being part of a group would make travel to remote locations easier and the company organizing the trip would arrange the air flights between cities. Still young enough to handle long days of sightseeing, we felt the places that we were to explore on this trip were calling, calling to us.

SARAWAK AND BRUNEI ON BORNEO

Let me start with Sarawak. We flew into Kota Kinabalu, a major coastal city on the island of Borneo. From the plane, I loved looking down on the lush jungle below. George, however, was not a happy camper riding in that little plane. But he wanted to go to Kota Kinabalu—one of the most unbelievable places we were ever to visit. This was *Adventure* with a capital A, and the two-engine plane was the only transportation available.

Our hotel in Kota Kinabalu was a two-story wooden building with only a narrow stairway leading to the sleeping level. We did have private bathrooms that functioned. The hotel was called Johnny's. Johnny was the sole proprietor. He was a large, outgoing man who was very proud of his hotel and greeted us personally as we sat down at our tables in the dining room that evening. Johnny proudly told us his hotel was the best in town. He was stating the truth; we saw no larger nor better hotel the next morning as we drove across town to a small boat landing.

At the landing, we boarded a boat that chugged slowly upriver into the heart of the dense jungle. Our objective was to see the longhouses of the Sarawak people.

Don't forget that George and I were serious-minded professors who got excited by things like this—and I still do! A longhouse is exactly what the name implies: a long house, only two rooms deep, with communal space in the front room and minimal private space in the back room. The Sarawak live together, maybe a hundred people in a house that stretches laterally. It is basically open-air, necessary in a region of high heat and humidity.

Our guide led us on a jungle trail to a longhouse. We had to climb a flight of stairs to visit it, for longhouses are built on stilts. The guide translated as the head chieftain described their communal form of living. Today, travelers can stay in a longhouse overnight, but I doubt whether it is as authentic a home as we saw in 1974.

George and I led our little group back along the jungle path to our riverboat. There was only one toilet on the boat; we wanted to use it before our group arrived. The toilet was in a cubicle so small that I could

33

not go in and lower my jeans. I just threw modesty to the wind and took off my jeans outside the cubicle, George shielding me somewhat from sight. Of course, the small quarters were not a problem for a man. What was a problem for both of us was the lack of any basin for handwashing, this before the days of hand sanitizers. The river water was not an option; it was filthy.

We explored the boat. At the stern was the kitchen where a woman was washing dishes—off the back of the boat in the river water. We both lost our appetites, for we knew that the toilet dumped right there into the river. Fortunately, dessert was bananas that we peeled ourselves. We did not try the plate of cold foods that was offered to us.

Despite the lunch and despite the toilet, George gave the day an A+; it was simply awesome. We did not realize that in the days to follow, we would experience places equally awesome.

The two-prop plane returned to fly us to Brunei, also on the island of Borneo. Brunei is a small sultanate. The sultan is purported to be one of the richest men in the world.

In some respects, our hotel in Brunei was more upscale than the one in Sarawak. It was four stories tall, it had elevators, and it overlooked the harbor area. But, we did discover an inconvenient flaw: the toilets did not flush, because there was no running water. The staff carried buckets of water to our rooms to use for flushing. We forgot about showering.

Still, we loved our visit there. The people of Brunei live in homes built on pilings right out in the river. In these water-based communities are schools, houses of worship, and stores. Boardwalks—on pilings, too—connect one building to the next. We just meandered on the boardwalks, smiling at the locals who were as pleased to see us as we were to see them.

In those days, the major museum honored Winston Churchill, who had supported the people of Brunei in their fight to escape from Japanese oppression during the Second World War. There was even a statue of Churchill in front of the museum. An aside—years later, when we were on a cruise, our ship made a stop in Brunei. By then, the museum told the story of the sultanate. The Churchill artifacts had been relegated to storage.

SUMATRA, JAVA, AND BALI IN INDONESIA

Our purpose in flying to Sumatra was to visit Lake Toba. This lake is in the caldera (or crater) of a supervolcano that blew its top about seventy thousand years ago. In the middle of the lake is a small island, which we were going to see.

After a rather lengthy coach ride through lush countryside, we arrived at our hotel. Our accommodation at the hotel was a pretty, rather romantic lakeside cabin that we had all to ourselves—just George and me. Our group dined communally in a lovely lodge, which also had a view of Lake Toba. All in all, the hotel was attractive and very clean. We were pleased with it, although our dinner the first night was "interesting." We were served a local fish, freshly caught that day in Lake Toba. We each got a fish with both skin and head still on it. That fish was more bone than flesh.

The next morning, we cruised across the lake. George thought it was rather exciting to be boating across a caldera. This was his kind of trip, and he listened intently as the guide talked about the eruption which was so massive that it affected the climate worldwide.

When we got to the island, we were met by mobs of young children. They surrounded us, urging us to buy something from them. We bought a crudely carved wood mask. We did not bargain; the youngster who sold it to us was asking only a dollar. I can look up and see the mask on the wall of my computer room as I type.

The housing on the island was unique. Each house was on stilts, the ends of the roofs were tilted upward, and the outer walls were decorated with colorful designs. As we walked the village, the children followed along. The young salesman who had sold us our mask grabbed my hand. I belonged to him!

The guide explained that the island was experiencing a population explosion; it is typical in Indonesia for a family to have many children, but here on Samosir Island, the population was out of control. As a result, poverty was a problem. Hearing that, George told me to give my young friend another dollar or two.

In the years to come, George and I often talked about our visit to Lake

Toba and the children living there. We wondered how the passing years had impacted the island. After all, that young entrepreneur would be middle-aged today.

Onward we went to the Indonesian island of Java. We landed first in the capital city of Jakarta. I remember only traffic and noise—nothing really exciting, nothing to compare with a volcano that had blown its top.

But Java is also home to Borobudur, the largest Buddhist temple in the world. Over the years we visited Borobudur several times; yet there is nothing like the first time. The temple is an impressive edifice carved out of rock, with huge "bells" cut from stone. Inside each bell is a carved, seated Buddha. We were young and climbed right up to the top to look down upon the lower levels. Interestingly in those days, on the landings leading to the top, vendors were displaying their wares. On future visits, we found that the vendors had been relocated to an area near the parking lots.

Our third Indonesian stop was Bali. George and I always called Bali the most beautiful island in the world. It has absolutely everything: beaches, temples, fascinating villages, rice paddies, fine wood carvings, and traditional dances.

Our accommodations were at the opposite end of the continuum from what we had experienced in Sarawak and Brunei. We had a small, private villa on the beach, with two levels. The lower level was for living; the loft was for sleeping. Both were decorated with wood carvings. The hotel dining room served fantastic food, especially delicious tropical fruits like the rambutan, which we had never tasted before.

We had a day to enjoy the sand, sun, and sea. Adjacent to the beach were some stalls where vendors were selling wood carvings. Awed by the fine workmanship, we bought a wood dragon mask, an exquisite carving of a fisherman, a pair of Balinese dancers, and a two-foot-tall statue of intertwining vines and small birds. For me now, these favorite travel purchases bring back memories of a beautiful day we spent in this island paradise.

The next day we toured. From the bus we saw terraced hillsides with rice paddies at each level, climbing upward, with green, green, green everywhere. We spied a farmer off in the distance working his rice paddy with a plow pulled by a water buffalo. We passed homes that had waist-high walls surrounding them. Within the walls were small, ornately carved shrines where the Hindu occupants could worship right in their front yards. We stopped to visit a large Hindu temple and a water palace. That evening, in the courtyard of our hotel, we watched traditional Bali dances: the monkey dance, the wedding dance, the fire dance, and the giant lion dance.

After spending the following morning on the beach, we headed to the airport to catch our flight to the Philippines. There, our escort told us our Garuda Indonesia flight was delayed. George, who you know was not enamored of flying, looked out onto the tarmac and saw our plane sitting there. On the wings were mechanics at work. George whispered to me, "They are suctioning the gas from the tanks." Sure enough, that was what was happening to *our* plane. And the mechanics were using their mouths to create the suction.

We sat and sat. Finally, after many hours, another plane landed. It was for a later Garuda flight to Manila. Fortunately, our escort managed to book us seats on that plane. My George was relieved.

MANILA AND THE PHILIPPINES

We arrived in Manila after dark. We quickly realized the significance of our late arrival when our bus was stopped at a police/military checkpoint and armed guards climbed on to check our IDs. No problem for us: We showed our United States passports and were waved on. This happened again—and then again—as we entered the city limits, for we were in violation of the nightly curfew.

We pulled into our hotel well after midnight. We knew we had a six-hour tour scheduled for the next day, which was already today. The tour was a drive into the agricultural part of the island on which Manila is located and then into the mountains to the volcanic area. In the countryside we were to see the way that different crops—coconut palms, banana, papaya, and coffee—were planted in the same fields, with shorter species nestled under taller ones to save space. We were to see

37

Taal Volcano, the smallest volcano in the world. It is billed as "a volcano, within a lake, within a volcano." This was a dream trip for any biologist/ geologist.

On arrival at our hotel, our escort announced that he was canceling the morning tour so we could catch up on our sleep. George's face dropped. Aghast, he spoke up, "No way. That tour is the reason we booked this trip."

Obviously, the guide did not want to get up early. He took George aside and offered to hire a taxi for us for the day; he would throw in money for lunch. George agreed.

A taxi picked us up a few hours later. We climbed in and headed out of Manila. Our joy was short-lived, for the taxi's engine began to sputter and then just died. Providentially, we were across the street from a small service garage. The taxi driver managed to push his vehicle into the station. The owner came out and asked George and me to make ourselves comfortable inside while he and our driver investigated our options.

Unfortunately, the taxi was too far gone to be repaired quickly, but the cab company, when called, promised a replacement within the hour. George and I settled down to wait in the service station. The owner's wife introduced herself, sat down, and began to chat. Shortly, the owner joined us. They were so happy to have real Americans to talk to about the economic and political problems facing their country. This was the time of the Marcoses—Imelda and Ferdinand—and a time of very little freedom for Filipinos.

Eventually, our replacement car arrived. George got to see how the crops were layered in the fields and to see the tiny volcano within the caldera of another volcano. We stopped for lunch at what was once a country club for American army personnel, when the Philippines were an American territory. At the time of our visit, it was a club for wealthy Filipinos; from there we had a lovely view of the volcano and the lake. Returning to the city, our driver stopped at a shop that sold every kind of souvenir that American tourists tend to buy; we bought capiz shell bowls and lamps because the Philippines are known for capiz shell products.

Back at the hotel, we talked to our fellow travelers who had stayed in the city. They were not happy when they learned what they had missed.

That day, too, we learned something fundamental about travel and tours:

- Speak up. Ask for what has been promised. This may be your only opportunity to see something important to you.

- What may seem like a low point can turn into a highlight—if you take action.

- When you travel, things do not necessarily go as planned. You must be able to bounce with the unexpected.

BANGKOK

On our round-the-world-by-air trip in 1969, George and I had flown into Bangkok and done the typical touristy things. We had taken a boat ride to the colorful morning floating market where women sell fruits and vegetables from their banana boats. We had visited the religious complex housing the great Emerald Buddha. We had spun around the city in a tuk tuk—a neat little motorized vehicle just big enough for the two of us. On our Southeast Asia tour we wanted to do something totally different. What we ended up doing was more than different. It was an adventure.

In our tour group was a woman who had been to Bangkok many times. Back home in the states, she was in the jewelry business. She had told us that when we got to Bangkok, she planned to telephone a company with which she had dealt in the past. They were going to send a car to take her to their shop.

"Do you want to come with me?" she asked. George and I jumped at her offer.

The driver and car arrived promptly—of course, because we were prospective buyers. When the driver pulled up before the jewelry shop, we sensed that something was not right. No one was on the street in front of the shop. The lights were turned off in the store; the showcases in the window were completely bare.

We knew that something was surely wrong when the driver pulled up over the curb and parked as close as possible to the front door. We knew that something was absolutely wrong when he told us to duck down as we got out and to run fast. He explained that there had been looting and shooting here the night before. The streets were still deadly dangerous.

We did exactly as the driver instructed. We ducked and ran. Someone was waiting at the door to open it, let us in, and quickly lock it behind us.

The morning was made even more unforgettable when the shopkeeper peeked out to see if anyone was lurking in the street outside before opening his safe and bringing out racks of rings, pendants, and pins. Thailand is known for its rubies, sapphires, and emeralds. Back in those days, colored gems—as they were called—were not very popular. As a result, the prices were far lower than they are today. I still have a small sapphire pendant and a ruby dinner ring—all bought that day and now kept in a bank safe deposit box.

We left the shop the same way we entered: We ducked down and ran fast. The driver put his foot on the accelerator and off we went! Truly, we had lived an adventure story that we would relate over and over again.

Chapter Six
TRAVELING ON GUIDED TOURS
1977-1991

Because George and I had enjoyed our escorted trip to Southeast Asia, we decided to investigate guided bus tours of Europe and North Africa. For a number of years, George had successfully driven us through Europe and Great Britain. Perhaps the time had come to let someone else do the driving and plan the route and activities. We had read about guided land tours. We decided to try that approach to travel even while we continued with our road trips and cruises during the same time period.

SPAIN AND MOROCCO

In 1977 we took our first bus tour. We chose a European-based company, Melia, and booked a comprehensive tour of Spain and Morocco. We agreed that driving ourselves would be more difficult in a country like Morocco where language differences would be a greater problem than in England or on the continent.

Going with Melia posed some problems that we did not anticipate, but in the end, the choice was a wise one. A guided bus tour is a good approach to travel if people prefer having someone else make the difficult choices about where to stop and do not have the time to research the countries they are visiting. The traveler sees more in a set amount of time, albeit in a regimented way.

To catch our Spain/Morocco bus trip, George and I flew to Madrid and booked into a hotel near the Prado Museum, which was convenient for city sightseeing. We had two hotel choices on the main square, a luxury hotel and a tourist-level one. We picked the tourist one. It provided good value for the money paid.

On our first day—a Sunday—we went to the Prado and then we walked through the park behind the museum. Although we found the art in the Prado Museum impressive, I delighted more in my "Sunday in the Park with George." Because it was the weekend, lots of folks were out enjoying the sunshine. Children were playing, running about, and laughing. It was May and flowers were just coming into bloom. The park was a perfectly magical place to be.

We had a second free day in Madrid before meeting our tour group. We used that day to take a local bus to Toledo, a walled city just north of Madrid, known for its factory that produces decorative steel swords and knives. The bus dropped us off outside the walls by the Tagus River. We found a tunnel in the wall that led into the city center and spent the day strolling the narrow streets and visiting the steelworks. Towering over Toledo is a fortress on a hill, the Alcazar. We did not climb up. It would have required considerable effort.

Early the following morning, we joined our tour group and set off to see three major cities in Spain: Cordoba, Granada, and Seville. In Cordoba we visited the former mosque that is now a cathedral with a flat, arched ceiling supported by hundreds of thick pillars. We perceived it as a mosque, for its structure is not at all cathedral-like. In Granada, we toured the Alhambra, an Arab palace and citadel built during the time when the Moors occupied much of the southern part of Spain. In Seville, our major stop was at the cathedral, which claims to be the resting place for the bones of Christopher Columbus.

These UNESCO World Heritage cities are fabulous. But of the three, it was Seville and its cathedral that provided us with one of the most memorable moments of our trip. Instead of following the guide from one side chapel to the next and listening to him explain the significance of each, we found ourselves a pew midway down the nave. The organ was playing and a large pendulum-like object was swinging back and forth across the upper space. We just sat quietly. We listened to the music and gazed at the beauty surrounding us. This was a time for meditation, a time to reflect and find peace within ourselves. The cathedral was so, so beautiful. Just sitting there brought happy tears to my eyes.

After spending a night in a hotel overlooking the Mediterranean Sea, we headed to Gibraltar, our crossing point into Morocco. The bus drove us to a spot where we could take clear photos of the famed Rock of Gibraltar. Shortly, we were on board the ferry and we were crossing the Pillars of Hercules, the strait separating Europe from Africa. This would be our first visit to Africa.

Overnight was in Tangiers in a hotel with a view of the strait. We had time to wander some of the narrow alleys and look into some of the shops in the souk. I have to say we were both excited, because we were looking forward to the Moroccan cities we were to visit: the capital city of Rabat, Casablanca, Marrakesh, and Meknes.

We started south to our first rest stop that was far out in the countryside. I was dressed in slacks with a sleeved top, but as I climbed off the bus, I could feel the eyes of the men who were sitting in front of a nearby shop following me. They ogled me as I walked past them to go to the restroom. Although we had been to India and walked through the crowded train station platform in Delhi, I had never experienced anything like this intense personal perusal. I told George right then and there that our decision to travel on a group tour of Morocco was absolutely right.

I remember visiting the royal palace in Rabat and being impressed by the perfection of the white marble structure glistening in the sunshine. I remember wandering the souks in Casablanca and the Medina, or old town, in Meknes. But it was the central square in Marrakesh, a city south of Casablanca, that provided our most vibrant memories of our Moroccan trip. We both rated our visit to Marrakesh a double *wow*!

The central square in Marrakesh is vast, truly vast. It goes by the name Jemaa el-Fnaa. In every part of Jemaa el-Fnaa there is action. Just think of a tremendous street fair, multiply that picture by fifty, and you will have an idea of what the square was and is like. Peddlers sell anything and everything. There are street performers of every imaginable kind: dancers, storytellers, and of course, snake charmers playing flute-like instruments to entice the reptiles to come out of their baskets and to sway to the rhythm of the music.

Our guide led us through the square and into the Medina behind the walls. Here were more upscale shops selling caftans, carpets, candies. In the carpet shop, we formed a circle while the salesmen—clad in their white gowns—threw one carpet after another onto the floor, hoping for a sale. We just enjoyed "the show" and the tea they served in glass cups. George and I lapped it all up, just like kids. I have to admit that, when the men ogled me at the first rest stop upon our entrance into Morocco, I had experienced culture shock. But this was different. This was culture heaven.

More was to come. When we entered the lobby and then the room of our hotel that evening, we felt that we had stepped into a scene from *Aladdin and the Arabian Nights*. Ornate? Oh my, yes. Even the shower enclosure in our bathroom was exotic. Glittering with mica-embedded tiles, circular in shape so that no shower curtain was necessary, it had a slim slit of a window tucked into the corner. The French onion soup we had that night in the hotel dining room was unbelievable. The moonlit views across the desert were more like a painting than real.

Some memories of things seen and done while traveling fade away rather quickly. Others last a lifetime. So many memories of Marrakesh are forever memories. Can you imagine remembering a bowl of French onion soup? Can you imagine remembering a shower enclosure?

Of course, not all forever memories are highlights. Some are "lowlights," memories of simply awful things that happen. And that thought brings me to something neither of us would ever forget.

Our tour was run by a European company, and smoking was permitted on the bus. This was often the case back in the seventies when smoking was an accepted fact of life, especially on the continent. A number of our fellow travelers smoked almost nonstop. We got off the bus each afternoon reeking of smoke, and I headachy from breathing in smoke all day. Thank goodness that today smoking is forbidden on buses and planes. At my age, now, I could not endure what we endured riding that bus. I called it a burning hell.

But the pleasures of travel outweighed the trauma of a smoke-filled tour bus, early morning calls to rise, and bags out by 6 a.m. As I mentioned in Chapter 1, in the summer of 1979, we took an overland tour of Kenya.

Because the trip was part of a Kean University program, smoking was not allowed on the bus. After our Melia tour in 1977, however, we always read travel brochures carefully and checked the important details. We checked the smoking policy, the number of meals included, the kinds of tours provided, and the number of travelers in the group.

FRANCE WITH TWA

By 1982 the two of us were ready for another organized land tour. This time we chose a bus trip around France offered by the airline TWA. Early in May, just after commencement at Kean University, we flew to Paris and then down to Nice where we had a couple of days on our own. We booked ourselves into a boutique hotel about a block from the seafront and set about relaxing. We even rented chairs on the beach to lap up some sunshine while our bodies adjusted to the time change.

The next day George and I found a public bus to take us to Monte Carlo. There is a route high up on the cliffs along the coast—the Grande Corniche—and a route lower down. We opted for the high road going, the low road for our return. Well, the high road was really high. The bus swooped along, coming close to the edge of the cliff (or that is what we thought). We clung on for dear life, remembering that it was on this cliff road that Grace Kelly, the American actress who became Princess of Monaco, had had her deadly accident. The views of the Mediterranean far below were spectacular. Each turn of a hairpin revealed a view that outdid the one before. Perhaps this was not a magical moment, but it certainly was an unforgettable one.

Arriving in Monte Carlo, the bus dropped us in the lower town. Not realizing that there is a series of escalators to the top, we walked up the path through the gardens to reach the upper town where the royal palace and the cathedral are located. We found some benches along the way; it was May, so flowers were already in bloom. We took our time, enjoying the views of the Mediterranean Sea.

When we reached the plaza in front of the palace, we watched the changing of the guard and then went into the cathedral where Grace

Kelly had married Prince Rainier back in the 1950s. I was a young woman in the fifties, just leaving my teenage years. To me, the marriage of Princess Grace was a fairy tale—a story of love and romance. I had seen Grace Kelly as the star of the Hollywood movie *True Love*, with Bing Crosby crooning the title song to Grace, a beautiful golden-blonde. The tale of Grace and her prince was the real thing! This was a fairytale moment for me.

But not for my George: He much preferred seeing the flowers in the gardens as we walked back down to catch our bus for our return to Nice. He was a bit disappointed that we did not have time to visit the aquarium that one of the former princes of Monaco had sponsored. George did eventually get to see the aquarium, but he had to wait about ten years until we stopped in Monaco on our second round-the-world trip.

Once we joined our TWA tour group, we drove north, stopping along the way to visit cathedrals in the major cities and chateaus when we neared Bordeaux. Our route often took us through countryside where the road was lined with European plane trees. The plane trees with their mottled bark formed a graceful arch of light green over the road: a pretty picture, especially on the spring days we were enjoying. The sun shone through the branches, casting shadows across the road. George loved that! It was much more relaxing than our drive on the Grande Corniche.

The most impressive city on our northward journey from Nice was Avignon. From our youth, we recalled hearing and singing the French tune whose lyrics go: "Sur le pont d'Avignon/L'on y danse, l'on y danse" ("On the bridge of Avignon, let us dance, let us dance"). We did not dance on the bridge at Avignon; rather we stood and looked out over the city while our guide explained that during the 14th century, Avignon was home to the papacy. The guide, like so many guides, told us a host of facts, which we knew we would never remember. What we would remember was standing on the bridge and hearing the guide sing the little French song we had sung as children. We would also remember seeing the Palais de Papes in the distance because of its distinctive architectural style.

The single most impressive object we saw on our tour of France was the Bayeux Tapestry. A huge tapestry composed of many, many panels, it chronicles the events leading up to the Battle of Hastings in 1066 and the actual events of the battle. Both George and I remembered learning about William the Conqueror, who crossed the English Channel and battled for dominance over England. His winning of the Battle of Hastings made him king of England and brought into the English language many words of French origin. The year 1066 was one neither of us had trouble remembering. Additionally, on one of our road trips through England, we had stopped in Hastings near the White Cliffs of Dover to view the memorial tower that commemorates the battle, so having the opportunity to see the tapestry was a treat.

The most memorable moment of our French trip—one that hit both of us hard—occurred during our visit to Normandy. Our tour took us first to a position high on the cliffs above Omaha Beach, one of the five beaches where the Allied forces landed on June 6, 1944, and one of two beaches where Americans landed. It was on these cliffs that the German forces had positioned their deadly guns and fired upon the incoming American forces. From there we could see the beach where so many men had lost their lives to liberate Europe. Still buried in the sands of the beach are remains of Allied ships that were blown to bits under the barrage thrown at them by German troops.

From the cliff top, we looked out on the waters of the English Channel and imagined what it must have been like for our troops. The day we were there, the seas were calm and sparkling. The day of the invasion, code-named Operation Overlord, the seas were rough, churned up by a storm off the coast. Our guide told us that about 2,000 Americans lost their lives in the invasion; total Allied deaths were nearly 4,500. I remember holding tightly to George's hand as we stood close together, feeling the horror that the soldiers, sailors, and airmen endured.

Leaving the cliffs, we made one of the most unforgettable stops in all of our many travels—the Normandy American Cemetery. At the cemetery are over 9,000 graves of Americans who died in battles in that part of France; the names of over 1,500 Americans missing in action are listed on a memorial wall. Arriving at the American cemetery, we looked out upon the crosses and stars of David that extend as far as the eye can see.

The tour guide gave us time to wander. And that is what George and I did, hand in hand. We read the notations on the crosses and stars, especially checking the year when each fallen warrior had been born:

1920, 1921, 1922, 1923, 1924. My George had been born in 1922!

We both had tears in our eyes as we thought about the men who are buried there; when they made the supreme sacrifice for their country and the world, they were about the same age George had been when he entered the service. They never had the opportunity to finish their schooling, succeed in a career, marry, be loved. When we got back on the bus, George whispered to me, "I could have been lying there, too. If circumstances had been different, I could have been there with them." And then I really wept.

After I had dried my tears, George told me how, when peace had been declared, he had gone looking for the burial site of Fred's brother, who was lost in the war. Remember that Fred was George's best friend with whom he took his first "cruise," the trip on the *Queen* that carried them both to war. George could not remember in which cemetery he had found Fred's brother, but he remembered taking pictures and sending them home to Fred's parents in New Jersey.

As we left the American cemetery and looked back at the crosses, these oft-quoted words of a World War I poem kept running through my head: "In Flanders fields the poppies grow/Between the crosses row on row." The crosses over which we had just wept were not World War I crosses. They were crosses for men and women of our own generation. Will people ever learn? Will we ever have a peaceful world?

Near the cemetery is the Omaha Beach Memorial Museum with a collection of tanks, landing craft, machine guns, and sidearms as well as helmets and uniforms from World War II. We spent some time there, but we were too emotionally drained by our visit to the American cemetery to appreciate the displays.

From Normandy, we headed to Paris. We had one day there with our tour group. On that day we did the typical tourist sites: the Eiffel Tower, Notre Dame Cathedral, the Arc de Triomphe with the Tomb of the Unknown Soldier. Since George and I had been to Paris, each of us before we were married, we were not as excited as if this were our first visit.

I do recall our leisurely evening walk down the Champs-Élysées. George kept remarking how different it was from when he had driven a jeep down the avenue in 1945. Then, his vehicle was the only one on the street. The area had been quiet compared to the noise of traffic and people surrounding us on our evening walk. I told George about when my sister and I, young women at the time, walked the avenue in the early evening. Groups of men had followed and tried to pick us up.

I also remember George's and my elevator ride to the top of the Eiffel Tower with our tour group. Neither of us had done that before. We both thought that the view gave the appearance of a three-dimensional map with the avenues radiating out in all directions and the roofs of houses looking like cardboard cutouts. And I remember well our visit to Notre Dame with our tour group. Before we entered the cathedral, our guide warned us to watch our possessions. Pickpockets might follow us until they saw an opportunity to strike. Forewarned, we identified a mother with a child in her arms who attached herself to our group.

As I write about this trip and about how George and I had begun to take for granted the opportunity to travel to fantastic and beautiful cities like Paris, I think of friends who are hesitant about going anywhere outside of the United States. As I have said many times to these friends, we live on an amazing planet, where the human mind has created structures as diverse as Notre Dame Cathedral and the Eiffel Tower, where Mother Nature has given us wonders as diverse as the White Cliffs of Dover and the Rock of Gibraltar. Wandering the world is a way to open the mind to differences in people and places. It teaches us to take in stride the disruptions in our lives, to be thankful for what we have, to face forward with hope.

EGYPT AND THE NILE WITH TWA

During the winter semester of 1984, George and I took a sabbatical, a semester off to pursue writing and travel. We had heard that Egypt was uncomfortably hot during summer months when we normally traveled. We decided, therefore, to investigate travel opportunities available during January, the coolest month in Egypt and the month our sabbatical from Kean began.

We settled on a TWA tour, since our trip to France with TWA had worked out so well: a knowledgeable guide, thoughtful fellow travelers, good food and accommodations, a nicely paced itinerary, and a price that fit our budget. We had heard that travel in Egypt was not up to European standards, but we thought that the sights to be seen would outweigh any inconveniences. We were absolutely right.

The morning I was to begin writing about our trip to Egypt, I lay in bed and thought about what we had seen there. It was as if a movie played in my mind—not a slide show but a movie with motion and even some sound. Scene by scene the movie played, with considerable detail but often without the names of the places we had visited. This kind of remembering does not always happen when I think back to a trip. It did in the case of Egypt because so much of the trip was beyond anything either of us had envisioned.

A temple on the Nile.

We flew into Cairo a day before we were to join our TWA group. We had pre-booked a car and driver to take us from the airport to Giza, famed site of the Pyramids of Giza and the Great Sphinx.

George and I had decided to splurge and had also pre-booked a room in a luxury hotel in Giza. It was a good decision. We were able to walk at our leisure from our hotel to see the raucous activity around the pyramids as camel drivers hawked rides and tour guides loudly spouted all manner of facts. We did not opt for a camel ride; we had been warned that the camel owner might demand a hefty tip before directing his camel to kneel so that a rider could get off. Neither did we take the walk up into the Great Pyramid, which we had been told could be scary if we were claustrophobic. We simply walked around the pyramids and then the sphinx. We marveled that the pyramids were over 2,500 years old, built when Egypt was one of the mightiest empires in the world.

The most striking scene in my mental movie of Egypt I call "Full Moon over the Pyramids." From our hotel we could see the pyramids outlined in the sky by a golden moon, with desert sands stretching far into the distance. "Magnificent," we both said. That sight was well worth the cost of the entire trip and the long plane ride. George later told me that never in his wildest dreams had he thought that he would travel to Egypt, which that night seemed to us to be the most exotic place in the world.

The next day our car and driver returned to take us to our tour hotel in Cairo—a Sheraton located on the Nile. That evening we had a short bus tour of Cairo. The bus made a quick stop at the tourist market before we climbed aboard a dinner boat that plied the waters of the Nile. Lights illuminated the banks of the river, and lights of other rivercraft sparkled here and there upon the water. The moon shone brightly above. Waiters clad in local attire served our meal. We felt that we had landed in a different universe.

But that night I paid the price. My intestines rebelled from something I had eaten, perhaps the custardy dessert. I knew I was in trouble. The next day, we boarded our tour bus for the long drive north to Alexandria.

I will never forget that drive! We had only one rest stop. Before the bus had come to a stop there, I was standing at the front, the first off and headed to the restroom. I can remember that as if it were yesterday. I do not remember much of Alexandria, other than that I stayed in our hotel room, looked out the window upon the Mediterranean Sea, and nibbled dry melba toast that we had brought from home.

After our return to Cairo, we took an overnight train south. TWA had reserved a private sleeping compartment for us on the train. Our compartment was beautifully appointed, and from the window we could watch the passing scenery. In the early dawn, we looked out to see people squatting on the banks of the Nile. The banks were the public bathroom. George just shook his head in disbelief. He was the one suffering culture shock this time.

I think that culture shock affects many travelers at some point. In a way, it may be a normal reaction to an environment totally different than our own and can have a positive outcome. Shock can trigger thought. Thought can bring understanding.

Now, back to our train ride along the Nile: Halfway through the morning, the train came to an abrupt halt. It did not move and it did not move and it did not move. George went to inquire why. He came back to explain that something was amiss on the tracks ahead and our tour guide was "working on it." Shortly, the guide came to the door and told us to gather our belongings; we were getting off the train and onto a bus that he had somehow commandeered. So in the middle of nowhere, carrying our luggage, we clambered off and walked—very, very carefully—across the tracks to our waiting bus. I especially remember George using his free arm to hang onto me for fear I would stumble.

Once we left the bus, we rode for several days on a Hilton Nile riverboat. We stopped at several small temples along the way. I have to admit that each temple began to look like the prior one, and today I have no distinct picture of any one of them—just general images of columns and carved facades and endless sand.

A few days later, we disembarked the Hilton riverboat in Luxor and checked into our hotel. That afternoon we walked among the tall columns and impressive stone carvings of Luxor Temple and the Temple of Karnak complex. Those temples are absolutely magnificent. I remember walking along an avenue lined with carved sphinxes; I remember an impressive obelisk at the end of the avenue. Yes, magnificent! Later in the evening we took a carriage ride to view the temples from the outside; the moonlight made them appear almost unworldly.

The next morning, we went to the Valley of the Kings to walk the area around King Tut's tomb and to climb down into one of the nearby tombs. "Amazing," I thought aloud, "so many tombs hidden under the sand."

George was feeling unwell by the time we returned to our hotel at noon. He finally had succumbed to the tummy virus—the last in our group to be struck down. I had been the first, and a doctor who was traveling with a suitcase of medicines had been the second. In the afternoon, our tour group was to take a felucca ride on the river to visit a park. George opted to rest at the hotel.

The felucca ride was quintessential Egypt! Because George was not there with me, I kept talking to myself: "I'm on the Nile in a felucca! Yes, I am! Yes, yes, I am." It was hard for me to believe.

Afterward, our group walked slowly through a pretty park on the opposite side of the Nile from our hotel. Then it happened. We saw a pack of wild dogs howling and running. Their prey was a young child who had become separated from her family. The child screamed. Three women from our tour group ran toward her. One grabbed the little girl. The other two went after the dogs. The parents came running and hugged those three brave women. This was the first thing I described to George when I got back to the hotel.

The next day, we flew south to Abu Simbel. I have a photo of George and me standing in front of one section of the Abu Simbel temples, which are carved into the rocks. This was the site we had come to explore. It was possible to walk back into the cliff to the temple area. I have no memory of the inside at all, just a mental picture of the impressive facade with its detailed carvings.

An unforgettable picture I do have is what happened when we got to the airport for the return plane trip to Luxor and on to Cairo. We had no assigned seats. Our tour group clustered by the door to the tarmac with a mob of other people. When the door opened, everyone ran. Obviously the flight was overbooked, but everyone in our group did get a seat. George and I were especially fortunate; our seats were in first class.

ENGLAND, BELGIUM, AND LUXEMBOURG

By 1990, we were ready to return to Europe. We chose two tours with Globus, one to the gardens and castles of England, the other to Benelux. We decided to do England again because George's cousins, Ralph and Ruth, had expressed an interest and said they would go with us. We chose Belgium and Luxembourg because, on previous trips to the continent, we had not touched those countries.

Recently, when I closed my eyes and attempted to run a movie in my mind of the stops we made on the gardens-and-castles tour, I came up with only one picture. It was of the courtyard in front of a hotel where the tour group had stayed for a night—a typical English country hotel, about three stories high and made of gray stone.

It was morning. George and I were first on the bus waiting for others to gather; the cousins had not yet appeared. Gradually the seats filled up, but still Ralph and Ruth had not boarded the coach. The guide, realizing the relationship we had with the no-shows, asked us what we knew. We had no idea, but I volunteered to call their room. Ruth answered, saying they were "running late"—the expression so many folks use as an apology for not being on time.

"Hurry up. Everyone is waiting," I said. I climbed back onto the bus, and eventually the cousins came running, dragging their hand luggage behind them. And this I will always remember: The other passengers on the bus began to stamp their feet in unison as Ruth and Ralph walked to the empty seats in the back. We had seen this happen to another late couple on our Morocco trip. I guess it is a common "punishment" meted out to folks who keep others waiting for the morning departure. The moral of the story: Don't be late when on a bus trip.

In rerunning our Benelux trip in my mind, I also retrieved just a single memory of Luxembourg. There we made a stop at the Luxembourg American Cemetery where General George Patton is buried and where there is an impressive memorial to him. As at our stop at the Normandy cemetery, the guide gave us time to walk among the crosses and stars. As at Normandy, we both were struck hard by the rows and rows of graves. We thought again how fortunate George and his friend Fred were to have had such long and productive lives, something that the boys interred there never had.

Once we were back on the bus, the guide said nothing. Rather, as we drove away, we heard a voice singing our national anthem over the public address system—"Oh, say can you see. . ." It was a powerful moment. No wonder it blotted out all other memories of Luxembourg.

But of course, no one could forget Brussels, the capital of Belgium, with its stately central market square—the Grand Place—and the stunning facades of the guild houses surrounding it. Those buildings were draped with flags and banners on the day we visited. Also in the Grand Place that morning, we saw women sitting on benches in front of shops that sold lace; these talented ladies were actually making lace by hand, using an intricate bobbin technique I had never seen before. Nor could anyone fail to remember a ride along the canals of Bruges or a visit to the main square in Antwerp, the Grote Markt, with its similarly ornate guild houses. Brussels, Bruges, and Antwerp are distinctly gorgeous cities, worthy of return visits.

Oh my! I nearly failed to mention the Manneken Pis in Brussels. I will leave it to a reader's imagination to figure out what this small statue depicts. Let me simply say that we all took pictures of this unique fountain, which is within walking distance of the Grand Place. George and I also carried home a round metal rendering of the Manneken Pis that hangs in our master bathroom even today.

THE NATURAL WONDERS OF THE CANADIAN ROCKIES

Did we want to travel in North America? Why not?

In 1991, we began planning a trip to the Canadian Rockies, an excursion that would focus more on natural wonders than on cities, cathedrals, and palaces. For our journey, we picked a tour company that collaborated with the grand old hotels of Canada—those managed by the Canadian Pacific Railway—and an itinerary with stops in Banff, Lake Louise, Emerald Lake, and Jasper.

The Banff Springs Hotel was our home for a few days. It is like a castle set in the hills high above Banff with great views down across the valley. *Stately* is a good word to describe the hotel lobby, which is paneled in dark, carved wood and has a soaring ceiling. Around the hotel is plenty of open space for hiking and gentle walking. From the Banff Springs Hotel, our group took the cable car up a nearby peak. The views were superb. George's facial expression, however, said it all. He was not happy about the gondola ride. He said he never trusted that cable cars were kept in good condition.

The next day we were off to the Chateau Lake Louise. Another of the grand hotels of Canada, it is constructed of gray, locally quarried rock and stands ten stories tall. It affords a great view of Lake Louise.

We lunched in the window-lined dining room and walked about the lake. We had anticipated great beauty. The views of the lake with its waters reflecting the surrounding, snow-capped mountains surpassed our expectations.

A short afternoon drive took us to Emerald Lake. Our lodgings by the lake were totally different from the Banff Springs Hotel and the Chateau Lake Louise. We stayed in rustic cabins, each with its own porch and wood-burning fireplace. We loved it.

In the evening, we wandered amid the park-like surroundings and along the shores of the lake. Yes, Emerald Lake is really emerald in color. A steward brought logs for the fireplace and lit a fire for us. Later, George and I sat in rocking chairs before our fireplace and watched the flames dance above the burning logs. The only sounds were the crackling of the fire and the creaking of our chairs as we rocked back and forth.

But for my George, the best was yet to come. As we drove back to the Lake Louise area to catch the main highway north, the guide asked the driver to stop in front of a tall cliff with layers and layers of exposed bedrock. The cliff was one that, if we had been navigating on our own, we would have passed as unremarkable. The guide explained that what we were looking at was the site of one of the most significant geologic discoveries: These rock beds were known as the Burgess Shale.

Immediately alert, George sat up! I did, too. We both knew that in those beds of rock were the oldest fossil remains ever discovered of the soft body parts of animals that had lived long ago. The guide could not show us samples of the rocks, because this was a national park and one could not just take a specimen. But simply being there was fabulous for anyone who had studied a lot of geology, as both of us had. George had even taught his geology students about the Burgess Shale.

Neither of us realized that we had a second exceptional experience ahead of us. We would actually walk on a glacial ice field on our way to Jasper National Park. At one point on Icefields Parkway, the bus stopped and we boarded a large, ungainly vehicle—an icemobile. It climbed up onto the glacier and took us to a point where we could get off to walk. This would have been fun even if we had never studied geology.

Jasper National Park was our stop for two nights. The Canadian Pacific hotel in Jasper is cabin-style and is set in a pine forest. The main lodge overlooks mountains laced with lakes and glaciers. The following day was ours to use as we wished. We walked around the lake, keeping alert for bears as we had been warned. We swam in the pool which had a unique feature: We entered it inside the building so as not to get cold, then swam through a tunnel to get to the outside section. Just imagine a swim in a heated, outdoor pool surrounded by ice-capped mountains.

We left Jasper by a train that wound around mountains and crossed bridges over deep ravines. Sitting near the front of the train, we could look out and see the rear cars as we traversed winding curves. We were on our way to Whistler, a ski resort near the Pacific. In a town called Kamloops—I had to check the name on a map—we switched to a bus. After a night in Whistler, a gondola ride there, and a train ride down the coast to Seattle, we were homeward bound.

As George and I flew home, we talked about our wonderful trip. And today, reliving it, I realize even more how fortunate I was to have a husband who loved nature and got excited about cliffs of fossil remains.

Chapter Seven

CRUISING OUR BASIC BUCKET LIST
1973-1992

While we were exploring Europe, Egypt, and Canada on guided land tours, we were also taking ten- to fourteen-day cruises to the Caribbean. As professors, we were able to book sunshine cruises when classes were not in session during the winter months. These were the kind that many folks equate with a cruise—a vacation to sunny ports with good food and accommodations at their fingertips.

However, by 1973, we were ready to cruise to places more exciting than the Caribbean. Like all avid travelers, George and I had a bucket list of trips we hoped to take. On our wish list were Saint Petersburg and the Baltic countries, the Greek Islands, Alaska, the North Cape, and Panama. Over the years from 1973 to 1992, George and I were fortunate: We were able to travel to each of the places on our wish list.

SAINT PETERSBURG AND THE BALTIC COUNTRIES

Early in the summer of 1973, George and I flew into Copenhagen, Denmark, to board a cruise to Northern Europe that the Royal Viking Line was offering. The one city highest on our bucket list was Saint

Petersburg. The Royal Viking cruise not only made an overnight stop there but also took us to other capital cities in the region: Oslo in Norway, Helsinki in Finland, and Stockholm in Sweden. We enjoyed all the cities. The most unforgettable were Saint Petersburg and Oslo.

On board the ship, before the *Royal Viking Sea* stopped in Saint Petersburg, the port lecturer warned us about what we should and should not do while in the city. Russia was a communist country with travel restrictions. We were not to bring any written matter like newspapers or books with us. We should not wander by ourselves, but rather take a guided tour, such as those offered by the ship.

That evening we chanced to talk to our dining stewards about the prohibitions that had been announced. They told us that the ship was supplying a bus for them. It would be parked just around the corner from the pier. Workers were permitted to walk around on their own. Did we want to come with them on the workers' bus?

Well, should we? We were younger and much more adventuresome then. The next morning, we each donned our oldest and darkest pants, old black polo shirts, black sweaters, and shoes that were scuffed from years of walking the streets of Europe. I pulled my hair back into a bun and put on no makeup. Disguised in what we thought looked like workers' garb, we walked down the gangway. At the bottom were Russian agents. They studied our passports and compared our pictures to our faces. When we had passed inspection, instead of heading to the rows of tour buses, George and I just kept walking, joining our dining-room stewards at the end of the pier. Sure enough a bus was waiting, and we got on with the workers.

The bus dropped us off along the Neva River, and we headed to St. Isaac's Cathedral and then to Senate Square to see the Bronze Horseman, a statue of Peter the Great that dominates the square. We walked and walked, following the canals, passing the Hermitage Museum, exploring to our hearts' content. No one stopped us. We tried to look like we knew what we were doing. Our main concerns were whether we could find our way to the bus pickup point and whether a bus would be waiting.

Thinking back, I do not know how the two of us law-abiding citizens had the audacity to do this! But that morning was the most memorable one of the entire cruise.

The next day, we took the ship's tour out to the Summer Palace. At one time, the palace was the residence during the summer months of the czars of Russia. Think Catherine the Great and Peter the Great. We were fascinated by the palace gardens. Hidden behind bushes that lined the pathways where we walked were trick fountains. If you happened to get in front of a triggering switch, a fountain spewed water at you. We both were careful where we walked, and we did not get wet.

The guide took us through the palace room by room; the place reminded us of the Palace of Versailles on the outskirts of Paris. Like many guides, he told us more facts than we would ever remember. What was most interesting, however, were his remarks about Saint Petersburg during World War II, especially how close the Germans had come to the city. He explained that the Germans had even taken over Catherine Palace, which was nearby, and stolen from it magnificent tiled stoves and art. Fortunately, after the war, these pieces were somehow found and returned.

Behind the Summer Palace, vendors had set up stalls. We bought a fine wool shawl for me and a couple of sets of Matryoshka dolls—dolls that nest one inside the other. Ours are exquisitely painted. One set bears a sequence of pictures that tells a folk tale and is signed by the artist. Anyone buying nesting dolls should look for the artist's signature on the base. They are the best ones.

When we got back to Saint Petersburg, the guide stopped the bus by the Neva River for a photo op. There a small oompah band was playing Sousa march music. It was a nice ending to another great day.

But, as we sat on the bus waiting for our group to gather, my George looked out the bus window. He saw an elderly woman who was dressed very poorly and was standing off by herself staring out across the river. She probably was younger than I am now, but she looked much older— wrinkled and gray. George said, "Quick, give me some dollars." On bus trips, for fear of pickpockets, he did not carry a wallet. I gave him some dollar bills. He rushed off the bus to give them to the woman.

Earlier, when we were riding to the Summer Palace, our guide had discussed the economy, and he had told us that poverty was rampant among senior citizens. Many of the older women did not have pensions and lived off the charity of others. That day, George gave one lady a little happiness and probably a good evening meal.

60

Toward the end of our cruise, we made a day stop in Oslo. Two things still echo in my mind from our stay in the capital of Norway: our visit to the Oslo City Hall, where the Nobel Peace Prize is awarded each year, and our walk in Frogner Park.

Oslo is a great city to explore on foot, and the public transportation system rates an A+. We got off the ship right by the City Hall and walked across the plaza to see the chamber where the Nobel Peace Prize is awarded. There was no charge to enter the hall where the annual ceremony occurs. We just strolled in and admired the chamber. It is a simple one with murals adorning the walls. Yet, we were impressed. Just to stand in the place where some of the greatest citizens of the world have been honored was a thrill.

We hopped a tram to get to Frogner Park. Once having climbed the massive marble staircase to enter and having walked through that park, no one could ever forget the sculptures displayed there. I had visited Frogner years before with my sister. I remembered it well and wanted to show it to George. I always called George "My Renaissance Man," for he knew so much about literature, history, and art as well as the sciences. He liked the unusual and was open to new ideas. Frogner Park was for him.

The more than 200 sculptures in the park extend across a vast area. They are modern works by Gustav Vigeland of men and women, girls and boys, all nude, often huddled together in distinctive groups. They represent ordinary people going about the everyday activities of life—propagating, giving birth, loving, playing, working at various occupations. The centerpiece is a towering pole of people, intertwined together, reaching toward the heavens. It sent a powerful message to George and me about the need for people to cling together to survive.

We walked a distance before finding the underground station that would take us back to the pier. On the way, we happened upon a statue of Sonja Henie, the Olympic prize-winning figure skater whom the Norwegians claim as their own. That is the wonderful thing about walking the streets of a city: You may stumble on an unexpected gem. Of course, the unexpected might be a shop full of hand-knit sweaters. Indeed, I bought not one, but two.

I cannot remember much from our days in Stockholm and Helsinki. My memories of those cities are dwarfed by my recollections of Saint Petersburg and Oslo. Obviously, in Stockholm, we loved our sail-in among the islands in the harbor; standing on deck when a ship sails into a city was always one of our favorite parts of a cruise. Then too, we enjoyed our stroll in the outdoor folk museum located on a hill overlooking the port. And we appreciated our walkabout in the old city and our stop at the Stockholm City Hall, where the annual Nobel Banquet is held.

From our day in Helsinki, I recall the strikingly modern Temppeliaukio Church and the Sibelius Monument. I remember the tram (with its clanging bell) that we took through the downtown. That is not much to remember of our day there; I guess we needed to return a few more times. One of the things to keep in mind when traveling by cruise ship is that often a day in a city is not enough. You cannot see everything in a day; better to relax, meander, and plan a return visit. "After all, tomorrow is another day."

THE GREEK ISLANDS

Greek Island cruises take travelers to islands such as Mykonos, Santorini, and Rhodes, as well as ports in Turkey and Cyprus. We chose the *MV Jupiter* for our first cruise into the Aegean in 1975. *Jupiter* was a small ship, part of a fleet owned by a Greek shipping line. We had to fly into Athens to catch the ship in the port city of Piraeus. Since this was our first time in Athens, we booked a hotel there and spent several days exploring before taxiing to the port.

We fell in love with Athens. It is a city that is easy to explore on foot. Yes, we climbed up to the Acropolis. At that time visitors were permitted to wander inside the ruins. Yes, we walked the narrow streets of the Plaka, the area just below the Acropolis, and then dined in a delightful taverna. Yes, we hired a car and driver for the trip out to Cape Sounion to see the ruins of the Temple of Poseidon that sits atop a point overlooking the sea. Yes, we even opted for a day tour to Olympia.

We had so many magical moments on this cruise, starting with those in Athens—too many to write about. Santorini and Kusadasi/Ephesus stand out. Both required lots of walking, so anyone following in our footsteps should be prepared for that.

Santorini is a geologist's heaven. The *Jupiter* sailed right into the natural harbor that is actually the crater of a volcano that exploded millions of years ago and since then has filled with water. Imagine sitting on a ship and looking up to the rim of the volcano high above. Imagine boarding a ship's tender to sail across a volcanic crater to dock at the pier. For us, imagination became reality.

When our tender reached the pier, George and I each hired a donkey and a handler to take us up the cliff to the rim of the old volcano. We each climbed on a donkey—George on his, I on mine. The keepers urged our donkeys forward. Off we went via a slippery cobblestone path that wound back and forth up the cliff. Of course, you may guess what made the path slippery and also gave the air a distinctive odor.

Once at the top, we walked around, passing shops and whitewashed houses and pausing from time to time to look down into the crater where our ship was moored. Today there is a tram that takes visitors to the top, but going by donkey was certainly more exciting. Today, too, there are many more big cruise ships plying the waters of the Mediterranean and Aegean seas, and the result is more crowded streets and noise.

If Santorini is a geologist's paradise, then the Kusadasi of today is for shoppers. Back in the seventies, however, when George and I visited for the first time, Kusadasi—near the ruins of the old city of Ephesus—was a sleepy port with few shops. We had to cross a sandy parking lot and go through a wire gate to get to the tour bus which was to take us to the ruins.

Scholars know Ephesus as the biblical city to which Paul the Apostle addressed his epistle—*Ephesians*—a book that is part of the New Testament. The ruins of Ephesus are worth exploring. We saw the remains of an amphitheater, the treasury, and some temples. But the most unforgettable ruins were of the bathroom with many holes cut side by side into a long marble slab. The guide explained that this had been a gathering place. People would sit and talk and "do their business." Customs change, don't they? What today is considered a private activity was, back then, communal.

If I seem to write often about bathrooms and rest stops, it's because, as we age and continue to travel, such stops become more imperative. I have to say, though, that customs associated with bathrooms are interesting, as are the differences in design found round the world even today.

ALASKA

Lots of Americans place an Alaskan cruise high on their wish lists. On an Alaskan cruise, there are great glaciers to see, whale-watching tours to take, good trails to hike, mountain railways to travel, and delicious salmon and crab to eat. Best of all, most cruises depart from Vancouver, Seattle, San Francisco, or Los Angeles. And of course, the ports are in Medicare country, which is something to consider as one gets older.

When George and I began to dream of cruising to Alaska, we dreamed of seeing Glacier Bay. That alone makes a trip to Alaska memorable, especially for folks who have not sailed the waters of Antarctica or Prince Christian Sound. That was true of us in 1976 when we took our first Alaska cruise. We chose the *Royal Viking Sky* out of Los Angeles, which included Glacier Bay in its fifteen-day itinerary.

The captain of the *Viking Sky* knew what he was doing. He sailed his ship up the long fjord to the face of Margerie Glacier. Once we arrived there, he held the ship in position in front of the face, as close as was safe, for a long time. He turned the vessel around periodically so that, regardless of what side of the ship we were on, we had great views of the blue ice riddled with crevasses. It was a brilliantly clear day, so the face of the glacier was reflected in the water. We saw huge chunks of ice break off from the face to crash into the water below with a deafening roar; the glacier was calving.

We could look far up to the top of the mountain where Margerie Glacier began; we could see tributary rivers of ice from side valleys join the main glacier. We could trace black streaks within and on the edges of the glacier high up into the mountains. The black streaks were masses of rock that the moving glacier had carved from the sides of the mountain and which had become embedded in the ice, forming moraines.

Too soon, we had to give up our place before the glacier and sail down the fjord. Only a few ships are allowed into Glacier Bay, and each is allotted a set amount of time. The bay is a national park, a protected habitat for animals that make it their home. It must be preserved.

Our morning in Glacier Bay was a wonderful experience for both of us, but especially for George, my in-house environmentalist. What a day it had been for him!

During our stop the next day in Juneau, George and I had the opportunity to see Mendenhall Glacier. The Mendenhall experience is different from the one at Glacier Bay. A bus drops passengers at a point where they can walk to see the glacier up close. Mendenhall does not end in a deep fjord, but in a tidal pool. When we repeated the Alaska cruise in June 1997, we returned to Mendenhall. The glacier had retreated up the valley, a victim of global warming.

Back in Juneau, we explored the streets on our own. That was something we both enjoyed—walking the streets with the opportunity to sit on a bench from time to time. In travel as in life, not all moments are powerful. Since George's passing, I realize that such peaceful moments are sometimes more valuable than the powerful ones.

A short distance from Juneau is Skagway, a mining town at the end of a long arm of the sea. It has the feel of an old western town with bars that have swinging doors and mirrored walls. In Skagway, we boarded an old railway car to take us up into the mountains along the path that the miners had hiked to get to the Klondike gold fields. From the train windows, we could see the narrow trail that the miners had followed.

The train took us over trestle bridges that stood high above deep ravines. It wound higher and higher until we reached the top of the ridge. At the summit, the train stopped, and we got out to stretch our legs and take pictures. Unfortunately mosquitoes were waiting. They struck with a vengeance—swarms of them; they seemed to love the smell of us. We clambered back onto the train and the mosquitoes followed. We used makeshift fly swatters to clear our railway car of the bloodthirsty pests.

Our train went back to Skagway the way it had come. The narrow-gauge tracks do not stop at the top of the mountain, however. They extend miles into the interior to Klondike Territory. This was the same direction that the miners took, loaded with the gear they needed to find and extract the gold. Those men had to have a lot of stamina to make the long trek; they had to have a strong desire for gold. History books tell us that more than 100,000 men made the journey into the Klondike gold fields in the 1890s.

We learned a basic travel lesson that day: Always carry insect repellent, because you never know when you will need it. However, regardless of those nasty and persistent pests, George and I loved the train ride. George kept talking about it as we roamed the streets of Skagway, the same streets the miners had walked as they prepared for their trek.

Sitka was doubtlessly our favorite town of all those we visited on our Alaska cruise. It is a perfect gem! What we enjoyed most was our walk in the Sitka National Historic Park, which is very near the dock. Here we saw striking totem poles on display in a quiet pine forest. Here we also saw Tlingits carving totem poles, which are really storytelling poles. Each pole has its own tale to tell—a story featuring a bear or an eagle or a hero or a maiden in distress.

We wandered a long time among the totem poles and pine trees. The earth was covered with needles and cones, and the air was redolent with the scent of pine. We felt at peace with the natural environment.

In the town itself, we went into St. Michael's Cathedral. The word *cathedral* does not really describe the small, wooden, domed structure we visited. A replica of the original that was lost when it burned in the 20th century, it houses paintings and icons salvaged from the fire. Built when Alaska was a Russian possession, the original structure was said to have been the oldest Orthodox cathedral in the new world. Its replica stands as a reminder of the town's early history.

Alaska is known for its special dark jade—jadeite. Of course, I left Sitka with earrings, a necklace, and a bracelet of jadeite, which is considerably different from the lighter-green Chinese jade. We also came home with a fine carving of a small totem.

Probably it is unusual to hear someone say that an important part of a cruise was the seafood. Because the ship picked up fresh salmon and crab in the Alaskan ports, those delicacies of the sea appeared on the menu almost every night, nicely prepared, really delicious. In Juneau, we went to a fishery where we saw salmon being boxed in ice to be sold and shipped. In Ketchikan, we took a tour that included an all-you-can-eat crab lunch. The crabs were piled in the middle of the dining tables. We helped ourselves, cracked open the shells, and enjoyed the best crab we had ever eaten.

When we returned to Alaska in 1997, we noticed how large numbers of cruise ships visiting a compact area can change the feel of a place. By the

1990s, more tourists clogged the sidewalks; more tour buses jammed the roads. We found more noise, less quiet peacefulness. George mentioned how glad he was to have seen the *real* Alaska back in the seventies.

NORWAY AND THE NORTH CAPE

The earth is truly a "many-splendored thing." The west coast of Norway, cut by majestic fjords and dotted with picturesque villages, is evidence of that splendor. Inland are snow-capped mountains, glaciers, and cascading waterfalls—earth's wonders dear to the heart of nature lovers. At the very top of Norway is the North Cape, the most northerly point in Europe that can be reached by road. Since so many of the interesting things to visit are along the west coast, clearly the best way to see this region is by ship. In June of 1978, to celebrate our tenth wedding anniversary, George and I traveled to Norway.

To get to the North Cape, we booked an Atlantic crossing on the *MS Sagafjord* followed by a cruise along the Norwegian coast all the way to the Cape. For George, our Atlantic crossing in the summer of 1978 brought back memories of his crossing from New York to Scotland during World War II. As we sailed the North Atlantic, he kept talking about that far different "cruise."

I would readily agree that there is nothing really spectacular about the North Cape when one stands upon it. It is simply a windblown, rocky promontory jutting into the Barents Sea above the Arctic Circle. We took a bus tour to the North Cape from the port village of Honningsvag, crossing stark terrain that even in summer seemed gloomy and foreboding. At the Cape is a rather striking monument in the shape of a large globe of the world. Travelers go there, as we did, just to know that they are standing at the top of Europe. We would have the same feeling when we stood at the southern tip of Africa, when we looked up at the southern tip of South America, and when we looked out from the most westerly point in continental Europe.

During the evening of our day at the top of Europe, the captain of the *Sagafjord* took us for a sail around the North Cape. It was the middle of

June, the time of the summer solstice and of the longest day of the year in the Northern Hemisphere. Remember, we were off the coast of "The Land of the Midnight Sun." George delighted in standing beneath the clock on the aft deck that showed the hour and having his picture taken at midnight. It was daytime bright!

As we passed close to the North Cape, we stood together at the rail and looked up. From this vantage point, the Cape was impressive. The thought that we were "there" made us shiver.

The great splendor of Norway, however, is found within the fjords, long deep arms of the sea carved out by glaciers that blanketed the land during the ice ages. We discovered that almost nothing compares to a ride up a fjord on a sunny day. And that is what we had—bright sunshine and a cloudless sky. We stayed on deck as we sailed our first Norwegian fjord, watching for waterfalls that cascade from steep cliffs formed by rivers of glacial ice.

When our ship dropped anchor mid-fjord, we hopped on a tender for the short ride to the edge of a cliff where we were to join a bus tour for a drive to the top. I remember that bus ride well. George always said that he too remembered it well. The bus navigated one switchback curve after another, with the views of the fjord getting better and better as we climbed higher and higher. I must admit that we were both scared, for there were no guardrails and the road was narrow. We just had to have faith in our driver and hope that the tires were good. The scary ride was worth the view from the top. We could see the *Sagafjord,* just a dot down, down, down there on the waters of the fjord.

I cannot remember for sure the name of the fjord we sailed that day. It may well have been Sognefjord, the deepest fjord in the world. I guess the name is unimportant, though. What does matter is the feeling of wonder we experienced. We had chosen this cruise to go to the North Cape. We got so much more.

On her way south, the *Sagafjord* docked in a number of small Norwegian cities—Bergen, Stavanger, Tromso, Trondheim—cities small enough to explore on foot. Our favorite was Bergen. It is a place that has everything one expects to find in a Nordic coastal town.

The port lecturer on *Sagafjord* had explained that the ship would dock at the far end of town and we would have to walk a considerable distance to get to the center. For that reason, on our first visit to Bergen, we opted for a ship-run city tour. We later realized that we could have walked the city on our own, but still there was an advantage in taking the tour. Included in it was a ride on the funicular up Mt. Floyen, the peak that overlooks the harbor and town. The tour had an assigned time slot for the funicular so we did not have to wait on line. We had plenty of time to walk around once we got to the top.

The tour spent time, too, in the Bergen Fish Market. Despite its name, we found little outdoor restaurants there and stalls selling things other than fish. After we had walked the market, our guide took us to nearby Bryggen, a quaint area of old wooden buildings with interesting facades and roof features. This is also an area of shops selling Nordic wares, especially knitted woolens.

In the afternoon, George and I took a small boat up an arm of the fjord on which Bergen is located. We passed cliffs with waterfalls cascading down. I remember that the captain blew the boat's horn as we passed below the cliffs. The sound echoed and re-echoed. It was a fun trip, but the scenery was not so striking as the scenery we had seen at our prior stop.

When she left Norway, *Sagafjord* sailed to ports in Holland, France, Portugal, and Spain before heading back to New York. We, however, disembarked in Oslo and transferred to a North Sea ferry. Our intent was to ferry to New Castle in England, catch the train down to London, and spend a few days in the city before flying home. We just wanted to have the experience of a ferry ride across the North Sea.

The ferry ride, however, was not the most comfortable; we had not anticipated that smoking would be permitted throughout the vessel or that our cabin would be so miniscule. The thing I remember most clearly, though, was looking out in the early evening and seeing yellow glows on the horizon—gas burning off the oil wells that work the North Sea and make Norway energy self-sufficient.

George and I returned to the North Cape and the Norwegian fjords in 1999 on a cruise on *Rotterdam VI*. That is a sure indicator that our first Norway cruise was a winner.

THE PANAMA CANAL

On board a ship, travelers commonly talk about the cruises they have already taken, especially the ones that they have liked best and the ones that they have liked least. From such conversations, we learned that the Panama Canal ranks high on travelers' wish lists. We resolved that we would transit the Panama Canal as soon as we had the opportunity. That opportunity came in March of 1992, when I was on sabbatical from Kean and George had retired.

Because this cruise was so high on our bucket list, we decided to go the luxury route; we booked a relatively new cruise line, Crystal Cruises, which was ranked number one by *Travel + Leisure* magazine. Our ship was the *Crystal Harmony*.

Most Panama Canal cruises stop in one or two Caribbean ports before sailing the canal and several ports on the west coast of Central America and Mexico after leaving Panama. Ours made two Caribbean stops: the Cayman Islands and the San Blas Islands. We did not bother getting off the ship at George Town on Grand Cayman. We had stopped there several times on Caribbean cruises and found it to be a great place for swimming and shopping. We decided it was easier to swim in the ship's pool and I did not need to shop.

George and I did, however, take the tender to shore in the San Blas Islands. The island where we stopped appeared to us more a tourist trap than a place where people actually lived. We found shacks and mud paths and women selling colorful appliquéd goods they had made. The quality of the sewn pieces was excellent, but as we were climbing off our tender, we saw local people arriving on the island laden with things to sell. It seemed as if they did not live there and were coming for the day to sell to the tourists.

It took several days to sail from Fort Lauderdale to Panama. Besides our two port stops, the cruise line offered lectures on the history of Panama and the building of the canal. The port lecturer was a true professional. She explained about the early efforts of the French to build a sea-level canal across the Isthmus of Panama. She suggested reasons those efforts failed: the impossibility of removing as much rock as would have been necessary to build a sea-level canal, the mosquito-borne diseases such as yellow fever that killed so many workers, the snakes, and the heat. She talked about the way the Americans had worked with the Panamanians against the Colombians to ensure Panamanian independence and about the treaty that President Roosevelt had signed with Panama that gave authority over the Canal Zone to the United States. She explained that Walter Reed and other American doctors had conquered yellow fever by discovering that the disease was transmitted by mosquitoes. As a result, it was possible for construction of the canal to resume. We went to each of her lectures, something we rarely had done on prior cruises. She was setting the stage so beautifully for our transit.

Late in the evening before the morning of our passage, our captain "parked" the *Harmony* at the entrance to the canal to await our turn to enter the first set of locks. George and I woke early on the morning of our big day. Looking out from our verandah at 5:30 a.m., we saw lights twinkling all around us. These were the lights of the other ships in the queue waiting to enter the Gatun Locks. These locks are actually three interconnecting chambers that raise ships from the Caribbean Sea to Gatun Lake.

At about six in the morning, we felt the *Harmony* begin to move. This was it! We dressed quickly and headed to the prow where we could watch the ship move into the first chamber of the Gatun Locks. Once we were in the lock, George and I ran to the stern to see the huge gates close behind our ship. Water poured into the lock and we began to rise. We sat by a window in the Lido restaurant to eat breakfast while *Harmony* inched upward.

When *Harmony* reached the top of the first chamber, the heavy gates in front of us swung open. Of course, by then we were at the prow, George taking pictures nonstop. This happened three times before we reached the level of Gatun Lake and then sailed into the lake that had been constructed by damming up the Chagres River. Gatun Lake is eighty-five feet above sea level. That is how high the Gatun Locks had lifted our ship.

Harmony docked in Gatun Lake, and we hopped onto a tender to go ashore. Our short bus tour took us to a viewing platform from which we could look down on the Gatun Locks and see other ships being raised up through the three chambers we had just navigated. Here our tour guide explained that the so-called donkey engines that are on the sides of the canal only guide the ships, which sail through using their own power. Is it not amazing what the human mind can conceive?

After crossing Lake Gatun, we sailed through the Culebra Cut. The Culebra Cut is literally an excavation through the highest part of the isthmus—the Continental Divide. It was this mountain ridge that foiled the French attempt to build a sea-level canal. The French were trying to cut the ridge down to the level of the Caribbean Sea, but that was an impossible task. The ridge was just too high; there was too much rock to be excavated and moved. Because the American plan was to use three locks at each end of the canal, the Americans had to remove considerably less material. A Panamanian historian had boarded *Harmony* as we began our transit; he explained all of this to us as we moved through the cut.

Near the end of the day, *Harmony* entered the locks on the Pacific side of the Culebra Cut: Pedro Miguel, which consists of two chambers, and Miraflores, which consists of one chamber. This series of locks lowered our ship to the level of the Pacific Ocean. As we went through each of the locks, George and I ran from the front of our ship to the stern. We wanted to see the great doors at the ends of the locks open and close. We wanted to see the locks empty; we wanted to see, as well as feel, our ship being lowered.

Having reached sea level on the Pacific side, we stood on the deck of *Harmony* and saw the Bridge of the Americas ahead. The Bridge of the Americas is a span across the canal that is a link in the Pan-American highway. We looked directly up at the giant arch as we sailed under the bridge. Of course, George snapped a great photo to add to the collection he took that day.

Both of us stayed on deck for most of the afternoon. We talked about those who, before the completion of the canal in 1914, had walked across the isthmus to get from the Atlantic to the Pacific. Feeling the intense heat of the sun as we stood at the rail of our ship and looking out over dense jungle terrain, we got some sense of how tough their journey must have been.

We thought about the workers who had lost their lives to malaria and yellow fever and who had died from construction accidents. We talked about the commitment of so many to turn a dream into reality. We talked, too, about President Teddy Roosevelt, who engineered the treaty that brought the United States into the picture, perhaps a bit illicitly.

That evening as we left Panama behind, George and I agreed that the day had been perfect—simply perfect. We agreed that we were so fortunate to have seen this engineering marvel. We never dreamed then that during our lifetimes we would sail the Panama Canal more than a dozen times.

The *Harmony* made several stops on the west coast of Central America and Mexico before docking in San Diego. First in my memory of those stops is a port in Costa Rica where George and I joined a bus tour over the mountains to the capital city, San Jose. The distance was considerable, but the scenery was lush green and rather striking. I can picture the little village that was our halfway rest stop high up in the mountains. It is a village that specializes in colorfully decorated donkey carts that tourists buy and ship home to use as foyer pieces.

I have memories, too, of San Jose. I especially remember the upscale homes and even the more moderate ones, protected by gated walls topped with barbed wire. I recall our visit to the museum housing artifacts from peoples who had lived in Central America thousands of years ago and to the theater, under repair, where we navigated carefully to avoid the construction debris. George remarked afterward that in our country we never would have been allowed entrance into a work area such as the theater, where we had had to tread so gingerly.

The second stop I remember is the city of Acapulco, a resort in Mexico. Again, since it was our first time there, we booked a short city tour in the morning that took us around the downtown section with a visit into the cathedral. The bus then drove us through the beach hotel area. This is what ships call a "highlights" tour, and it works if one wants a short overview. In the afternoon, we explored the handicraft market on the pier.

Few ships stop today in Acapulco. Crime is a serious problem. We sensed that when we repeated our Panama Canal cruise in December 1992. On that trip, we walked the area just behind the pier. A young fellow must have identified us as possible targets to mug; he began to follow us. George had with him a Spanish-language guide that listed useful phrases; in it he found the phrase that means, "Get away from us!" He turned, faced the fellow, and bellowed the Spanish expression. George's pronunciation must have been understandable, or it may have been his body language, but the young man stopped in his tracks, turned, and fled.

I remember, too, our stop in Cabo San Lucas, at the tip of the Baja Peninsula. Here we boarded a small boat for a sail into the bay to view a rather striking natural arch that rises out of the water. It was a simple excursion, but enjoyable. Returning to Cabo, we settled on the beach and swam in the ocean. This was not a very smart thing to do, as George discovered. That evening he suffered a case of Montezuma's revenge. We assumed he had swallowed water while he was swimming. After that on our trips, we took greater care about where we swam; in developing areas, sometimes they dump sewage directly into the sea, without any attempt to clean it up. In those instances, we stayed away from the beaches and used the ship's pool.

Chapter Eight
EXPLORING CRUISING OPTIONS
1992-2001

Most of the ships on which we traveled during our first years of cruising were ocean-going liners carrying between 700 and 1,300 passengers. These would not be considered large by today's standards, as new ships are being built to carry 5,000 or more. But in the seventies, eighties, and nineties, our ships would have been categorized as large. During our early cruising years, too, we chose ships based primarily on their itinerary, sailing date, and price. In doing so, we sailed with a variety of cruise lines: Swedish American, German Lloyd, Royal Viking, Cunard, Norwegian America, Crystal, Celebrity.

In the 1990s, although we continued to sail the larger ships, we also began to choose another kind of cruise experience. We began to pick a cruise based on a ship's characteristics rather than her itinerary—just to see what it would be like. We sailed a doubled-hulled vessel, some small yacht-like ships, a sailing vessel, and a riverboat during the years 1992-2001. When I think back on those cruises, most of my memories are of the ships themselves.

RADISSON DIAMOND: 1992

On Memorial Day 1992, I chanced on an ad in our local paper. A company called Diamond Cruise in conjunction with the Radisson Hotel chain had launched a unique ship—the *Radisson Diamond*. The *Diamond* was a double-hulled vessel with a catamaran design. It carried about 350 passengers. The shakedown cruise, a voyage intended to identify problems and correct them, was slated for mid-June. The ship would run at half capacity, passengers would occupy only the verandah staterooms, and the cost for the fourteen-day voyage was half the expected price of the maiden voyage which was to follow. The cost for the shakedown cruise was ten thousand dollars for two people. I knew that we would never pay twenty thousand dollars, the full cost for a fourteen-day trip for the two of us.

I showed the ad to George. He nodded his approval. By the next day, we were booked and fully paid. That afternoon, I told my sister about our expensive bargain, a trip that would begin in France, make stops in Spain and Portugal, and end in Lisbon. She booked. I called George's cousins. They and another member of their family booked. We were a group of six. We had two weeks to prepare.

The six of us flew into Paris, where we were met by a Radisson agent who escorted us to a bus that would take us to our ship. It was docked downriver, waiting for us. Our first impression of the *Diamond* was of a giant crab hovering over the water. We had never seen anything like it. Grabbing our carry-on luggage, we climbed the gangway. We were on! I do not know how we managed such a fast getaway, but we did it.

We were ecstatic when we saw our stateroom. This was deluxe living, far more luxurious and spacious than George and I previously had experienced. We even had a good-sized verandah. It was a far cry from our cabin on our first Christmas cruise, when we were so far down in the bowels of the ship that our feet were below the waterline.

The formal dining room was the most magnificent ship's dining room we had ever seen. Located aft in the ship, the room was several stories high, with floor-to-ceiling windows across the complete stern and with Grecian columns adorning the expanse.

We were not so impressed with the main lounge, which also served as the entertainment center. It was small and the sight lines were awkward.

We also thought the casino took up too much space on the main deck. All in all, though, we were very happy travelers.

Because it was a shakedown cruise, we hit some minor glitches; for example, the air-conditioning in our cabin gave us problems. The management, however, immediately switched us to another cabin, which was equally extraordinary, if not even better. The service in the dining room the first night was not up to par, for the staff were all new and learning the ropes. These, however, were really minor inconveniences.

The major glitch, which in the end proved to be advantageous, was a mistake by the captain. An important stop on our itinerary was the French city of Bordeaux. Bordeaux is situated on the Garonne River, and the ship was supposed to take us upriver to dock right in the city center. However, the captain had misjudged the tides. The water in the river was not deep enough for our ship to enter when we reached the mouth of the Garonne.

The decision was made to offload us at a town at the mouth of the river and bus us into Bordeaux—at no additional cost. The ship would move upriver when the tide came in and pick us up at the regular city dock later in the day. Our group of six liked that idea because we would get to see the countryside, which we had not anticipated.

When we arrived in Bordeaux, the bus dropped us off in the heart of the old city, a convenience that enabled us to see the major attractions and then walk slowly back to the pier. We had all day, for the *Diamond* was not expected to reach Bordeaux until three in the afternoon. We arrived at the pier early, thinking we could just sit there and enjoy the sunshine. We were surprised, however, to see a huge crowd of people amassed on the pier. Inquiring, we learned that a local TV station had run a story the night before about this ship with the weird look that was to enter Bordeaux that afternoon. The crowd was waiting to see *our* ship!

And then, there she came, up the river, horn blowing, ship's flags flying! We had not seen the *Diamond* in motion. It certainly was a strange sight, not at all like the ships we were accustomed to seeing. We stood on the benches we had been sitting on, looking over the heads of the French people. We stared, amazed just as they were.

Once the ship had tied up, crew members set up a red carpet and a ropeway through the crowd. The carpet and ropeway were for *us*, the passengers. We marched through like celebrities to the cheers of the French who had gathered for the "show." They actually clapped. George chuckled at this sendoff. He patted me on my shoulder and said, "You really picked us a different cruise."

Standing hand in hand on the bench in Bordeaux and watching the *Diamond* steam upriver toward us is one of the most unforgettable memories I have of our cruising days together. It is a precious memory, one I often replay in my mind.

SONG OF FLOWER: 1993-1995

It was on *Radisson Diamond* that we learned about the 250-passenger vessel named the *Song of Flower*. *Song of Flower* was a small ship constructed on the hull of an old ferry. Operated by Radisson Seven Seas Cruises, it was about the same size as the "yachts" of the luxury line Seabourn, but half the price. We had always wondered what it would be like to sail on a ship of this size. Because the price was something we could handle, we decided to book the ship for a fourteen-day cruise in the western Mediterranean for the summer of 1993 and a fourteen-day cruise in the eastern Mediterranean for the summer of 1995.

What we appreciated most about the *Flower* was the exceptional service. One example that I remember clearly: I had just climbed out of the ship's small swimming pool and was standing on deck putting on my wristwatch. A deck steward rushed over. "Madam, may I help you with that?" he asked. And he did. The crew members seemed to enjoy talking to us, too. They were friendly as well as efficient.

Although many cruisers swear by such small ships, we did find *Flower* limiting. There was almost no entertainment in the evening, something we liked and I still like on the larger liners. There were few little nooks and crannies where one could sit and read. The small size, though, had one major advantage, and that advantage was the reason we chose her for our second cruise in 1995. Being small, the *Flower* could go where larger ships could not.

One place *Flower* could go was through the Corinth Canal, the canal that connects the Aegean Sea with the Ionian Sea and separates the main section of Greece from the Peloponnese. The transit of the Corinth Canal was on the itinerary of the 1995 cruise. George had read about that canal, and it was something he wanted to do. Additionally, the ruins of the old city of Corinth were close enough to one of the cruise stops for us to tour them.

Both George and I always loved to sit on a ship and watch the world go by. That is what we did as we transited the Corinth Canal. This canal is a narrow cut through solid limestone, so at times there are tall, sheer, rock cliffs on each side. Like the Suez Canal, it is a sea-level canal; there are no locks. Like both the Suez and Panama canals, there is an amazing bridge spanning it. The canal is only four miles long, compared to the fifty miles of the Panama Canal; it is very narrow, just eighty-one feet wide.

Our passage through that four-mile, one-of-a-kind waterway was the high point of our trips on *Flower*. Because the channel is so narrow and the rock walls so high, making the transit of the canal was like sailing through a roofless tunnel. A caveat: I admit that a roofless tunnel, by definition, does not exist—which just goes to show why George and I felt we had slipped down the rabbit hole that day and entered Wonderland with Alice.

An aside: Both the *Diamond* and the *Flower* have gone on to different lives. Both have been sold and now sail Asia. The *Diamond* does short gambling trips out of Hong Kong. I guess the large casino turned out to be a plus after all.

WIND STAR: 1994

Having seen the *Wind Star* anchored in harbors in the Caribbean and in the Mediterranean, George and I decided to book the four-masted sailing ship for our Christmas holiday in 1994. I recall our flight to Miami and onward to Barbados, but I do not have any clear memories of our port stops during the ten days we spent on *Wind Star*. I do, however, have one indelible memory of the ship.

Our first evening aboard, after a good meal in the main dining room—and I remember it was good—we looked for some form of live entertainment, but came up dry. We found no combo playing in the small lounge, no piano-bar action, nothing. We chalked that up to the fact that it was the first night, and often on ships, the entertainment is minimal as passengers settle in.

The next evening, however, was the same story. By chance, however, we wandered up to level four to see what might be happening on the open deck. We found absolute quiet. We heard no engine noise, because *Wind Star* was relying on her sails, not her engines, which were used primarily on windless days and nights. That evening the warm breezes of the Caribbean filled the sails. Few people were on deck. The sky was star-studded. The moon glowed. It was a gorgeous night!

We settled in a pair of deck chairs and leaned back to contemplate the stars. At one point in his teaching career, George had taught astronomy, so he could identify the most obvious constellations for me—Orion, the Big Dipper, the North Star, and the Little Dipper—as well as the lesser-known clusters. This was our entertainment for the evening; we could not have asked for better. It was to be our entertainment for the eight nights to follow. Each evening we would seek out "our" deck chairs, push them close together so we could hold hands, and enjoy the sea, the air, the stars, the peace.

We discovered, too, another advantage of the *Wind Star*. Being small (she carries about 135 passengers), she could sail into pretty, beach-lined coves and anchor there. We could tender from our mooring to the beach and enjoy the water, the sun, and the sand. *Wind Star* and ships like her are really ideal for beach lovers, swimmers, and snorkelers. Probably, too, she is more suited to couples and those traveling in small groups than to the single traveler.

Earlier in 1994 during spring break, George and I had joined our cousins Ralph and Ruth for a seven-night cruise around the Virgin Islands. We did that cruise on the *M/V Yorktown Clipper*, a small ship that carries about the same number of passengers as *Wind Star* but does not use sails. We had the same reaction to it as we had to *Wind Star*: It is great for swimming and sunning, perfect for beach lovers. Often, *Yorktown* would anchor and drop a platform off the side. We could use flotation devices to keep safe as we swam in the warm waters that surrounded the ship. One day, a big turtle even came to look us over and to swim with us. Again, evenings were quiet. In 1994, however, we were part of a group; in the evenings our group would generally gather in the lounge to talk.

A RIVERBOAT ON THE RHINE: *2001*

During our years of what I think of as "togetherness travel," George and I were often asked if we had taken any riverboat cruises. Until 2001, our answer was "no." In that year, we decided to explore Europe by riverboat so that we could see towns and cities not located on the coast.

We chose Uniworld riverboats and booked two cruises back to back—one on the Rhine, followed by one on the Danube. Our plan was to fly into Switzerland and pick up our Uniworld boat there, then cruise the Rhine River into Amsterdam, and finally hop a plane to Berlin for a short land tour before embarking on another Uniworld boat trip in Nuremberg.

About a week before we were scheduled to fly to Europe, however, we got a shocking call from a Uniworld agent. The agent told us that they had made a mistake and the cost was actually eight hundred dollars more than they had quoted and what we had already paid. We could not board the ship unless we paid them the eight hundred dollars.

When I re-ran the numbers, I figured out that Uniworld had made an honest error. They had failed to include in our original price the cost of the flight between Amsterdam and Berlin, where our second leg was to begin. We had not, however, factored into our budget another eight hundred dollars. We asked to talk to a supervisor, who took responsibility for the mistake. She said that management would agree to split the eight hundred with us because it was their error; we could pay just four hundred. Actually, since we had a contract with Uniworld, we were not obligated to pay anything more. But time was flying. We authorized the company to charge the four hundred to our credit card. We were not happy about the added expense, but we did realize theirs was an honest mistake.

We boarded our riverboat near Basel in Switzerland to sail north, downriver. Here are some of the most memorable stops we made along the Rhine.

From Ludwigshafen we toured to Heidelberg by bus. The stately castle up on the hillside is what comes to mind when I think of Heidelberg. I think also of our group gathered around tables in a beer garden having lunch community-style, a scene reminiscent of the operetta *The Student Prince.*

In Rüdesheim am Rhein, we walked from the ship up the hill to visit Siegfried's Mechanical Music Cabinet, the "neatest" little museum we have ever visited. Siegfried Wendel over the years had collected music boxes, decorative player pianos, hand-cranked carnival instruments, and organ grinders. He had opened his collection to the public. True or not, the museum guide—a big, strapping guy who spoke enthusiastically about the major pieces on exhibit—introduced himself as Siegfried and told us how he had started his collection. He set some of the mechanical pieces in motion, so the museum reverberated with music.

Back on the boat, we cruised through the Rhine Gorge, a pass through high mountain ridges with steep cliffs on each side and with castles dotting the hillsides. We listened for the Lorelei, the mythical woman who is said to haunt this part of the Rhine and is cursed forever to call out to approaching ships. Of course, we both claimed to hear the Lorelei as we sat on the upper deck, watching the passing scenery.

In Koblenz, which is located where the Moselle reaches the Rhine, the ship's tour director led us to the major sites by foot. He then let us loose to wander on our own, warning us to be back at the cathedral a little before noon. At noon the cathedral organist was to present a free concert. I remember sitting in a pew with the rest of our group, enjoying the glorious sounds of the organ. I remember, too, thinking that without the guide we would not have known of the concert and would have missed this emotionally moving moment.

In Cologne the guide took us on a walking tour up and down the streets, ending at the magnificent Cologne Cathedral. Here he gave us an hour on our own. George and I spent most of our time sitting peacefully in a pew before wandering into some of the shops on the square. During the hour, I kept checking my watch to be sure we returned on time. The guide had warned us that he could not wait for any latecomers. The tides in the river controlled our boat's departure time. I recall that he actually gave us directions to the railroad station where we could catch a train to our next stop downriver if we missed the bus. One lady failed to show. Until she arrived back on the boat, we all worried about her.

We had lots of other great moments; it would take too long to note them all. A few general points, however: An advantage of a European river cruise like ours is that the boat docks right in town. The disadvantage is that you walk, walk, walk. Bus trips from the ship are rare, other than when sights to be seen are a distance from the dock, as in Heidelberg.

A RIVERBOAT ON THE DANUBE: *2001*

Arriving in Amsterdam after our Rhine cruise, George and I transferred to the airport and caught our flight to Berlin. We arrived in the city three days before our short pre-tour and our Danube cruise would begin.

In planning this leg of our trip, we had discovered that the pre-cruise hotel in central Berlin that Uniworld had booked for us was *Expensive* with a capital E. With a little effort, we found a more affordable hotel in the suburbs that was on the tram line. We booked there for the three nights we were on our own. It was a serendipitous choice. From the window of our hotel, we could look down on the square below. There we saw what appeared to be a high mirrored wall that went on and on. What was it?

When we walked out that evening in search of a place to dine, we investigated. Etched into the huge mirrored structure were names. They were names of Jewish people who had lived in this section of Berlin and been rounded up by the Gestapo to be transported to the death camps. We stood and read name after name, so many for just one small neighborhood.

During our supper in a little restaurant we found around the corner from the memorial, George and I talked about the horror of that time in Germany. George had given three years of his life to be part of the American force sent to liberate Europe, so seeing the mirrored memorial was personally meaningful. We agreed that in our attempt to save money, we had stumbled on a meaningful memory, a powerful one that neither of us would ever forget.

Two days later, we rode the tram into central Berlin and checked into our tour hotel. The next morning, as we were told to do at check-in, we gathered at the front of the hotel to meet our fellow travelers. Two guides were waiting. They introduced themselves as local guides who would be in charge from Berlin to Prague. We would meet our Uniworld escort in Prague.

Our bus trip to Prague went via Dresden. On our way there, George reminded me of how the Americans and Brits had firebombed Dresden during World War II in retaliation for the German destruction of Coventry. We had visited the English city of Coventry during a self-drive road trip and had seen the ruins of parts of the old cathedral—the destroyed parts now enclosed within glass walls as a memorial to those killed in the attack.

In contrast, Dresden had been totally reconstructed so that it looked just as it had before the bombing. The guide, however, held up photos of the city after the bombing. Both of us wondered, as we listened to him speak, why the Americans and Brits had done this.

The guide explained that there had been no industrial plants in the area. It had simply been a city with beautiful architecture and with ordinary men and women and children, just like in Coventry. Having seen the similar pointless destruction of Coventry, I kept asking myself, "Why? Why do civilized peoples continue to do this to one another? Is revenge so important?"

We pulled into the courtyard of our Prague hotel in late afternoon, tired. Our two guides from Berlin bid us farewell and told us that our Uniworld escort would meet us in two days outside the hotel. Then they left.

We all trudged to the front desk to check in and get the keys to our pre-paid hotel rooms; our accommodations for two nights were part of our original tour cost. We could not believe it when the desk clerks would not let us check in until the room cost for all of us was guaranteed by a credit card. *There was no Uniworld agent with a credit card!* We all stood around, not knowing what to do. We did not want to get slapped with the cost of a hotel for which we had already paid.

Unbelievably, one of our group stepped forward with his credit card in hand. He told the desk clerks, "Put the group costs on my card. I am the one in charge."

When we gathered that night for our going-away dinner in a private dining room assigned to us, the man who had saved the day explained that as soon as he got to his room, he had called his credit card company and canceled the card. It was an extra he carried for emergency use. We clapped. What a brilliant move! You can imagine the earful the Uniworld escort got when he met us two days later.

We explored Prague on our own the next day. I had been to Prague before George and I were married, so I had a good idea of the major sights and how to get to them. We rode the underground from our hotel to the city center. Several flights down, the underground was accessible by a rickety wooden escalator. We walked the Charles Bridge over the Vltava River from Old Town to the Prague Castle on the other side and then back again. We waited for the astronomical clock in Old Town to strike the noon hour so we could see the little figures circle round. And we found an inexpensive cafe for lunch, one patronized by locals.

"This was our kind of day," George said as we rode the creaking escalator down to the subway platform to catch a train back to our hotel. And indeed it had been.

Eventually, the Uniworld escort made his appearance, and our tour group departed Prague. We were on our way. Our destination was the riverboat landing on the Danube with a short tour of the city of Nuremberg en route.

In Nuremberg, the bus made a stop in front of the Palace of Justice. I remember sitting on the bus as our guide told us about the trials of Nazis accused of war crimes, which took place in the Palace of Justice at the end of the Second World War. Nuremberg was chosen for the trials because the city is generally considered the birthplace of the Nazi party and the Palace of Justice was the place where huge Nazi rallies had been held before and during the war. Many of the accused were responsible in some way for the Holocaust.

Neither George nor I had realized that there were twenty-four accused. We did know about Rudolf Hess, who was found guilty and sentenced to life in prison before he committed suicide. We also knew about Hermann Goring, who was sentenced to death by hanging.

The bus covered a considerable distance before arriving at our boat landing. On our bus journey southward toward the Danube, George and I shared our own stories with each other. George told me about his time stationed in Germany after the war. He described how local Germans who were employed at his army base would stand outside the mess hall and wait for the Americans to dump their food scraps in the trash. They would beg for those scraps to take home to their wives and children. George said that he could imagine how those Germans felt, begging for survival from people to whom they had lost the war. He explained that some of the Germans had been conscripted; they had been forced to fight. He told me about two distant German cousins who were conscripted when they were in their sixties, sent to the Russian front, and never heard from again.

In turn, I described to George a visit I made in 1967 to a Polish concentration camp near Krakow—a camp named Plaszow. Plaszow was the place where Jewish people from the ghettos of Krakow were brought, some to work as slave laborers and some to be shipped on to the death camps. In the same vein, we recalled the mirrored wall in the Berlin suburbs that we had just seen.

How fortunate we were to have each other at that powerful moment, to be able to talk together about what we were seeing and to make connections to events from the past. We were blessed. I miss those conversations.

That evening we boarded our riverboat and steamed south to Melk in Austria, the site of a noted abbey which is located on a rocky promontory overlooking the Danube. The next morning, we sat on the upper, open deck of the riverboat as we sailed toward our landing. The view up to Melk Abbey was truly fabulous. Buses were waiting to take us up there.

Both George and I were unhappy with tours where we had to stand and listen to a guide drone on. But this was different. First, the Baroque-style Melk Abbey is stunning. Second, the guide did not dwell on each and every artifact. We liked the library best; it reminded us of one in Trinity College in Dublin where we had viewed the Book of Kells—high ceilings, shelves lined with books, dark wood walls, and some cases with the most valuable manuscripts on display. A visit to Melk was made for us because we both loved libraries, I particularly.

Vienna—the city of the waltz king, Johann Strauss—was next. The evening of our arrival in this gem of a city, the ship sent us by bus to a concert hall. I think it might have been a hall in the Schloss Schonbrunn, the summer residence of the Hapsburgs. We sat not in a regular theater, but in one of the stately rooms on gilt chairs. The performers were in evening attire and played Strauss waltzes. Afterward, we drove through the city streets, passing the Vienna State Opera House and the main government buildings, which were aglow with lights. Teachers that we were, we rated the evening an A+.

The next day we had free time to wander the streets. We walked around the opera house and stepped into the lobby. We passed the town hall and went into St. Stephen's Cathedral. A memory: Standing outside the cathedral, looking up at it, George was struck by pigeon droppings. Plop, onto his shirt. I cleaned him up. We both laughed, glad that it was only his shirt that had been hit, not his head. Weird, isn't it, what we remember years later? Not the interior of the cathedral nor its facade, but the pigeons.

My memory of Budapest is not so unusual: the sail down the Danube so we could get a great view of both sides of the city (Buda on our left, with its government buildings, and Pest on our right), and the bridge connecting the two sides. After we tied up, the ship's tour guide took us around the city by bus, a slow circle with a few inside visits.

On the pier was a small market. We explored it and bought paprika, a lead crystal bowl, a colorfully embroidered blouse, and a garnet bracelet —all things for which Hungary is known. We wanted a few concrete memories of our trip as well as all the images we had been filing away in our heads.

The best, though, was the view of Buda and Pest at night. We sat on the open deck in the quiet of the evening and watched as the lights of the city began to flicker on. The Danube served as a mirror, reflecting the beauty of Budapest. This was our last night before we disembarked the next day and flew home. The trip had had a rocky start but a picture-perfect ending.

Guess on which ship we were: Diamond, Flower, Wind, Star, or Riverboat. The clue is the stunning dining venue.

Chapter Nine
TAKING LONGER CRUISES

From the time we were married in 1968 until 2001, George and I took numerous cruises and land tours. Other than our honeymoon round-the-world-by-air trip, these tours and cruises generally lasted fewer than thirty days, and our destination was either the Caribbean or Europe. In the summers of 1998 and 1999, however, we decided to try cruises that were a bit longer. Luckily, in 1995, we had discovered a cruise line that offered itineraries to more exotic ports, the Holland America Line—HAL, for short. The price was often half what we had paid on the luxury lines. Because the price was less, we could take longer voyages.

OUR THIRTIETH ANNIVERSARY TRIP

Our first longer cruise started with an Atlantic crossing in 1998. The ship, *MS Rotterdam VI* of the Holland America Line, sailed from New York City, which was ideal for New Jersey residents like us. *Rotterdam* made stops in cities on the Mediterranean and then steamed through the Dardanelles to Istanbul and into the Black Sea, going as far east as the Ukraine. Our cruise ended in Athens, where we caught a plane home; the total trip was thirty-three days.

Our sail-away from New York City in mid-May 1998 was exciting as always. We had the New York skyline on our port side—the Trade Center buildings still standing—and soon the Statue of Liberty on our starboard side. This was the last time we would see the skyline with that profile as we started a cruise.

The entrance to the Black Sea from the Aegean is through the narrow passage called the Dardanelles. As we sailed the Dardanelles, we stood on deck to see Gallipoli high on the hill above us. In the distance up there, we could make out the monument commemorating a series of World War I battles that took place between Turkish and Allied forces. These battles were for control over the strait that *Rotterdam* was navigating. The end result was a resounding defeat for the Allied forces and hundreds of thousands killed on both sides.

The Dardanelles leads into the Sea of Marmara and from there into the Bosphorus and the Black Sea. We went up on deck for the sail-in to Istanbul. George and I had sailed into many harbors. We always put the Istanbul sail-in on our most impressive list along with New York City, Sydney, Hong Kong, and Rio. The sail-in is impressive because Istanbul spans two continents and because the skyline is riddled with minarets and the domes of so many mosques. We picked out the Blue Mosque, Hagia Sophia, and the towers of Topkapi Palace; then, as we turned to go up toward the Golden Horn, we saw the spires of the huge Suleymaniye Mosque.

Rotterdam docked in the new commercial section so that, from our stateroom, we could look out on the Old City and the Galata Bridge that connects the new with the older parts of the city. That evening as the lights twinkled on, Istanbul became a fairyland. We did not even have to leave the ship to enjoy the view.

The next day we joined a morning tour. Perhaps because I love food, when I recall that tour, my mind goes first to lunch in a Turkish restaurant. The restaurant was located on the fifth floor of a building overlooking both the Galata Bridge and our ship docked across the channel. George and I recalled walking the old Galata Bridge back in 1969, when it was a pontoon bridge that moved with the currents. The bridge we saw in 1998 was a new one, built to carry increased traffic. We also recalled having passed the old Galata Tower that we could now see

89

from the windows of the restaurant.

The restaurant provided a view down on the plaza where we had just visited the New Mosque and the Egyptian spice market. Outside the mosque, we had seen men performing ritual washing of hands and feet before they entered. We had heard the call to prayer echoing from the minaret. Inside the spice market, we had seen huge bags of spices lining the floor, each redolent with the smell of a familiar or unfamiliar spice. In short, the view from the restaurant was really a visual tour of the area.

The food was tasty, too. George said it reminded him of the meal he had eaten back in 1969 when he had ventured forth on his own to find a restaurant where he could enjoy genuine Turkish fare. That was on a night when I had chosen to dine in the hotel because I was too tired to go out.

In the afternoon, we shuttled to the Grand Bazaar—a place we knew from prior visits and where I had bought tiny sapphire earrings in 1969. In 1998 we made another purchase. We saw a large, brass, teapot-like pitcher in one of the shops. We bargained, paid, and waited while the salesman wrapped it in newspaper. We left it wrapped until we arrived home, only to find that the salesman had pulled a switch. Instead of a shiny new pitcher, he had wrapped a dented, discolored one with a lid that was loose. To put a positive spin on this story, you could say ours was the "real thing," a well-used pitcher, not one made for the tourist trade. We learned a valuable lesson that day: Never let an item out of your sight once you have bought it.

An itinerary hint: Istanbul is an amazing city—an exotic place to visit and revisit. It has the flavor of both the east and the west. For anyone wanting a different travel experience, Istanbul provides it. And don't forget to try a Turkish restaurant with a view of the Golden Horn and the Galata Bridge.

When our captain backed *Rotterdam* out of Istanbul, he headed east through the Black Sea toward Sevastopol, a tender port in the Ukraine on the Crimean peninsula. In the past, Sevastopol has been on cruise ship itineraries because Yalta is nearby. Yalta was the scene of the weeklong conference toward the end of World War II attended by Churchill, Roosevelt, and Stalin. It was the place where the Big Three carved up eastern Europe and Germany. George and I wanted to visit Yalta.

I have a very clear mental picture of a palace-like structure where the Yalta Conference was held. I can visualize a very long whitish building, a couple of stories tall. It has a name, which I did not remember and had to look up: the Livadia Palace. Livadia had been the summer home of Czar Nicholas II. I particularly remember seeing the long oval table about which the three leaders and their aides had been seated and the pictures on display showing them conferring about what postwar Europe would look like.

We also drove to a point from where we could see the Swallow's Nest, a castle that looks like something from a Disney movie with highly decorated towers and walls. It perches on the very edge of a cliff overlooking the Black Sea. Some older women had set up folding tables where our bus stopped. Our guide explained that these women were selling family possessions to survive. We bought a very old set of Russian nesting dolls, which we did not need but loved on sight. Rather than bargaining, we added a tip to the asking price.

A day later we were in Odessa, a city in the Ukraine. My most vivid memory of our stop there was climbing the Potemkin Stairs, located rather close to our docking site. We did the climb in stages, sitting and resting when our legs cried out in protest. I also remember walking the boulevard at the top of the 192 steps. George and I did the walkabout on our own. Although we were not certain, we guessed that the ornate, stone buildings that lined the boulevard were apartment complexes; they reminded us of similar buildings along Riverside Drive in New York City.

Compared to our day in Odessa, the one we spent in Romania was pretty much a disaster. The ship docked at a distance from the city of Constanta. From the port lecturer, we had learned the number of the bus to town. We thought we were all set to see Constanta on our own. But we erred! We did not get off the bus at the stop for the main city, and once we missed that stop, the bus zoomed off with us aboard. It was a long distance to the next stop and a long hike back to where we should have hopped off. We spent a considerable amount of time walking through the industrial section of the city.

Then, of course, we needed a restroom; and, of course, we could not find one. We walked and walked looking for signs, still without success. Finally, we went into an office building and asked if we could use theirs.

The receptionist kindly showed us the way. This was our first lucky break of the morning.

We had been told to visit the casino—not to gamble but just to see the flamboyant, stone building that has towers and domes and arches flying in all directions. To us, it looked like a giant piece of fluff, something designed by an architect gone a little mad.

It was closed! All we could do was walk around the grounds and peer in the windows.

By then it was getting late; we had wasted most of the morning on our endless walk through the industrial section. We decided to head back to our ship. Walking to the bus stop (and we did find it), we had our second lucky break—a great photo op. We stumbled upon the Cathedral of Saints Peter and Paul just in time to see several women washing the church's Persian rugs on the pavement out front. Dressed in long gray skirts and cumbersome jackets, they were using heavy brooms and soapy water to scrub the rugs. We gave these hard-working women a thumbs-up, and they nodded back at us.

In retrospect, George and I agreed that we should have been better prepared for this stop. We should have studied the guide books and realized that, given the distance between the dock and the city, it would have made sense for us to have signed up for a tour. Live and learn.

We fared much better the next day when our ship stopped in Varna, which is an attractive Bulgarian resort on the Black Sea. I remember lovely, tree-shaded streets that were perfect for strolling. And that is what we did. We sat on park benches from time to time, enjoyed an impromptu band concert on the central square, and popped into a shop or two. It was a warm, clear day. In travel, we reminded each other, we have to take the bad with the good. Our delightful day in Varna made up for our disastrous day in Constanta.

We sailed back toward the city of Istanbul on our way out of the Black Sea. We passed the palaces that line the northern shore of the sea as we neared Istanbul. George spotted the Dolmabahce Palace built by a sultan of the Ottoman Empire, which we had toured during one of our earlier visits to Istanbul. We steamed under the Ataturk Bridge and then we waved farewell to the spires of the mosques that dot the skyline. We could never get enough of this view.

We had a couple of sea days for relaxation before we disembarked in Athens. For us, it had been a fabulous thirty-three days, with only one low point, our day in Constanta.

THIRTY-SIX DAYS ON *ROTTERDAM VI*

In 1999, George and I opted for a thirty-six-day cruise comprised of three back-to-backs:

1. Rome to London;
2. London to the Baltic countries; and
3. Norway to the North Cape.

The catalogue distributed by the cruise line showed each as a separate cruise. It is easy, however, to put together a long cruise by booking a series back-to-back.

We chose these three back-to-backs knowing that there would be no Mediterranean, Baltic, or Norwegian ports on our itinerary that would be first-time visits. We had been to all of the ports, had enjoyed them, and had wanted to return.

On the itinerary of the first cruise in our series was Valletta, the capital of the small country of Malta and one of our favorite Mediterranean ports. Malta is a small, independent island country. It is located south of the boot of Italy and, until rather recently, was a British possession.

Valletta is on our list of favorite cruise cities because the sail-in is unique. We learned from our first visit to Valletta to stand at the rail on the top deck of our ship in the morning and "watch the parade pass us by." The old city—where St. John's Co-Cathedral and the Grandmaster's Palace of the Knights of Saint John are located—is several flights of stairs above the water level. As a result, the top deck of a ship is about even with the upper town. Standing at the rail atop our ship, George and I could look over the city walls and into the old town. It was just like being there, walking about the city. We have never seen anything like that in any other place in the world.

The first time we visited Valletta, we had booked an excursion to

93

the upper town that included inside visits to the co-cathedral and the Grandmaster's Palace and a guided walk along the main avenue and side streets. The co-cathedral of Valletta is unique: It has hundreds of graves under the marble floor, each with an ornate, flat, casket-shaped memorial stone on top that identifies the knight buried there. During our first visit, we spent considerable time walking across the stones, reading the inscriptions, and admiring the designs. The floor is absolutely exquisite.

The Co-Cathedral of St. John has a sister cathedral in the city of Mdina; the floor of St. Paul's Cathedral has the same highly decorated covering of flat gravestones as the one in Valletta. We wanted to see St. Paul's Cathedral, so on our 1999 back-to-backs, we booked a morning bus tour to Mdina and the surrounding areas. As we drove there, our guide told us that Mdina is known as the Silent City. Out of respect, we should be very quiet during our visit. When we arrived, we discovered hundreds of children enjoying Mdina. As most youngsters do, they ran, and screamed, and . . . So much for the Silent City. But we were happy we had made the trip. The floor of St. Paul's Cathedral was even more magnificent than we had expected. There were lots of lookout points, too, that provided views of the sea and the countryside.

Walking back to our bus, George spotted a sign on one of the buildings we were passing: The Sisters of St. Dorothy. Here was an order of nuns bearing my name—a name meaning gift of God. George called to me, "Stand under the sign, Dorothy. I want to take your picture." It was a good idea! I have that picture to bring to mind our day in Malta.

Tunis was also on the itinerary of the first segment. During our previous stop in Tunis, the capital of Tunisia, we had taken an all-day tour to see everything! We had visited the museum and walked the winding alleys of the Medina. We had explored Carthage and looked out on Tunis Bay from the Roman aqueduct. We had lunched on Tunisian specialties and roamed the streets of a pretty blue-and-white village perched on a cliff overlooking the bay. We had indeed seen the major sights for which Tunis is known. On our visit in 1999, therefore, we decided to taxi to the walled city and slowly explore the Medina and all its shops on our own.

Once off the ship, George and I bargained with a taxi driver who was parked by the pier: one way, two people, a total fare of five dollars. We hopped in, and the driver started down the causeway that leads straight to the city gates—the entrance to the Medina. We recognized the causeway because that was the route we had taken on our prior visit.

But then, the driver cut across the causeway, turned left and turned right and turned . . . I started screaming, "This is not the way. No! No! Go back to the causeway!" I kept screaming, but to no avail.

George whispered, "When he stops, be ready to move fast. Get ready to get out." I had in my hand the five dollars plus tip, so I was ready.

The driver finally came to a stop in a plaza that we thought might be behind the Medina. We both had kept track of the direction we were traveling and, having been there before, were reasonably sure where we were in relation to the Medina.

We hopped out fast. I was still screaming like a banshee on attack. The driver said, "This is the Medina."

I screamed, "*No*, it isn't!"

He said, "The ride was ten dollars."

George said, "No, five." I threw the five-dollar bill at the driver, without a tip! We ran!

Catching our breath, we stopped to look around. We realized we were in a residential area adjacent to the Medina, but how to find our way in the winding maze of alleys?

I spied a lad who was about ten years old. He smiled at me. I smiled back and said, "Medina?" I pointed to him, to us, and then in the direction I thought the Medina might be.

More smiles. The boy nodded his head and gestured to us to follow him. We did. This way and that way, we wove through the maze until we recognized that we were in the Medina. The lad stopped, smiled, pointed at the area ahead. We sighed with relief, shook his hand, and gave him a five-dollar bill. More smiles.

That night at dinner, we shared our story with our tablemates. All of us talked about how important it is when traveling not to wear good jewelry or expensive clothes, and to carry identification but not too much money. Someone at the table explained that she carries her tote bag with the outline of the ship on it when she and her husband go off on their own. She shows it to the cab driver when returning to the ship at the end of the day. Someone else brought up how we should all be aware of things going on around us. We decided that a wise axiom for travelers is to enjoy but keep your eyes open. We decided, too, that smiles often are as good as words—perhaps even better at times.

The rest of our cruise pales in excitement when compared with our morning in Tunis. In Oslo, we crossed the inner harbor on a boat to explore three museums: the Kon-Tiki Museum, the Viking Ship Museum, and the Folk Museum where old houses brought from all over Norway have been set up to show life in prior days. We also could not resist going back to Frogner Park to wander again among the unique sculptures of Gustav Vigeland. In Stockholm, we made sure to be on deck as the *Rotterdam* sailed in; we remembered the lovely views to be enjoyed as a ship navigates among the many small islands. In Saint Petersburg, we visited the Hermitage and the Catherine Palace and even made a stop at the Church of the Spilled Blood, places we had not visited on our previous cruises to this Russian city. In Copenhagen, we strolled the area where we were docked to see again the Little Mermaid sculpture and to sit on a bench overlooking the harbor. In coastal Norway, we took a train ride through a succession of tunnels to an overlook where we could view the fjords far below us.

These were lovely, relaxing days for us. We sometimes took tours as we did in Russia; we sometimes meandered on our own; and sometimes we simply stayed on the ship and enjoyed the scenery from the crow's nest. Regardless of what we chose to do, we realized the value of returning to places to dig deeper and to review.

Chapter Ten
GOING IN GRAND STYLE: SOUTH AMERICA

In late December 2001 a few months after 9/11, I retired from Kean so we could take even longer trips. George had retired in 1989. At my retirement, I was sixty-seven years old, and George was eighty. We had to travel while we were still able.

On December 27, 2001, three days after I cleared out my office at Kean University, George and I were standing on our verandah aboard Regent's *Seven Seas Mariner*, looking out over the Fort Lauderdale harbor. We were both excited. *Mariner* was to take us on a complete circumnavigation of South America. We would not get home until February 19; we would be on the ship fifty-four nights.

Cruises such as this are often called Grand Voyages. They are special in that luggage pickup and delivery are included in the base price. That means you label your bags and set them on your front porch. The next time you see your bags is in your stateroom aboard ship. Grand Voyages are also special in that, periodically during the cruise, you find a gift on your pillow—something nice to take home as a remembrance of the voyage. The ship provides activities not generally found on short cruises: crafts, watercolor classes, games, bridge instruction. At many ports, a local entertainment group comes aboard to perform. When the ship docks at a distance from the city center, a complimentary shuttle to town is often provided. As I remember this voyage, certain places, people, and events stand out. It is stories of these that I will share—our unforgettables.

MAKING *MARINER* OUR HOME

My first memory of our South America cruise is of something that happened as our ship left Fort Lauderdale. Standing by the rail of our verandah, I heard a woman calling to us from a few cabins away. "Hi, there. I'm Mary Ellen and this is my husband, Frank. Who are you?"

We waved and replied, "We're Dorothy and George from New Jersey."

We chatted back and forth, and then Mary Ellen asked us to meet them in the lounge before dinner for cocktails. In the lounge that evening, we found Mary Ellen and Frank waiting for us. Another couple sat down, too—Franz and Lois Tyack from Arizona. The Compass Rose, the formal dining venue on *Mariner*, has no assigned seating, and so it was natural for the six of us to go to dinner together. Our new friends suggested that we do a repeat performance the following evening. Again we met in the lounge outside Compass Rose. Another couple joined us for the cocktail hour, and then the eight of us went into the dining room for supper.

This became our evening dinner group. Dining together, talking together, even touring together in some ports—our group became an unforgettable part of our South American voyage. We learned that building new and even lasting friendships is easier on longer voyages than on shorter ones.

The first evening, after dinner, we explored the ship with Frank and Mary Ellen Diaz. We located the two reservations-required dining rooms—the French restaurant and the steak-and-seafood restaurant—as well as the buffet restaurant on the lido deck. We found the swimming pools, the small presentation lounge at the stern, a number of bars, the small library, and the large showroom at the front of the ship.

That night in the showroom, the cruise director introduced the entertainment staff. Ray introduced the bridge instructors, the dance instructors, and a couple who would be teaching watercolor painting every sea day in the morning. Ray also introduced the cast of singers and dancers who performed a few numbers, and then he sang and shared a few salient points about himself. He was English, had performed on the West End in London as a singer, ventriloquist, and puppeteer, and had been cruise director on a number of lines before coming to Regent. George and I, forever after, rated Ray Solaire the absolutely best cruise director on the high seas.

Back in our suite—Regent calls all its staterooms "suites"—we could not help being impressed with what was to be our home for the next fifty-four nights. Our suite had its own verandah, a bedroom and a lounge separated by a curtain if we wanted to divide the space, a huge walk-in closet with drawers and shelves, and a very large bathroom with lots of mirrors, one in the tub area so we could see ourselves in all our nakedness. And ours was the cheapest suite on the ship!

The next morning we went to watercolor class. Our teacher was an attractive young woman; her husband was there to help with materials—paper, brushes, paints, art books—all supplied at no extra charge. That morning, she started with the basics: the color wheel and color mixing. Shortly, she was teaching us how to paint sky, sea, birds, flowers, palm trees, buildings, glaciers ... She told us that, back home in Connecticut, she ran an art school for children. That was good for me; she knew how to handle beginners. But George, who had considerable talent, appreciated her step-by-step instruction, too. We attended each sea day, skipping not a single lesson.

Mariner stopped at a couple of Caribbean ports on her way to the Panama Canal—all ports we had visited before. This was our fifth transit of the canal, so we did not run around trying to see everything. Often, we sat on our verandah to watch our progress. Once through the canal, we made a few stops at South American ports and read up on Machu Picchu, where we were to take an overland trip when we arrived in Callao, the port for Lima, Peru.

FLYING HIGH: MACHU PICCHU

The high point of our first South America cruise, both literally and figuratively, was our Regent three-day tour from Lima to Cusco and Machu Picchu. We brought home so many memories.

Our hotel in Cusco was the Monasterio, a luxury hotel that was once a monastery, as the name implies. On arrival, we were offered a cup of coca tea, which was to help with altitude sickness. Cusco is at least 12,000 feet above sea level, and we had been at sea level just a few hours before. So we drank coca tea liberally before we dined in splendor in an impressive, dark wood-paneled refectory. This was where the brothers had eaten in days gone by. Our dinner that evening was a great beginning to our overland trip—really our first significant memory of it.

Our hotel room was not that ornate. After all, it had at one time housed a brother. I recall awakening there in the middle of the night feeling that the room was rocking and rolling. George diagnosed my problem as altitude sickness and called the front desk to order oxygen. Wow! I inhaled and felt better. Although George felt no ill effects of the altitude, I urged him to take some whiffs. Afterward, we jested that on our first night in Cusco, we got "high" on oxygen.

The next day was the most important one. Our guide escorted us to the railway station early and onto a train car reserved for our tour group. The car was equipped with tables set between facing seats. We sat with Kay and Paul, who proved to be lovely companions for the day, for the cruise, and even on a future cruise. As we were served snacks and coffee, the train carried us down—not up—to the place where Machu Picchu is located. Fortunately for those of us who had been suffering from altitude sickness, Machu Picchu is at a lower altitude than Cusco. As our train chugged along, we kept our eyes glued to the view. We were in the Peruvian Andes, and the scenery was spectacular.

Arriving at the village at the base of the mountain where Machu Picchu stands, we boarded a bus for the drive up to the ruins of the ancient Inca fortress. Switchback after switchback after switchback! Higher, higher, higher! Our driver knew what he was doing. He got us safely to the top where our guide escorted us from point to point, explaining what we saw spread out before us.

We both had pictures in our minds of Machu Picchu, pictures we had seen in movies and guide books. But being there in person? It makes me shiver just to remember. The guide said we could climb up higher if we wanted to. I said no! George would have done it by himself—at eighty years young. Again I said no! The trail up was steep, the path was uneven, and there were no handrails. Instead, we sat on a bench that faced out over the valley and absorbed the tranquility and the magic of it all.

After lunch in a restaurant that overlooked the valley below, we boarded the bus for our trip down. When we got to the first switchback, a young lad darted from the hillside and let out a shriek and waved to us. Then he darted back into the brush and started to run down. We were riding around the switchback. He was cutting directly down, so that at the next curve, there he was again, shrieking and waving. A lot of switchbacks, a lot of shrieking, a lot of waving. When we got to the village at the base, the youngster popped out of the woods to give a final wave and shriek. Of course we gave him a tip. And of course he climbed onto the bus with tourists going up to the ruins, to repeat his feat.

We had time to stroll the Native Peruvian market located in the village. We bought a handmade, woolen wall hanging and necklaces made from old Peruvian coins. Then we boarded the train for our ride back to Cusco—or so we thought. After a time, the train stopped, the guide urged us off, and we climbed onto a bus that was waiting. Our route was another winding road as we climbed higher to reach Cusco. Our new friend Kay was still suffering from altitude sickness. Add to that the sway of the bus, and you can understand why she had to ask the driver to stop, and to stop fast.

Day three of our overland trip was hectically busy. We boarded an early flight into Lima, toured a set of ruins nearby, wandered the museum attached to the ruins, and enjoyed lunch on the premises.

The afternoon saw us on a bus, riding south down the Peruvian coast to rejoin our ship, which had sailed late the night before. We passed irrigated fields where fruits and vegetables were being grown for export to the United States. I never sleep on buses; neither did George. We were so tired from our three days of on-the-go traveling that we both admitted afterwards we had missed at least half the bus trip.

When we got "home"—that is how we now referred to *Mariner*—the cruise director had a huge *Welcome Home* sign strung atop the ship. All the ship's workers were lined up in two rows from the gangway to our bus. As we climbed off—hot, dirty, and tired—the men and women of the *Mariner* cheered and clapped and called, "Welcome home!" Our own cabin stewards were there and came up to welcome us with hugs.

A postscript: I just walked into our TV room to look at our Machu Picchu wall hanging—a great memento of three wonderful days when we were literally flying high. George called them Super-A-Days. Reminiscing afterwards, he repeated what he had said when we were in Egypt: "Sweetheart, I never dreamed that in my lifetime I would see Machu Picchu."

CRUISING GLACIER ALLEY AND THE HORN

George and I had cruised Glacier Bay in Alaska and thought it wonderful. Imagine four glaciers—not just one—located along a series of mountain ridges and then extending down into the clear waters of the channel you are traversing. That is exactly what we saw as *Mariner* steamed through the Beagle Channel and down Glacier Alley toward Ushuaia, Argentina.

We had chosen the location of our suite just for this day. The glaciers are on the north side of Glacier Alley. Because our suite was on the port side of our ship, we could stretch out in lounge chairs on the verandah to watch our progress; we literally had a front-row seat to watch the show. We could see the sun sparkling on the blue ice of the glaciers' faces. We could see the reflection of the glaciers in the icy waters below. Both of us had learned about aretes, moraines, fissures, and calving in geology classes. We were seeing what we had read about and what George had taught about.

We spent the next day in Ushuaia, walking the village, getting a little cold from the strong winds. The following morning, our captain announced that we were going sight-cruising. He turned the ship and set a course that brought us directly under Cape Horn. The Horn, which is at the very tip of South America, is not a promontory; it is an island with cliffs that tower above the sea. Hearing of the vicious seas that early navigators had faced as they rounded the Cape, we expected the worst. Instead, we got the very best. That day the sea was like glass. We could see the monument marking the southernmost point of South America high above us on the cliffs.

Passport stamp from Cape Horn.

Hoping that we would have calm seas, the captain had collected our passports the night before. Because Mother Nature was in a peaceful mood, he lowered a tender and sent a few of his able seamen ashore. They came back with our passports stamped "Isla Hornos." Another set of great memories and a priceless souvenir—our stamped passports.

That evening in our suite we found a fine cashmere blanket in a delicate beige color—another priceless souvenir. It was our special cruise gift from Regent. I love to wrap myself in it on cold winter evenings.

WALKING WITH THE PENGUINS

On this voyage, we did not get into the Falkland Islands, a port where many ships drop anchor so passengers can walk with the penguins. Instead, we went to a lesser-known spot on the east coast of Argentina. I cannot recall the name of this island. It might well have been Camerones Island, but I am not certain.

Wherever we were, we saw thousands and thousands of Magellanic penguins. Members of this species are small, much smaller than the king penguins we saw years later in the Falklands. They are found mainly on islands off the coast of Argentina.

Our morning at what I will call the unknown island was a biologist's dream. From the tender wharf, we strolled just a short distance on a boardwalk to a spot where the birds literally surrounded us. The noise they made as they called to one another was deafening. The smell was overwhelming. Even on the boardwalks that crossed the fields, we had to watch where we stepped.

There were mothers with babies cuddled up to them, others scratching at the earth by our feet, and still others burrowing in the ground. In every direction were penguins, more penguins, and more penguins. Although after 2002 George and I went twice to Antarctica and once to the Falklands where we saw penguins galore, we never again experienced anything quite like walking among those masses of penguins that day. The sights, the sounds, and the smell of Camerones still remain with me.

MONTEVIDEO

Montevideo in Uruguay is an ideal city for sightseeing on foot. Remains of the *Admiral Graf Spee*—the German ship that was sunk in the harbor during World War II—are right at the pier. The city itself is compact, with many of the important sites on the central plaza or just down the avenue from there. What makes Montevideo even more convenient for sightseeing is that a leather goods store generally provides a free shuttle service up to its shop, which is more than halfway into town.

We had heard that Montevideo was the place to buy leather jackets, so after photographing the *Graf Spee* plaque and artifacts, we climbed onto the shuttle to the shop providing the free transfer. We found that the store was packed with *Mariner* passengers, and the prices seemed high, given the quality of the jackets we tried on.

We left the store and walked up into the main plaza and down the boulevard to visit the cathedral. Returning to the plaza, we walked completely around the shopping arcade and admired the statue of national hero Jose Artigas in the middle.

As we were photographing Señor Artigas, an older man approached us, proffering a card and saying, "Leather, leather jackets. Go here." He pointed up the boulevard and then gestured to the right. "Good prices," he added.

What did we have to lose? We would be walking main streets with other pedestrians. We could look into the shop before entering. And so we started out. Although we noticed that the older man was following us, he kept his distance. Arriving at the shop identified on the card, we looked in. Two nicely dressed women were sitting inside. They were sewing leather garments.

"OK, let's go for it," I said.

Our decision proved to be a good one: The quality of the leather jackets was far better than in the prior shop, and the prices were lower. George tried on a number of black jackets. I tried on some brown ones. George found one that was a perfect fit. I found one I liked, but the sleeves were too long. The older of the two women—probably the mother—told us that was not a problem. She could shorten the sleeves while we waited.

After a little gentle bargaining, we agreed on a cash price in American dollars. I explained that I needed to go into the fitting room to get the cash. I gestured to my chest. She understood. When I came out of the fitting room and counted out the American dollars, she looked at me and said something I have never forgotten: "In our country, the husband carries the money and pays." I did not try to explain to her that we had figured out long ago that it was safer for me to carry our cash in what is known as a "bra pack." Pickpockets would probably expect the man to be carrying the money in a wallet in his back pocket.

With our bundles in hand, we walked through the main square and then down the hill, through back streets, over uneven pavement to our ship. We did not have the audacity to return to the shop providing free shuttle service carrying jackets we had purchased elsewhere.

RIO DE JANEIRO

Say the word "Rio" to seasoned travelers and they will respond with Sugarloaf, the Christ the Redeemer statue, Copacabana, and Ipanema—and their eyes will light up.

George and I were ajitter with excitement the morning of our first sail-in to Rio. It was still dark. Then slowly the sky began to lighten, and we could see the vague outline of Sugarloaf, the mountain that stands guard over Rio harbor. As we sailed closer, the sky brightened even more and we could see a cable car swinging high up above Sugarloaf; we could see Christ the Redeemer on Corcovado Mountain. Closer yet, and we could see Copacabana Beach on our port side and ahead the beach at Ipanema. *Mariner* turned to go into our docking site. We had arrived.

A morning tour supplied by our travel agency took us along Ipanema Beach to the base of Sugarloaf Mountain, where we boarded the first of two cable cars to the summit. Once we reached the top, we looked out in all directions. We had thought that nothing could be more exciting than our sail-in, but the view of Rio spread out at our feet goes down in my memory book as unforgettable—not five stars, but ten.

The day got even better. Once we climbed off the cable car at the base of Sugarloaf and got back on the tour bus, our guide took us on a sightseeing spin around Rio. At noon, we stopped at a restaurant to have lunch. The restaurant, situated on a second floor, overlooked a lovely lake. We could enjoy the view as we lunched with friends.

That evening—compliments of *Mariner*—all the passengers went on a special outing to the Copacabana Hotel for cocktails in the main ballroom. Afterward, we had the opportunity to cross the road and walk along the famed beachfront. Ah, a warm breeze off the ocean, stars above, friends to be with, and a husband who cared. What more could a woman want?

On our second day in Rio de Janeiro, George and I hopped on a shuttle bus from the pier to town. It was a complimentary one offered by a jewelry firm with stores in many South American cities. After touring the facility and looking at the gems—mostly colored stones mined in South America—we headed back "home." Of course, I took back with me a lovely citrine ring that George had picked out. The shuttle was not free after all.

Sail-away was at four in the afternoon. Our great captain announced that he was taking us sightseeing: He would steer *Mariner* past Sugarloaf so that those on the starboard side could see the city. Then he would swing *Mariner* around and sail back so those on the port side could enjoy a last view of Rio. George and I already had decided that this was not to be our last view. We were coming back! We had to return to take the tram up Corcovado to see the giant statue of Christ that stands atop the mountain.

SALVADOR DA BAHIA

Salvador da Bahia is the Brazilian city on the most easterly hump of South America, the area closest to the African continent. When we stopped in Salvador on our 2002 voyage, *Mariner* docked at a pier very near the general market on the lower level of the city. We walked the short distance to a large elevator that we took to the upper level of Salvador. I recall we paid ten cents for a one-way ride.

Going up was a little scary; I clung to my pocketbook, and George stood close to me. We were the only tourists on the dark, enclosed, crowded elevator, but we really had nothing to fear. Our unfounded fear was the normal unease of the unknown.

We got off at the top level and had a lovely walk around the main square, visiting two large churches and sitting on a bench in the plaza to enjoy the sunshine. We walked along adjacent streets lined with colonial-style buildings and took pictures of women who were dressed in colorful bouffant skirts and white peasant blouses and who balanced trays of fruit on their heads. We thought that they were paid to dress this way to add a colonial ambiance, which they certainly did.

Before taking the elevator down to the lower level, we stopped at an art shop on the square. George spied a carved mask on the wall: a superb piece by a local artisan, rendered in the African style. I can look up on the wall of my study as I type and remember the day when . . .

Our elevator ride to the lower level of Salvador did not seem scary at all, not after George and I had had such an enjoyable stroll. Once down, we walked the aisles of the general market. We bought a couple of what the vendors called "slave pins" that were made of an inexpensive alloy. We found nothing, however, to compare with the carving we had bought at the fine art store.

George and I visited Salvador several times after that on later trips. By then, the pier had been moved a considerable distance from the market and elevator. We had to take a bus to the upper level of the city. Think of what we would have missed if we had not visited here before large groups of tourists arrived.

THE AMAZON

Mariner stopped at a number of other large cities and small towns as we worked our way up the east coast of Brazil. We strolled the streets in most of them and shared lovely days together. One evening, our captain announced that we would soon be entering the waters of the Amazon. We might not even realize that we were in the river, for at its mouth, the Amazon is many miles across from one bank to the other. There would be good-sized islands in the channel, so we might not be able to see both banks at the same time.

He warned us that the bed linen would not be changed so often, the swimming pool would be emptied, and personal laundry service would be suspended. We all were to be careful in our water usage. The captain explained that the ship could not take on water from the Amazon to desalinate and use in the laundry and waste systems.

When we opened the drapes the next morning, we knew we were sailing the Amazon. The water was reddish-brown. Hunks of floating debris, even large trees, were coming at us as *Mariner* plowed up the river. Our trip toward Manaus, our ultimate destination on the Amazon, took several days. During those days we spent many hours sitting on our verandah watching the rainforest go by, reading, and using our developing watercolor skills to sketch and paint postcard-sized pictures of the Amazon.

As we steamed upriver, the ship's naturalist gave a series of lectures that we attended in order to understand the ecology of a rainforest. One fact we learned from her is that malaria is not a huge problem along the Amazon. The acidity of the water does not provide a good environment for mosquitoes that carry malaria. She said that, unless we intended to hike deep into the rainforest, we really did not need to take anti-malaria medication.

The lecturer also explained about the Meeting of Waters, a phenomenon we were to see twice on our river trip. Near the city of Santarem, there is a tributary, which is bluish-gray in color and flows into the brownish Amazon. For miles, the waters of the two rivers flow side by side, not mixing because of differences in temperature, speed, and acidity. The naturalist told us that we should be on deck as we came into Santarem to see the Meeting of Waters and the distinct "line" between the two merging rivers. Once in town, from a pier extending out into the river, we would be able to see this phenomenon even more clearly.

Near Manaus, the Rio Negro, which is black, flows together with the Amazon, which is brown. For miles, they flow side by side, not mixing. Again we were up on deck to see the second Meeting of Waters. Some friends took a little boat out into the deeper water. Their craft carried them across the place where the two waters flow side by side. We decided we would do that "next time."

MANAUS

Our first morning in Manaus, George and I hopped on the shuttle bus offered by a local jewelry company to its location in a resort hotel about twenty minutes from the city. The bus drove us by major landmarks such as the opera house and the ornate mansions constructed by the rubber barons as well as through poorer areas. Once we left the city, we passed military bases and at times caught glimpses of the Amazon. In short, we had a free highlights tour.

Reaching the resort, we were pleasantly surprised. Just outside the hotel was an arcade of small shops where I found a pair of wood earrings—two pairs, to be truthful—that called to me. Inside we visited a branch of the jewelry concern where George had bought my citrine ring in Rio. There I saw an amethyst pendant that I also could not leave behind.

Usually, as we traveled, we paid in cash. We would bring a rather hefty amount of American dollars and, when necessary, change those dollars into local currency on the ship. Unfortunately, not expecting to make a major purchase, we had not brought enough cash with us that morning to cover the cost of my amethyst. We used our credit card to pay, feeling comfortable having this upscale business handle our card. We never used our credit card for small purchases or in stores of unknown reliability.

Located on the grounds of the resort was a small zoo that housed monkeys, sloths, lizards, birds, and other animals native to Amazonia. George was not pleased with what he saw. The animals were in small enclosures that gave them little space to roam or fly. "Not good at all," he said.

George and I returned to the port via the complimentary shuttle bus to rest up for the excursion the ship was providing that evening. But in the end we did not rest. We hung over the railing of our verandah to watch the show unfolding on the pier. There, small riverboats, which catered to local people's need for transportation up and down the Amazon, were loading cargo and passengers. We could see hammocks slung on the decks; this was where Amazonians slept when traveling the river.

The sounds were as exciting as the sights. We heard workers hollering back and forth; we watched boats jockeying for position on the pier. By the way, this was a floating wharf; it rose and fell with the tide.

As we relaxed in our suite, the phone rang. The call was from the front desk telling us that someone from a local jewelry firm was at the gangway asking for us. We hurried down to speak with him—the salesman with whom we had dealt in the morning. He explained that they had hit a snag; our credit card company had rejected the charge we had posted for my amethyst. The representative of the company said that they would send a private car the next morning to take us back to the store, where we could call Visa and verify our purchase. We had planned on spending our second day walking the streets in Manaus, so returning to the store would not be a problem.

Back in our suite, we dressed in formal attire, because this evening was special: The entire complement of passengers was going to the Teatro Amazonas (known to cruisers as the Manaus opera house) for a performance by the local philharmonic orchestra. Because this would give us an opportunity to tour the building, which is a major sightseeing attraction within the city, George, I, and our new friends the Tyacks caught the first bus. Once we had walked up the grand staircase into the lobby, we were greeted by waiters offering champagne. Glasses in hand, we entered the performance hall. Magnificent! Simply magnificent! Around the edges were private boxes where the rubber barons and their guests had always been seated. Since we were among the first in, we selected a centrally located box, entered, and sat down to chat and sip champagne.

I recall that the concert was lovely. Equally lovely was sitting in a VIP box, champagne glasses in hand: We felt like royalty—Franz and George dressed in tuxedos, Lois and I in our best gowns. Our evening at the Manaus opera house rates among the most unforgettable nights in all our travels.

The telephone call we placed the next morning, from the jewelers to our credit card company, remedied the problem. We were soon in a private car heading back to the pier. Our original plan for the day had been to walk around the municipal market near the pier. The limo driver was pleased to drop us there, and we were able to explore on our own. Mainly a fish, meat, and vegetable market, the renovated building is constructed of cast iron; it even has stained-glass windows at one end. We walked from stall to stall, eventually sat on a bench, and then meandered back to the pier through congested, noisy streets. I held my pocketbook close to my body because we did not feel completely safe walking the crowded streets.

Back in our suite that evening, we talked about our credit card fiasco. We realized that we had made a major mistake. Before leaving the states, we should have called our credit card company to alert them that we were traveling out of the country and given them the names of the places to which we would be going, as well as the dates. Knowing that we would be in Brazil on the date we posted the charge, the company would have been less likely to reject it. Also, we should have had a card that carried no out-of-country currency exchange fee. Ours carried a 3 percent fee, which added to the cost of the purchase. At least by then we had auto-pay. Each month the credit card sends our bill directly to our bank for payment. This is important when one is away from home for many months.

PARINTINS

The next day at about noon, we arrived in Parintins. Again, this was a special-event port; all the passengers were to attend the Boi Bumba show, compliments of Regent. We had learned the previous day the advantages of getting to an event early, so we caught the first tender and then the first bus to the arena where the show was being staged. The arena was circular and had tiered seating around the circumference. Beautiful young women lined the entry to the theater—young women who were bare-breasted and who wore colorfully plumed headdresses and grass skirts.

George said he wanted a seat on the ground-level tier; it would be better for filming. He picked a seat middle-center, and we settled in with our friends Mary Ellen and Frank to await the opening act. What an act it was! The women who had welcomed us on arrival danced to the pounding music of drums. Handsome men in loincloths not only danced but did acrobatic jumps. Floats decorated with colored crepe paper and flowers moved among the dancers.

Toward the end of the show, a huge paper dragon appeared in the doorway. Dragon really did look like one, but with the feet of a half dozen men showing below. He swayed and pranced and ran around the arena floor. I was amazed when he stopped right in front of me and bobbed his head up and down. Then Dragon put his face right into mine. In his mouth he held a box that obviously contained a compact disc. George said, "He wants you to take it!"

George's choice of a seat, mid-center, first tier, was fortuitous. I am still the proud possessor of a CD of Boi Bumba music. For years after, that music filled our car, blasting from our Toyota's disc player as we drove.

About ten years later, George and I went back to Parintins and booked tickets for the same Boi Bumba show. But it was not the same show. The women were no longer topless. The theater was a simple auditorium right on the pier with no tiered seating. We had to wait in line before we were allowed to enter. It was hot and humid inside. George remarked that we were fortunate to have "done" the Amazon before cruising the river became so popular. We saw the river "as it really was."

There is a saying, "You get what you pay for." Our round-South America cruise with a top-of-the-line cruise company was not cheap. It was more expensive than other circumnavigations we did in years to follow. We did, however, experience the exceptional—days far beyond the ordinary and events that were really special.

Speaking of the cost of travel, which is something all cruisers must consider, I want to say that the price of an overnight excursion such as ours to Machu Picchu can be hefty. However, overland trips add another dimension to cruise travel. We learned that on this cruise. In the years to follow, as long as we were physically able to handle overland travel, we spent the extra money for tours we really wanted to do. We just considered the cost of an overnight excursion as part of our total expenditures.

Chapter Eleven

GOING IN GRAND STYLE: ASIA/PACIFIC

George and I arrived home from our South America cruise on February 19, 2002, and we started immediately to plan for our trip around the Pacific Rim, which was scheduled for late September 2002. Our planning included trips to doctors and dentists to make sure we had all our prescription drugs and were up to date on our medical exams. That is when we hit a serious snag.

In April, George was diagnosed with prostate cancer. In the urologist's office, Dr. Schwarz tried to break the news gently. Just a few seconds after he began to give us the diagnosis, I could tell from his body language that it was bad news. I will never forget helping my sweetheart down the steps when we left the doctor's office. In the past, George had always helped me down, although he often referred to me as his young bride. This time I held his arm to give him support. This time I led him to the passenger seat of our car and then got into the driver's seat.

The doctor had explained treatment options. We discussed them and made decisions. And then George asked, "What about our Asia/Pacific cruise in the fall?" He loved traveling the world as much as I did, and he was determined to do that trip.

"It will work out," I assured him. "You'll be OK, and we have plenty of time before final payment to change our plans if we need to." But I have to admit I was nervous, and I had my fingers crossed.

George's procedure took place in June. At our first post-op visit to the doctor, George asked about whether he would be able to travel by September. Dr. Schwartz reassured us, "Something else will get you before the cancer. Take your cruise. Live your life!"

Arriving home, we sent in our final payment for the Asia Pacific Explorer Cruise with Holland America. We were going exploring. We were going to live our lives.

On September 23, 2002, as George and I stood on the deck of *MS Volendam* in Vancouver Harbor and watched the skyline disappear into the evening sky, I gave my dear husband a big hug. "You did it, George!" I said.

"Yes," he replied. "*We* did it!"

ALASKA

Volendam headed north toward Alaska, where she made only one stop on her way to eastern Russia—in the capital city, Juneau. Since we had been to Juneau before, we limited our sightseeing to a short walk around the port area. We used the rest of our time to settle into our cabin and to lunch with our new dinner tablemates. We had chosen a table for six people at the early dining hour—5:30 p.m. Our friends Frank and Mary Ellen were on board, too, but they preferred the later seating—8 p.m.

Leaving Juneau, *Volendam* went full steam ahead; it would take a number of days for us to reach our next scheduled port, a port in Russia. But a rumor began to circulate. *Volendam* was going to make an emergency stop at Dutch Harbor, in the Aleutians. Why? Every kind of rumor imaginable spread around the ship: a passenger was sick; a crewman had had a serious accident; someone had died.

When we anchored in the bay at Dutch Harbor, most of the passengers were on deck to see what would happen. We saw a lifeboat being lowered with several people on board. It headed toward the pier and then returned—minus one man. The captain made an announcement over the public address system that everything was OK: We would get to our Russian stop on time, and he would be giving everyone a glass of champagne at supper.

The next day we learned the reason for the unexpected stop we had made. An eight-page, eight-and-a-half by eleven-inch version of the *New York Times* was available each morning. That morning in the *Times* was a brief article reporting that a HAL ship had been forced to stop at Dutch Harbor to offload a priest who had been convicted of child abuse and who was fleeing the United States.

The authorities had caught up with the man, just in time. The next day we would have crossed from American into Russian waters.

PETROPAVLOVSK-KAMCHATSKY, RUSSIA

Petropavlovsk-Kamchatsky is a city on the Kamchatka Peninsula, which is north of Japan. Few travelers go there; even our cruising friend Jim, who has visited more cities and countries than I can count, told me it is one place in the world where he has never been.

After passing through the Bering Strait, *Volendam* dropped anchor in the harbor of Petropavlovsk-Kamchatsky. It was a cold, windy day; there was even snow on the volcanic peak that stands sentinel over the city. Knowing that our mode of transportation would be our feet, we dressed warmly and set off.

We had been told by the ship's lecturer to go to the museum/shop a block away from the main boulevard. George and I did not want to get lost, so we approached some teenagers, who were standing on a corner by the pier, and asked directions. We used gestures and carefully enunciated English. Unbelievably, the girls replied in good English.

Taking advantage of that, we began to chat. We asked them what they were doing on this corner in the morning when school would have been in session. They explained that they had been released from school just for this purpose—to talk to visitors from the cruise ship and practice their English. They not only explained how to find the museum/shop but escorted us there.

Inside were other high school girls who, in English, told us the price of three little painted boxes we wanted to buy. Yes, we bought the three boxes, and when we got home, we gave one to the internist who had discovered George's cancer.

The girls pointed out the scenic way back to the pier. We followed their directions and found a statue of Lenin mounted on a pedestal in the main square. Behind the statue was the snow-tipped, volcanic peak we had seen in the early morning from the deck of *Volendam*. It made a striking scene for George to photograph.

"What a nice morning," I said as we boarded *Volendam*. "We got lucky when we asked directions from those teenagers by the pier." Those girls are what I remember most about our day in Petropavlovsk-Kamchatsky, a city whose name I have difficulty remembering and pronouncing. It is easier for me to say Peter and Paul, which is what the name means in English.

JAPANESE PORTS: KUSHIRO, HAKODATE, AND TOKYO

Steaming south, *Volendam* took us to the port of Kushiro on the Japanese island of Hokkaido. I have but one picture in my mind of our stop there: the fish market with aisle after aisle of individual stalls, each loaded with every kind of fish we could imagine: salmon, halibut, pollock, shark, mackerel . . . Of course, the place was redolent with the smell of fish. I recall that the ship offered a shuttle to the downtown area so we could enjoy what we liked doing most—walking the streets of the city.

Steaming even farther south, we stopped next in Hakodate, still on the island of Hokkaido. Again, we had an easy morning. We took the ship's shuttle to the center of the city. And again, I can conjure up just one picture of our walkabout: a busy square with lots of traffic and noise and with a covered arcade-like area that is the Japanese equivalent of an American food court. We wandered about, sat on a bench, and watched the people.

The next morning, we awoke to find our ship tied up at a dock in the port for Tokyo. Because the port is a considerable distance from the central city and we had spent time roaming about on our own during our honeymoon trip in 1969, George and I opted for a ship-run highlights tour to refresh our memories. Our first stop was the Imperial Palace, the residence of the Emperor of Japan. We crossed the bridge and walked the palace grounds, which we remembered clearly from 1969. Another stop was at a typical busy intersection crowded with people and cars. We remembered the colorful neon signs and large, flashing television screens mounted high on the buildings. And we remembered especially the noise and the hustle and bustle.

Of course, there was the obligatory shopping stop at an expensive pearl store. Both of us recalled the simple room on the Ginza, in a third-floor walkup, where we had selected pearls and had waited while the proprietor strung them: That again was in 1969. I still have my string of pearls, which I recently had restrung. I paid more for the restringing than I originally paid for the pearls. Of course, back in the sixties, the dollar/yen exchange rate was unbelievably in favor of the dollar.

OSAKA AND KYOTO

In 1969, George and I had spent a couple of days in Kyoto. In addition to visiting with the president of Kyoto University, we had walked the grounds of the golden Kinkakuji temple, sat and contemplated at the Ryoan-ji rock gardens, walked across the creaking floors of Nijo Castle, took tea in the Japanese formal style, and stopped at the Kyoto Handicraft Center. At Kyoto Handicraft, we had bought a gorgeous four-panel painting of a persimmon branch, signed by the artist. It is done on gold-colored silk. The price then was only seventy-five American dollars, shipping included. The painting came with papers documenting its authenticity. On our land tour in 1976, we had stopped there again and bought a similar but smaller piece at twice the price. We thought—just maybe—we would like one more four-paneled painting done on silk.

We opted, therefore, for a day tour from the port of Osaka to the old city of Kyoto that took us back to the gardens, palaces, and temples we remembered so clearly—and to Kyoto Handicraft. No matter how many times we have sat quietly and contemplated the placement of the rocks in the quiet of the rock garden, we have always found inner peace. No matter how many times we have walked through the gardens surrounding the exquisite Kinkakuji and have viewed the golden temple itself, we have always been awestruck. Actually, in our den is a machine-made tapestry of the temple that we bought on our first stop in Kyoto. I still adore our Golden Pavilion.

But we were disappointed at Kyoto Handicraft. We did not buy another painting. The large ones like our persimmon branch now bore a price tag of more than two thousand dollars and the quality did not compare with our four-paneled painting. When we returned home after our cruise, George and I made a special point of studying our persimmon branch. It is such a beautiful piece of art.

BEIJING, CHINA

The main reason George and I booked our Asia/Pacific cruise was to visit Beijing. *Volendam* would stay in the port of Xingang for two days. Passengers could disembark there and take a two-day, overnight trip to Beijing. This was our opportunity to make our dreams come true.

The ride from Xingang to Beijing is rather long; the bus made one rest stop on the way. For most of us ladies, that stop was a culture shock: The toilet looked more like a porcelain hole in the ground. Women had to squat, not sit. At the same time, we had to hold up our jeans to keep them off the floor and keep them dry. The odor was overpowering. Interestingly, when we took a similar tour in 2013, we made the same rest stop. It was a totally different experience, with some toilets in the western style and without the odor.

An hour after our rest stop, George and I were standing in Tiananmen Square. The square is huge—the largest in the world. It faces the Forbidden City and is rimmed by modern buildings, such as the Great Hall of the People. Some locals were out enjoying the sunshine, groups of school children were on field trips with their teachers, and vendors were hawking kites.

Our guide gave us a brief explanation before letting us explore on our own. We did just that, walking about, buying a paper kite from a vendor, and—yes—thinking. It was in 1989 that military forces, brought in to quell a peaceful protest, killed thousands of students in the square. That was only thirteen years before our visit, yet the guide had not mentioned the Tiananmen Square massacre in his explanation. He had just talked about the size of the square and identified the surrounding buildings. George guessed that the government strategy was to play down the massacre and that guides had to follow the party line.

The time passed quickly. Too soon, our guide gathered us together and walked us across Tiananmen and through the gates into the Forbidden City. Constructed in the fifteenth century, the Forbidden City is a vast complex of buildings that housed the Emperors of China for more than 500 years. The buildings are colorfully ornate, decorated in golds and reds. The roofs curve upward, and dragons look down from the eaves. We walked through one chamber after another, one courtyard after another. It was fascinating.

Lunch was in a restaurant located behind the Forbidden City. Food was served communal-style; we sat in groups of ten around circular tables with rotating centers—lazy Susans, as we call them at home. The waiters brought in bowls of steaming food for us to share. We ate and used the restroom there; we did not know when we would see another Western-style facility.

Our afternoon destination was the Temple of Heaven. I remember the lovely path arched with trees that leads into the temple, the vast courtyard we had to cross, and the circular, three-tiered structure at the core of the complex. After a brief explanation, our guide again set us free to explore. That was perfect for George and me; we could go at our own pace and return to the bus at our leisure.

Vendors, of course, were active in the bus parking lot. One young vendor approached us, displaying a gold-and-black scarf. It was silk, large, and gorgeous. In her hand, she also had a stack of other scarves; she counted them out—one, two . . . nine, ten. The price was ten for ten dollars. I asked her to unfold another one. She displayed that one, too. I took from her the two scarves she had opened and gestured toward the other eight, which she handed over. I gave her an American ten-dollar bill. Of course, the other eight were small squares, nothing to compare with the first two. Still it was a great deal; forgetting about the eight small pieces, I actually paid only five dollars for each of the two large scarves.

Driving by Tiananmen Square again, the bus took us to the Beijing Hotel, an immense hotel up the street from the square. When we checked in, our guide told us to be ready in one hour, because he was taking us to a Peking duck restaurant for dinner. Our dinner outing was the least satisfactory part of our overnight excursion. The restaurant was a super-huge emporium that was serving hundreds of tourists. George joked that the allotment was one small duck per table of ten.

We slept well that night. The Beijing Hotel was luxurious, the beds comfortable, and the bathroom shiny and bright.

THE GREAT WALL OF CHINA

Up early the next morning, we boarded our bus by 8 a.m., and we were off. We had an hour's drive to the Great Wall of China through an area that was rather mountainous. And then, there it was—the Great Wall. Our guide led us from our bus along paths lined with vendors and finally up a couple of sets of uneven stone steps. Standing on the wall, the guide provided us with a brief explanation and again let us wander. Most of our group walked up higher. I walked a short distance and then gave up when faced with a steep incline. George, of course, was pumped full of adrenaline, and he walked a considerable distance along the wall. I found a nook where I could sit and look at the Great Wall as it wound up into the hills. A lovely morning, blue sky, a view of the wall—I was Dorothy in Oz.

When George returned from his trek, we "hit" the shops. We found a red, wooden dragon mask, a walking cane just like ones we had seen a gentlemen using the day before, a string of blue and white ceramic beads, and several narrow cloisonné bangle bracelets. George got a T-shirt emblazoned with the words "I Climbed the Great Wall." We were buying lasting memories to go with our visual ones of the Great Wall.

Dragon mask.

George and Dorothy on the Great Wall.

Lunch was at another emporium-style restaurant on the road back to Beijing. We ate quickly because I had spied a small cloisonné owl in the gift shop and I needed time to make my purchase. We also visited the restroom with the hope that we would not have to use the odiferous, squat toilet at the rest stop on the highway back to the ship.

Our trip "home" took four hours. The views from the bus were especially interesting as we neared Beijing. We saw row after row of high-rise buildings under construction; everywhere there were cranes perched on rooftops. The guide told us that this was a time of rapid expansion outward. Local city neighborhoods, the hutongs, were being demolished to make way for office buildings, and residents were being forced to move from their neighborhoods to apartment blocks.

Both of us were tired after two long days. On the bus, we napped a bit, and we talked. George was convinced that we had not had sufficient time to see Beijing. He announced, "We have to come back." I agreed.

HONG KONG

George and I had made two prior stops in Hong Kong, one on our round-the-world air trip in 1969, and one on our air/land tour of Southeast Asia. This visit was our first by ship. For that reason, we left our cabin early to go on deck for the sail-in. It was unbelievable. We saw miles and miles of high-rise apartment and office buildings on both our port and starboard sides. The building complexes "climbed" up the hillsides, claiming every inch of land. George told me he had read that Hong Kong has more skyscrapers than any other city in the world. From what we observed, that was plausible.

Ahead we saw the Ocean and the Star Ferry terminals. We recognized these from our prior visits. The captain swung *Volendam* around and backed her into our slot in the Ocean Terminal. It was a tricky maneuver.

Volendam stayed only a day in Hong Kong. On that day, we wanted to go to Stanley Market, which we had heard so much about but had never visited. Following directions supplied by the ship's port specialist, we took the Star Ferry across the harbor from Kowloon, where we were docked, to Hong Kong Island on the other side. At that time, senior citizens paid nothing to cross over by ferry, and the ride is always fun. Once on the island, we found the public bus terminal and the location of the local bus to Stanley Market. We did not want the express bus that goes through tunnels to get there; we wanted the local that climbs the mountain with views down to the fishing village of Aberdeen. The port expert on the ship had advised this.

The ride over the mountain is an adventure. The road is narrow. The pace is fast. George and I had chosen the front seats on the upper level of the double-decker bus. We just hung on as the bus whipped around curves and rushed down inclines. But we felt that the views were worth it. We decided, too, that on our next trip to Hong Kong we would have to go to Aberdeen to ride one of the sampans we saw bobbing in the harbor. Yes, we knew we would come back!

At Stanley Market, we shopped for hours. The market is huge and prices unbelievably low. We bought bow ties for George for formal nights, several basic blouses and shirts, and a pink Chinese evening jacket for me.

In the afternoon, back in Kowloon, we strolled the area adjacent to the Ocean Terminal. This is one of our favorite parts of Hong Kong. Right there is the Peninsula Hotel with its classic lobby, where we could sit, relax, and "take tea." Nearby, too, is the park where senior citizens enjoy tai chi together, and just across from the park is our favorite shop selling carved figurines. On this visit, we recognized the shopkeeper from our prior visit and, of course, we bought a carving—one of a Japanese fisherman made from bone. Across Nathan Road, which is the main avenue on the Kowloon side of Hong Kong, are the Chungking Mansions. "The Mansions" is a misnomer. They are really a maze of rather dark, narrow alleys on the ground floor of a business complex. The alleys wind around, and it is easy to get lost.

In Hong Kong, to enjoy the city, a traveler must be able to walk. On this trip, after George's cancer encounter, we were happy that we both could cover distances without a struggle. George and I often talked about how wise we were to have started traveling when we were young enough to explore city streets independently.

The first part of our evening entertainment that night in Hong Kong was a light show. From the ship, we could look across the harbor and watch colored lights dance across the buildings on Hong Kong Island. Reds, greens, blues, yellows, and whites filled the evening sky. Sitting on deck chairs, George and I held hands and quietly watched.

The second part of the entertainment was a show staged on the pier. Costumed dancers performed for us. The best act was a massive dragon propelled by eight men who worked as a unit. As did the dragon in Parintins in South America, this one dipped and dived, supported by long sticks that the men—within the body of the puppet—carried. With music from the pier as an accompaniment, *Volendam* pulled away and moved down the harbor. The sail-away was as phenomenal as the sail-in.

BROOME, NOT BALI

Leaving Hong Kong, *Volendam* headed south to Indonesia, the country from which Holland America draws many of the men and women who serve as stewards on the ships of the line. Our destination in Indonesia was Bali, the island I consider one of the most beautiful in the world.

For many of the passengers on our Asia/Pacific cruise, Bali was a place to which they looked forward with eager anticipation. For the Indonesian crew members, Bali was a part of their homeland.

When a HAL ship docks in an Indonesian port, the crew are allowed to entertain their families on board during the days the vessel is tied up to the pier. You can imagine how excited our Indonesian stewards were as *Volendam* got closer and closer to Bali. Many had families who were flying in from other Indonesian islands to be with them. Some of the men and women who helped us every day had not seen their families in months. Some had not even seen their babies who had been born after their last visit.

A few days before we were to dock in Bali, we got the bad news via television. This was 2002, and 2002 was the year of the terrorist bombing of an Indonesian nightclub in Denpasar, the capital city of Bali and our port of call. Our Indonesian men and women were heartsick, because they knew what that meant. Shortly, the captain announced over the PA system that the top brass in Seattle had canceled our Bali stop. Instead, *Volendam* would be stopping in Broome, Australia.

This was a moment on our cruise that George and I never forgot. We often talked about how sad our stewards were for days after. When we would talk to them about our missed port, we could see tears in their eyes. Some would open their wallets and share pictures of their wives and children, mothers and fathers. Our hearts ached for and with them.

Volendam steamed past Bali and south to Broome, which is in Western Australia. She tied up at a dock several miles from Broome, and so Holland America supplied a complimentary shuttle to town. For us this worked well. On the way in, we saw a mob of wallabies hopping in a field right by the road. The bus driver stopped so that camera buffs could take pictures. It was the first time either of us had seen wallabies in the wild.

Broome turned out to be a town rather similar to those seen in old western movies. The sidewalks were boardwalks. The bar looked like the ones we had seen in Juneau, Alaska, with a swinging, louvered door and a big mirror on the wall. The barbershop was a stool on a street corner. Fellow travelers, knowing how costly haircuts were on board *Volendam*, lined up for a trim.

There was not much to do in Broome—other than walk up one side of the street and back down the other side, looking in shop windows. For us, though, it was a unique experience in a part of Australia we had never expected to see. Returning to the ship, we stopped again to photograph another mob of wallabies, relatives of kangaroos found primarily in Australia.

CAIRNS, AUSTRALIA

Cairns is on the east coast of Australia in the state of Queensland. It is a port from which tourists can take a catamaran out to see the Great Barrier Reef. *Volendam* docked in Cairns, and George, I, and many of our fellow passengers transferred in the port to a catamaran. The catamaran was large, with rows and rows of seats in an inside cabin and some seating on an outside deck. Since the wind was chilly and blowing with force, we chose to sit inside.

It did not take me long to realize that we were in trouble. We were barely out of the harbor when our catamaran began to rock violently. I looked around and saw a squad of young people, who were dressed in smocks, standing in the back with paper bags in hand. A woman near me hollered, "I need help," and one of the emergency squad came running with a paper bag and a wet cloth—just in time. I was next! George managed to hold out for a time; actually, he was among the last to be stricken with *mal de mer*.

At the Great Barrier Reef, we transferred to a semi-submersible. Passengers walked down a ladder into the body of the boat and looked out from side windows as the vessel moved along the reef. I decided it was best to be the last on the boat, so if I felt sick, I could go up topside and get air. That was a wise decision!

Back on our catamaran, George and I found benches on the open-air aft deck and stretched out. Then I remembered: In my tote bag, I had a packet of seasickness pills that HAL had distributed during some rough seas. We each took one. I offered the third pill from the packet to a woman who was also stretched out on a bench; she looked green, far worse than we did. She took it, which shows how ill she was—to take unknown medicine from an unknown person. Later we heard that a couple had been so desperately sick that they had paid several hundred dollars to be helicoptered back to Cairns.

Actually, the return trip was not so bad. It may have been the pill combined with the fresh air, combined with our being stretched out prone, combined with the sea calming. Whatever the cause, by the time we pulled into Cairns, George and I felt well enough to walk about the shops adjacent to the pier.

SYDNEY, AUSTRALIA

Our entry into Sydney Harbor rated an A+++. Seasoned travelers had encouraged us to be up on deck early, because entry into Sydney is like no other.

On the day of our arrival—our first of many such Sydney sail-ins we did over the years—the sky was bright blue, and the waters of the harbor sparkled as the sun bounced off the waves created by *Volendam's* wake. As *Volendam* progressed up the harbor, George and I saw the white, sail-like outline of the Sydney Opera House portside and then ahead Sydney Bridge, known to locals as the coat hanger. What a gorgeous view! Absolutely glorious! Perfect in every way!

After our barrier reef debacle, we deserved a bit of good luck, and we got it. Our captain pulled right into our dockage spot. He did not turn the ship around to back in. That put our cabin on the side facing the Sydney Opera House; we could see the building from our small window on A-deck. We also were lucky because there is only room for one ship in Darling Harbour. If a ship does not get that desirable spot, the captain has to dock farther from the main attractions.

Because we were "right there," we could walk to the major sites. George and I walked around by the ferry slips and picked up a ferry schedule to help us in our explorations the next day. We then headed toward the opera house. We climbed up the stairs, strolled around the building, and then walked down the steps where we stopped to gaze back. The Sydney Opera House is unique with its soaring sails; it is an architectural gem.

Following our map, we meandered in the direction of the Royal Botanic Garden. I decided when we got there that I needed a rest, so we found a bench to sit on before walking the paths of the garden. As we sat, George pointed out bats—lots of them—hanging from the branches above our heads. Seeing them, I decided I did not need a rest after all.

George and I took a different route back, one that passed through the section called The Rocks. The Rocks is where Sydney started, thus an interesting area of old buildings for wanderers like us. The common denominator in our explorations that day was *walk*. We followed a route marked on a map being distributed at the pier. We had learned early in our travels to pick up a map before setting out on our self-directed walking tours.

And now the real high point of our day, more thrilling even than our sail-in! In the middle of the night, I awoke and for some reason felt compelled to open the curtains and look out. Before me was a fantastic picture. In the distance was the Sydney Opera House, the full moon casting a shimmering glow upon it. Close by our window, illuminated by the ship's side-beaming lights, were hundreds of white seabirds. The birds seemed almost to be dancing: Gracefully, they dived down to the water and then soared upward—over and over again. George had to see this. I woke him up, and for almost an hour, we looked out our small window at a scene I call "The Dancing Seabirds of Sydney."

BAY OF ISLANDS, NEW ZEALAND

When *Volendam* left Sydney, the captain followed a northeasterly course that led us to the Bay of Islands on the northern tip of the North Island of New Zealand. This was a tender stop, so from the tender we could view the small islands in the bay.

I have one very clear picture in my mind of our stop at the Bay of Islands. To our right, as we rode in, we saw a park-like area with a largish building almost hidden among the trees. We saw the New Zealand flag flying overhead. This was our destination for the morning—The Treaty House—where the Treaty of Waitangi between the Maoris and the United Kingdom was signed in 1840. That treaty granted the native Maoris citizenship rights.

George and I explored the Treaty House, which is now a museum, and the Maori meeting house, which is also on the grounds. It was the meeting house, called a *wharenui* by the Maori, that fascinated us the most. Lining each side of the rectangular building are very tall statues—tikis—carved from wood and decorated with mother-of-pearl eyes. Tall, the tikis extend from floor to ceiling. George guessed that the tikis are supposed to scare away evil spirits. There were carvings also on the outside of the meeting house, making it impressive both inside and out.

AUCKLAND, NEW ZEALAND

By sea, Auckland is only a short distance from the Bay of Islands. Auckland is often referred to as the City of Sails because so many small sailing boats are moored in the harbor. The Auckland sail-in is nothing like the Sydney sail-in, but nice just the same with all the sailboats.

George chose our outing in Auckland. He wanted to see the Waitomo Glowworm Caves located south of the city. Because the caves are a distance from Auckland, we opted for a ship's tour. We always felt more secure on a ship's tour when our destination required a long bus ride. We worried about getting back to the ship in time for sail-away. The ship will wait for a delayed ship's tour bus. If you are on your own, you *are* on your own. See you at the next port.

Again, I have a single picture in my mind of our visit at Waitomo—a picture of me with George and others in a large rowboat, looking up at the ceiling of a cave sparkling with the light emitted by thousands of glowworms. Our guide in the caves was a Maori, who told Maori stories as we glided through one underground channel after another. He assured us that the light was a natural phenomenon; worms were actually generating it. By the way, according to George, who looked it up when we got home, the scientific name for these critters is *Arachnocampa luminosa*.

In a gift shop connected with the Waitomo Caves, I found a small wood carving of a tiki on a cord for George to wear around his neck. We also found a fifteen-inch carved tiki that today hangs in our kitchen with our other Polynesian treasures.

ON THE *VOLENDAM*

When *Volendam* backed out of her berth in Auckland, she headed east across the Pacific, the largest and deepest ocean on earth. For George and me, this was our first South Pacific crossing. We had only three port stops left, but many sea days to get us across the Pacific—more days without making landfall than we had ever experienced. This was the time for us to enjoy the ship and its activities, and to relax.

On our first sea day, we noticed passengers wearing lime-green T-shirts with the gold design that was the logo for our Asia Pacific Explorer Cruise. I really wanted one; it would be great to wear when I got home to remind me of the days George and I had shared on *Volendam*. I went to the shops, but the clerk told me that the T-shirts were not for sale: You had to win them playing trivia. We had seen trivia listed on the daily program on this and prior cruises, but we had never gone to a game.

That afternoon, naively, I sent George up to play trivia and told him to win a lime-colored T-shirt for me. I say "naively" because a dozen or more teams often compete and, as someone told us afterward, on Holland America ships, trivia is a "bloodsport."

About an hour later, George returned with a T-shirt and a story. He had found the lounge packed with people waiting for trivia to begin. Most were grouped in teams of six. George spied a group of five ladies and asked if he could join them. Yes, they were short one player because their sixth team member was not coming that afternoon. George said "his" ladies really knew their movie, music, television, and sports trivia, and given that there were some science and geography questions, he had been able to contribute answers they did not know.

"We won," he proudly announced, "and I helped them win."

George's ladies had told him that on the last afternoon of the voyage, the cruise director was going to give every player a lime-colored T-shirt. We had to attend trivia each afternoon until the end of the cruise, George explained, so we could get two more. For a couple of afternoons, George and I sat alone at trivia, but soon others joined us. We had a team, a group of new friends for the remainder of the cruise.

From then on, we became trivia regulars. In the years to come, we became rather good players and won some games, too. More importantly, we made some lifelong friends, people with whom we continued to travel year after year and with whom I still regularly exchange emails.

On sea days, in addition to trivia, passengers could select from a menu of activities: cooking and bridge lessons, watercolor and dance instruction, crafts, swimming in the pools, crazy games like Call Out, lectures, and interviews with the entertainers and staff members. Back in 2002, there was a theater for movie buffs, a large library with a book swap, and computer labs.

And now let me describe evenings aboard the ship. The evening of our first sea day after leaving Auckland was designated a formal night. George and I donned our dress-up duds, and about a half hour before dinner, we headed to the Ocean Bar for our pre-dinner waltz. Neither of us really knew how to dance, but we could handle the waltz; we had practiced dancing it in our stateroom on our first cruise after we were married in 1968 and had become rather good waltzers. For any other music, George had his own steps. Since he had rhythm and I could feel it when we danced together, we just did our own thing when the piece was not a waltz. George often wondered aloud how I ever knew what he was going to do when he didn't know himself.

After dinner—perhaps with lobster because it was a formal night—most cruisers headed to the show lounge. We liked the fact that we could walk from the stern of the ship to the prow to get to the entertainment venue and that it was a short walk to our cabin after the show.

On many formal nights on our cruise, passengers found a gift on their beds. The first formal night after our departure from Auckland, our present was a small stuffed kangaroo with a joey in her pouch. During the cruise, our gifts included a large tote, a duffel bag, a daily journal, a lapel pin with the cruise logo, and a poncho, to name just a few. In more recent days, cruise companies have cut back on the number of gifts they provide. I would guess that cost is a factor.

Let me now talk about the parties, which are an integral component of a grand cruise. George and I had booked our Asia/Pacific cruise through a discount travel agency affiliated with American Express. American Express had sent a couple to serve as escorts for travelers who had booked with an affiliated agency. That couple hosted cocktail parties periodically during the voyage—an especially nice idea when sea day follows sea day. We found that other agencies did much the same thing, and even with these perks, the cruise cost was actually lower than if we had booked directly with the cruise company.

Holland America also hosted parties for us. First were the general parties, such as the welcome-aboard cocktail reception. In addition, the shipping company hosted what were called Mariner Receptions. Most cruise companies have a rewards program that honors those who have cruised many times with the line. The ship's captain and hotel director recognize frequent cruisers at invitation-only parties and luncheons. The nice thing is that, as we accumulated days with the cruise company, we also got some other nice perks—perks such as free laundry service.

George and I did another kind of partying on our way home across the vast Pacific—private partying. Most ships offer a specialty dining room; the surcharge for dinner back then was about thirty dollars per person, and for lunch half that. Today on most lines there are other specialty dining venues, and the surcharge is higher.

Earlier during this cruise, we had not dined in *Volendam's* specialty restaurant, which is basically a seafood and steak house. We had too much else to do. Now we had more time, so as we were leaving Auckland, we made reservations for dinner with our friends Mary Ellen and Frank. Since then, over the years on grand voyages, we have found that dining in an extra-charge restaurant is a wonderful way to celebrate special occasions with friends.

POLYNESIA

This morning, September 25, 2020, I woke up imagining us back in Polynesia on a picture-perfect beach that George and I loved—Matira Beach on Bora Bora. The water at Matira is so calm, so warm, so clear. We could walk far out into the lagoon, for the gradient is gentle. Swimming, we could look up at the volcanic projections towering above the hillside. Matira Beach is a little piece of paradise.

At Matira, I always swam with a song running through my head, a song from the musical "South Pacific" about the way Bali Ha'i calls to one's heart. On the morning of the twenty-fifth, I heard that song in my heart, urging me to come away.

I had crawled into bed on September 24 during the pandemic knowing that the next day I was going to travel virtually to Bora Bora, which is my favorite beach spot in all the world. And so Bali Ha'i was calling to me as I thought back to our first visit to Bora Bora. When James Michener wrote the novel *The Tales of the South Pacific*, it is said, he had in mind Bora Bora in Polynesia—fabulous, fantastic Bora Bora!

Because 2002 was our first time there, we opted for a highlights drive around the island. The open-air bus tour was offered by our American Express travel agency escorts, Pat and Bill.

From that day, I remember the striking views that met our eyes as our bus circled Bora Bora, absolutely heavenly views. I remember seeing somewhere on our drive a clothesline on which were pinned sarongs of multiple designs and colors. We stopped to look and buy because sarongs are almost synonymous with Polynesia. And I remember our stop at the famed restaurant Bloody Mary's, named for a character in "South Pacific." We sat and had a drink there.

I recall, too, a rather crazy thing that happened after our stop at Bloody Mary's. The bus let us off at the side of the road by a lovely beach where folks were swimming. "Ah, to swim in that water," I said to George.

Our escort felt the same way, but she took action. Stripping off her shoes but still fully clothed, Pat jumped in. She frolicked in abandon and called out that the water was wonderful. I knew absolutely that we would return for a full day at the beach. It would have to be sometime soon.

133

Because we had joined a circle-the-island tour in Bora Bora, we decided instead to wander about Papeete, the capital of Tahiti and the city where *Volendam* docked next. The best part of Papeete is its market which is housed in a huge two-level building. In it, vendors sell flowers, meats, vegetables, black pearls, T-shirts, wood carvings, and practically anything else one could want. On the second level, George and I discovered a musical group performing island dances, so we sat on a bench for a while to watch and listen.

We also found wood carvings that were a little far out—literally. The carvings were of fully aroused males with greatly exaggerated equipment. We wondered who in the world would display a carving like that in their home. Interestingly, on our return to Papeete a few years later, the risqué carvings were gone.

Nuka Hiva in the Marquesas Islands was the last stop on our 2002 Asia/Pacific cruise. It is a tender port. Knowing that and also knowing that sometimes lines form to board a boat, George and I were up early to catch the first one. The port lecturer had explained that the island was small and that no tours were being offered; we should just walk the shore area, go into the church, and look in the few stalls we would find under a tent erected in a field.

We investigated the stalls first, because the port lecturer had told us that the Marquesas Islands are known for wood carvings. Entering the tented area, we saw tables set around the inside perimeter. On one table George spied something that looked like a war club. Primitively rendered, it had a carved handle to which—with a simple cord—was tied a hefty stone. The price was twenty-five dollars, which seemed steep. We did not, however, bargain with the seller, who through gestures and a few words told us that he had made it himself. George really wanted that war club, and we saw that it was the one and only club for sale.

For a time, with George clutching his prize, we followed the path that led around the bay away from the village. We stopped in the church, and George took a few pictures. That was enough. It was so hot and humid that we were drenched from our own perspiration.

Heading back to *Volendam*, we met passengers who were just starting to explore. Of course, they remarked on George's war club.

"Where?" a woman asked George. George explained that his club was onc of a kind. "How much did you pay?" she continued.

When he said twenty-five dollars, she said she would give him twice that much. When he refused the offer, someone who had overheard his conversation offered a hundred. The man wanted the war club for his grandson. George figured he had made an excellent purchase. I agreed. His war club was priceless.

George and I returned to Nuka Hiva on several other Pacific crossings, but the small quintessential Polynesian village of our memories had changed. Just a few years later there was a large building near the pier where vendors were selling fine carvings—nothing like George's original war club. By the pier, ladies were selling black pearls. And a short way down the street, drivers were offering to take passengers to the top of a nearby hill to look down upon the ocean.

To show the contrast, George and I succumbed; we bought an exquisitely carved wooden knife in one of the new shops. It cost seventy-five dollars. That carving hangs on the wall in our living room. George's war club is on the wall in the kitchen in a location where he was able to look at it from his seat at the table.

HOMEWARD BOUND

Leaving Nuka Hiva, our captain set a course for Los Angeles. George and I both felt differently now; we had a sense of winding down. That was the general feeling we sensed among our friends as well. Many of us started to organize our things for packing and asked our room stewards to bring our luggage out of storage. Earlier, we had completed forms indicating our travel arrangements once we reached LA. Based on what we had indicated on the forms, we had been assigned disembarkation numbers.

The morning of our penultimate day aboard *Volendam*, all the passengers gathered in the theater for a special farewell. The cruise staff, the stewards, and some of the officers paraded into the main show lounge and up onto the stage. As they arrived and we saw our dining and cabin stewards, we clapped and cheered. Amid more clapping and cheering, the cruise director and the captain spoke. And then the grand finale! Everyone on stage joined hands and sang "It's a Small, Small World." At the same time, they waved the flags of their countries. We—the passengers of this grand voyage of sixty-four days—had tears in our eyes by then. These wonderful people, who had made the voyage so splendid for us, had become like family.

In the afternoon, George and I went to trivia to pick up our T-shirts. We found Frank and Mary Ellen for final hugs and promised to keep in touch. We dined with Herb and Betty, and then we went with them to the showroom where the production cast gave a short performance. After that, it was off to our cabin. We put our labeled suitcases into the hall to be picked up in the night by the crew and organized the next morning on the pier, where we would claim them. George gave me a big goodnight hug, and then we were off to dreamland.

In the morning, I got up to see the lights of Los Angeles come into view. We were back in our own beloved country!

In Los Angeles confusion reigned on the dock; the longshoremen, who handled the luggage, were on slowdown; to make a long story short, George and I missed our flight from LA to Newark. We did catch a later flight, but to say the least, we had an anxious hour when we did not know whether we would be stuck in the airport overnight.

A veteran traveler once told us to bounce with the flow, to focus on the good things, not the bad. The chaos we experienced at disembarkation proved the soundness of his advice. Despite the rough time we had retrieving our luggage on the pier, we had had marvelous days and weeks. On our Asia Pacific Explorer Cruise, we had seen parts of the world we had only dreamed of.

As we waited in Newark for our limo driver to pick us up, I looked at my George and thought that only nine months before he had been diagnosed with cancer. And here he was, still traveling and even talking about where we would go next. Life was good.

INTERMEZZO

From the time we had married in 1968 until our return from our South America and Asia Pacific Explorer Cruises in 2002, George and I had kept on the go—traveling as much as we could during college breaks, mostly on shorter trips to the Caribbean and Europe. However, our South America and our Asia Pacific cruises introduced a new dimension to our travels. After my retirement, "the world was our oyster." We could travel farther from home, and we could travel for longer periods.

Of course, we still took shorter cruises. In 2003 and 2004, we cruised the Caribbean, the Mediterranean, and the Baltics. These were trips we had mostly booked on board the *Volendam* before disembarking in 2002. We had discovered that, by booking on board, we got added shipboard credits for a cruise. Within the same time frame, we took some shorter family cruises and some voyages with friends, which sailed out of New York City. We liked the idea of not having to fly to the ship.

But in the back of our minds, we harbored our dream of returning to China. I kept in my mind, as well, the possibility of a world cruise and transiting the Suez Canal. George was hesitant about a world voyage; he talked of seeing Africa.

At the end of 2003, we began to investigate land tours of China. We had friends who swore by a company called Grand Circle, so late on a Friday afternoon in January of 2004, I placed a call to ask for pricing on their twenty-one-day China tour scheduled for April. George and I agreed that the itinerary was perfect for us: Beijing, Shanghai, Wuhan, the Yangtze, Xi'an, Guilin, Hong Kong. The GC agent quoted a price that I thought was within reason. I said what I always said when getting pricing: "I have to check with my husband, and I will get back." By Tuesday, we had decided to book the trip. George had been given a clean bill of health by his oncologist on our return from our Asia/Pacific cruise, we both wanted to see more of China, and the price was within our range.

Imagine my surprise when I called the next Wednesday to discover that the price had gone down considerably since the prior Friday. George was standing by me as I wrote down the new price. He took out his credit card and handed it to me so I could place a deposit.

Little did we realize that the reason for the price change was something called SARS, a virus in the same family as COVID-19 which was impacting travel to China. Well, we did not know that and learned about SARS only when we got to China. Today, as I shelter at home and recall our 2004 China trip, I realize the irony of my doing this; here during the time of the COVID-19 pandemic, I am recalling a trip to China that we took during SARS.

Our China trip would open new and even wider windows in our travels of the world—windows that would take us not only to China, but to Africa, to the Middle East, through Suez, and yes, eventually around the world. Throughout this phase, I began to keep a journal, and so in traveling virtually during COVID-19, I could "begin" a trip by reading what I had previously written as we traversed the world. In Part Two of my memoir, I will share the high points and low points of our adventures from 2004 forward.

Singapore during World Cruise 2009.

Part

2

OPENING
WINDOWS WIDER
2004–2016

Chapter Twelve
TRAVELING CHINA

We were in the park that surrounds the Temple of Heaven in Beijing. It was Easter Sunday morning, 2004. Three Chinese gentlemen were playing their violins. Couples were waltzing. George turned to me; he bowed and held out his arms. "Shall we?" he asked.

And then we waltzed—two smiling and happy Americans on a sunny day in the park, surrounded by waltzing Chinese. Something must have been inspiring my husband, for he danced me about in perfect time with the violins. He twirled and swayed, and I had no trouble following him. It may have been the place. It may have been the time. It may have been the sunshine or even the cherry blossoms just breaking into bloom. But we two serious-minded professors waltzed as we had never waltzed before.

The Chinese dancers stopped to watch us. Probably few Americans had ever joined their Sunday-morning dance in the park. When the violin music ended, our audience clapped for us and smiled broadly.

Neither of us ever forgot the Easter morning we danced at the Temple of Heaven. It was truly a little piece of heaven for us. Friends have asked how we could return to a city or a country or a place and still find pleasure. The answer was simple: We knew that there was a special moment like "Waltzing in the Park" waiting for us.

BEIJING

When I was trying to decide which of our wonderful moments was the one that led all the rest in my memory bank of China 2004, my choice was between "Waltzing in the Park" and "Rickshaw Ride in the Hutongs of Beijing." The hutongs are old neighborhoods of the city crisscrossed by narrow lanes; the lanes are lined with homes that were built years and years ago and are slowly being demolished to make way for high-rise apartment and business complexes.

Our rickshaw ride and the stops we made in the hutongs were unforgettable. Our young driver liked to be the leader of the pack; he pedaled fast and wove in and out of traffic to get ahead of the other rickshaws in our cavalcade. The Wild One, as I quickly named him, drove us to two old towers where he let us out to catch our breath and walk around one of the old neighborhoods. We were followed by vendors who hawked pocketbooks, hats, vases, T-shirts. George bought two hats—a baseball cap marked with a "genuine fake" Olympic Games 2008 emblem and a pot hat with lots of pins from various regions of China.

Then we were off again, holding tightly to each other as The Wild One rounded corners and even raced automobiles. Exciting, yes, and a morning not to be forgotten!

But the day got even better. Our tour bus stopped in front of an elementary school, where we visited a classroom. The children read to us from their English books so we could hear how well they could pronounce English words. Members of our tour group read from the same books so the children could hear their pronunciation. One of our group was a music teacher. She decided that we should all sing, and so she led us in a rousing rendition of "Old MacDonald Had a Farm." We were enthusiastic as we sang the familiar lines: "with a moo, moo here, and a moo, moo there," and "with a cluck, cluck here and a cluck, cluck there." Then she turned to the children and motioned for them to join in. All of us smiling and singing, we were an example of how easily people of different cultures and ages can enjoy a common activity.

On our way back from our visit to the Great Wall the next afternoon, we had another unforgettable moment—this one sad. We stopped at a martial arts school where the boys and girls performed for us. They gestured and jumped as if fighting. Younger children, who sat with us, mimicked the moves of the older ones. All of them did acrobatic jumps.

One young man tried to split a thick board with his bare hand by slamming it into the wood. He failed once, twice, and then a third time until he finally gave up in obvious pain. After the show, we saw him walking away, sad and embarrassed. His hand was purple and enlarged. We all gave him a round of applause, a resounding cheer, and smiles. He smiled back. But we all felt saddened for this young man.

Of course, during our stay in Beijing, our group walked Tiananmen Square, the Forbidden City, the gardens of the Summer Palace, as well as the grounds of the Temple of Heaven—all sites George and I had visited in 2002. But memories of "Waltzing in the Park," "The Wild One," "Old MacDonald Had a Farm," and "The Boy Who Had to Accept Defeat" were the most striking ones George and I carried away from our second visit to Beijing.

SHANGHAI

George's fondest memory of Shanghai was of a performance of the Shanghai Acrobatic Troupe. The costumes were beautiful, the backdrops were unbelievably colorful, and the acts were phenomenal and varied. I especially remember the scenes involving spinning teacups, swirling umbrellas, and acrobatic jumps. The human pyramids, in which layer after layer of performers balanced on the shoulders of those below, defied gravity, especially when the one at the top was seven levels above the lowest. The most frightening act involved four motorcyclists who rode at top speed around and around inside a transparent sphere. When their speed was great enough, they sped around the very top, literally riding upside down. That was the part my George really loved.

My fondest memory of Shanghai was of a visit to a preschool/kindergarten. When we arrived at the school, we saw children lined up on the sidewalk, waiting to greet us. As each of us clambered off the bus, a little one stepped forward, grasped our hand, and led us into a large gathering room. We sat down and the show began: They sang, they played musical instruments, they recited, and they danced. During the dancing, my little one came back to me and pulled me into the circle to dance with her. The others did likewise.

Then the children led us into the room where they napped. My hostess climbed up to her top bunk and pretended to sleep. She was showing me that this was her place. Finally, she escorted me back to our bus. The little ones stood and waved goodbye as our bus pulled away. It was a touching experience that brought happy tears to my eyes.

Of course, during our three days in Shanghai, our guide Jack took us to the sites to which all visitors to the city should go: the Shanghai Museum with its collection of antiquities; the Yuyuan Garden and the adjacent shopping area; the Bund; and Nanjing Road. We were always on the go, and we often returned to our luxury hotel late in the evening. By the way, our hotel was an upgrade. Because of SARS, hotels were running far below capacity, and Grand Circle had booked us into a deluxe venue rather than the tourist one we had expected.

On our third day in Shanghai, Jack escorted us to a lovely town that was nearby—Suzhou. We went by train, which proved interesting, again because of SARS. As we entered the train station, we had to pass through a temperature checkpoint, as did the Chinese people boarding the trains. We noticed that most of the Chinese wore masks.

In Suzhou, we rode an excursion boat along the Grand Canal. It was an easy, pleasant way to see the town, given that the sun was shining and the sky bright blue. We also toured a silk-spinning factory, heard an explanation of silk production, and enjoyed lunch at a plentiful buffet. Later we wandered through the Humble Administrator's Garden, and later still we listened while an older gentleman spoke about his experiences during the Cultural Revolution—which for us was the high point of the day because he explained events so forthrightly. By the time we got to our hotel that evening, George and I were more than ready for a good night of sleep.

WUHAN AND THE YANGTZE RIVER

From Shanghai, we flew into Wuhan to board the *Princess Elaine*, a riverboat that plies the waters of the Yangtze. It was dusk by the time we walked down the ramp and located our cabin on the *Princess*. The cabin was small and the beds were narrow and hard, but we had private facilities with a shower. We were more than satisfied. Having already dined in the revolving rooftop restaurant of what was then the Wuhan Holiday Inn, George and I tumbled right into bed. It had been a super-great but long day.

We awoke the next morning to the strains of *Butterfly Lovers* which was the morning wake-up call on the boat. That day—April 15—we spent relaxing. Lecturers talked to us about the Three Gorges Dam Project, the crew presented a folkloric show, and we watched the scenery as we steamed upriver.

The following morning, we again awoke to *Butterfly Lovers*. Our tour group was up on deck when the *Princess Elaine* went through the first lock and then docked so we could disembark to visit the Three Gorges Dam. We stood at a lookout where we could view the five-step lock system through which ships must pass to go around the dam; then we viewed the structure itself.

In the afternoon we steamed through the first of the three gorges. The water level had been raised in the first gorge, but not to its ultimate level, which would happen when the dam project was completed in 2008. In 2004, we could still see the beauty of the gorges. We had come just in time.

Our third day on the Yangtze was the absolute best. In the morning, we took an extraordinary ride on a peapod boat up one of the tributaries of the Yangtze. Peapods are long, narrow vessels that hold about eight people. When we were there, the boats were poled up the tributary, or what is really a lesser gorge, by men who wore only briefs and shirts. We wondered why, but at the point when they jumped into the water, we understood.

The trip was spectacular. We were in a deep gorge with cliffs rising steeply from the water and with ancient hanging coffins up high on the cliff sides. Eventually, we came to a place where, if we dipped our hands into the water, we could touch the rocks in the riverbed. There the boatmen jumped into the water, harnessed themselves together with ropes, and pulled us farther

145

upriver. As they pulled, they chanted, their voices reverberating off the cliffs. When our boatman, dripping wet, climbed back into our peapod, he gave each of us a pebble from the riverbed. Earlier I wrote that the boat ride was spectacular. It was unbelievably so! George graded it ten stars.

Back on *Princess Elaine*, we continued to work our way upriver. We passed suspension bridges under construction and large apartment complexes high up on the hills above the Yangtze. The apartments housed those whose homes were previously at river level—homes that would be flooded when the project was completed.

CHONGQING

We disembarked the *Princess Elaine* in Chongqing, a large city that was the home of the elite air squadron, the Flying Tigers, during World War II. I have a couple of images in my mind of the brief time our tour group spent in Chongqing before we flew to Xi'an.

The first is of pandas munching on bamboo leaves and stems at the zoo in Chongqing. The pandas were so cute. At the same time we were there, a group of young girls, who were laughing and smiling, were visiting. They wanted to have their pictures taken with the pandas and us.

A group of Chinese women were also at the zoo. They approached and asked to have their pictures taken with one of the men in our group. He was short and had a large round belly—like the Buddha. The ladies politely asked if they might rub our friend's belly; it might bring them luck. He was more than happy to oblige.

The second mental picture I have is of something that happened in the main square of the megacity—and it is a megacity, although before we went to Chongqing we thought it a village deep in the interior of China. In the city square parked next to us was a bus filled with American couples holding Chinese baby girls in their arms. These couples had come to China to find daughters to adopt. They were so proud of their babies that they held them up to the windows of their bus so we could see how beautiful their new daughters were. First cute pandas, then cute babies!

XI'AN — TWO EXTRAORDINARY DAYS

The Terracotta Army! Yes, here we were at the very place where thousands of Chinese warriors, horses, and chariots crafted from terracotta more than two thousand years ago are lined up row upon row upon row! Discovered in 1974 by a farmer who was digging in his garden, the site where the warriors stand is extensive. It is much, much larger than George and I had ever imagined, with three digs to visit and an explanatory movie-in-the-round to view. Granted, many of the terracotta warriors on display have been reconstructed from fragments; still, the effect is striking. All were crafted in amazing detail. Our guide explained, for example, that no two warriors have the same face.

We had plenty of time to explore the huge covered areas that house the digs—areas that resemble airplane-factory floors in their vastness. And we needed that time just to walk the grounds and to get pictures. George took so many pictures that I told him to look with his eyes and not through the lens of his camera. Again, we walked and walked to see it all.

In our travels around the world, George and I had been to Abu Simbel in Egypt, Angkor Wat in Cambodia, Borobudur in Indonesia, Machu Picchu in Peru. The Terracotta Army in Xi'an rated right up there with these other world heritage sites.

We liked our lunch stop. The food was good and included noodle soup; a chef demonstrated noodle making; and just inside the door was a bazaar with lots of shops. The price for jade pendants was lower than we had just paid an hour earlier, so I bought still another to give as a gift.

We had an unexpected pleasure awaiting us in the afternoon: a visit to the Giant Wild Goose Pagoda. Expecting a simple wood pagoda, we found instead a stone structure with more than a dozen tiers. It is located in a lovely park filled with a number of outbuildings that display the arts and crafts of the region. An art lover, George was fascinated by the shop displaying and selling scrolls and paintings. He selected a piece he wanted—a horizontally laid-out painting of an emperor riding in a horse-drawn chariot with two foot soldiers running ahead and two cavalrymen on horseback leading the way. It is at least six feet across and a foot and a half high; the artist had signed it with his chop. Bargaining, George bought it for fifteen dollars.

The painting, which we named *The Emperor Warrior*, held a position of honor in our old house, which we sold when we moved into a retirement community in 2009. When our house was on the market, a Chinese realtor brought a potential buyer to look at it. The customer unfortunately was not interested in our house. Later, however, we got a call from the realtor. She told us that if ever we were interested in selling *The Emperor Warrior*, we should call her.

In our new retirement home, *The Emperor Warrior* reigns in the foyer. My dearest friend Jenny, who was born in China, came to view it. She pointed out the numerous chop marks in red ink on the perimeter of the painting. She explained that those chop marks were put there by successive owners of the piece. Our painting has lots of chop marks; ergo it is old and probably valuable.

That evening, our guide Jack escorted us to the Tang Dynasty Palace restaurant and theater for dinner and a show. The food was exquisitely presented; the performers were beautifully costumed. George was carried away: He filmed the entire production and the successive courses as they were placed before us. I'm glad to say, though, that he did take time to eat.

The next day was equally jam-packed. We walked the city walls in the early morning and then visited a lacquerware factory/sales center. At the lacquerware center, we saw craftspeople carving pieces of soapstone used to make the faces, headdresses, and clothes that they then mounted on black-lacquer tables and screens. George and I found the demonstration satisfying. I say *satisfying* because on our 1969 round-the-world, forty-day trip, we had bought a large four-paneled lacquered screen and end tables in Hong Kong. We paid about one hundred fifty American dollars for the set, which included shipping charges to New Jersey. Our guide explained that screens like ours were now selling for over a thousand— just for the screen.

Lunch was not included in our tour package. For that reason, Jack dropped us off in the Muslim section of Xi'an where we would find inexpensive lunch venues. Nibbling on nuts and candy, George and I skipped a noon meal so we could walk about the area.

We chanced on a fine arts store that sold paintings. The shop was run by two women; the younger one could speak enough English to help us. We fell in love with two square paintings of children in an outdoor school; the paintings are done on silk. Then George spotted a painting of an ancient warrior, done on rice paper. The young woman told us that the warrior was the best of the three; the artist was the professor, she explained, whereas the paintings of children were by a student. We got all three for fifteen dollars. Of course, the American dollar had more value then. And of course, it cost five times that to have the three framed once we got them home.

Oh yes, and the one by the professor has lots of red chop marks! It hangs in our foyer with *The Emperor Warrior*. Our black-lacquer screen is there, too; the faces of the figures on our screen, though, are ivory.

GUILIN

That evening, we flew into Guilin. We went there to take a boat ride on the Li River.

Both George and I had eagerly anticipated our cruise on the Li. Having studied geology, we knew that along the river are karst limestone hillocks with deep depressions between. It is a unique kind of topography, which is striking and is often pictured in Chinese paintings. We lucked out; the weather was perfect—sunny and the sky blue with just a few puffy clouds. That, however, might also have worked against us. Hundreds of small boats were on the Li early that morning. They jockeyed with one another and caused general havoc. The karst hillocks were beautiful, but the river lacked the serenity we had anticipated.

We disembarked in an area of shops. Again it was noisy and crowded. I bought a small cloisonné elephant to add to our growing collection of pachyderms. Practical George bought a suitcase to fill with all our purchases.

Back at our hotel, Jack explained that we had two choices for the remainder of the morning. We could walk around the area by the hotel on our own or we could take a tour to a tea garden. We chose the walkabout.

Our hotel—The Garden Hotel—was located by a lovely brook, not in the central city but in a quiet suburb.

On our walk, we stumbled on a preschool down a little alley. The children were outside doing exercises. We stood and watched them. An older woman was sitting on the curb outside. She held a child in her lap and had him wave to us. We waved back. As we watched what was going on, the local folks looked us over; we were the "big noses" from the West.

The afternoon, in contrast, was busy. We visited the Reed Flute Cave. We had to climb up to get to the entrance, and we had to wait our turn to enter. Once we went in, we saw massive limestone columns, stalactites, and stalagmites.

Leaving the limestone caverns, we stopped to see the home of a farmer and his family. To us, it seemed primitive. The toilet was only a slit in the floor, with some boards above to balance on when one squatted. The farm animals lived in close proximity. Before heading to the airport for our late-evening flight to Hong Kong, we stopped at a hotel for supper. George remarked on the contrast between the farmer's house and this hotel, where we dined in luxury. But, he added, the farmer might well have thought himself fortunate. He had a home of his own, family, enough rice, and land to farm.

HONG KONG

Our tour group arrived after midnight at our hotel in Hong Kong. Up early the next morning, we hopped the bus for a morning tour of Hong Kong Island. Having been there twice before, George and I did not need an excursion. We decided, however, to take the tour with our group. A ride on the Star Ferry and one up the tram to Victoria Peak are always fun, and the view of Kowloon and the harbor from the top is always special. And yes, on the tour we finally got to sail on a sampan in Aberdeen.

That afternoon, Jack said that he would take our tour group for a walk down Nathan Road. George and I decided to go on our own. We just took off. We walked around the famed Peninsula Hotel and down

Nathan Road to the shopping area called the Mansions, where George had bought me a string of jade beads on a prior visit. I was looking for a similar strand for my sister. I saw loose jade beads in the window of a jewelry shop there; of course, they had to be strung. Inside, we talked to the two women shopkeepers—a mother and daughter. They explained that because of SARS, tourism was way down and the economy was suffering.

I picked out the actual jade beads and one gold clasp-bead for my sister's necklace. The price was low, because the women had probably not had a customer for days and were desperate for a sale. George and I sat and talked to the shopkeepers as the daughter strung the beads. As we were leaving, the mother told us to tell our friends back home to come to Hong Kong. It was safe.

Our last day! Sunday, April 25, 2004. George and I spent most of the morning wandering the back streets between the mosque on Nathan Road and the Peninsula Hotel. We came upon the same shop where we had purchased a bone carving on our last visit. We even recognized the shopkeeper because George had filmed him then. We saw a fine carving of a Chinese god. He represents longevity, so we bought him as a good-luck charm. According to my friend Jenny, he is one of the three Chinese star gods who bring good luck; the other two represent prosperity and happiness. Since we could afford only one, we felt that at our stage of life, longevity was the most important god to carry home with us.

Back at our hotel, we rested before taking a farewell walk by the harbor. There are now escalators and elevated walkways all over Hong Kong that make walking easy. As a result, we did not have to cross traffic-filled streets. We found a bench and sat down just to contemplate Victoria Peak and Hong Kong Island. We were impressed by the amount of building underway. On our first visit in 1969, the city was so different—a sleepier, quieter place.

Sitting by the harbor, we talked about some of our best moments on this trip. We talked, too, about how important it is to travel when one is young enough to walk miles and miles without getting overly tired. George and I had been the oldest on our China trip. We had made the journey just in time to enjoy the long days and the full schedule. We talked, too, about some of our purchases. We had bought so many wonderful things; but what we were really taking home were memories. Ah, and we were taking home a good-luck omen—good luck for a long life.

Chapter Thirteen
CRUISING VIKING LANDS

To veteran HAL cruisers, "The Voyage of the Vikings" means a summer or early fall cruise generally out of Boston with stops in Maine, Nova Scotia, Newfoundland, Iceland, Ireland, and Norway. Additionally, a few other places are added to the mix each year. The outbound route typically goes around the north coast of Iceland, the homeward route along the south. Usually a transit of Prince Christian Sound and stops in Greenland are part of the itinerary, too.

George and I took the VOV in June of 2004, just a few months after our return from China. The 2004 VOV departed that year from New York City—a perfect embarkation port for New Jerseyans.

ON THE WAY: HEADING NORTH

Standing on deck on June 6, 2004, at sail-away, George and I looked out at the New York City skyline on our port side. This was our first sail-away since 9/11 had changed the configuration forever. At least we could remember what it used to look like.

Our ship *Rotterdam VI* steamed north to dock in Boston. For me, Boston is a familiar city; I grew up in a small prep-school town in New Hampshire, and my family used to go to Boston to shop. George and

I decided to take a highlights tour so I could revisit the Boston Public Garden—the home of the cast-iron ducklings that are the characters in *Make Way for Ducklings*; the Old North Church and Paul Revere's statue; and Fenway Park with its statue of Ted Williams and his teammates.

On tour, we had the opportunity to take pictures. I was the first off the bus to see Mrs. Mallard and her eight ducklings—Jack, Kack, Lack, Mack, Nack, Ouack, Pack, and Quack. *Make Way for Ducklings* is one of my favorite children's books. I used it as an exemplar when I taught children's literature to future teachers at Kean University.

We crossed the Charles River to Cambridge and the Radcliffe Quadrangle at Harvard. We also passed some of the buildings of MIT. Again, we hopped off for picture-taking, as we had done in the cemetery behind the Old North Church.

In Portland, Maine, *Rotterdam* offered a tour to three lighthouses. Having lived as a child near the Nubble Lighthouse in Maine, I had often gone to the Nubble on family outings. Something about a lighthouse beckons me, perhaps because lighthouses are beacons of safety or because they are symbols of New England where my Grant ancestors landed in 1630. At any rate, I wanted to see lighthouses rather than trek city streets.

We were able to climb up into one of the lighthouses near Portland and to walk the surrounding areas. It was a warm June day, so this was an ideal outing.

Sydney, Nova Scotia, was our first stop outside the United States. On the pier is a large welcoming hall where local craftspeople display and sell their wares. Inside the building is a small performance center where a group of Cape Bretoners sing, dance, and play the fiddle. George and I decided that attending their show would be a different way to spend the morning. We had stopped in Sydney once before and remembered it as the port with the giant fiddle on the pier. Now we added one more dimension to our memory of Sydney. As I sat there lightheartedly tapping my feet to the music, I never imagined that, a dozen years later, Sydney would be the site of the saddest of all my cruising memories.

ON THE WAY: HEADING EAST TO ICELAND

Rotterdam made port in a small village in Newfoundland, Red Bay, before heading east toward Iceland. We enjoyed a few sea days during which we attended lectures about Iceland, played trivia twice a day, read a bit, relaxed, and dined. The North Atlantic treated us well, with no exceptionally high waves or strong winds.

When George and I wed, my husband brought to our marriage several large atlases. I contributed a couple, too. One of mine was a children's atlas with maps covered with small pictures showing points of interest in each major area of the world.

George loved maps and so do I. We both would study maps of areas to which we were going before we started a trip. We also carried a world map to hang on our stateroom wall on longer cruises as well as an almanac with a section of maps in the middle. We knew before we married that we shared major interests. We did not realize that we both enjoyed a love affair with maps.

Before our VOV cruise in 2004, we got out our atlases to study maps of Iceland. To geologists/geographers, the map of Iceland is fascinating. The northern coast is fingered with deep fjords that were carved into the sides of mountains during the Ice Age. The southern perimeter is a volcanic area, where—according to my children's atlas—the Strokkur geyser is located. On our VOV cruise, we would make stops in both areas, so we would see Iceland's stark contrasts.

When *Rotterdam* entered Iceland's northern coastal waters, our captain slowed down and took us on an early morning scenic cruise up a major fjord to the town of Isafjörður. We anchored there in the harbor. Not knowing what to expect, we booked a short tour that included a drive along the edge of the fjord to a fishing village. In the village, we stopped at a small museum with displays of native animal life, especially arctic foxes, and we visited a typical wooden church to hear a young woman sing Icelandic songs. Our final stop was at a local restaurant for coffee and sweets. Although the museum itself was not that impressive and we saw only one fox that hid its head when we all tried to take its picture, we felt we had a good morning. The scenery alone was worth the cost of the tour.

Leaving port in the late afternoon, we enjoyed scenic cruising of the Isafjörður fjord. Because George and I had a window table for dinner, we had lovely views from the aft of the main dining room as we steamed out into the sea.

That evening *Rotterdam* crossed the Arctic Circle. On our cabin door the following morning, we found certificates—signed by the captain—indicating that we were among the few in the world who had traveled into the Arctic.

The next morning, *Rotterdam* dropped anchor in the harbor of Akureyri. My memories of Akureyri are of three stops we made while on tour. Leaving the harbor, our bus drove us across Eyjafjordur and then along the edge of the fjord. From there, we drove up into the mountains, crossing the Vikurskard Pass, from which we could look down into the valley below. George and I agreed that the scenery was even more impressive than what we had seen the day before.

We made our second stop at a mighty waterfall, Goðafoss. We had to walk up a rather steep path to view the falls, but the walk was worth it. Brilliant sunshine made the crashing waters sparkle; there was even a rainbow.

Equally unforgettable were the steaming lava flats that we visited next. In my files I have a picture of me in front of striking lava formations and engulfed in steam that smelled of sulfur. I am wearing my wooliest sweater and a plastic rain bonnet to protect my hair from the wind and the steam.

REACHING EUROPE

Our next few ports could not compete with the Icelandic ones in terms of scenery or impact. In Douglas, on the Isle of Man, George and I rode the steam railroad to a lookout above the town. We picked this activity because both of us liked old railways and our ride was in a Victorian railway car. In Stavanger, Norway, we just walked around the port. The major things to see were near our dock so we could do a leisurely self-guided tour on foot.

Rotterdam, in the Netherlands, is a big port city. The pier where we docked was on the river right downtown, but neither of us was excited by the idea of walking busy city streets. The ship advertised a bus trip to the Kinderdijk windmills, where nineteen old windmills are lined up along the waterfront. The windmills were once used to pump rising water out of the village and into the nearby canal.

The drive to Kinderdijk was interesting because sometimes the road is below sea level, and the sea is restrained by dikes. Once there, we walked the pretty grounds and climbed up into a windmill—something nice to do, but still not so striking as our waterfall/hot springs tour in Iceland. Both of us decided that the Icelandic segment might well be the high point of the VOV cruise.

IRISH MEMORIES

Our route took us around the south coast of England up to Dublin and Belfast. We had one sea day before we made landfall. George and I spent time just relaxing and reminiscing about other times we had been in Ireland.

I asked, "Do you remember when you drove me around Ireland and we stayed overnight in Dromoland Castle?" Yes, he remembered it well. He remembered, too, that our room was in the lower, new section near the horses. And he remembered the flies that had stayed there with us.

"Do you remember driving the Ring of Kerry?" Yes, he remembered that well.

"What about our bus trip around Ireland with Ralph and Ruth?" George prompted, thinking back to a tour we had taken with our Hennings cousins. Yes, we both remembered looking over the Cliffs of Moher on a cloudy, blustery day. And yes, we both recalled seeing the *Book of Kells* in the library of Trinity College in Dublin on the same land trip in 1992.

"Nassau Street, across the way from Trinity College? That is where I bought you your wool, patchwork Irish cap. George, do you remember?"

And we remembered Grafton Street nearby and the statue of Molly Malone.

George and I decided that when we arrived in Dublin, we would revisit our memories. *Rotterdam* supplied a shuttle to the far end of Nassau Street. We walked until we reached the shops we knew so well. We dropped into a few. George spotted a small porcelain replica of an Irish cottage with a man repairing the thatched roof. Appropriately named *The Thatcher*, it is part of The Irish Heritage Collection. The detail is delightful: a ladder leaning against the cottage, a pile of thatch on the ground soon to be part of the roof, the thatcher with his blue overalls, the strands of thatch on the roof. We had seen cottages with thatched roofs as we had driven through the Irish countryside. We would take *The Thatcher* home.

We walked into the central courtyard of Trinity College and sat on a bench to catch our breath before strolling down Grafton Street. The street seemed familiar, but we never could find the statue of Molly Malone. I think we did not walk far enough. After a brief stop at a pub, we retraced our steps back to the shuttle stop.

Relaxing on board in the afternoon, we studied our purchase, our Irish cottage. We both agreed that we had bought a fine memory of our day in Dublin as well as of our prior driving trips in the Irish countryside. *The Thatcher* sits today in my sunroom under the small white Christmas tree that I keep there year-round. I call it my tree of hope.

The next day, *Rotterdam* pulled into Belfast, the capital of Northern Ireland. It was our first visit. We considered taking the long trip out to see the Giant's Causeway, a geologic site we both had studied. Afraid that it would be cold and windy, we opted for a highlights tour of the city. The most striking mental picture I have of Belfast is of the apartment complexes that the guide pointed out—a complex for Catholics and a separate one for Protestants. The guide explained that he could tell who lived where by the flag waving over each. The guide also took us to see the murals that chronicle events in the religious disputes that have riddled Northern Ireland for so many years, and he pointed out places where there had been bombings. It was not really a happy tour, but one that made us more aware of the problems and prejudices that Northern Ireland has faced.

BACK TO ICELAND

Two days later on our westward journey home, *Rotterdam* anchored in a harbor off the southern coast of Iceland, near the village of Vestmannaeyjar on Heimaey Island. Actually, I am not sure whether our visit to Heimaey might have been on an earlier crossing of the North Atlantic in 1978 rather than on the 2004 VOV. When one repeats cruises to specific areas as we often did, it is hard to recall during which cruise a particular stop occurred.

Be that as it may, what I am certain of is the unique experience we had on the island. Heimaey was the site of a volcanic eruption that spewed lava down over the village of Vestmannaeyjar in 1973. The eruption lasted about six months, and during that time the villagers were evacuated.

On our arrival in Vestmannaeyjar, we tendered ashore. Locals came out to welcome us and point us in the direction of the lava fields. To our amazement, we walked on very hot, steaming lava, something we had never done before. Roped off was another area where the lava was still so hot that it glowed red.

Strolling through the village, which had been rebuilt after the destruction of 1973, we could see the volcanic cone that had formed at the time of the eruption and that now towers menacingly above the village. In Vestmannaeyjar itself was a large mural depicting steps in the commercial preparation of fish; the island's economy today is based on the fishing industry.

Since our visit to Vestmannaeyjar, I have never seen a cruise with this small village on its itinerary, which makes me think that our visit may have been in 1978, not in 2004. Perhaps there was concern about safety or even about preservation of the site itself. Regardless, this stop had been extraordinary; we had walked on steaming lava!

Arriving the next day in Reykjavik, the capital of Iceland, we decided to do something equally wonderful. We took what is known as the Golden Circle tour. Our first stop was at Thingvellir National Park, a UNESCO World Heritage Site. Both of us were excited as we approached the park, for it is here that the Eurasian and North

American tectonic plates meet at the surface of the earth. It is the only place in the world where people can walk the fault—the cut in the earth formed by the drifting of these two continental plates.

We were fortunate. The weather was perfect for a walk through this rift in the rocks along a path bordered on both sides with igneous cliffs. We sauntered as slowly as we could to extend the moment. Some might wonder at our childlike delight at walking between two walls of rock. We even heard a fellow tourist say in disappointment, "We came all this way to look at rocks?"

But we two were ecstatic, particularly so because later in the next year we were to visit St. Helena, an island in the middle of the South Atlantic Ocean at the juncture of the Eurasian and North Atlantic plates. It lies on the Mid-Atlantic Ridge that extends all the way up to where we stood in Iceland.

Dorothy in Iceland, clockwise from top left: Geyser flats, falls, the fyords, and the faults.

Wending our way through the fault in the earth—a visible cut far lengthier than we had imagined before our visit—we saw in the distance the Icelandic flag, with its bright red cross. The flag was waving above the site of the oldest surviving parliament in the world, the Althing. Our guide explained that the Althing was an outdoor assembly that had met for the first time in 930 A.D. The flag stands there today as a proud reminder of Iceland's early democratic foundation.

From Thingvellir Park, our tour took us to Gullfoss falls. Magnificent! Smashing! Loud! The waterfalls of Iceland are mighty, with spray blowing skyward and rainbows shining. If waterfalls were all that Iceland had to offer scenically, they would be a great enough attraction to entice visitors to this island country.

But of course, there are also the geysers. Arriving in the Geysir Geothermal Area, we waited impatiently. And then it happened. With a little rumble that built to a crescendo, a geyser only a short distance from us began its show. First a little tower of water, then higher and higher to over ninety feet, the hot waters of the geyser gushed upward.

Hearing a rumble from up ahead, we watched as another geyser erupted and then another. At our feet were pools of steaming water, spewing sulfur fumes. We were in an active geothermal area, with emphasis on the word *active*.

Across the highway from the geothermal area and facing it was our luncheon venue. There we could enjoy salmon steaks and watch the continuous show the geysers were putting on. George made sure we sat where we had a view out the windows over the Geysir Geothermal Area. Indeed, it is called a geysir area. *Geysir* is the Icelandic word from which the English language derives the word *geyser*.

On our way back to the pier we enjoyed lovely scenery: snow-capped mountains in the distance, heath and farmlands close by, and greenhouses heated with geothermal energy. The tour had been a long one—eight hours—but it was ideal for us. We saw nature at its finest, we saw the beginnings of a nation, and we dined rather splendidly.

HEADING HOME

As we cruised westward, eventually we entered Greenlandic waters. *Rotterdam* was scheduled to navigate Prince Christian Sound, a glacier-lined fjord which wends its way north off the southern coast of Greenland. Unfortunately, we were too early in the season. The channel was ice-filled and dangerous. Our captain announced that a transit of Prince Christian Sound was out of the question. He would treat everyone to a glass of champagne that evening and drop anchor the next day at Nanortalik, a small fishing village on the south coast of Greenland.

Reaching Nanortalik, George and I ambled around the village, stopping in an old timber church and in a clothing shop where I bought a shirt with a modernistic rendering of Greenland's red-and-white flag on the front. Nanortalik is a small, compact village, great for a slow walk.

Our captain set a southerly course and in a day reached the port of Saint Pierre and Miquelon, a French overseas collectivity. A small island group, the territory lies off the southwest coast of Newfoundland and is the only French foothold on the North American continent. We tendered in to find a town larger than Nanortalik, with a pretty little harbor and a park with benches. The streets are lined with colorful houses—some pink, some light blue, some yellow, some light green. We figured that this could be a harsh place to live during the winter, and the attractively colored houses might lend cheer on dark, dreary days. We spent a pleasant morning walking up and down the streets and then sitting on one of the benches in the park overlooking the harbor. Having taken daylong tours rather recently, we found that this was a pleasant change.

Back aboard *Rotterdam*, George and I settled in for the short hop to Halifax, the capital of Nova Scotia. We had been to Halifax at least three times before, once on a land tour of the Maritime Provinces. We had seen the major sights: the Citadel on the hill, the government buildings, nearby Peggy's Cove, and the cemetery with the graves of people who lost their lives when the *Titanic* went down.

Halifax has a broad boardwalk along its waterfront that begins at the passenger terminal with its produce and craft markets as well as a museum that tells the Canadian immigrants' story. We wandered the craft market briefly and then struck out to stroll the boardwalk.

On our arrival in our final port, Newport, Rhode Island, we went through United States immigration procedures before heading for our tour bus. For George and me, this was a first visit to Newport, and we wanted to see The Breakers, the grand mansion built by Cornelius Vanderbilt in the late 1890s. A tour was the simplest way to do this.

The bus took us first along Ocean Drive to look out across some of the famed beaches and the nearby rocky shoreline. Then we were off to The Breakers. Before entering the mansion, we walked around the grounds to take in the lovely view across the back lawn down to the sea. Inside, the entry hall is spectacular, with huge crystal chandeliers and marble trim; so are the ballroom and reception rooms. But what really impressed us were the bathtubs. The bathtubs are freestanding and made of porcelain with carved sides; they have four taps, not two—a tap for cold water, a second for cold salt water, a third for hot water, and a fourth for hot salt water.

At the end of the nineteenth century, the wealthy made Newport their summer playground, a place to escape the heat of New York City or Boston. They called their mansions *cottages*. George and I smiled when our guide explained that to us. By these standards, our three-bedroom cottage in Warren, New Jersey, was a hovel.

We followed our guide along Cliff Walk, looking back at other cottages. The phrase *conspicuous consumption* came to my mind as we passed one mansion after another. I could understand people wanting to enjoy great ocean views from the windows of their homes, but did they really need so much? George—"My Renaissance Man"—told me that the Sixteenth Amendment legalizing income tax was added to the United States Constitution in 1913. Before that, industrial tycoons paid little or no taxes; as a result, their money could multiply, and there was almost no limit on their spending.

LOOKING TO THE FUTURE

The next morning we pulled into New York Harbor. We were home after thirty-four days of travel that had taken us across the North Atlantic and back again. The trip had given us the opportunity to stand on hot lava and walk through the fault formed by the action of the North American and Eurasian plates—which we both agreed had been the high points of the cruise. Could we handle a world cruise of over one hundred days? George was not ready to commit to such a long cruise. What about part of a world cruise where we would be away about fifty days? To George, this sounded doable.

Arriving back in Warren, we checked cruise brochures that had accumulated while we were away. We booked an eleven-night cruise to the Caribbean for December 2004. It would leave from and return to New York City—no flying, just a little vacation. Then we bit the bullet and booked a fifty-four-night segment of Regent's world cruise—Hong Kong to Fort Lauderdale—on *Seven Seas Voyager* during the winter of 2005. We would start with a long trans-Pacific flight, but that was something we could handle, because United Airlines had begun nonstop flights from Newark to Hong Kong.

A few days later, with all our cruise reservations in place, George presented me with a card he had created years before. He kept his masterpiece in his top bureau drawer and gave it to me over and over again, when the spirit moved him. My dear husband had made the card from an advertisement for scientific equipment that he had transformed into a love note. On the front is a merry-go-round horse and the words, "Travel in the best circles." Inside is a three-dimensional, pop-up carousel, under which George had clipped a paper with his words, "Ride with me, sweetheart, on my merry-go-round of life! I love you." Next to those words, George had drawn a heart and three kisses. I still have the card.

Ah, the magic of memories. They can carry me back to when . . .

Chapter Fourteen
EXPLORING HALF THE WORLD

George and I flew business class on United Airlines to Hong Kong, upgrading with frequent flyer miles. Overnighting in Hong Kong, we boarded *Voyager* the afternoon of February 26, 2005. *Voyager* is a gem of a ship. Regent is an upscale line—the line we had used on our circumnavigation of South America in 2002. We knew that we would get top-notch service.

On *Voyager's* itinerary after she left Hong Kong were some wonderful ports. Many, such as Vietnam, were first-time-ever visits for us.

VIETNAM

The rather long ride into Ho Chi Minh City from the port where *Voyager* docked in Vietnam was more interesting than we had anticipated. On the drive in, we noticed that many of the buildings lining the roads on the outskirts of the city had only limited frontage. The buildings—far deeper than they were wide—looked like elongated boxes. We asked our guide why this was. He explained that property taxes were levied based on the length of the frontage, so architects had devised this scheme to keep taxes low. I guess no one likes paying taxes, no matter in what country he or she lives.

Getting into the central city, I remarked to George that the government buildings looked like ones we had seen on the avenues in Paris. Of course, that would be so, he reminded me. France had been the controlling power in Vietnam for many years.

And then we began to notice the motorcycles. The streets were filled with them. What was amazing was the number of people piled onto one vehicle: We saw entire families with a couple of children clinging on. In some cases, the riders were even balancing large packages. The motorcycle drivers did not navigate slowly, either. I remember that one motorcycle, piled high with packages and people, swerved right in front of our bus. And I remember that the roar of motorcycle engines was deafening.

In Ho Chi Minh City, we visited a war museum to see tanks, guns, and other artifacts of the American War. Our guide called it "the American War," not "the Vietnam War." As we exited the museum, I recall that an older Vietnamese man leaned across a fence and said to us, "Do not believe everything they told you in there. We like Americans."

Our next stop was more upbeat. We attended a water puppet show that was different than any we had seen before. The puppeteers were hidden behind a curtain; telling a story of old Vietnam, they manipulated colorful puppets that were suspended above a pool of water. At times the puppets dipped below the water to emerge a short time later across the pool. Sometimes they skated gracefully on the water in time with music. It was just fun to watch.

My clearest memory of Vietnam, however, is a rather silly one. The guide dropped us off in front of the central market in Ho Chi Minh City, or Saigon as it used to be called. The market sells everything— clothes, shoes, household goods, fruits, vegetables, and souvenirs.

Entering the market, I saw a pair of whitish, textured slacks that I loved on sight. Gesturing to them, I caught the saleswoman's eye and pointed to myself. Nodding vigorously, she took them down. I spread my hands to show her I needed a larger size. She nodded and found a larger pair. Again, I spread my hands to indicate that even that pair was not large enough. She nodded and found a still larger pair.

As she held them up across my lower body, she said—in all seriousness—"For big bum!"

Every time I wear those slacks now, I think, "Yes, for big bum—mine!"

When our tour guide had dropped us off at the front of the market, he had pointed the way down the avenue we were to walk after our allotted time there. He had told us to meet him in the lobby of the Rex Hotel at the end of that avenue and had suggested that we take the elevator to the bar at the top of the hotel and look out at the view. He had explained that the Rex was a watering hole for American officers during the American War.

Once we left the market, we walked in that direction, passing lovely shops. I have an exquisite cane that George picked out in one of those shops and that we brought home with us. I also have a clear memory of standing on the top floor of the Rex, looking out on Ho Chi Minh City below—the post office across the way, the church in the distance, and the tree-lined avenues. We brought that picture home, too.

Oh, yes, and from our tour the next day, we brought home a memory of China Beach, the beach on the South China Sea where GIs went for rest and relaxation during the Vietnam/American War. George and I walked along the shore, and I thought out loud, "What a peaceful place!" The waves were rolling in gently from across the South China Sea. The air was balmy, not really hot or humid. The people in our small tour group were the only ones on the beach. Quiet reigned. It was a scene of beauty, not of war.

George and I talked about how American soldiers must have felt when they got a short respite from the fear and agony of the war. My colleague at Kean University, Thomas Banit, had been one of those GIs who had gone to China Beach for R and R; he had told me how much it had meant to him, a first lieutenant with the United States Marine Corps.

Vietnam is not a really happy place to visit, especially for those of us who are old enough to remember the American War. George and I remembered.

BANGKOK

George beckoned for me to come and see the view from our window at the Shangri-La Hotel. Our room overlooked the Chao Phraya River, or in English, the River of Kings. We had just checked into the hotel for a night that was part of the world cruise package Regent provided to all passengers on *Voyager*. We were in Bangkok, Thailand, what had been called the Kingdom of Siam in days gone by.

From our window we could watch the action on the river as small boats came into view and then disappeared from sight. Just imagine! We could see this without leaving our room in our deluxe hotel. George and I had stayed in top-of-the-line hotels just a few times during our prior travels, but this one was truly awesome. George was so impressed that he took pictures of our posh accommodations as well as of the action on the river.

We did not tarry long admiring the view, for we had only the afternoon to explore Bangkok. Once out in the street, we hailed a tuk tuk and asked the driver to take us around the city for a couple of hours. We explained that we wanted to go to the Golden Buddha and the Reclining Buddha, and then to any other significant sites in the immediate area of the Shangri-La. Since we had been to Bangkok on our round-the-world-by-air trip in 1969, we remembered the morning market, the Grand Palace, and the Emerald Buddha, and we did not need to repeat those. Off we went! Our driver could speak a little English, so we were in good hands.

Returning to the area surrounding our hotel, George and I hit the nearby shops. Today in my closet are four sarong-like long skirts, one with a top to match, which we bought that afternoon. I wore the sarong with the matching blouse that evening to the banquet Regent gave for us. The gala evening was in a ballroom overlooking the River of Kings. The view at night was even more magical than in daylight. We felt that we were surely in Shangri-La, the fictional paradise that James Hilton described in his novel, *Lost Horizon*.

The next morning, Regent had a line of buses waiting for us in front of the hotel. Once we were on our bus, it took at least an hour for us to get to the harbor, which is a considerable distance from Bangkok. We were back on *Voyager* by noon and settled into our suite when the captain announced he would cast off shortly. He reminded us that our next port of call was Singapore.

SINGAPORE

Arriving in Singapore, George and I hopped into a cab for the short drive to Chinatown, our destination for our morning walk. The cab drove us along avenues with tall apartment complexes and business buildings. Everything was so clean. We were impressed.

Chinatown was a delight with its paper lanterns and colorful buildings adorned with red dragons and roofs with eaves that pointed skyward. George and I just puttered around the lanes, stopping in shops and exploring a few temples in the area. In one shop, we bought a couple of old Chinese wall scrolls and then sat to chat with the proprietor, who served us tea.

This was our kind of morning. We had a map in hand so we could locate the three main temples—the ornate Sri Mariamman that we viewed from the outside and two others that we entered, the Thian Hock Keng and the Buddha Tooth Relic. At one point, a mini-parade marched by. We never did find out what was being celebrated, but the parade was the capstone on our morning outing.

PENANG, MALAYSIA

A day later, George and I were in Penang in Malaysia. Our tour took us to see a golden reclining Buddha that reminded us of the reclining Buddha in Bangkok. Somewhere I have jotted down that it is 108 feet long. We also visited a heavily ornate temple embellished with pieces of colored porcelain and another temple with a four-armed goddess. I think by then we had seen enough temples.

The best part of our short tour of Penang was a visit to a Chinese settlement that is suspended over water with buildings supported on pilings. We strolled along a boardwalk that winds among the homes. We passed children who were playing and fooling around as children do all over the world. They were eager for us to take their pictures.

We made a final stop at a hotel for tea. We all agreed that the tea service was the low point of the afternoon. There was no comparison at all to tea time on *Voyager*.

FERRYBOAT PEOPLE

As you may remember, George and I had joined *Voyager* in Hong Kong. The ship had left Fort Lauderdale at least a month before. A small number of passengers had disembarked in Hong Kong, where we and a number of others had boarded. Of course, in the month before we boarded, passengers had bonded; friendships had been established. The full-cruise passengers viewed the new arrivals—George and me among them—as interlopers. They actually had a name for us: the Ferryboat People.

Anticipating the situation, I kept alert for others who had joined in Hong Kong. On deck at sail-away, George and I chatted with a lovely couple from Australia. We introduced ourselves and shared with each other where our homes were. We seemed compatible, and so I asked them to dine with us that evening. They were as glad to befriend us as we were to befriend them.

The first sea day in the afternoon after we had boarded, I looked around the lounge and found a trivia team that had lost two players in Hong Kong; they welcomed us, especially when they realized that we had been professors and might know some answers. Playing trivia, bridge, or other organized games is a good way to make shipboard friends.

A day or two later, George and I went for a swim in the pool. There was a gentleman already swimming. We introduced ourselves to him and the three of us began to talk as we swam. We liked him. He seemed to like us, and so we asked him if he and his wife would dine with us and our new Australian friends that evening. "Yes," he said, obviously pleased; he told us he and his wife were from Ireland and their name was Kavanaugh. They had just boarded in Hong Kong, too.

My story has a happy ending. We had a lovely evening together and arranged to meet again the next night for supper. We were six Ferryboat People who had found each other—ferryboaters from Australia, Ireland, and the United States. Later, when we got to Mumbai in India, our dinner group picked up a young English couple, Theresa and her husband Roger, as well as an English couple living in Spain. They had just boarded *Voyager*. Now we were ten.

In traveling, I have learned that it is possible to find compatible people if one extends oneself. Even as latecomers, we found friends who expanded our horizons. Conversely, travelers need to reach out to newcomers. It is so easy to withdraw into our comfort zone—our bubble—with our current friends. It is so easy to fall into the trap of thinking that for some reason we are "better" than others—better than the Ferryboat People of the world.

KOCHI IN GOA

Ah, Goa, a section of India impacted by Portuguese explorers and immigrants. I consider Kochi in Goa a favorite place to visit. Kochi, a port on the west coast of India also known as Cochin, was a major stop on the Europe/China route in the Age of Exploration. It was a major stop for us in 2005. George and I, unsure of our ability to wander on our own in Kochi, opted for an easy boat ride in the harbor followed by a guided walk and then a bus ride through the old parts of town.

My first memory of Kochi I call "Fishing Nets in the Harbor." Fishermen in Kochi employ an unusual technique. They suspend very large nets on wooden racks and then fling them down into the sea through a system of counterweights. We had seen those Chinese fishing nets in operation as we came into port. We stopped on tour to watch the action close up. It was an incredible scene, made more memorable by the fact that vendors were swarming around us and St. Francis Church was only a short distance away. This church is said—at one point—to have housed the remains of the Portuguese explorer Vasco De Gama.

My second memory—a fun one—I call "Elephants on a String." When we hopped off our little boat in the old section of Kochi, we were surrounded by young vendors. They were hawking small, stuffed cloth elephants strung together on a colorful beaded cord with a small bell on the end. One dollar! We could not resist these young salesmen who followed us down narrow streets lined with interesting shops. Seeing that some of the strings included stuffed-cloth birds, horses, and even zebras, we had bought six strings by the end of our walking tour.

My fondest memory I call "Entertainment under a Tent." In the afternoon, Regent loaded the entire passenger contingent onto buses and took us to a hotel located on a spit of land that juts out into the bay. There we found large tents, where we sat to enjoy a lively martial arts demonstration and a dance performance that told a story of old India; of course, there was food. We shared our table with our new Australian friends. What a special afternoon—with entertainment, conversation, and friends.

MUMBAI, INDIA

George and I had booked our Regent voyage with the same American Express affiliate we had used for a number of other cruises. This agency was one that sent an escort on longer trips and provided special events and tours. On our first morning in Mumbai, our American Express affiliate provided us with a tour that included lunch. Here is a list of what we saw on the tour.

1. The Large, Steaming, Outdoor Laundry: Yes, you read that correctly. We clambered off the bus to stand looking over a railing and down on a vast, vast hand laundry in action. Across the entire area, plumes of steam rose from giant cauldrons of boiling water in which clothes were soaking. Men were pounding clothes to get them clean. Garments were spread on the ground for drying. Never had we seen anything resembling that; it

looked like a scene from hell.

2. The Streets Themselves: Cows are sacred in India; they wander freely everywhere—on every road and in every lane. They were even sleeping in the streets.

3. The Mahatma Gandhi House and Museum: We walked through the home, feeling as if we were in a sacred space. Peaceful protest—that was what Gandhi believed in . . . not violence. Our guide told us the story of Gandhi's March to the Sea, a protest against the British salt tax. We knew the story, for our minister at home, whose husband is from Goa, had shared it in one of her sermons.

4. The Jain Temple Up on the Hill Overlooking Mumbai: I will never forget seeing a man sitting on the floor of the temple and counting grains of rice. Perhaps his patience is something we all need to emulate during difficult times.

The absolute high point of our day in Mumbai was lunch in the Taj Mahal Palace Hotel. The bus stopped in the square across the street from the Taj, so we could walk first around the Gateway of India, a giant arch on the waterfront. We were followed relentlessly by men and women begging. A woman carrying a baby hitched onto me and followed as George and I walked the square. A man who appeared to have a crippled leg followed George. Our guide warned not to give alms. If we did, we could be mobbed.

The lobby of the Taj Hotel was luxurious beyond belief. The dining room was charming. The food was delicious. The contrast was striking: outside the beggars, inside the world of wealth and privilege.

The next day was a Sunday, and most shops were closed. We went outside the terminal area and talked to a taxi driver parked at The Green Gate. Could he drive us to a shop selling shirts and blouses? "Yes," he responded, so we climbed into his cab.

The taxi driver took us to a section that was not touristy at all and parked in front of a seedy-looking building. He pointed to a stairwell leading to a dark upstairs area. Given that there were no store signs visible, George decided that he should investigate before I went up.

He was gone only a short time, returning with a smile that said all was well. And it was. On the second floor was a simple shop with shelves and shelves of shirts. The shopkeeper showed us what he had, and we both bought a couple of inexpensive tops.

Returning to our ship, we had a surprise waiting for us. On our telephone voicemail was a message from Theresa Price, a young English woman with whom I had been communicating for months on the chat site CruiseCritic.com. She and her husband Roger had joined *Voyager* that afternoon, and she was saying "Hello." I returned her call and we made plans to dine together that evening. We found over the years that CruiseCritic.com was a great site for making friends with others who were planning to take the same cruises we were.

DUBAI, UNITED ARAB EMIRATES

Ornate gold necklaces, heavy gold chains, wide gold bangles, gold charm bracelets, elaborately crafted gold rings hanging in the windows of jewelry shops—one shop after another: This is my forever memory of Dubai and its gold market. Dubai gold is more brilliant orange in color than the lighter yellow gold found in American shops. It is so vibrant that an entire shop window overflowing with gold jewelry is more than the eye can absorb.

The gold souk is almost surreal. George and I were surrounded not only by gold, but also by men dressed in flowing white robes and by women in black robes with black, cloth coverings over their faces and heads. If anyone was wearing gold, it was well hidden beneath the robes. We were amazed, though, to see women's dress shops with window displays of mannequins attired only in panties and bras. That hit us as a strange juxtaposition.

We followed the narrow walking street within the covered gold souk to its far end where there was an aromatic spice shop. We went in just to look and smell. We crossed the road to watch the action on the creek that bisects the city. The creek was bustling with activity as small boats ferried people to the other side. In my memory bank I have a map of this area, as clear to me today as it was when we strolled there in 2005.

We had gone in the morning to Sharjah and Fujairah, two other of the seven United Arab Emirates, to visit a museum and a souk and to drive through the surrounding desert area. The museum had displays depicting life in the Emirates before oil made the area rich. The souk sold goods brought in mainly from nearby India—pashmina scarves, shirts, silk jackets, and blouses.

The drive was eye-opening, too. We traveled via modern motorways, and we passed modern apartment and business complexes. Again we were struck by the contrasts we saw, this time between the old way of life on display in the museum and the new oil-driven economy we were viewing firsthand. We enjoyed the morning, but our tour was not so striking as our walk through the gold market in the afternoon. That was one of a kind.

MUSCAT AND SALALAH, OMAN

South of the Emirates is Muscat, the capital of Oman. My most significant memory of our day there is of the mosque on the outskirts of the city and the handsome, handwoven Iranian carpet that covers the entire floor.

George and I had bought our first nine-by-twelve hand-woven Persian rug, a Kerman, the year after we were married. Soon after, we bought a Kashan and a second Kerman. We always loved our rugs, so you can imagine our delight in seeing the magnificent Iranian carpet stretching wall to wall across the floor of the mosque. Rendered in greens, blues, beiges, and browns—the same hues as our rugs—the carpet is adorned with geometric and botanic designs. These colors and designs also grace the ceilings and walls of the mosque. The overall effect is simply exquisite. As we walked the perimeter, because we were forbidden from walking on the rug, our guide told us that the total worth of the carpet was eight to nine million American dollars.

The drive to and from the mosque was similar to the one in Dubai—modern motorways, upscale apartment and business buildings, desert surroundings. On our return trip, our tour group made a brief stop at a fish processing plant and then at the central souk. In the market, which was really a narrow, uphill, covered pathway, were stalls selling shoes, sunglasses, gold, men's shirts, women's blouses, shawls . . . Many items had been made in nearby India, where the prices were far lower, as we knew from our shopping excursions a few days earlier.

The city of Salalah is just down the Arabian Sea west of Muscat. George and I toured the area; what stands out from that tour are the frankincense trees. At one point, our guide stopped the bus and, using a knife, cut a narrow slit into a tree. We could see sap oozing out. The guide explained that when the sap congeals, it becomes frankincense.

In a small nearby market where we later had time to wander, we saw bags of frankincense being sold. I bought a bag to take back to the minister at our church so she could show it to the children in the religious education classes.

Before a Mosque.

SAFAGA AND SUEZ

Fast forward. *Voyager* sailed out of the Gulf of Aden and followed the coast of Yemen into the Red Sea. With Saudi Arabia on our starboard side and Eritrea and then Sudan on our port side, we headed north toward Safaga, Egypt.

We were up early the morning of our arrival in Safaga. All of us had a long day ahead, because this was a special-event stop. Included in our cruise package was an overnight trip to Luxor to see the Valley of the Kings, the Temple of Luxor, and the Karnak Temple complex. From our verandah, we looked down on at least twenty-five buses, parked side by side on the pier. The entire passenger contingent was going on tour.

Even George and I, who had been to Luxor in 1984, were eager to go. We decided it would be wise to be on the first bus. That way, we would be the first to leave and would have longer at the sites. It did not work out the way we had planned. We sat until all twenty-five buses were loaded. A ship representative explained that we were to go caravan-style for security reasons.

Eventually, we were off. Several police cars led the way, with more following behind and an armed guard riding shotgun in the front seat of each bus. Our caravan never stopped during the entire three-hour ride to Luxor. Police sirens blaring, the buses sped through intersections where more police held back cross traffic. Since our bus was first in the caravan, we had a front-seat view of the action.

Having been to the Valley of the Kings, Luxor Temple, and the Karnak complex on our 1984 land tour, we appreciated the "review course." From our prior trip, we remembered the heat of the desert, the smells of the donkey droppings, the cacophony of sounds that are Luxor. But our experience in 1984 was far more genuine than the one in 2005. Imagine pouring 800 cruisers into each of the sites at one time. You get noise, crowds, and confusion.

Again, fast forward. *Voyager* left the Red Sea and began its transit of the Suez Canal. Because Suez is a sea-level canal, there are no locks, just a slow passage through the narrow cut between Africa and Sinai that was deepened and widened when the canal was built in the mid-

1800s. On our starboard side was the Sinai—mostly sand with a few military encampments and monuments. The most interesting was the monument commemorating the Six-Day War between Israel and Egypt in 1967. On our port side was Africa with a number of towns and cities.

As the sun set and stars began to twinkle above us, we saw the lights of Port Said in the distance. The Egyptian city sits on the southern coast of the Mediterranean, rather near the Nile Delta. We did not stop in Port Said. For George and me, that would have to wait another year or two. *Voyager* just picked up speed and headed north to Kusadasi, Turkey.

REVISITS TO KUSADASI AND ATHENS

Since George and I had taken the tour to Ephesus on a prior cruise, we stayed in Kusadasi when we pulled into this popular Turkish port. Nonetheless, I have a short story to share.

George and I had been away from home now for a number of weeks, so I decided that I would telephone my sister in New Jersey when we made landfall in Kusadasi. I remembered from an earlier visit here that in the square just outside the souk was a telephone booth. So we headed to the square. Indeed, a man was selling phone cards for five dollars; better yet, he was sitting right by a phone booth. Before buying, we studied the directions. We had to enter a slew of numbers, but it seemed doable. Very, very carefully, I put in the numbers. I heard her phone ringing in New Jersey. From almost halfway around the world, I heard my sister asking, "Where are you?"

We had a nice chat, and then right there in the square, I heard the call to prayer from a nearby mosque. "Barbara, do you hear that?" She did. Can you imagine hearing the call to prayer over the phone from so far away? It seemed surreal.

After crossing the Aegean Sea, *Voyager* docked the next morning in Piraeus, the port for Athens. We had been to Athens on prior visits, but we decided to take a refresher course in the form of a highlights tour sponsored by Regent.

On our tour, George and I climbed up the Acropolis hill to revisit the Parthenon. The climb seemed steeper and harder this time; of course, that was because we were both a few years older. But we were disappointed when we got to the top. Now we could walk only the perimeter of the Parthenon and not go into the temple ruins. Our guide explained that this was a way of preserving a world treasure; lots of people tramping through the inner core could damage this heritage site for future generations. We were so fortunate to have visited the Parthenon years earlier, when we could wander within its walls.

THE STRAIT OF MESSINA, STROMBOLI, AND SORRENTO

Voyager's route took us across the Ionian Sea and into the Strait of Messina. It was a delightful cruising day, and we could see a bit of Italy afar on our starboard side and Sicily on our port side. Obviously, we could not discern any landmarks, other than the Sicilian city of Messina in the far distance, but for geography-loving travelers, it was still exciting. George and I had a map of the strait in our hands. As we steamed through, we pinpointed our position on it.

That same evening, our captain announced that we would shortly be passing Stromboli, an active volcano off the west coast of Italy. George and I had passed Stromboli before, but we had never seen any activity. Nevertheless, at the appointed hour, we were at the ship's rail, hoping to see a fiery burst lighting up the night sky. George held his video camera in readiness.

Suddenly . . . "There, there, George, did you see it?"

"Yes! Yes! I got it! I got it!" George not only had taken videos, but he had recorded our excited voices on his camera. Last evening, I played that video for the first time in years. What a treasure to have, especially our voices echoing from the past! It is a real-life record of our long love affair with the world and with travel.

The following morning, when we stepped out on our verandah, we saw Sorrento high on the hill above us. We were anchored in the harbor and the tendering service to shore had already begun. We had decided that this would be a leisurely day. At our convenience we took the tender into the pier and then a shuttle bus up to the town. We spent only an hour or so strolling the streets and shops. On long cruises, we had found that it paid to vary what we did, sometimes touring, sometimes walking on our own, and sometimes just staying on the ship.

MONACO AND GIBRALTAR

A day later, we were in Monaco, anchored in the harbor among myriad yachts and liners. Here, there was to be another special afternoon/evening event for everyone on *Voyager*. The ship was taking all of us to a reception being held in the Oceanographic Museum that is part of the complex of royal buildings atop a hill overlooking Monte Carlo. A grandfather of Prince Rainier sponsored the building of the aquarium in 1911. An avid naturalist, the former royal prince loved everything about the sea, but especially the fauna. We were excited about the excursion because we had missed seeing the aquarium during our 1982 visit to Monaco.

Glad that we would be taken by bus up the hillside, George and I tendered in early so we could wander the square in front of the Prince's Palace before entering the aquarium. We also wanted to spend time in the aquarium itself before the reception in the great hall. I think that my George videotaped every fish swimming in every display. Biologist as he was, George was in his glory. His videos of the fish are among the best he ever took.

After George had taken his videos, we headed to the reception hall for refreshments and conversation. By then, many passengers had arrived. George and I went to the buffet table; we were followed by a couple with whom we had talked off and on during the cruise, starting weeks before in Singapore. Making conversation, the woman turned to us and said, "This event should have been just for us—the full-world cruisers. It should not have included the Ferryboat People." We gasped, smiled, and talked about the fish in the aquarium. She obviously did not realize that George and I were happy ferryboaters!

The following evening as *Voyager* made her way to Malaga, we told the story to our dining companions, who were all ferryboaters like us: the Prices who were from England, the Kavanaughs who were from Ireland, the Constantines who were retired Brits now living in Spain, and our Australian friends. We all agreed that we were the fortunate ones on the cruise; we had found one another.

Two or three nights later, *Voyager* passed The Rock of Gibraltar on our starboard side. Since our suite was starboard-facing, we stayed on our verandah and watched as our ship sailed by. We recalled seeing the Rock on our Spain/Morocco tour years before. Our night-time sail through the Pillars of Hercules, which is what the strait between Spain and Morocco is called, added a different dimension to our memory of Gibraltar. As the ship left the Rock behind, we both felt a bit nostalgic. We were homeward bound. The end of our trip was coming soon.

MADEIRA, BERMUDA, AND THE BAHAMAS

Voyager docked in three ports on our way home: Funchal in Madeira, Hamilton in Bermuda, and Nassau in The Bahamas. All three are pretty islands; all are places we had visited many times. Perhaps because our cruise was winding down and I was even beginning to organize our things for packing, from those stops I cannot recall any memorable moments— what in my mind I was beginning to call "Stromboli Moments." We enjoyed walking through the flower market in Funchal, visiting Crystal Caves in Hamilton, and strolling the straw market in Nassau. Lovely, yes, but these activities did not compare with seeing a Stromboli eruption.

On board the *Voyager*, there were special events and entertainment. The rumor on the ship was that some well-known personality had boarded in Funchal and would entertain us toward the end of the cruise. The rumor was correct. Mark Russell—the political satirist, singer, and pianist who at that time worked the Washington, D.C. clubs and performed on TV— had boarded. He presented his show before a packed house.

In the final days of the cruise, George and I went to a few special buffets, both of us continued to play trivia with our team, and I eventually got down to serious packing. We had bought a large duffle bag in Kusadasi to fill with our newly purchased possessions, so I threw those into the duffle and then packed up most of our other belongings, ready to offload in Fort Lauderdale.

George and I spent considerable time enjoying the sea air on our verandah during our final days of the cruise. We talked especially about our Stromboli Moments from our half-a-world cruise and about the cruises we had already booked for late 2005 and 2006. We had booked an October/November/December 2006 cruise adventure along the west coast of Africa. It would take us to countries that we had never visited. It was *only* forty-six nights. This was an exciting prospect. Equally exciting was the prospect of doing a full-world cruise. Might we do that, too?

I am always up early on the last morning of a cruise. I watch to see the first lights from shore. When those lights are shining from an American port, I really am excited. In the past, I would wake up George, so we could watch as we came closer and closer to home.

"It was a good trip for us, wasn't it, George?" I asked.

"Yes," George said. "Sweetheart," he added, "let's book the *Amsterdam* world cruise for 2007." That was a Stromboli Moment for sure.

Chapter Fifteen
EXPLORING AFRICA

Speaking of Stromboli Moments, we had one after another on our West Africa/South America adventure in 2006. Our ship for this voyage of a lifetime was *Prinsendam*, the smallest vessel in the Holland America fleet. At the ship's helm was Captain Turner, one of the most experienced captains of the line. Our departure port was Lisbon in Portugal; our return port was Fort Lauderdale. The first Africa stops were in Morocco.

CASABLANCA AND AGADIR, MOROCCO

Over the years, George and I visited Casablanca many times. I have a favorite shop there, tucked within the walls of the old city and near the clock tower. Each time we arrived in Casablanca, we would gaze out from the top deck of our ship to see the Hassan II Mosque with its tall minaret outlined against the city skyline. On one trip, George and I had stood in the plaza in front of the mosque to listen to the call to prayer that is sent forth five times a day.

So in 2006, upon our arrival in our first North African port of call, we stood for a time looking out from the ship onto the city and the minaret. Then we hopped into a cab for the short ride to the clock tower near "my" shop. Entering it, we saw an old woman down on her knees scrubbing the floor. She was dressed in dark garb that covered her from head to toe. What we could see of her face was wrinkled from years of hard work. She never took her eyes off me as I slipped a red-and-gold caftan over my clothes to check for fit. To her, I must have looked foreign and youthful, although I probably was older than she was. To this day, when I think of that morning in Casablanca, I conjure up an image of "Woman on Her Knees," the actual position of women too often in the past and even in the present.

We spent the morning wandering from stall to stall inside the walls of the medina. We bought George a pair of handmade shoes and me a couple of fake silver bracelets. People watched us, as we watched them going about their daily chores. When we were ready to go "home," George spotted a couple carrying Holland America bags and asked to share a cab with them to the ship. That cut our cost in half.

Our second landfall in Morocco was Agadir. This was a new port for George and me, so we opted for a tour that promised a view from the hilltop casbah, or fortress, and a guided walk through the Berber market.

Well, the ride to the casbah was an adventure. Hairpin curves, no guardrails, no idea as to whether the bus had good tires and brakes—we breathed easier when we got to the top. But not for long.

In the plaza, where we climbed off the bus to view the town far below, was a charmer with a large, ugly snake wound around his neck. The guide had warned us to keep our distance from the snake charmer, or we might end up with *his* snake around *our* necks! Obviously, it would cost something to get him to reclaim his reptile. I got right back on the bus. George took some pictures, but he, too, did not linger long to admire the view.

Our guide led us next into the Berber market. Here she told us to stay close to her. "The market is a busy place," she warned. "I do not want to lose anyone."

Intrigued, we walked the narrow aisles that were jammed with people. Because trash was everywhere, our guide kept calling, "Watch your step. Rough ground!" We obeyed; we kept our eyes on her and watched where we put our feet. She was an assertive young woman, who at one point stopped for a full-fledged altercation with a merchant who was blocking our path with his handcart. She was dynamite.

Back on the bus, she explained that some men resent seeing young women working at such a responsible, well-paying job as hers. The label I put on my mental image of our Agadir guide was "Woman on the Way Up," to contrast her with the "Woman on Her Knees" we had seen in Casablanca.

MAKING FRIENDS

We had two sea days before our next port of call. The first of those days was packed with social activities.

On the first morning at sea, we met with our CruiseCritic.com chat group. We had been posting on the web for about six months, using code names to identify ourselves. Now on the ship, we sat in a circle and introduced ourselves. As chairperson of the group, I started: "We are Dorothy and George Hennings, educators from New Jersey. My online name is Blue Whale."

When all of us had introduced ourselves, we began to talk about our experiences in Casablanca and Agadir and about our touring plans for upcoming ports. Our group size was perfect for this kind of informal give and take—fifteen in all. We decided that we would keep meeting on sea days to share ideas, especially about what to do while in port. The members of the group were also interested in hearing more from one couple, the Garsons. These fine folks had told us that at each port they were planning to go to missionary centers to distribute goods they had brought along—computers, books, paper, pencils, and even clothing.

The afternoon of our first sea day, we also got together with the four other members of our trivia team. We had "found" one another at the first trivia match of the voyage, which had been held after we had departed Lisbon. The unique thing about our trivia team was that one couple were birders. At each port of call, their plan was to hire a cab and go to garbage dumps. That was where the birds were. Gathering in the afternoons after shore days, we would be entertained by our birders and their stories of visits to dumps.

Before dinner on the first sea day, George and I attended a cocktail party given by our travel agency escort, Tom. Tom hosted a number of parties during the cruise and also offered tours in some ports. This was the first time we had traveled with this agency. It was a wise choice, for Tom also hosted coffee chats on sea days. The agency had a large group of clients on board, so we had the opportunity to meet lots of interesting people.

After the party, we headed to our dining table—a table for six in the smaller of the two dining rooms on *Prinsendam*. Assigned to our table were Eloise and Dom. Amazingly, they had lived most of their lives in New Jersey and were alums of Kean University where George and I had taught until retirement. The other two were from Ohio and were avid travelers. As a result, conversation flowed easily each night at dinner. We were fortunate, too, for ours was a window table so we had a front seat for sail-aways, which often happened during dinner.

DAKAR, SENEGAL

On October 23, *Prinsendam* tied up in Dakar, the capital of Senegal. George and I did not feel comfortable traveling on our own, away from the city and into the countryside. This was our first sub-Saharan port of call, and we did not know what to expect. We, therefore, opted for a ship's tour to a lake that was pink in color, to a village where we would see how people lived, and to an area of sand dunes.

We were in for an eye-opening adventure. Escorted by a motorcycle policeman, we traveled on an old bus with no air-conditioning. This dilapidated vehicle took us through areas of extreme poverty—really extreme poverty—and then stopped at a motel where we transferred to an old French military truck with seats along the back and big, balloon-like tires. The driver started his vehicle by touching wires together on the battery.

Pink Lake was not very pink, but biologist George found it informative, nonetheless; he learned that the pink shading was caused by the sun reflecting off bacteria in the lake. George had never heard of that phenomenon.

At the village stop, we peeked into what the guide called the "sleeping houses." These were small, round, straw dwellings topped with conical, thatched roofs. Interestingly, inside were western-style beds and bedding. The toilet—a metal chair with the bottom cut out and a bucket below—was in a separate building and was shared with others in the community. In a central area of the compound, a young boy was manually lowering a pail on a rope into a well and hoisting it up filled with water.

Back in our French military truck, we headed to the dunes. Our drive over them was like a roller coaster ride; the driver sped up one side of a dune and down the other—fast. He kept doing that, climbing one dune after another, shifting gears, and revving his motor to a roar. We just held on tightly! This was more an adventure than a Stromboli Moment, but it was something we both remembered and talked about for a long time. George, however, was not really happy about our dune ride; as an environmentalist, he was concerned about what the trucks were doing to the dunes, which faced the Atlantic Ocean and served as a protective barrier.

Our driver took us back to the motel so we could transfer to our bus. Vendors lined the courtyard and hopped up when they saw us coming. We bargained for a sand painting that showed a village scene of houses with conical roofs similar to those we had just seen. We priced an exquisitely carved mask; the vendor followed us after that, lowering his price to ten dollars just before we climbed onto the bus.

When we arrived back at the pier, we found that numerous vendors had set up for business. We spotted three masks we liked: an ornate round one embedded with metal and stones, a second with an elongated face and a pointed chin, and a third with a crown. They were very different from the one we had bought in the countryside, so exotic that we went wild and bought all three. In the afternoon, we considered going the short distance into Dakar, but we decided not to when we heard that other passengers had been mugged on the pier where we had bargained for our three masks just a few hours earlier.

Our morning in the countryside near Dakar set the stage for many other days filled with exciting adventures. From those adventures we brought home almost unbelievable memories—memories so different from anything we had ever experienced on prior travels that we began to call them "West African Moments."

THE GAMBIA AND GHANA

The Gambia is the smallest country on the mainland of Africa. It was our destination as we sailed south. We learned that it is just a finger of land on each side of the Lower Gambia River.

Our tour was to an animal reserve in the countryside. George and I chose it because we wanted to drive out beyond the capital city of Banjul to see how ordinary Gambians lived. After our day in Dakar, we knew we should take a tour and not wander streets on our own.

Our drive to the Abuko National Reserve took about an hour, and every minute was fascinating. The main road was roughly paved, but the side roads and the areas between the homes were red clay and mud. The houses and shops were small, often with tin roofs and siding; they stood at the very edge of the main road on which we were traveling. There was little car traffic, but numbers of people were walking. Despite the red clay that was everywhere, the women walking in the road were garbed in flowing, very clean, very colorful cotton dresses. Generally they had their hair bound up in patterned bandanas. Goats, cows, and chickens roamed freely. Mesmerized, George and I kept our eyes glued to the passing scenes; we did not want to miss one "West African Moment." By contrast, the animal reserve was just ho-hum. If there were any animals other than monkeys in residence, they heard us coming and disappeared into the brush.

Returning to town, we asked the guide if we might stop at a stall where we could buy local goods, especially wood carvings. Responding to our request, the bus driver left the main road and turned down a back street that was deep with red mud. It had rained the night before, and with no drainage system, the side street was nearly impassable. So we did not have to wade through the mud, the driver took us right to the front of the one and only shop.

As we got out, George announced, "No more masks! We already have four." Instead of another mask, we bought a carved wood plaque. It depicts a wistful young boy in a contemplative pose sitting beside a conical-shaped house, very much like the ones we had seen the day before during our village visit. The plaque is a splendid visual reminder of sub-Saharan Africa.

In nearby Takoradi in Ghana, George and I took an afternoon tour called "Culture and Castles." By bus, we were driven to a small village for the "culture" segment of the tour. On our way, at first the road surface was just red clay, and our progress was slow. Eventually a tar surface replaced the packed clay, and progress was faster. Lots of potholes, however, made for a jolting journey.

Nonetheless, George and I were so glad we had taken this tour. What we saw was worth any discomfort. We passed lots of markets and small villages with tin or stucco houses clustered close to the road on which we traveled. The houses had no real windows or doors, just wide openings to the outside. We wondered about sanitation, electricity, and water. There was considerable street activity; as in The Gambia, goats, cows, and chickens roamed freely.

After a lengthy ride, we arrived at our village stop where we first explored independently. In one area, we saw young boys sorting small, silvery fish. In another, we watched youngsters organizing the fish on racks to be smoked; the fish looked a lot like sardines to us. On the other side of the compound, we observed women and girls who were squating on the ground as they peeled, washed, chopped, and cooked cassava—a source of tapioca. Seated together in a row were the village elders and their chief. Our tour group paraded by to shake hands with the important men of the community. Then we lined up and the elders and the chief paraded by us to shake hands again. Our guide explained that this was a local custom.

We were supposed to visit the village school. That did not happen because, as our guide explained, "The teachers are on strike." As a result, the children were working at such everyday tasks as sorting fish and peeling cassava.

Our second stop was at Cape Coast Castle, a large walled fortress jutting into the sea. Inside were a shop, a museum, and some dark dungeons where men and women had been imprisoned at the height of the slave trade. Cape Coast Castle is a UNESCO Heritage Site; the city where it is located—Cape Coast—was once the capital of Ghana. Despite George's warning the day before, we left there with another mask to add to our growing collection.

Before returning to *Prinsendam*, we stopped for a photo opportunity at Elmina Castle—a large castle, black with mildew. Extreme humidity is a problem there, and it was a problem for us, too. By the time we returned to the ship, we were hot and very sweaty. George said to me several times that evening, "I am so thankful I live in America." I agreed. Travel is a powerful eye-opener.

LOMÉ, TOGO

The next morning, George and I awoke to the sound of drumming coming from the pier beneath our verandah. *Prinsendam* had just docked in Lomé, Togo. We opened the draperies to see drummers and chanters performing on the pier and colorfully costumed dancers swaying in time to the drumming. Their dance, we thought, was telling a story about sowing seeds and harvesting grain. Costumed stilt walkers strutted among the performers. It was a scene right out of the pages of *National Geographic*.

A morning tour took us to a fishing village. This was by mistake because our driver got lost and could not find his way to the fish market on the pier where we were supposed to go. We learned later that our buses in Lomé were the same ones we had used in Ghana and The Gambia; the drivers were taking their buses overland from port to port at night since there were not enough local vehicles in each port to meet our needs.

On the way to the fishing village, George saw a man standing stark naked by a pile of garbage at the side of the road; the man was scavenging for food. At the village we saw shacks made from twigs and branches, the homes of fishermen and their families, who kept dismantling and moving their houses to follow the fish. Our driver eventually found the market, where women were waiting for fish to take back to their villages to sell. It was a hectic, noisy scene on a pier where fishermen were bringing in their morning catch.

Then our guide took us to a nearby beach, where we stopped to watch men pulling in fishing nets and chanting as they pulled. Some from our tour group pulled too, as we took their pictures. We all knew we would remember this beach scene, but we wanted an actual photograph of "Pulling in the Nets."

The most uncomfortable event of the day was next. The tour stopped at a small museum on Independence Square. Many women in our group by now were more interested in finding a restroom than looking at displays. We were directed up a flight of cement stairs in a windowless, unlit stairwell. As we climbed up and up with no handrails for security, it got darker and darker. We women decided that under no circumstances were we going any farther into a darkness where creepy crawlies could be lurking. Staying close together, we carefully made our way down to suffer in silence. When the guide realized our discomfort, he made a special stop at the Hotel Palm Beach so we could "ease ourselves." We loved that euphemism.

After our impromptu rest stop, our driver lost his way for the second time that morning. We ended up at the border crossing between Togo and Benin. Before the driver could turn his bus around, people waiting at the border began pounding on the sides of it. We never found out why—perhaps they thought we were going to cross the border and wanted a ride over. Whatever the reason, our driver turned his bus and got us out of there as fast as he could.

Yes, we were soon lost again—for the third time that day! Eventually, after much backing up and turning around, our driver found the fetish market where voodoo goods were on sale. We saw rows and rows of animal skulls, dolls with pins to use to cast a spell on others, and fluffy-tailed thingamajigs for waving a hex away. We did not buy anything. Perhaps we should have: A dried animal skull would have made an interesting addition to our growing mask collection.

When we arrived back at the pier, vendors selling more "normal" goods were waiting for us. George and I bought beads, masks, belts, and pocketbooks. Notice the plural nouns and the word *masks*! But with a genuine leather belt selling for three dollars and prices lower than in prior ports, we could not resist. My favorite purchase of the day was a small, brass, medallion-like piece, which I later learned is a passport mask. A passport mask identifies the tribe to which the owner belongs. It is small enough for me to hang on a shoelace and wear as a pendant.

Our day in Togo was the first of four days that were the most unforgettable and unusual in all our years of travel. People often ask what we felt was our number-one trip. George and I agreed that "The Taste of Two Continents" rated right up there because of our out-of-the-ordinary days in Lomé, Togo; Cotonou, Benin; Douala, Cameroon; and Libreville, Gabon. The ports in these countries are in a category of their own.

COTONOU, BENIN

Another group of elaborately costumed drummers and dancers welcomed us to Cotonou in Benin. Because our cabin was portside, we could again watch the show from our verandah.

Our excursion in Cotonou was to Ganvie Stilt Village. We were on one of the buses from the day before that had been driven overland to catch up with the ship at the next port. Leaving the pier, we passed tin and stucco houses with red sand paths between. They were similar to those we had seen the day before. As in the prior ports, the women we saw along the road were attired in long, colorful, cotton dresses—very clean cotton dresses despite the red-sand surroundings.

Again the bus driver got lost going from the pier to the cutoff for the stilt village. Eventually he found the way. Arriving at Ganvie, our tour group climbed onto motorized boats for a fifteen-minute ride to the village, which is constructed on pilings over a lake. As we motored, a fisherman came by to demonstrate how he cast his net so that it swirled wide in a big circle above his head and then spiraled down into the lake.

When we got to Ganvie Stilt Village, we clambered up onto a small pier. There we wandered among the homes, the restaurants, the stores, and even a hotel. A gentle breeze was coming off the lake, so it was a bit cooler than we had expected.

Before leaving, we headed to the "restroom." It was a square hole in the floor in a small wood-enclosed single cubicle. You could see the water of the lake down through the hole. Before leaving, too, I bought the requisite souvenir, a handmade, appliquéd piece that the saleslady said she herself had sewn.

Once back in Cotonou, our guide took us for a ride through the main areas of the city. We passed the local produce market, which was a mob scene because it was Sunday and the people were out doing their weekly shopping. Our guide announced that under no circumstances were we getting off the bus; it was too dangerous. Instead, he took us to a craft market consisting of individual little shops connected by a boardwalk; there the vendors practiced aggressive bargaining. Of course, I found something to buy—a wood plaque to pair with the one we had purchased in The Gambia. This carving is of a mother with her baby strapped onto her back, something we had seen over and over again in The Gambia, Ghana, and Benin.

We were hot and sweaty by the time we got back to *Prinsendam*. The bus had not been air-conditioned. According to our guide, it was "air-cooled," which meant that we could open the windows. Before going up to our cabin, we left our wood purchases at the top of the gangway. This had been the protocol in our prior West African ports. The ship kept all wood items in the refrigerator for several days to kill any termites the items might contain.

Before supper and before we cast off from the dock, *Prinsendam* lost power as Captain Turner transferred from one system of generators to another. As a result, supper was delayed, as was the evening show. Much, much later as we sat in the theater waiting for the movie to begin, we heard the engines start up and felt the ship moving down the channel.

Then it happened! We felt the ship bump, vibrate, and list.

Captain Turner immediately came on the PA system. He explained that although *Prinsendam* had been in the middle of the marked channel and had had a local pilot aboard to guide her out, she had struck a sandbar on the starboard side. The captain announced that he was turning back to have the hull checked. We were nervous, to say the least, and returned

192

to our cabin to wait for an update. I even began to collect our valuables and medications in a pillowcase—just in case we had to abandon ship.

Shortly, Captain Turner came back on the PA. The crew had made an internal check of the hull. We were not taking on water. He had checked with the home office in Seattle. The decision was not to turn back. It was more dangerous to go back than to go forward. Returning to port, we might hit another uncharted sandbar. Or we might hit another on our way out.

The next day—a sea day—we were still afloat. On our door was a letter from Captain Turner. Here is what it said: "As you may know, upon departure from Cotonou, ms Prinsendam touched bottom on an uncharted sandbar at the harbor entrance for a brief moment. As is typical upon arrival and departure, a local pilot was on board to assist with the ship's navigation. We have conducted tests and examinations to ensure the integrity of the hull and there was no damage to the vessel. We are sailing to Douala, Cameroon. We will arrive as scheduled on Tuesday."

The Captain later came on the PA to warn about going onto the outer promenade deck after dark. He explained that he had ordered all deck lights turned off and that it would be dangerous for us to walk outside. He had had the lights turned off as a precautionary measure against marauding pirates; he also had posted armed guards on both sides of the ship, patrolling all night long. He was charting a course more than eighty miles from the coast. We were passing Nigeria, which was a pirate attack zone, and he was taking no chances.

That evening before climbing into bed, George checked that our verandah door was locked, the outside lights were off, and the drapes were tightly closed so no cabin light was visible from the sea. Captain Turner had directed us to take these precautions as we passed through pirate-infested waters.

What an amazing two days it had been!

DOUALA, CAMEROON

The following morning, we rose early to be ready to leave the ship as soon as it docked in Douala. Because of the tides, *Prinsendam* had to sail by 2 p.m., so tours had to be back by then. This was our first stop with overcast skies and thunderstorms predicted in the afternoon. We had had a spectacular lightning display with rain on our eventful departure from Benin, so we were happy to see no rain as we boarded our bus for our morning tour.

Driving through the streets into the city center, we encountered heavy traffic, something we had not found during our prior stops in West African ports. We also saw many high-rise office buildings and apartment complexes.

Our first stop was at a large craft center. The stalls there had wood and metal carvings galore, with some designs we had not seen before. We stopped next in the central square to walk about and take pictures of the Catholic cathedral.

In the square, before she opened the doors of the bus, our guide issued a warning. "This is a dangerous area," she said. "If you decide to get off with me, leave your valuables on the bus and stick to me like glue. Or just stay on the bus. Look out the windows and decide what you want to do." Although we saw many, many young men loitering in the square, most of us walked with her, clustered closely together.

We got back to *Prinsendam* on time and without incident. Others did not fare so well. One of the buses in our group had stopped just outside the port. The driver had announced that he did not have enough gas for the trip, and he would need to stop to fill up his tank. But he had a problem: He did not have any money to pay for the gas. He had demanded that the passengers contribute cash for a fillup. The passengers had refused. Eventually a supervisor had come to the rescue, and the tour had continued, albeit in shortened form.

Several couples, who were touring independently by taxi and who had stopped to take photographs, had been pulled over by the police. They had broken the law, the policemen had announced, by taking pictures of a bridge—a *little* bridge over a *little* creek. The so-called lawbreakers

194

could pay a hefty fine right then and there or be taken to the police station where their cameras would be confiscated. They paid!

Even the ship experienced a "shakedown." HAL had to pay a huge sum to offload its garbage, far more than at any prior port in which the captain had docked. The cost was twenty-five thousand dollars.

In Douala, four young male vocalists joined our ship. They had flown in a day before and stayed in a local hotel. These men were big, strong guys. They told us that once they arrived, they never left their hotel; the streets outside were too scary.

When George and I got home to New Jersey, I checked the itinerary of the Holland America circumnavigation-of-Africa cruise slated for 2008. The stop in Cameroon had been scratched. Similarly, that country was not on the itinerary for the 2022 circumnavigation; neither was Togo nor Benin. We felt very fortunate to have gone into these countries and come home safe and sound. Our country-counting friends, who keep track of the number of countries they have visited, envy us our adventures in West Africa.

LIBREVILLE, GABON

Libreville in Gabon was far less frightening. Our buses were air-conditioned and a step up compared to the ones we had had in Ghana, Togo, Benin, and Cameroon.

George and I had booked a short morning tour that included stops at a craft market, a museum, the central square, and the main church. The tour cost $135 per person, high for a third-world country. We also had to pay about a hundred dollars for a visa, with an added assessment of fifty dollars by the agency procuring it for us. All of these costs, of course, were in addition to what we were paying for the cruise itself.

The market we visited in Libreville was for tourists, not locals. Our guide was a young university student with a wide smile and excellent English. He said that he and his friends could not afford to shop there. We bought a souvenir mask, some beads, and a length of fabric. To us, the prices in the tourist market did not seem high at all.

We made a stop at the local museum. Although small, it did have interesting displays of local crafts, especially wood carvings which we had come to love.

Our bus drove us up the main avenue past the huge presidential compound and the government buildings that had been constructed mostly with Chinese money. Our young guide warned us not to take pictures; it was against the law. After what had happened to our fellow travelers in Cameroon, all of us heeded the warning.

Then we headed to the Catholic church, which is known for its intricately carved wood columns. Luck was with us. It was All Souls' Day and a service was in progress; we could hear chanting and singing echoing forth.

We were able to go inside and walk around the building to view the columns. The carvings were amazing, exquisite beyond belief. But it was the scene itself that fascinated us. Worshippers were dressed in their best holiday attire; they swayed to the music as they sang. Their voices reverberated from the rafters.

Outside, after the service, we saw nuns dressed in white garb trimmed with green. There were lots of other people milling about—men, women, and children—who were out for a holiday stroll. They eyed us—dressed in jeans and T-shirts—as if we were from a different planet. In a way, we were.

WALVIS BAY, NAMIBIA, ON THE SKELETON COAST

When we awoke in the morning three days later, we were in Namibia. I turned to George and said, "This is your day, Sweetheart!" That was so true. George and I were going to Moon Valley, a part of Namibia noted for its "moonscapes" and unique flora. The area was a veritable wonderland for naturalists.

Driving in a six-minivan caravan, our small tour group went north along the Atlantic coast—along what is known as the Skeleton Coast, in part because of the bones of early Portuguese seamen found on the beaches there. We passed miles and miles of sand dunes and stopped once so that each of us could feel the sand. Dune sand here is very fine. It actually originates in the rivers of South Africa, is blown by the wind into the ocean, and is carried by ocean currents north to Namibia. The sea waves then bring the sand onto shore, where the wind builds it into dunes.

Our route carried us north and east to Moon Valley. Dolomite is a major igneous rock found here. It is very hard, much harder than other rocks in the region. The dolomite, being harder, better withstands weathering and stands out as sharp dark ridges. The result is a dramatic "moonscape."

Our leader was a driver, a guide, and a naturalist rolled into one. He steered his van up, down, and then over rises in the road; we enjoyed wonderful views at each rise. It was as if we were traveling into a different universe. The earth looked so weird that a five-year-old riding in our van asked his mom, "Where are we? What are we doing here?"

Our naturalist/guide/driver was a blond Afrikaner with red cheeks burned by the sun. He knew desert flora and would stop the caravan from time to time so we could get out to see the few small plants growing in this inhospitable environment. He showed us lichens, which are a combination of algae and fungi. Reaching for his bottled water, he poured some on the lichens growing on rock surfaces. Reacting, the lichens sprang to life, opening up and absorbing the droplets. The reason that the lichens can survive in this harsh terrain is that, when morning fog rolls in from the ocean, they absorb it. The fog provides enough water to sustain them.

But the *piece de resistance* was *welwitschia mirabilis*, a cross between a tree and a flower. George's botany-loving friend Fred had been to Namibia the year before and had told George about this very long-living plant. Some scientists claim that a welwitschia plant can survive as long as twenty-five hundred years. Now George was seeing it for himself in its natural habitat. He was ecstatic. Yes, truly ecstatic! For him, this probably was the high point of our entire forty-six-day cruise.

Before we got out of the van to view these plants, the guide explained that the roots of welwitschia are very shallow; they spread laterally across the ground so that they can absorb what little water there is. To preserve this shallow root system, naturalists had placed a ring of small rocks around each plant. We were not to step over the rock ring onto the root system. It could destroy these rare and precious plants.

Some people are amazing. A woman from another van in our caravan stepped directly into the forbidden area and onto the roots to have her husband take a picture of her with the welwitschia. My husband was aghast and actually reprimanded her—albeit in a gentle tone of voice.

As we rode through the more rugged areas of the moonscape, George kept telling me to look at the rock beds. With so little plant growth, we could easily see the rock layers, folded upward to form ridges. Later, we stopped at one of the higher dunes that we had passed on our outbound journey. Some from our tour group attempted to climb to the top of the dune. Because the sand is so fine, climbing is difficult, but a few strong folks did make it to the summit.

Back in Walvis Bay in the afternoon, our driver stopped at a lagoon where flamingos live. Fortunately, George had his binoculars with him. Using them, we could distinguish the two types of birds—taller pink flamingos and shorter gray ones.

Yes, this surely had been George's day.

CAPE TOWN, SOUTH AFRICA; LUDERITZ, NAMIBIA

The sea was rough as we plowed southward toward Cape Town. We had expected this because, as Captain Turner had warned, winds coming off Antarctica whip up the ocean waters and create turbulence.

Prinsendam arrived in Cape Town mid-morning after a day at sea. The sail-in was fabulous—the sky blue, the sun shining. There was not a trace of a cloud over Table Mountain; often there is a white cloud draped over it. The locals call that *the tablecloth*. Because our ship was not overly large, she could berth right at the Victoria and Alfred Waterfront; our cabin faced Table Mountain. We could walk off the ship directly into the waterfront center.

George and I spent a splendid afternoon puttering around the waterfront. We stumbled upon a local instrumental group and sat down to listen. We found, too, the plaza with statues of the four South

Dorothy and Table Mountain.

Africans who had won the Nobel Peace Prize: Mandela and de Klerk in 1993, Bishop Tutu in 1984, and Lutuli in 1960. We took time to read the quotations by these great men; their words are embedded in the surface of the plaza.

That evening, from our verandah, the two of us watched the lights of the city begin to twinkle on and Table Mountain gradually fade into the darkness. We had to pinch ourselves to believe that we were actually here in Cape Town, docked just below Table Mountain.

In 2002 George and I had sailed Cape Horn, an island at the tip of South America. Now we wanted to go to the Cape of Good Hope, very near to the most southeasterly point in Africa. Our full-day tour to the cape took us out of the city and along the scenic route via Chapman's Peak Drive. The tour brochure had promised us "some of the Cape's most magnificent views." That was not an exaggeration.

Reaching the Cape of Good Hope Nature Reserve, we took the

funicular to the top of Cape Point. Again the views were as dramatic as the tour brochure had promised. From Cape Point we could almost "see" where the Indian Ocean by definition meets the Atlantic Ocean. Obviously, we saw only an expanse of open sea; we had to tell ourselves that the Indian was on the left, the Atlantic on the right.

We lunched at a restaurant with floor-to-ceiling windows looking out on the Indian Ocean; we visited a colony of braying jackass penguins that live on a violently windy expanse of Boulders Beach; and we walked through the grounds of the Kirstenbosch National Botanical Garden, which is on the eastern slope of Table Mountain. By the time we reached the gardens, I was exhausted. George, however, was still full of energy and really excited about seeing the numerous plants that are indigenous to South Africa.

Back on *Prinsendam*, George and I tidied ourselves and headed to dinner. My cousins, John and Patricia from Florida, were joining us for the second half of our cruise, and I was eager to greet them. They also would be joining our dining table each night for supper.

Prinsendam was supposed to leave port late on day two, but the need to refuel and sail out of the harbor when the winds were not so violent delayed us—first by a few hours and then by a day. George and I spent our unexpected day strolling the Victoria and Alfred Waterfront.

At 1:30 a.m. the next morning, Captain Turner started the ship's motors and backed his vessel away from the pier. We were leaving Cape Town, bound for Luderitz in Namibia.

Luderitz is a small town settled originally by Germans. George and I decided to explore the town by foot. The most interesting place to see was the Lutheran church with its colorful stained-glass windows: Embedded in each was the name of the donor. We used the pews of the church as a place to rest before walking back down to the ship. For us it was a safe, easy walkabout day with no really outstanding moments. Oh, yes, a few youngsters approached us for "a dollar to buy bread." We surmised that, with cruise passengers coming to town, the boys had found an easy way to make a little money.

ST. HELENA AND THE ASCENSION ISLANDS

The sea turned rough as *Prinsendam* headed west. We were scheduled to make landfall at St. Helena in the mid-Atlantic after a couple of sea days. Jamestown in St. Helena has two claims to fame. First, it is located on the Mid-Atlantic Ridge, a ridge formed by the drifting of the Eurasian and American continental plates. The ridge extends from Iceland in the north to island groupings in the South Atlantic. George and I had walked the fault in Iceland caused by the pulling apart of these two major continental plates, so we were eager to stand on St. Helena. Second, St. Helena is the island to which Napoleon was sent after the Battle of Waterloo. It was there that he died.

The sea was still turbulent at 10 a.m. when tendering from ship to shore commenced. George, Patricia, and John grabbed the first tender over. I stayed on the ship because I had a headache that was affecting my equilibrium. I did not want to take a chance riding a bouncy tender, and I knew that sooner or later we would return to St. Helena.

George, Patricia, and John came back to the ship with pictures of what they had seen. John and Patricia had climbed Jacob's Ladder, a steep set of steps—699 in all—that go up to the top of the island. George showed me a picture of the cousins as they made the demanding ascent. All three of them had survived the bouncy tender ride unscathed, although one passenger was not so fortunate. She had stood just as the tender slammed against the pier. She had sustained an arm injury—or that was the rumor that ran through the ship.

The following day, Captain Turner attempted to land in the nearby Ascension Islands, another spot in the mid-Atlantic formed by the drifting apart of the continental plates. This time, our captain decided he was not going to try for a landing; the seas were too violent. As he explained his decision over the public address system, Turner made an important point about cruising. If someone really, really wants to visit a specific port, he or she might be wise to fly in. Given the vagaries of the sea, a captain cannot guarantee a landfall in a port.

The captain then told us that he was canceling our scheduled stop in Natal in Brazil. Because of drought conditions, there was not enough water in the Natal harbor for *Prinsendam* to enter. Instead, our ship would stop in Parintins on the Amazon.

The captain's announcement reminded us that we were on our way to Brazil, the second continent we were visiting on our cruise called "The Taste of Two Continents."

FORTALEZA: SUNDAY ON THE BEACH WITH JOHN

In 2002, George and I had stopped in Fortaleza, Brazil, on a weekday and shuttled to the huge, downtown market and to the cathedral, which is across the avenue. In 2006, we docked on a Sunday. The downtown market was closed, but a local jewelry firm was running an afternoon shuttle to its shop on the beachfront. Patricia, John, George, and I decided to take advantage of the free transfer.

The beach is a beautiful one. It was packed with Sunday sunbathers and swimmers. The four of us enjoyed a leisurely walk on the sand. From the beach, we could look at the condos and apartment buildings of Fortaleza in the distance. It was great to walk with my big, tall, bearded cousin John in an area where we had been warned of pickpockets. With him as our escort, we felt safe.

Eventually, we headed back to the hotel that was the pickup point for the shuttle to the ship. Eloise and Dom, our evening tablemates, were there. Dom showed us a red abrasion on his neck and told us that as they were walking, a young man had jumped on him from behind and had tried to rip his gold chain and cross from his neck. Fortunately, Dom was able to grab the chain before the would-be thief took off with it. Unfortunately, during the scuffle, the chain had cut into his neck. As the shuttle bus drove us along the avenue back to the ship, Eloise pointed out the young thief and his companion in crime. They were sauntering along, we assumed on the prowl for another victim.

BELEM: A STROLL ALONG THE AVENUE

When we arrived in Icoaraci, the port for Belem, John, Patricia, George, and I chose a leisurely stroll down the main avenue of Belem to the Theater of Peace as our outing for the morning. Since the ship docked in Icoaraci, about a forty-minute drive from Belem, we figured the ride via the free shuttle would provide an overview of the area.

On the bus, I sat behind the Brazilian lecturer from the ship. Climbing off, I asked him which was the best way to the theater. He said, "Follow me!" He led us down the main avenue, showing us the original custom house and other sites of interest. Before leaving us, he pointed out the theater far down the avenue.

The four of us meandered along, enjoying the street stalls geared for the locals as well as the souvenir shops for tourists like us. The streets were packed with people, but we did not feel threatened in any way. Of course, we had big John with us, and he does look rather formidable with his bald head and long beard.

Arriving at the far end of the avenue, we entered the lobby of the theater to view the impressive main staircase. It reminded George and me of the stunning staircase at the theater in Manaus that we had visited in 2002. Both of these were built with money contributed by rubber barons who wanted to bring European music and culture to Amazonia.

Realizing that we had a long walk to the shuttle pickup point, the four of us made our way back along the avenue. The shuttle was waiting. The driver, who spoke English, was talkative: He supplied a running commentary as he drove us to the port. The most interesting point he made was about the mango trees growing on each side of the road. They formed an arch of green almost completely across it. The driver told us that the mangos were dangerous. If a mango fell and hit someone, it could cause serious injury. The driver also stopped briefly before the Church of the Nazareth so George could take pictures.

All four of us were happy with our day, which I had named "A Stroll along the Avenue with Cousin John." We had seen what we had wanted to see. Also, at the last minute before we'd reboarded our ship, John had made an extraordinary purchase—a very long, genuine blowgun! John had bargained for it with a man—not a shopkeeper—who was fishing from the pier with his blowgun at his feet.

UP THE AMAZON TO SANTAREM AND PARINTINS

That evening, *Prinsendam* steamed out of the Para River, where Belem is located, and into the Atlantic toward the mouth of the Amazon. When we awoke the next morning, we were already cruising the mighty river. We did not realize it, because we could not see the riverbanks. At that point the Amazon is very, very wide—at least six miles from one bank to the other.

As we made our way upriver, the waters of the Amazon became reddish-brown and contained floating debris. Soon we thought we could see a bank on one side; the lecturer said that what we saw were islands. It got too hot and humid for us to sit on the verandah, although cousin John would often come and sit out there. From Florida, he was used to the heat. We just sat before our sliding glass doors and watched the waters of the Amazon flow by.

Santarem is a good-sized city on the Amazon. We steamed into Santarem after again seeing from our verandah the Meeting of Waters—the flowing together of the brown Amazon with the clearer waters of the Tapajos. As we had seen on our trip around South America in 2002, here the two rivers meet but the waters do not immediately mix; rather they run parallel, brown next to clear, for a considerable distance. We were as excited to see it in 2006 as we had been in 2002. After all, we were deep in the rainforest, sailing the storied Amazon.

After *Prinsendam* docked, the four of us caught a cab and rode into downtown Santarem. George and I looked for the market stalls on the river side of the road. We remembered live chickens and other produce being sold there. But the picturesque stalls we remembered were gone; perhaps the outbreak of the bird flu had led to their demise. In the removal of the waterside shops, however, something distinctive had been lost.

While John and Patty walked about, George and I sat on a bench in the city square in front of the Cathedral of Our Lady of Conception, the oldest building in Santarem. It dates back to 1761. We spied a few souvenir stalls on the square where we found a cheap pair of wood earrings—nice design, good price. But what I remember most clearly is the two of us just sitting, relaxing, and picturing in our minds the exact spot on our wall map where we were at that moment—on the Amazon.

The next morning George and I awoke to a loud, boisterous welcome. Sounds of incessant drumming were coming from the floating pier across the water from where we were anchored. On it, minimally clad young women were dancing to the rhythm of the drums. We were in Parintins.

John had suggested that we sightsee by tricycle cab. We agreed. After bargaining for five dollars a cab, John and Patty hopped into one; George and I hopped into another. We set off for a spin around the small town— past the cathedral, the Boi Bumba arena, and the cemetery. It was a fun hour, and we even had time to browse the shops on the pier.

George and I tendered back to the ship. The cousins stayed ashore to browse some more. To our amazement, a few hours later, cousin John came to our cabin with a massive, finely carved wood chair. He had just bought his fabulous find and wanted to leave it on our verandah so that when he visited us in the next couple of days, he could sit on his one-of-a-kind Amazonian chair. I have to say the chair was impressive. I could just picture him sitting on it on his wraparound porch back home in Florida, his blowgun lying at his feet and a satisfied smile on his face.

That night Captain Turner plotted an eastward course back toward the mouth of the Amazon. A few days later, on December 2, *Prinsendam* steamed into Fort Lauderdale. George and I watched the coast of Florida come into view. Standing there in the early morning, we thought about "The Taste of Two Continents." We both agreed that our days in West and South Africa were among the most remarkable ones we had ever experienced.

What was ahead? We would be leaving in a little over a month on our first full round-the-world cruise. We knew that our colleague and friend from Kean University, Madelyn Healy, would be on the ship. Better yet, cousins John and Patricia had decided to sail with us.

"Life is good," I said to George, as I often did when we were headed home from a successful cruise.

"Yes, it is," he replied. "Yes, it is!

Chapter Sixteen
SAILING THE WORLD
2007

January 14, 2007: George and I were standing on the promenade deck of *ms Amsterdam* as she pulled away from Fort Lauderdale to begin her circumnavigation of the world! We would be away 104 days. We would sail the Pacific, the Indian, and the Atlantic oceans; the Panama and Suez canals; the South China, the Mediterranean, the Caribbean, the Red, and the Arabian seas. We would visit ports on six continents. The number of countries? Too many to count! We were both excited. We were finally taking our first complete world cruise.

THE SOUTH PACIFIC: EASTER AND PITCAIRN ISLANDS

Amsterdam transited the Panama Canal and stopped in Ecuador and Peru before heading west to Easter Island. For two days after we left Lima, we saw neither land nor other ships—not even birds. The Pacific Ocean is vast. Our ship was a small dot in the largest ocean on earth. Traveling across it, we felt insignificant.

We had a number of South Pacific Islands ahead of us. The first was Easter Island, a possession of Chile and part of Polynesia. Would

George and Mo' Ai

Amsterdam be able to get us into Easter Island? Early in the voyage, our captain had explained that about half the ships attempting to anchor off the island and to tender in their passengers succeeded. The seas are often rough in this part of the world.

Our captain was successful!

We went to Easter Island to see the Mo'ai, large stone statues of human figures that the Rapa Nui people had erected between 1250 and 1500 CE to honor their most revered ancestors. Each statue, which can weigh as much as eighty tons, embodies a sacred spirit, or so the people of Rapa Nui had believed. To see some of these distinctive statues, George and I signed up for an all-day tour offered by the ship.

On tour, we saw Ahu Hanga Te'e, the site of some unrestored Mo'ai. Our guide, an archaeologist with a wealth of knowledge, walked us across a grassy field where we stood in awe beneath the figures. He explained that the islanders had moved the Mo'ai from the quarry where they were carved to locations such as this one.

From Ahu Hanga Te'e, we traveled to the quarry, a good distance away, to see where the islanders had gotten the stone. Reminding us of the weight of one Mo'ai, the guide explained that it is still an open question as to how the islanders managed to move the Mo'ai from the quarry to the sites where the figures stand today.

At Ahu Tongariki, perhaps the most impressive of all the Mo'ai sites, we saw and photographed a row of fifteen restored figures, standing side by side. Each was different from the next, some with hat-like stone objects on their heads. Each had a big head out of proportion to its body; the guide explained that these were "living faces" honoring ancestors. Those fifteen Mo'ai, standing shoulder to shoulder, are one of the most magical memories George and I carried away from our world cruise. They were just awesome, we both agreed.

At Anakena, we visited another striking display of restored Mo'ai. These are located near a beach where it is thought that the first people landed in the Easter Islands. In this beautiful location, we ate lunch under a tent set up by a local hotel. I bought a black T-shirt in a souvenir stall there, expensive but worth every penny. It is adorned with embroidered Mo'ai and is a splendid reminder of our day on Easter Island.

After lunch, we changed focus. Our guide took us to a volcano that had blown its top. Today, it is a crater lake that is a mile across and very deep. The waters are a lovely green.

The ride to the crater and eventually back to our ship was exciting. It had begun to rain heavily, and the road was narrow, curvy, and slippery. Driving to the tender pier, we saw private cars on the sides of the road resting in muddy ditches. Our driver knew to slow down, and we got back safely. We figured we had been wise that day to book the ship's tour, although it was considerably more expensive than private tours some friends had booked on the internet. We had had it all: an excellent guide, a fine driver, a good bus, fantastic Mo'ai, and a delicious lunch.

Several days after leaving Easter Island, *Amsterdam* dropped anchor off Pitcairn Island, where Fletcher Christian and his fellow mutineers had settled after they took over the *Bounty* and set Captain Bligh adrift in the Pacific. We passengers could see Pitcairn in the distance, but we were not allowed ashore; there were so many of us that we would have overwhelmed the island. Instead, inhabitants of the island came aboard in the morning with their wares and set up stalls on *Amsterdam's* pool deck. One of the local Pitcairn women who came aboard was said to be a great-granddaughter of Fletcher Christian. Whether that was true we will never know, but everyone snapped her picture, my George included.

The pool area that morning was bedlam. Everybody wanted to buy something, although the only items made locally were the ones carved out of wood. Years later, when George needed a cane, he used the carved wooden one he had bought from a Pitcairn islander. But I doubt whether it was crafted by hand on the island. When we arrived home, we discovered that a neighbor had the identical cane that he, too, had bought on Pitcairn.

Our captain declared the next day "Mutiny on the Bounty Day." The dining room was decorated with a buccaneer theme and most of the staff dressed as pirates for the evening. Even the trivia questions were about pirates. Themed nights such as this were common on sea days during the world cruise.

THE SOUTH PACIFIC: BORA BORA, AMERICAN SAMOA, AND FIJI

Westward we went to Bora Bora. George and I had toured the island on our Asia Pacific Explorer Cruise in 2002. We remembered that Matira Beach on Bora Bora was the best for a morning swim, so that was our destination.

"Remember your hat," I told George before we left our cabin.

"Do you have the suntan lotion?" he asked.

The sun is powerful in the South Seas, and George's balding head could take a beating from the burning rays. I had in hand my sun visor, and we both carried old white T-shirts. We knew that we would be foolish not to wear T-shirts over our bathing suits to protect our shoulders from the sun while we swam.

After tendering to shore, George and I hopped on a vehicle called Le Truck that took us to Matira. We had the beach and the water to ourselves. The water was calm and the lagoon bottom had no sudden dropoffs. The views of the island from there were quintessential

Polynesia. George even took his camera far out with him into the water to videotape the stunning views of Bora Bora he saw as he swam in the lagoon.

On February 7, the *Amsterdam* docked in Pago Pago in American Samoa. George figured out that, since this was America, the American dollar and the English language would work. His plan for our day in Pago Pago was for us to hop on a public bus that circled the island—an inexpensive but different way to sightsee.

I got my dollar bills ready and, once on shore, we boarded a local bus with one other couple from the ship. We did not know exactly where we were headed, but we were glad to be on our way. The bus stopped from time to time, and Samoans climbed on and off. We stayed on, for the driver had told us the bus would make a circle of the island and eventually would get us back to our point of origin. We saw lots of lush scenery, including the Flowerpot Rocks—hillocks in the bay covered with bushes and trees. Our driver pointed out the burial mounds in almost every front yard. The custom in American Samoa is to bury family members right there at home.

At one point, we could tell that we were headed back to Pago Pago, the capital city where we had started. It was almost noon when the driver told us he was going to stop briefly to pick up his daughter from kindergarten. Well, when he stopped, we were ready to go. Off we went to visit a couple of classes, talk to the teachers, and take pictures. It was rush, rush, rush, but we loved every minute.

The other couple from the ship was still on the bus with us. They asked the driver if we could stop for five minutes in a local supermarket. At the market, we hopped off with them. The supermarket looked exactly like the ones at home, with brand-name products we knew. When I mentioned that, George shrugged his shoulders and asked, "Why not? This is the United States of America."

Our tour lasted a good two hours and cost us seven dollars for the pair of us, including the five-dollar tip we gave the bus driver for his daughter. She had talked nonstop to us once she got on the bus. It was the best tour we had taken, or ever would take, around a South Pacific island.

In Fiji, George, I, and our friend Madelyn took a "regular" excursion offered by our travel agency. By boat, we motored up a river to see the countryside and see how Fijians live. This was a real village, not one set up for the tourist trade. We walked the village and witnessed a ritual kava ceremony in which a liquid concoction is made and drunk. Then the three of us headed back to the boat landing. On the way, we got tired and spied some folding chairs in the shade beneath a house that stood on stilts. As we rested there, down the stairs from the floor above came a very, very well-rounded, big man with a carved wooden knife in each hand.

What was this about? It did not take us long to figure out that he had carved the knives himself and wanted us to buy them. They were crude, but we bought one and Madelyn bought the other. Ours hangs on our kitchen wall next to our war club from the Marquesas Islands.

AUSTRALIA: SYDNEY, CAIRNS, AND DARWIN

Onward to Australia! Our entry into Sydney harbor was as gorgeous as George and I had remembered from 2002: The opera house was glistening in the sunshine and the Sydney bridge was ahead. This time, instead of roaming the area around the Opera House, we decided to take an excursion to the Blue Mountains. Our cousins went with us.

Nearing the mountains, we saw blue in the distance, which comes from the reflection of light off particles in the air. Once there, we looked out over the Three Sisters, a distinctive rock formation, and then took the tram down deep into the canyon. The ride was spectacularly scary, for the tram tracks are the steepest in the world. Reaching the bottom, we walked with our guide along a trail through what he described as a warm, temperate rainforest. My personal biologist George explained to me that, although the rainfall is very heavy here, the foliage in a temperate rainforest is not so dense as what we would see soon in the tropical rainforest we were booked to visit near Cairns. The Blue Mountain region is also filled with evergreens and laurels. Of course, the Blue Mountains are located in the temperate zone, not in the tropics.

When we arrived in Cairns, we knew what *not* to do. We remembered

211

the absolutely awful catamaran trip we had taken to the Great Barrier Reef in 2002, when we both had gotten violently seasick. Instead of re-attempting that disaster, George and I, along with Madelyn, John and Patricia, opted to go with our travel-agency group north to a tropical rainforest. Our route was along a coastal road from Cairns to Port Douglas. Although the ride was of the white-knuckle variety, the scenery was striking; George and I agreed that our trek through the rainforest was well worth any discomfort we felt in getting there.

During our walk, we took a break at the Silky Oaks Lodge, in the heart of the forest, to sit on a covered porch and enjoy morning coffee. The porch was open on all sides, so we could look out upon the rainforest to see orchids, ferns, bamboo, and bromeliads all around us. As we enjoyed our coffee, it began to pour, which made the forest around us sparkle because the sun was still shining.

When the rain stopped, our group strolled slowly back to the bus. The sun was shining on us at that moment, literally and figuratively. As we walked, we saw the most amazing thing: startlingly blue butterflies. They were a gorgeous robin's-egg blue like nothing we had ever seen. Patricia took some fantastic butterfly pictures and gave me copies when we got home.

Also on our tour's itinerary that morning was Mossman Gorge. We walked the gorge deep in the rainforest for about a half hour. There were several viewing points that allowed us to look out over the Mossman River rapids. I had been nervous about walking in the forest, fearful of its being muddy and slippery. Fortunately, the paths were paved with a non-slip tar, and there were railings to provide support.

Before returning to Cairns, we made a brief rest stop in the small village of Mossman, which seemed to have more bars than houses. George suggested that imbibing might be a great way to fill time way out there in the rainforest.

That evening, George and I got another taste of the region's culture, this time in *Amsterdam*'s theater. On a world tour, the cruise director has a budget to bring in local entertainers; the performance we viewed that night featured the Tjapukai Aboriginal Cultural Group. The performers danced, drummed, and played the didgeridoo. They also explained that the didgeridoo's hollow inner column is eaten out by termites—a fact that we had never heard before that evening.

A few days later, we sailed into Darwin Harbour, a return visit for us. This time, we stayed in town and hit the shops. We also explored Parliament House and stumbled upon a display of aboriginal art. We discovered that the nice thing about making a return visit was the opportunity to take a relaxed approach to our day. We just sauntered the streets, found a sunny bench to sit on, and picked up two souvenirs—a boomerang and a card with an aboriginal design that we could use as a model in art class.

As George and I walked back to our shuttle stop, a young woman came up to us, followed by a cameraman. She explained that she was from a local television station and was doing a story for the evening news on tourists' impressions of Darwin. She asked us a lot of questions: What did we like about Darwin? What had we bought? How did we like the shopping? We could hardly believe that we had been selected for an interview halfway around the world from New Jersey. We wondered if our interview had ended up on TV. We would never know, for by then we were steaming north toward Indonesia.

INDONESIA: BALI AND SEMARANG

If George and I had been asked to identify the most picture-perfect place in the entire world, we would have named the island of Bali in Indonesia. We remembered Bali from our air-and-land trip of 1974 as a gorgeous spot, but in 2007 we found the island even more striking. At every turn of the road, we encountered an absolutely stunning, picture-postcard image: terraced rice fields stretching up the hillsides; a farmer working his fields with a single-pronged plow powered by a water buffalo; small Hindu temples within the walls of every front yard; a magnificent palace situated on a lake that reflected the beauty of gardens and statuary; an old craft village; walls of colorful, scary masks in shops; a craftsman etching Balinese figures into the slats of a wall hanging.

From World Cruise 2007, George and I came away with another kind of memory of Bali, equally striking and even more touching: hundreds of Indonesian families waiting patiently on the pier to board *Amsterdam* and spend a few hours with the men and women who served as dining and cabin stewards on the ship. In the week before our Bali stop, these wonderful workers had been eagerly counting the days and hours until they would be able to hug their families. Some had not seen their spouses or children in nearly a year, having signed eight-month contracts. Many of the visitors had flown in from other Indonesian islands, making a considerable journey for just these few hours of family love.

During our Asia/Pacific trip in 2002, our ship had been scheduled to stop in Bali. The stop was canceled because a nightclub bombing had occurred just a few days before our anticipated landing. The gloom on the ship then was overpowering. This time, in contrast, our stewards were ecstatic because they were going to see their families. When we returned to the ship after our tour, they brought their loved ones to meet us— their shipboard families. They were so proud to show off their children and spouses. Later that evening, however, our dining steward told us that waving goodbye to his wife had left him heartbroken. He knew he would not hold her close again for months.

The next day, *Amsterdam* docked in Semarang on the Indonesian island of Java, and George and I boarded a bus for a day tour to Borobudur. The bus drove us through beautiful countryside—verdant rice paddies with volcanoes visible off in the distance. We stopped for morning coffee at a restaurant/shop high in the hills, where the vistas were unbelievably wonderful.

It took us two hours to get to the Buddhist temple, the largest in the world and one we had visited in 1974. We had a police escort that bypassed slower traffic, and did we move fast! The bus driver was skilled; he swerved around other vehicles, missing them by inches.

The temple at Borobudur has nine levels. I did not know whether I could get to the top, although I knew that my George, at age eighty-five, could and would do it. Success! I made it to the top, with George giving me a hand as we neared the uppermost level. The views from there are impressive, and the temple itself unbelievable. Its most striking feature is a series of stone bell-like structures, each sheltering a carved Buddha within.

Lunch was at a lovely Javanese resort set in a park-like compound. George and I sat at a table with my cousins. We looked out over green farmlands and far-off volcanic hills. Yes, we were in Indonesia. Yes we were! Cousin John shook his head, hardly believing he was there.

Of course, vendors were waiting for us in the bus parking lot; I could not resist and bought puppets, masks, and two long caftans. That evening at supper, we women saw ourselves coming and going, for we had all bought the same dress; at five dollars for one, why not?

HONG KONG—AGAIN

Three days later, after crossing the South China Sea, *Amsterdam* docked at Ocean Terminal next to the Star Ferry in Hong Kong. During the sail-in, George noted that there were many more skyscrapers on the hills of Hong Kong Island than when we had last visited. Later, as we walked the streets of Kowloon, we both kept remarking about the way the city had changed since our first visit in 1969. Then, it was your quintessential large Chinese village with street vendors selling one hundred-year-old eggs and shoemakers selling their wares on the corner. By 2007, it had become a vast and busy metropolis.

We were familiar with the alleys along Nathan Road and enjoyed roaming the shops that afternoon. Better yet, from the deck of *Amsterdam* in the evening, we watched the skyscrapers of Hong Kong Island light up with changing colors.

On prior visits to Hong Kong, we had heard about the Giant Buddha on Lantau Island. In the past, getting to Lantau required a lengthy trip, first by sampan and then by bus. That would have been too great a struggle. By 2007, however, a bridge had been constructed between Kowloon and Lantau, and there was a cable car that ran up to the Buddha. This we could handle.

The cable car took us six miles up and over the hills to the site of the Buddha. The ride was spectacular—truly spectacular—and from the cable car, we could see the Buddha as we came closer and closer. Once at the site, really a little village surrounding the huge structure, we wandered on our own and stopped for some lunch. The Buddha was at the top of an endless stairway—you might call it a stairway to enlightenment. George walked up to the first landing to take pictures. I just sat in the square and serenely contemplated, my usual approach to being in a magical place.

Stanley Market was our destination the next day. As we had done on a prior visit, George and I caught the Star Ferry to Victoria and then a public bus to the market. As he had done before, George climbed on quickly to get the front seat on the second level—best for picture-taking. By now, both of us were getting used to curvy roads with few guardrails, but this road was still exciting to travel. Arriving at the market, we wandered the shops for "only" three hours before returning to *Amsterdam* with a few bags of purchases.

VIETNAM

When Americans think of Vietnam, they probably conjure images of the Vietnam War. George and I wanted memories of Vietnam that were far different than the ones we still retained from that awful period of history. Ergo, when we arrived in Nha Trang on the South China Sea, we opted for a tour offered by our travel agency, which gave us a glimpse into the way Vietnamese people live. It was a wise choice. We visited a kindergarten in a small village, a bakery that offered us samples of freshly baked rolls, a mat-weaving shop, a rice paper-making establishment, and finally a private home. The home with its altar memorializing the life of a family member who had recently passed away was a genuine residence. We were able to walk through the rooms to see the outside kitchen area and even the bathroom.

We made a stop, too, at a temple complex on a hill overlooking a bay filled with fishing boats. Like the other temples we saw there, it was exquisitely carved out of red sandstone and was replete with human and godly figures. There were lots of stairs, but we managed to get to the top level where we could look down on the bay below.

Back on the pier was an extensive market. In the afternoon, we wandered the stalls. Shopping is part of the fun of most cruises, but it is an integral part of a world cruise that goes to so many ports rich with exotic goods. Here, we bought necklaces, Vietnamese boxes, and lacquerware, as well as some fine blouses that I still wear. In my file, I have a great picture of George and me, back on the ship that evening. We are each wearing a new batik shirt we had bought from a street vendor in Bali and a necklace we had purchased that afternoon in Vietnam.

KUALA LUMPUR AND PENANG, MALAYSIA

I have two photographs in my dining room from our 2007 visit to Kuala Lumpur, the capital of Malaysia. One is of George and me in front of the Petronas Twin Towers and the second is of the two of us relaxing in the lobby of a luxury hotel where we had lunch. These color prints were both taken on our day tour of the city, which made stops at the Royal King's Palace, the old Victorian-styled railway station, a restored Malay timber house, a pewter factory, and, of course, the Petronas Towers.

For sure, George and I never forgot those towers; art deco in style and joined together via a sky bridge, they look like something out of a Disney theme park. At one point, and for just a short time, the Petronas Towers were the tallest buildings in the world.

George and I did not visit any gardens while in Kuala Lumpur. We left that for the following day, when we docked in Penang. Our day there was a biologist's dream: On our schedule were three different kinds of gardens.

First were the Penang Botanic Gardens—a vast park-like area through which we strolled on our own. Leaving this preserve, we went north by bus, passing some rather beautiful scenery along a coastal road. Second was a butterfly garden, a screened enclosure filled with plants and butterflies that hovered over them and us. Some of those fragilely lovely butterflies even came to rest on our fingers, shoulders, and noses. Third was the Tropical Spice Garden, where we saw plants grown to be used as spices, thriving in their natural habitat.

At the spice garden, we had time to browse in the gift shop, where I found something really special—a cane with a small brass tag bearing this engraving:

Sir Jefferey
British
1941
East India
Hillpig-Smyth

The cane is green and brown with a mottled camouflage pattern. It has a slight crack in the handle, perhaps from someone's use of it during World War II, given the 1941 date. The cane unscrews in the middle to fit into a British Army pack. It has gone with us on each cruise since 2007. Because it can be unscrewed to form two pieces, it is a perfect travel cane. I still tuck it in my suitcase on long cruises, and when I do, I remember "The Day of the Three Gardens."

Dorothy and George at the Petronas Twin Towers.

KOCHI, INDIA

Friends often ask what our favorite cruise or trip was among all our world travels. While that seems impossible to answer, I do have some top choices when it comes to specific types of experiences. Here is my list of favorites:

Beach:	Matira, in Bora Bora
African Market:	The Indian Market in Durban
Continent:	Antarctica
Place:	Machu Picchu
Moment:	Waltzing with George at the Temple of Heaven
City:	Hong Kong
Island:	Bali
Country:	China
Shopping City:	Kochi, in the Portuguese section of India

The final item on that list explains why George and I were excited the morning of March 17, 2007, when *Amsterdam* docked in Kochi. Because this was our second time in Kochi/Cochin, we knew exactly what we wanted to do: shop. Told of our plans, John and Patricia decided to join us for our shopping adventure, and we offered to expand our morning itinerary to include a few must-see sightseeing stops for them.

Disembarking in Kochi, the four of us headed to the line of tuk tuks next to the pier. We went to the head of the line and negotiated with the first two drivers for a shopping trip to the area near the synagogue, where we knew there were lots of shops. We included in our negotiations stops at St. Francis Church and the famed giant fishing nets. We made a deal for a three-hour trip; each tuk tuk was to cost ten dollars, although we actually planned to give each driver fifteen. Deal made, we hopped into our tuk tuks and off we went.

Or so we thought. On the other side of the port gate and around the corner, our tuk tuks came to an abrupt halt. Both drivers got out and approached John. Because he was the big guy, they assumed he was our leader. They tried to renegotiate for an entire day's tour of the old and new cities that would cost much more. Big John was intimidated; he had never encountered this way of doing business. Pointing at me, John said, "No. No. Talk to her."

The drivers came to work on me. I put on my sternest schoolteacher face and shook my head, saying, "No way. Take us back to the pier. We were here last year and know exactly what we want to do and how long it should take." We all just sat tight.

Having given it their best try, the drivers agreed to our original terms, and off we went again. We had a productive morning. We stepped briefly into the old synagogue and then began hitting the shops. In a massive souvenir emporium, we found a gorgeous (and heavy) black wood elephant encrusted with red and blue pieces of glass. Sold. We watched carefully as Mr. Elephant was wrapped up, to make sure that the carved elephant we took home was the one we had picked out. He was expensive, close to fifty dollars even after bargaining, but George wanted him.

Down the street, I saw a lightweight, black wool jacket embroidered with fine pink and green flowers. It was hanging just outside one of the stores. I tried it on. It fit. Sold. We walked into one shop after another. I bought a few cheaper shirts for me and George. Patricia and John were finding treasures, too. Our tuk tuk drivers stayed on the corner waiting to take us to see the church and the fishing nets. We knew never to pay until the end. That way we were certain that our driver would not leave with our money in his pocket and search for another fare.

We still had time, so we stopped to walk into St. Francis Church and then out onto the wharf where the fishermen were working their nets. George and I had "been there, done that" two years before, but we still appreciated the revisit. Also right on the fishing wharf were more vendors. We bought a few of those small soft elephants that dangle about five to a string; we had bought some on our prior visit but had not seen them for sale again, even in Mumbai. John and Patricia bought a few as well, for they make great gifts.

It was time to go back to the ship for lunch, so we climbed into our tuk tuks for the exciting drive back. A return tuk tuk ride is always exciting, for drivers want to get back to the pier to pick up another set of tourists. They go fast! Once there, we paid our drivers, adding a good tip. Big John offered to carry Mr. Elephant back to our cabin; he could see it was far too heavy for George to handle with ease.

That afternoon, George and I rested. It takes energy to shop and negotiate. Patricia, however, headed back out. She had learned how to negotiate for a tuk tuk and bargain in the shops. She spent the entire afternoon at work, returning late with bags full of purchases. She had bought one blouse that I loved. I told George I would buy one like it the following year. And I did!

MUMBAI, INDIA

When we docked two days later in Mumbai, a full brass band—traditionally attired in red jackets with gold-braid trim—welcomed us. The band was playing Sousa marches. This was a big contrast to our welcome in Kochi, where three ornately "dressed" elephants were on the pier with a group of male dancers and drummers.

Our destination the first morning was Elephanta Island, which lies just beyond the harbor and is the site of a series of temples carved into rock cliffs. Our tour bus dropped us off at the majestic Gateway of India, where we boarded a small boat to take us to Elephanta. Once on the island and at the base of the temples that are high up in the cliffs, we hopped into sedan chairs to be carried on poles by four husky men to the temples at the top. The temple walls are finely cut with images that tell religious stories; our guide walked us from place to place and explained the meaning of the carvings. It is an amazing area to explore because it's a reminder of what the human mind can conceive and the stories the mind can create.

We walked down the steps from the temples; we could handle that. I would have had trouble climbing up, however, for it was a considerable distance.

On our second day in Mumbai, George and I walked out through the green pier gate into a mass of taxi drivers. It was a frenetic scene with lots of noise and activity. We bargained with a driver, who spoke good English, for a three-hour visit to shops and some riding around the area to see the sights. Before we had driven far, the driver stopped and tried to pull a switch. He wanted us to move to another taxi that was there on the side of the road. Supposedly, the driver was his brother.

George and I refused to budge from our taxi. Finally, the driver gave up. George figured that "the brother" probably could not speak English very well and would have had trouble getting riders on his own. In a way, this was very much like the switch that the tuk tuk drivers had tried to pull on us in Kochi.

Coincidentally, when we asked our driver to take us to a shop that sold moderately priced blouses and shirts, he took us to the same second-floor store in the same seedy neighborhood we had visited in 2005. He also took us to Fashion Street, where we wandered from stall to stall, looking at the merchandise, buying a few shirts and blouses, and taking in the lively street scene. When we got tired, Jimmy—we were now on a first-name basis—drove us past some of the stately old Victorian-style buildings on the main avenue that date from the time when India was part of the British Empire. Before hopping out of the taxi at the pier, we made a date with Jimmy to return that evening to take us and our cousins on a night tour of Mumbai. At 7:30, the four of us went out to the Green Gate. Jimmy popped up out of the darkness and waved to us so that none of the other drivers could steal his customers.

Driving in Mumbai is an adventure in survival, but Jimmy knew how to do it. He drove us back to the Gateway of India, where we briefly walked around and took pictures of the monument illuminated with spotlights. Then he drove us along Marine Drive, which was glittering with lights—lights that were reflected in the waters of the bay. Again, we climbed out to walk and take pictures. Jimmy took us high up to a lookout spot above the city; the view down was spectacular. We would have been leery of venturing so far in the dark with someone we did not know, but by then we knew our driver and felt comfortable. On the way back to the pier, Jimmy took us past the Hanging Gardens, a number of impressive temples, and Gandhi's house, providing a running commentary about what we were seeing.

We were back at the pier by 9:30. The four of us felt we had had quite an adventure. John and Patricia hired Jimmy to return the next morning to take them to the outside laundry and some shops.

The next day, George and I just walked the pier, where shops had been set up. I spotted a lovely carved table that, when collapsed, would fit into a suitcase. It would make a unique end table. Actually, it was not for sale; a vendor was using it as his desk. Nevertheless, that carved table stands in our living room today.

Of course, I bargained for the table. At supper that night, Patricia admitted she had failed to bargain for a linen dinner jacket that John had bought that morning. I remember her slapping her head and saying, "I can't believe I forgot. We paid too much." Jimmy must have been happy though; he doubtlessly earned a nice tip from the shopkeeper for bringing in a customer who paid full price. But in the end, John and Patricia got something special in return. Jimmy had taken them to see his home and meet his wife.

EXOTIC DUBAI, UNITED ARAB EMIRATES

If someone had told George and me a few years earlier that we would sail the Arabian Sea, the Gulf of Oman, the Strait of Hormuz, and the Persian Gulf more than once in our lifetimes, we would have said, "Impossible." But here we were doing just that and our destination again was Dubai, one of the seven United Arab Emirates. Since this was a repeat visit for George and me, we journeyed out of the city and into the desert on the first day of our stay.

The stops we made on our desert trip were unique. We went to an archaeological site dating back to 2500 BCE. That is the same time period when the Great Pyramid of Giza was constructed.

We walked through a souk in bordering Oman that was not intended for tourists but for locals—a market so unbelievably exotic that we felt we had taken a trip back in time. We also sat down in an oasis that Omanis still use for relief from extreme desert heat.

We visited a museum associated with the royal family of Dubai, as well as a royal palace. The palace was different from those in the west. It had numerous compounds, because the last ruler who had called it home had had four wives and eighteen sons. The guide did not say how many daughters. He probably thought that the number of girls was too unimportant to mention.

A camel market was another unusual stop on our way back. We saw camels in numbered cages, waiting to be sold. They were dromedary camels (or Arabian camels as they are sometimes called); all were tall and had one hump. Every once in a while, one would open its mouth and yawn in our faces. I guess camels get bored waiting around. On our way back, too, we stopped to walk across the sand dunes, which took on a reddish glow in the late-afternoon sunshine.

Our first day in Dubai had been a double *wow* day. I do not know enough adjectives to describe how we felt as we climbed the *Amsterdam* gangway that afternoon.

The next day, George and I hopped into a cab for the short ride to the gold souk. We had been there in 2005, but we wanted to return to take a boat ride across the creek that is near the spice market. From the other side, we could grab a cab back to the ship. Even though we had walked most of the route in 2005, we enjoyed the Middle Eastern feel of the souk. Best of all, our self-guided excursion was inexpensive—ten dollars for two rides in cabs and one on a boat. But, of course, the cost was a bit more, given that we bought a gold ring for George, a couple of pashmina scarves for me, and a couple of canes for our growing collection.

ALEXANDRIA, EGYPT

After a day in Salalah in Oman and a day in Sharm el Sheikh in Egypt, *Amsterdam* transited the Suez Canal. She then cruised into the Mediterranean Sea and made landfall in Alexandria, Egypt. Again, this was a repeat visit for George and me. On our prior visit, however, I had not been well, so we did not get to see very much. This time, George and I wanted to tour the major sites. We decided that our best option was to hook up with another couple and bargain with a taxi driver for a three-hour excursion. We bargained in American dollars.

We asked our driver to stop first at a bank so we could convert our dollars into Egyptian pounds to use for entrance fees. Across from the bank was Abu al-Abbas al-Mursi Mosque, the oldest and most important mosque in Alexandria, according to Brian and Louise with whom we toured that day. Our driver told us that we could go in if we took our shoes off. We women would have to cover our heads and enter by the back door while the men went in the front. No way were we women going to separate from our men. We simply took off our shoes at the front entrance, donned head scarves, and followed the men in. No one stopped us, so we were glad we had insisted. The dome of the mosque was beautiful, with delicately painted, golden floral and geometric designs. Because it was early morning, we were the only ones in the mosque, so we could enjoy the quiet.

Alexandria is known for its catacombs. The four of us walked together down a winding stone staircase into the caverns that hold the bones of previous generations of Egyptians. To say the least, it was an eerie and different place to be. Alexandria is also the site of the only remains of a Roman amphitheater in Egypt. We were able to walk through the ruins and then view Pompey's Pillar from afar.

The library of Alexandria is well known both for its collection of documents and its architectural style. George and I explored the outside, where we could study the design of the building, while our friends went in. We found we had made what for us was a good choice, because groups of schoolchildren were gathered in the square. With the permission of their teacher, we were able to photograph them as they waited to enter the library.

Before returning to the ship, we drove along the corniche by the sea and stopped at the point of land where the great lighthouse of Alexandria, one of the Seven Wonders of the Ancient World, once stood. From there we could look out across the Mediterranean Sea.

We also stopped at the market on the pier, our shopping destination for the day. That night when I dressed for supper, I put on my new necklace made from carved camel bone. George had bought it for me at the pier market that morning.

ASHDOD AND HAIFA, ISRAEL

Finally the day had arrived when we would be in Bethlehem and Jerusalem. Very early, George and I were up and on a bus heading from the port of Ashdod to Bethlehem, the town where the Bible tells us that Jesus was born.

The long drive to Bethlehem was an eye-opener. We expected to see mile after mile of desert. Instead we saw "a land of milk and honey." With the assistance of intensive irrigation, the Israelis have turned arid lands into productive and green agricultural areas. The guide pointed out the new Israeli settlements up on the hills, which were more extensive than we had anticipated. From a distance, they looked like high-rise apartment complexes with no charm at all.

Nearing Bethlehem, we saw the monstrosity of a wall created to separate the Jewish section of the country from the Palestinian. Before the bus could go into Bethlehem, which is in the Palestinian section, our Israeli guide hopped off and a Christian guide got on. The Israeli was not allowed to go through the checkpoint in the wall and enter Bethlehem. How sad it is that there are walls dividing people.

Arriving in Bethlehem, our tour group walked to the plaza in front of the Church of the Nativity. George and I stood quietly together, away from where the guide was reciting his facts. Facts were not so important as the realization that the birth that occurred here and the life of one man had had such a powerful impact on the history of the world.

The church was crowded with pilgrims from all over the world because this was Holy Thursday. We walked through the sanctuary and saw the display showing the original level of the church. We did not attempt to go down the stone stairway to the lower level where Mary is said to have given birth in a manger that once was located there. The stairway was packed with people standing shoulder to shoulder on the steep, uneven steps. To go down was too dangerous at our ages; if one person were to fall, others would go down, domino-style. Instead, we sat in a pew and drank in the beauty of the sacred space, especially the beauty of the lamps hanging from on high and casting a warm glow over us.

From Bethlehem, we drove to Jerusalem. In the city, we stopped to walk through the Church of All Nations, the Gardens of Gethsemane and the Mount of Olives. We walked from the gardens to a viewing platform. From there we could look down on the Dome of the Rock. That view of the golden dome sparkling in the sunshine is probably my most striking memory of our entire day.

The bus took us down to the old city. We walked through the gates and along lanes within the walls to see the Jewish, Arab, and Christian sections. We passed markers showing the Stations of the Cross. We stood at the Wailing Wall where hundreds of people were gathered. This was a holy time for Jews and Christians alike, so hundreds of people had come to pray.

Our guide took us to a display that showed the successive layers of the city from past periods and walked us through lanes lined with souvenir shops. When it was time to climb back on our bus, the guide apologized; the coach had not been able to park close to the old city. Instead, it was parked way up on Gethsemane—a two-mile hike for us. Needless to say, George and I were really tired when we climbed off the bus that evening.

The next day we docked in Haifa. We had chosen a morning excursion to Acre, an old walled city with buildings dating from Crusader days. In Acre, we visited the mosque, the old baths, the tunnel the Crusaders had built as an escape route, and the old walled Arab section. We walked on the walls to look down on the sea and finally "escaped" through the Crusaders' tunnel.

I have a distinctively personal memory from our walk along the lanes of Acre. As our tour group walked through one large plaza, I spied a tall crook cane. It was the kind often pictured in nativity scenes, carried by the shepherds as they came in from the fields where they were tending their sheep. I called out, "How much?" The vendor said, "Three dollars." I responded with "One dollar." The vendor turned away in disgust. I had insulted him with an offer that was too low.

Reaching Haifa, the bus drove us to the top of Mount Carmel. From the heights, we could look down on the lovely Baha'i Temple and Gardens as well as on the city and sea far below. Some in our group— our cousins among them—walked down through the gardens and back to the ship. I was too tired, so we climbed on the bus to ride to the pier.

DUBROVNIK, CROATIA

Leaving Haifa late in the evening—the Baha'i Temple and Gardens on the hillside ablaze with lights—*Amsterdam* headed to Kusadasi in Turkey, to Piraeus, which is the port for Athens, and then to Dubrovnik on the Adriatic Sea. On every world cruise, Holland America Line organizes a special event for its guests. Dubrovnik was the scene of that event during our 2007 world cruise.

In Dubrovnik, *Amsterdam* docked at the stern of the cruise line's *ms Prinsendam*, the ship on which we had sailed to West and South Africa just a few months before. It was the first time that Holland America Line had two of its ships prow to stern in a harbor, with each ship in the midst of a grand voyage. On our arrival in the early morning, George and I walked off *Amsterdam* and onto *Prinsendam*. We went up to the Lido restaurant to have coffee with Eloise and Dom, Kean University alums whom we had met while we were on *Prinsendam* in the fall and who were again sailing on that ship. We were so excited to be together.

Then we headed off via shuttle bus to revisit Dubrovnik. George and I just roamed the city and walked its walls, which we had done before but which is always fun.

In the afternoon, we gathered on the lido deck of *Amsterdam* with passengers from both ships to enjoy the festivities associated with the cruise line's special event. The deck was decorated with flags and balloons. Wandering minstrels, mimes, men on stilts, and puppeteers entertained. Booths were set up where passengers could play games and win prizes. The orchestras from both ships were playing. Food and drink were plentiful. Later we went to the showroom to hear Holland America's CEO, Stein Kruse, talk about future developments and changes occurring at the company. The future looked so rosy then for the cruise industry. Later, with COVID-19, so much changed.

CIVITAVECCHIA, ITALY

Late on the evening of our day in Dubrovnik, *Amsterdam* sailed into the Adriatic and through the Strait of Messina to dock in Civitavecchia, the port for Rome. On a Mediterranean cruise we had taken in the past, we had ridden the bus into Rome. We had walked through St. Peter's Basilica and stood reverently before Michelangelo's *Pieta*. We had entered the Sistine Chapel and looked up at the magnificent ceiling. We had wandered the Colosseum and the area of the old Roman Forum. I actually have a photo of us in the Colosseum listening intently to our guide.

So having visited Rome and having wonderful memories of the city and even a photograph of us there, George and I chose to go instead to the Etruscan hill towns. Our bus took us past fields of wheat and vegetables, since this is a farming region. We saw several towns up on the hillsides. Eventually our bus climbed up and drove through two lovely villages. We had the opportunity to walk about in one, Tuscania. We explored on our own, taking photos of the lanes and houses.

Back on the bus, we traveled to a farm in Canino. This farm specializes in olive and olive oil production. It has a great location with wonderful views in every direction. George and I and John and Patricia sat together on the verandah of the farmhouse and lunched on cheese, ham, fresh tomatoes, and toast with olive oil. We rated this an A+ morning.

LIVORNO, MONTE CARLO, FUNCHAL, AND PONTA DELGADA

It was day eighty-nine of our voyage. If someone had asked how many days we had been cruising, I probably would have guessed fifty. Time goes quickly when days are packed with such a variety of things to do. On April 14, we stopped in Livorno, the port for Pisa and Florence. Having been there before, we chose just to walk the avenues of this old Italian city. The thing that I remember was how affluent the people looked and how expensive the goods in the shops were. Of course, we had been spoiled by prices in the Far East.

The next day was a Sunday and we were in Monte Carlo, where we had been in 2005. Nevertheless, we took the escalators and elevators up to the rocky promontory upon which the Cathedral of Monaco and the Prince's Palace sit. Lady Luck was with us: We were able to slip into the cathedral toward the very end of Sunday Mass, and we were able to hear the mighty organ and a hymn by the choir. We even were able to walk behind the altar at the end of the service to pass the tomb of Prince Rainier III, who had died about two years before.

When we returned to the ship, rumors were rampant: *Amsterdam* might skip our projected stop in Casablanca. There had been a bombing in this Moroccan city and threats to cruise liners. The captain came onto the public address system in the late afternoon to confirm the rumor. He announced that, in lieu of Casablanca, he would take us to the Azores on our way home. He added that we were now on our way to Funchal in Madeira, the next port of call on our original itinerary.

Imagine sitting in a wicker sled and speeding down regular roads cut by cross streets, the sled held back only by two men who guided it with ropes they held in their hands. On several prior visits to Funchal, George and I had considered doing the sleigh ride. In 2007, we decided that the ride would be a fantastic finale to our world cruise.

Our excursion started with a cable car ride to the top of the mountain that overlooks Funchal. The views from the cable car to the town and ocean below were gorgeous. At the top, we transferred to a sleigh. Exciting is too tame a word for the ride. I screamed the entire way down, and especially loudly at the cross streets. George just hung tightly onto me in an unsuccessful attempt to make me feel safe.

Several days later, we were in the Azores. Because George and I had been to Ponta Delgada before, we remembered the town very well. We remembered the sidewalks paved with black and white stones to form mosaic patterns similar to those in Lisbon. We remembered, too, the church on the main square that is adorned with blue-and-white tiles. The hand-painted tiles are exceptional, really outstanding for a small church in a small town on a small island in the Atlantic Ocean.

HOME

That afternoon, I began to pack. We had five days until we would reach New York City. We had brought several fully packed suitcases with us when we had boarded in Fort Lauderdale one hundred days before. We had shopped steadily during those hundred-plus days, and Holland America had given us gifts each formal night. Fortunately, one of those gifts was a large blue duffle bag. We each received one, and Madelyn had given us hers. I felt better when I got most of our treasures stowed in our duffle bags.

During the last few days of the cruise, we did a lot of partying. We lunched with some new friends and had dinner with others. We exchanged email addresses and telephone numbers. We promised one another we would keep in contact. Much of the conversation on those final days at sea was about how fortunate we were to have made this world voyage.

Better yet, on the morning of the penultimate day, George said, "Let's do this again! Let's book World 2008." I quickly ran down to reserve a cabin for us. This time, George said he wanted a verandah cabin. Our large inside stateroom had been good, but wouldn't it be fun to sit on our own verandah and look out upon the oceans of the world as we crossed them? Yes, emphatically yes! Already, in my head, I was planning for and dreaming about next year.

On Friday, April 17, after an early morning sail-in, we disembarked in New York City. The Statue of Liberty, her torch held high, welcomed us home.

Chapter Seventeen
SAILING THE WORLD
2008

A friend who loves to travel recently told me that a trip has three capital A phases. First is the Anticipation Phase, during which travelers look to the future and dream dreams of what they will see and do. Anticipation can involve reading about places to be visited, surfing websites that describe tours, and studying brochures from both the travel agency and the cruise company that tell about excursions they offer.

Most importantly, world travelers have to be sure their passports will be valid for six months after the projected return date and have enough blank pages for all the entry permits to be stamped into them. Travelers may also have to secure visas for countries that require them. George and I found that it was rather easy to go to our local post office to renew our passports. We usually paid a company recommended by our travel agency to secure the necessary visas.

Second is the Actual Phase—the traveling, the doing, the seeing, the listening, the recording, the videotaping, and the exploring.

Third is the Afterward Phase. Returning home, travelers recall events— the magical moments of their trip. For me, this often happens when I walk through our house and look at things we bought while traveling. It also happens when I don a blouse or necklace or scarf bought on a trip. Memories of a voyage sometimes pop up out of nowhere, triggered by something that someone is saying or that I am seeing.

The Anticipation Phase for our 2008 world cruise began almost immediately after George and I returned from World '07. We received a description of tours our travel agency was offering and saw an overland trip to Angkor Wat in Cambodia. We decided that World '08 was the time to do that; a rigorous excursion, we had to take it while we were able to walk long distances. We also looked into tours in ports we had not visited before and ones in some of our favorite stops from the past.

ACROSS THE WIDE PACIFIC

When George and I booked World '08, we viewed the first three weeks of the 113-day cruise as an escape from the cold of winter. When we left New Jersey on January 3, 2008, snow was falling; when we arrived in Fort Lauderdale, Florida, our embarkation port, the sun was shining. For the next twenty-one days after we boarded *Amsterdam*, we sailed warm Caribbean waters, navigated the locks of the Panama Canal, and enjoyed repeat visits to balmy and beautiful Polynesian islands like the Marquesas, Tahiti, Moorea, and Bora Bora. During these vacation days, we often sat on our verandah and watched the sea and the sky. Our friend James Smith, whom we met on World '08, wrote a serial haiku based on our Pacific days. Each stanza is a three-line haiku and adheres to a five/seven/five syllable pattern. I quote it with his permission:

> wavy white foamed wake
> stretching out in zigzag course
> trails behind the ship
>
> undulating waves
> cradled rocking to and fro
> white caps foaming breath
>
> flashing silver streak
> skimming ocean's surface swells
> flying fish at play

Watching the wake and the waves, watching for flying fish, even watching the stars at night—those are the peaceful aspects of days on the Pacific.

On those first twenty-one days, we reconnected with old friends and made new ones. In port, we strolled streets and markets that we had walked before. We swam in warm lagoons and in the pool aboard the ship. These weeks were a true vacation.

THE ISLANDS: SAMOA AND TONGA

On the morning of January 25, *Amsterdam* steamed into Apia, the capital of Samoa. The skies were overcast and the streets were wet from a recent downpour. George and I had booked a tour—a drive into the countryside with a visit to the house where Robert Louis Stevenson had lived in retirement and where he had died.

In Apia, our buses were primitive, wooden vehicles with hard benches and plastic windows that we could open in lieu of air-conditioning. From time to time during the morning, it rained, but fortuitously, whenever we climbed off the bus, the weather cleared. Actually, things worked out rather well.

The Stevenson house proved to be a lovely home with wraparound porches overlooking expansive lawns. We walked through the rooms to view the living space and furnishings. What an interesting idea, we thought, a retirement retreat in the South Pacific. Toward the end of our visit, we settled down to watch a Samoan dance production.

On the way back to our ship, the bus made three stops: at the local market, at a beach for a short walk, and in the countryside for picture-taking. We were functioning on "island time," so there was no rush, no hustle, but also no standing around and waiting.

Our day in Tonga was a stark contrast. A friend who does not cruise once asked us, "Did you ever have a really bad day on a cruise?" Of course we did—our day in Nuku'alofa, Tonga, being one. Here is my blow-by-blow account of our hurry-up-and-wait, horribly awful, bad day.

Amsterdam was supposed to dock. The seas were rough, so we tendered instead. Tendering was no fun: We had to wait in the crowded lounge at least an hour before the boats were ready to load, and as a result, all tours started late.

To get us to our first stop by the ocean, our bus driver took us down a one-way, muddy lane. From there, we walked through the mud to look out over the coastline: Because of the rough surf, the view down to the sea was something to behold. Our Tongan guide had given us fifteen minutes for the round-trip walk, so everyone in our group rushed and arrived back on time. But about ten vehicles had followed us down that one-way lane and walled our bus in, so we sat and waited, and waited, and waited. We waited until all the people on all the buses that had parked behind us had walked to the ocean and returned to their coaches. Unbelievable!

Then came the fun. Imagine about ten vehicles, each in turn trying to back out of a narrow lane deep with mud that the buses were churning up. It was hot. It was humid. And we waited some more while the buses maneuvered.

I have to admit that there was something good about the day: We stopped to see blowholes—places along the coast where the ocean crashes onto strangely shaped rocks that are interlaced with cracks. The sea runs beneath to gush skyward through the cracks. A dramatic scene!

At our next stop at a lovely beach, our Tongan guide again gave us fifteen minutes. Getting back on time to the assigned pickup point, we waited, and we waited, and we waited some more. This time we stood by the side of the road to wait because there was no place to sit.

I hate bats. Our final stop was to see flying foxes, the nice name for bats. There were hundreds of them hanging from the branches of trees under which our bus dropped us off. Needless to say, I stayed on the bus.

On our return to the ship, we passed the Royal Palace. Yes, this is a kingdom; there is a king, who obviously does not have an office of tourism to prevent fiascos of the type we experienced.

THE NORTH AND SOUTH ISLANDS OF NEW ZEALAND

The feature that attracted us to World '08 was the itinerary with stops in four major New Zealand cities—Auckland and Wellington on the North Island, Christchurch and Dunedin on the South Island. The *piece de resistance* was Fiordland National Park.

We had a superb sail-in to Auckland harbor—a repeat for us, since we had stopped here once before. This time our entry was even better. We were blessed with blue sky and bright sunshine, and the harbor was filled with sailboats—as it should be, given that Auckland is known as The City of Sails. The title of our tour that day was "Coast to Coast," because the excursion made stops on both the east and west coasts of the North Island.

On "Coast to Coast," we stopped at a family farm where we had morning tea and were entertained by the owner, who sheared a sheep for us. Then he demonstrated how New Zealanders use border collies to herd their rams and ewes. The entire family—including the grandchildren and grandparents—welcomed us.

We drove from the coast, where the farm was located, across verdant farmlands to the opposite side of the North Island. Once there, we climbed to a vantage point overlooking the Pacific Ocean where gannet birds roost. The views continued to be picture-perfect.

We had expected New Zealand to be beautiful. That day it exceeded our expectations. Our coach was an air-conditioned Mercedes that practically floated, and our guide knew his material. This tour was exactly right for us: I appreciated the farm visit with morning tea, and George the gannet colony.

Both of us enjoyed our day in Wellington, New Zealand's capital city, even more. There, Holland America gave all the passengers who had booked a verandah cabin a complimentary excursion: HAL loaded about 300 of us onto buses for a comprehensive city tour. We passed the parliament building, what New Zealanders call "The Beehive," and stopped at an old wooden church—a delightfully quaint structure with exposed wooden rafters from which flags and colorful banners had been strung. The small church was a quiet haven within a city filled with busy people. The bus then drove us along the seaside and climbed up Mount Victoria to provide us with a bird's-eye view of Wellington. "Ah, what a beautiful city!" I exclaimed, as we stood on the heights and looked down.

My dear husband and travelling companion nodded in agreement. "Awesome," he replied.

Lunch was at the town hall where, with much pomp and ceremony, we were served an elaborate meal. The mayor of Wellington welcomed us to her country and city; then she introduced a representative from the HAL Seattle home office, who had come all that way to greet us and distribute gift bags containing red-and-black scarves made from New Zealand possum. Between courses, we were entertained, first by Maori folk dancers and then by New Zealand farmers. The farmers demonstrated sheep shearing, cow milking, and the herding of ducks by dogs. On the stage of the town hall (all at one time!) were sheep, cows, dogs, ducks, and farmers. We all agreed that Holland America Line had outdone itself that day.

The weather did not treat us quite so well in Christchurch. Up by 5:30 a.m. the next day, we were off the ship by seven, everyone carrying an umbrella. Our tour was with our travel agency and escorted by Tom, whom we knew very well by then. That morning we took the Christchurch railway train, called The TranzAlpine, up into the Southern Alps of New Zealand. The train carried us across the lowlands before it began its ascent up to Arthur's Pass. Unfortunately, the good weather of our two prior New Zealand stops had deserted us; the tops of the tallest mountains were hidden in the clouds.

Once we were high up in the mountains, we transferred to coaches for the return trip. Somewhere in the hills, we stopped for lunch under a tent; we guessed that the tent had been set up just for us because no restaurant was large enough to accommodate our group. Once in Christchurch, the bus took us along the major avenues so we could see the main sites as well as the Avon River that flows gently through the city.

Two full-day tours back-to-back: We had said we would never do that, but we did. Both of us were exhausted but happy by the time we returned to the ship. We managed to go to the dining room for supper, but afterward, it was off to bed.

I remember waking up the next morning in Dunedin to see the sun shining. After our train ride in the rain the previous day, the sun was a very welcome sight. That day we had a scheduled visit to the Settlers Museum in downtown Dunedin, where we walked through a full-scale replica of the kind of sailing ship that brought Scottish settlers to New Zealand. It was so little that neither of us could conceive of spending months aboard a ship that small. We made stops to photograph Robert Burns' statue and First Church before we headed out onto Otago Peninsula.

Before this, we had taken many tours to view scenery. Sometimes one blended with the next in our minds, but I clearly recall our drive via the high road along the hills overlooking the bay. The scenery was gorgeous, truly gorgeous. I recall, too, the lovely little inn and the gardens where we stopped for morning tea, scones, jam, and clotted cream—delicious, truly delicious. This being an area settled by the Scots, a group of bagpipers performed during tea. Their show was in sharp contrast to the entertainment in Wellington that harkened back to the Maori origins and the farm-based economy of New Zealand.

We followed the low road back to Dunedin as in the Robbie Burns song, "Oh, ye'll take the high road, and I'll take the low road, And I'll be in Scotland afore ye . . ." In our hearts, we thanked friends who had urged us to see New Zealand. The country is as welcoming and wonderful as they had promised us.

NEW ZEALAND'S FIORDLAND NATIONAL PARK

The port lecturer on board *Amsterdam* had explained that Fiordland National Park—on the southwestern coast of New Zealand—receives hundreds of inches of rain each year; we were exceedingly happy, therefore, to see the sun as we began our sail through Fiordland. George and I breakfasted in our cabin with the drapes open as we sailed through Dusky Sound and around Resolution Island. We passed low-lying mountains covered with green; we passed islands practically at our fingertips. We could look back to see our winding wake, the result of our turning into the sound from the Tasman Sea.

I am wearing my passport mask from West Africa as a necklace and earrings from Costa Rica.

At mid-morning, we entered Doubtful Sound. It had warmed up by then, so George and I sat on our verandah to watch the passing scenery—stunning scenery that had been carved out by glaciers during the Ice Age. We now saw snow on the mountain peaks, which were much higher than the peaks we had seen in Dusky Sound. Each moment, the "picture" in front of us got more spectacular. I kept saying to George, "Look! Look!" Travel can't get much better than this. We were so close to the rock cliffs on our port side that they seemed to be right there. Ah, and the waterfalls—heavenly!

George was videotaping almost nonstop; with my little camera, he also took some pictures of me standing near the rail with the mountains behind me. In one, I was wearing my brand-new, red-and-black possum scarf. I think of our ride through New Zealand's Fiordland each time I wear that warm scarf on cold New Jersey evenings.

Leaving Doubtful Sound, we spent a couple of hours in the Tasman Sea before turning in to Milford Sound in the afternoon. Milford Sound has steeper walls cut into the granite—granite that sparkles with the quartzite it contains. Milford is even more spectacular than Doubtful

239

and Dusky. Again we sat on our verandah to watch our progress up the channel and then back down to the sea. The port lecturer delivered a running commentary that was broadcast over our television set, so we could listen as we watched in comfort.

Our friend Jim Smith composed a haiku to memorialize our passage through this phenomenal national park. He gave me permission to quote it:

> glacial, granite cliffs
> weather beaten waterfalls
> inaccessible

The evening was perfect, too. Given the fantastic day we had all enjoyed in Fiordland and given that we had completed the New Zealand segment of our world voyage, conversation at dinner that night flowed easily. Our tablemates had done different things in each of the ports, and they were eager to share their experiences and impressions.

The water was like glass as we headed out over the Tasman Sea toward Australia. As the sun dropped into the sea, George took a picture of the sunset from our verandah. I took a picture of him taking a picture of the sunset.

AUSTRALIA

World '08 took us to three ports in Australia: Sydney, Melbourne, and Fremantle. It was our stop in Melbourne that stood out for both of us. My in-house biologist wanted to see Australian animals in their natural habitat, so we opted for a bus tour to two animal sanctuaries. The first was a forty-five-minute bus ride from Melbourne. The coach drove us across flat, dry plains before we arrived at the park. The protocol for our visit was to drive around and then clamber off quickly when the guide spotted kangaroos, wallabies, and/or emus. We saw mobs of kangaroos that were grazing and hopping and bounding across the road. We had to walk into an enclosure to see the wallabies. The emus just sauntered along beside us when we got out to view the billabong, a watering hole where magpie geese were roosting.

Following Jim's lead, I wrote a haiku in the three-line, five/seven/five syllable pattern, no punctuation necessary:

> emus kangaroos
> wallabies perform for us
> hopping 'cross our path

The bus dropped us off at a picnic spot where we enjoyed morning refreshments: tea, coffee, pastries, and cookies. Amazingly, parked close by was a catering truck. Our morning coffee break was catered.

After our coffee stop, the bus drove to a second state park, this one the home of koalas. We had anticipated seeing lots of koalas, but it was not like that at all. A couple of young rangers had been tramping the park in search of koalas to show us, because the animals are rare and hard to spot. We followed the two women rangers into the bush and looked up when they pointed. There in eucalyptus trees were koalas curled up into tight balls, but it was almost impossible to see their faces. The rangers explained that this is the way these animals live in the wild.

> curled up in tight balls
> koalas cling to branches
> shy Aussies alone

We did not have a chance to sightsee in Melbourne. As George said, "We'll do that next year." My eyes lit up. He had already decided we would do World '09, with Melbourne again on the itinerary. He had been thrilled with our trip to the animal sanctuaries. He had loved the emus, kangaroos, wallabies, and koalas. Australia was calling—calling to him to come back.

BALI, INDONESIA, AGAIN!

Breakfasting at home on a morning in October 2020 and knowing that day I would travel virtually to Bali in Indonesia, I looked up at the wall above my kitchen table and saw three dragon faces glaring down at me. On World '07, George and I had bought these three ugly pieces of art in Tenganan, an old walled village in Bali. Two are colorful reproductions; one is a more valuable, old, faded piece. Ugly as they are, I love to look up and share breakfast time with them.

We returned to Tenganan when World '08 made a one-day stop in Bali. Again we walked the main lane between two parallel rows of houses that form the central part of the village. We stopped to watch craftsmen etching storyboards that tell old Balinese tales through a series of pictures on the front side. On the back are the stories written in Bahasa, the language of Indonesia. We also talked to a vendor we recognized from 2007 and purchased a wall hanging similar to one we had bought before; now we would have a pair.

George took pictures of cows sleeping peacefully in the lane, of chickens and dogs roaming freely, and of two men carrying a live pig in an elongated straw basket. Tired, we paused to sit on a wall to watch the Balinese go about their daily lives. Our 2008 visit surpassed in pleasure our visit in 2007. We were less pressed for time; we could wander, rest, watch, and even listen for the rooster to crow.

Our 2008 tour also took us to the Kerta Gosa Klungkung complex that consists of the Royal Court of Justice and a floating pavilion. We had been told to bring scarves to wrap around our waists while we were there; so, as a sign of respect, we tied them around us as we entered. *Beautiful* is too ordinary a word to describe what we saw. Flowering plants and lush greenery were everywhere. The buildings, with their painted ceilings and ornately carved exteriors, were magnificent. It did not matter that it had begun to drizzle. The rain only added to the beauty, coating surfaces with droplets that shimmered.

Our tour group also visited the terraced Pura Kehen temple complex dating from the eleventh century. The drive to Pura Kehen was wonderful, with gorgeous views of Balinese countryside visible at every curve in the road. George kept nudging me and pointing, "Look, Sweetheart! Look!"

At the temple complex, we had to climb numerous steps. George took my arm and got me to the top. There, sweet-faced children peeped out at us, and our handsome guide—and indeed he was handsome—explained what we were seeing. Knowing I would forget the details, I just absorbed the beauty while the demonic face of Kala Makara, carved into the facade, stood guard over the temple and me.

Somewhere in our travels that day, we stopped for lunch at a lovely restaurant high in the hills. The floor-to-ceiling windows framed dramatic views—views of rice fields, terraces, and far-off volcanic peaks. That day, George and I again rated Bali as the most beautiful island in the world. Ah, it surely is.

BRUNEI AND MANILA: TIME MARCHES ON

Having been to Brunei and Manila in the 1970s, George and I looked forward to our revisit during World '08. We recalled the Churchill Museum and the water village in Brunei. Lo and behold, by 2008, the Churchill Museum now honored the royal family of the Sultanate of Brunei. Here we saw a gorgeous golden chariot, ornate costumes, and local artifacts. All signs of Churchill were gone, even his statue in front of the building. When asked, our guide said that the Churchill things had been "put away."

The water village—a village built on pilings out into the river—was still there, just as we remembered it. We strode again on the wood planks of the boardwalk connecting houses, schools, and stores. This time, we had the opportunity to step into one of the homes—one that was tastefully decorated with western-style furnishings. We could have been in a home anywhere in the United States.

We did not remember the mosque. Perhaps we were not taken there or allowed to visit it in the seventies. The mosque in Brunei has twenty-four domes covered in pure gold, a number of stately minarets, sparkling white marble floors and walls, a vast courtyard, and a reflecting pool. We women had to robe up to go in, and all who entered had to take off their shoes. Beautiful, indeed: The Brunei mosque is considered one of the most beautiful in the world.

We did not remember the city having so many hotels and tall buildings. We did recall the hotel where we had stayed in the seventies, remembering that water was carried to our room so we could flush the toilets. We looked for that hotel, but we did not find it. Probably it had been torn down to make room for a new one.

The Manila of 2008 was far different, too, from the Manila we had visited back in the 1970s. In this case, we were not sure that change meant progress. We hopped on the ship's shuttle bus to go to the Mall of Asia; the ride took forever as the bus sat motionless in traffic for minutes on end. The mall is humongous, the largest in Southeast Asia. It was your typical mall, which could have been found in any big city in the world. Charming? Not at all.

A distinctive memory, the best of the day: Back on the pier, we saw a booth advertising inexpensive telephone rates for calls to the United States. We sat down and gave the couple running the booth the 201 area code and a number to call. Recognizing the area code as one in New Jersey, they told us that, for six months of every year, they lived in Bergen County, New Jersey. They spent the winter months in the warm Philippines.

After we had made our call, we sat and chatted with these friendly folks. We told them we were from Jersey and had worked as professors at Kean University. The woman's eyes lit up. She said that her son had graduated from Kean. What a small world it is!

We really enjoyed our time with this lovely Filipino couple. Before we left their booth to reboard *Amsterdam*, they gave us a colorful refrigerator magnet with the words "Mabuhay! Philippines" and the Philippine flag on it. After lunch, we ran down to the pier with a Kean bookmark for them.

HA LONG BAY, VIETNAM

When the forces of nature work in harmony across eons of time, the result can be a landscape that defies the imagination. That is true of Ha Long Bay in northern Vietnam. Our first glimpse of the famed island hillocks and cliffs of Ha Long Bay was at dawn during sail-in.

George and I were on our verandah as the mist lifted, the sky began to lighten, and the hillocks gradually emerged and were reflected in the calm, greenish waters of the bay. We had anticipated this moment for over a year. It was a perfect Stromboli Moment, well worth waiting for.

Shortly, small wooden junks pulled up alongside *Amsterdam*. George and I climbed onto one. It pulled away from the ship and chug-chugged its way among other boats and out between the cliffs and hillocks. I have a favorite photo in my album of George sitting under the overhang on the back deck of the boat. In the picture, he is wearing a navy T-shirt with the karst mountains of the Li River of China adorning the front. He has a broad smile on his face, and he looks so content. Until now, it never dawned on me that George had intentionally chosen to wear that T-shirt on that day, because the Li River hillocks and those in Ha Long Bay share a common feature—underlying limestone beds.

Our wooden junk kept chug-chugging until it reached one of the island hillocks formed from the limestone. We climbed off to explore a cave that nature had cut into the rock. The cave was the kind with little lakes, stalagmites, stalactites, and limestone columns—all illuminated with colored lights. We felt as if we had dropped into an underground corner of paradise.

George on Ha Long Bay, note the junk and hillocks on the right.

245

In this paradise, unfortunately, we had to walk and walk and walk. Emerging from the cavern, we had to locate our junk among all the others jostling for a place at the little dock. There were lots of boats, but here the others added to the ambiance. Our junk took a circuitous route back to *Amsterdam*, ducking in and out among the island hillocks and allowing many opportunities for us to take pictures of this UNESCO World Heritage Site.

ANGKOR WAT, CAMBODIA—A FAIRYTALE TRIP

Because our three-night trip to Angkor Wat was almost like an adventure in Wonderland for us, our story of going there during World '08 begins as many fairytales begin, "Once upon a time."

Once upon a time, George and Dorothy stepped into Wonderland, not by falling down a rabbit hole—as in Lewis Carroll's *Alice in Wonderland*—but by flying from Ho Chi Minh City. The two of us had left *Amsterdam* in Vietnam to fly into Siem Reap, Cambodia, with a group led by our travel-agency escort, Tom.

There was even a fairytale feel when we reached our hotel in Siem Reap. We smelled the odors, heard the sounds, and enjoyed the sights of Southeast Asia as soon as we stepped into the lobby of the Sofitel Royal Angkor. We were greeted by a row of musicians sitting under the portico outside the hotel; garbed in Cambodian attire, they were playing marimba-like instruments. Filled with the smells of sandalwood and spices, the lobby opened onto a park-like area with a man-made, lily-filled pond and a bridge over which we walked to get to the room where we were to stay for the next three days. The room was unbelievably exquisite. It was huge with marvelously shiny wood floors, hand-woven throw rugs, sliding glass doors that looked over the lily pond, and a bathroom the size of our cabin on *Amsterdam*. There is no way to describe the beauty.

That night we enjoyed a buffet supper in the main dining room with cousins John and Patricia and our newly made, shipboard friends Pete and Jane. Then we took off. With Pete and Jane, George and I hailed a vehicle that was powered by a motorcycle, and we headed to the night market. The cost was eight dollars for the four of us—two dollars per person for the evening. Patricia and John were in the cab behind us, but once we left the hotel portico, we lost them: We did not see them again until our return to the hotel.

The cab, with the four of us packed in, drove down a traffic-filled boulevard. Darkness enveloped us, with just a few city lights along the street to illuminate our way. The driver kept going and going and finally stopped on a street lined with stalls, where we climbed out. The four of us stayed together as we walked from shop to shop—just in case. Tom had told us that it was safe to be out at night. We found that to be true.

We bargained for sequin pillow covers, puppets, and pocketbooks. My most cherished find that evening was a small, round, brass face. I knew that the next day we would visit a temple adorned with faces carved into the stone of a temple. My brass face is similar in shape to those we would see; hung on a shoelace, it is a one-of-a-kind pendant.

Our ride back to the Sofitel was slow due to evening traffic. Arriving at the hotel, we gave the driver a nice tip, for he had walked with us among the stalls—probably to pick up gratuities from the shopkeepers from whom we had made purchases. But that was acceptable. His presence had made us feel secure.

Early the following morning, we loaded onto buses—fifteen to a bus—to tour the main temple, Angkor Wat. Angkor is actually an area where many temples are located, the biggest being Angkor Wat, which our guide Sam told us was built 1,000 years ago by Suryavarman II. It is huge. We walked up and up and over and around. We had to watch our step since the terrain was rough to navigate and there were many stairs to climb—stairs made of uneven stone without handrails.

The climb was worth the effort, for what we saw was beyond belief. Most outstanding was the bas-relief called the Churning of the Ocean of Milk, a depiction of the conflict between good and evil. It stretches yards and yards along one side of the first level. From that level, we kept climbing. When the group started up another flight of steps, I sat down by a pillar and waited for them to go up and come down. This was perfect for me, because it provided an opportunity to rest and contemplate. I cannot get the "feel" of such a place while walking and watching where

I put my feet. Sitting in a quiet corner, with only a few Cambodians worshiping nearby, I let the aura of Angkor Wat envelop me.

Walking to our buses—and again the walk was lengthy—we looked back at the carved temple that is Angkor Wat. Yes, it is huge, and we had climbed and walked much of it. George and I could not conceive, even as we stood there, how vast and old Angkor Wat is. *Awesome* is too tame a word.

Later that day, our group visited a series of other temples:

- the Terrace of the Elephants with a frieze depicting an elephant hunt;
- the Terrace of the Leper King with friezes depicting a king who had leprosy;
- Angkor Thom, a fortified city built in the 10th century by Jayavarman VII;
- the Bayon, which is considered the single most outstanding monument of Khmer culture and which is covered with carvings of faces of a benevolent ruler—faces like the one on the pendant I had bought the night before;
- Ta Prohm, which is also known as the Jungle Temple because huge roots of trees snake their way between and among the carvings, the towers, and the walls.

To see these temples, we walked and walked. Again it was worth the effort. We saw so much beauty and so much history revealed in stone. We had never realized that the Angkor area has so many finely carved stone temples. We had thought we were going to see only Angkor Wat. We saw so much more than we had expected.

Back in the Sofitel that evening, our tour group dined together on the lighted terrace in front of a reflecting pool. The tables were decorated with flowers; even the chairs were "dressed" in cloth covers and ribbons. Discreet lights hidden in the bushes cast a glow over everything and everyone. Between the entree and dessert, beautifully costumed young people performed Cambodian dances.

Up early the next day, we set out to see the 1,000-year-old temple called East Mebon, where there are numerous carved elephants—life-sized ones—guarding each corner. We climbed to the second level over uneven steps to look down on the surrounding area. When Sam began to climb to a third level, I bailed out and carefully made my way to the base. Across the road was a row of shops that were calling to me. I had just enough time to bargain for four silk scarves and two pocketbooks before George and the others started to board the bus and I had to run to join them.

Perhaps the most exquisite temple we saw in Angkor was Banteay Srei. All on one level, the various structures of the temple complex are carved into rose-colored sandstone. Banteay Srei is known for the intricacy of the stone carvings, which are perfectly preserved. Sam explained to us the symbolism of the figures depicted.

On our way back to our hotel for lunch, we stopped at a small village. We walked between the houses and even entered a home. How little these people have; how basic their way of life. We learned, too, how important a fresh water well is to their existence. Cambodia, the guide reminded us, was the scene of the "killing fields," where many people died in past years. In 2008, the country was still recovering from that terrible period in its history.

Our afternoon adventure was much different. We drove out to the Tonle Sap, the largest lake in Southeast Asia, for a boat trip to visit a floating village. The road we traveled was filled with potholes and covered with dust. The houses we passed were very small, often just one room divided into areas by curtains—really only huts made out of thatch with some metal siding.

Arriving at the water's edge, our group of fifteen climbed into a boat that took us out into the lake. There people live on floating houseboats, which do not rest on pilings as do the houses in the water villages of Brunei and Penang. This is important during the rainy season, for the level in the lake rises many, many feet, and of course, the houseboats rise, too. Schools, temples, restaurants, and shops are all part of the floating community.

The lake water was muddy. We wondered what good it did for the people to bathe in it. Yes, we did indeed see adults and youngsters washing themselves in the lake.

Our boatman was a relatively young fellow; his assistant was a boy about eight years old. The boy manned the pole as we pushed away from the land and when we returned. In the interim, the child curled up on the front deck and napped. As we rode from one area of the village to the next, a small craft drew up alongside ours. A couple of very young children boarded our boat to sell beer and soft drinks. After these five- or six-year-old boys had "worked" our boat, the father came alongside to pick them up and take them to another boat following us across the lake.

As in most fairy stories, not all was rosy in our Cambodian tale. We saw the stark contrasts between our plush hotel and the homes that dotted the roadside. We saw young children, who should have been in school, working. Sam, our guide, reminded us of the Communist takeover of Cambodia starting in the late 1970s. During the takeover, hundreds of thousands of Cambodians were killed—hence the term *killing fields*. It was not until 1993 that peace came to Cambodia and tourists like us could visit Siem Reap to see the magnificent temples and to feed needed dollars into the economy.

Our tour group stayed another night in our fairytale hotel. The next morning we flew via Phnom Penh to Singapore to reboard *Amsterdam*; our ship had sailed there during our three-night stay in Cambodia. Yes, storybook land was unbelievable, but our ship felt like heaven when we walked up the gangway. To us, after so many days of voyaging, *Amsterdam* was home.

CHENNAI AND MUMBAI, INDIA

Question: What is the opposite of a fairytale?
Answer: Grim reality!

George and I went from our fairytale experience in Siem Reap to grim reality when we arrived in Chennai, India, three days later. First, the local immigration authorities were delayed in clearing our ship, so we waited and waited for the bureaucracy to function. Then when we finally stepped off the gangway onto the pier, we found we were stepping into black muck—tar, oil, and whatever else you can imagine, made worse by a recent rainfall. Once we were aboard our tour bus, the guide announced that the microphone was not working; we would have to listen closely. He also explained that because of our delayed disembarkation, he was canceling our stop at the dance school where we were to have been entertained.

At last we were on our way. As our bus pulled into the city from the port, we saw piles of garbage littering the streets and numbers of people for whom home was the sidewalk. They lived beneath sheets of plastic that protected them from the elements.

Our guide took us to a series of old Hindu temples. We walked through a cave temple with a bas-relief depicting figures of gods and animals watching the downward flow of the Ganges River from the Himalayas. We went to a shore temple carved into a monolith with an inner area that we explored. We continued to a temple with several buildings cut into rock. Our guide explained what we were seeing, but we had trouble understanding his explanations. We decided that Sam, our Cambodian guide, had spoiled us for all future guides. Sam had been the best.

Lunch was al fresco style. Our group sat at long tables set up under a tent of trees. We were served a variety of local dishes that waiters ladled from buckets onto broad banana leaves, which served as our plates. This might sound exotic, but fearful of our stomachs, George and I only pretended to eat.

The return trip was as eye-popping as our outward journey. We passed more streets cluttered with waste, and we saw more people who lived amidst the clutter. Our earlier visits to India had taken us to the west coast—to areas like Goa—where life is less grim for poorer people. I have to admit that here I experienced culture shock.

Back on the pier, we had to walk across an area still covered with black gunk. George and I took our shoes off before entering our cabin because we did not want to drag any of the dirt inside with us. George spent a half hour cleaning our shoes with an old toothbrush.

Here is my account of our day in serial haiku form that Jim taught me to write:

thick gunk on the pier
our intro to the city
we watch where we walk

home is the sidewalk
the reality of life
lived in poor Chennai

George toothbrushes shoes,
scrubs the grime but not the grim
reality time

rude awakening
for all those who have so much,
life is not equal

Three days later we were in Mumbai. There, too, we saw the stark contrast between the haves and the have-nots. George and I bargained for a taxi to take us to the Taj Mahal Hotel. Once there, we walked through the hotel lobby and then to Colaba Causeway two blocks away. The lobby of the Taj was populated by tourists and by wealthier Indians; the shops in the hotel displayed upscale and expensive merchandise, too pricey for us to buy. In contrast, the causeway area was a beehive of activity and noise: Beggars followed us; naked youngsters did their business over a street grate; street vendors hawked their wares.

In a shop down an alley off the causeway, George bought a few shirts for five dollars apiece. To get there, we passed an open sewer, and inside the shop, the odor from the sewer was overpowering. On the floor was a king-sized mattress on which the shopkeeper suggested we sit as we decided on our purchases. George later suggested that the shop was both a business and a home. The mattress was where the man and his family slept at night.

When we left the shirt shop, again beggars surrounded us. We had been warned never to give alms. It could be dangerous. But George, when we arrived home, wrote a check to Doctors without Borders. He said that this group, which had been awarded the Nobel Peace Prize in 1999, helped needy and ill people around the world, people like some we had seen in Chennai and Mumbai.

TO AND THROUGH SUEZ

After stops in Salalah in Oman and Safaga in Egypt, *Amsterdam* cruised north up the Gulf of Suez and, on the evening of March 25, dropped anchor at the southernmost point of the Suez Canal. There we waited for our assigned time to make the transit of the canal. Looking out that night, we saw the lights of other ships waiting to go caravan-style through the canal the next day. As we looked out from our verandah, too, we saw white gulls gliding in the light our ship was casting across the water. This was a marvelously perfect moment, beautiful and serene.

At 6 a.m. on the morning of March 26, we felt *Amsterdam* begin to move. Opening our drapes, we saw Port Suez on the port side, a container ship ahead of us, and numbers of ships behind. We were on our way, the second ship in the caravan.

Although this was our third transit of Suez, it was the first we had made in a verandah cabin on the port side—the Egyptian side—of the canal. On the Sinai side there is mostly desert with a few military encampments. On the Egyptian side are settlements, highways, and railroads.

The first part of the northbound transit is through a long, wide, straight ditch that is the result of the dredging and widening that occurred when the Suez was constructed in the mid-1800s. Eventually we came to the Little Bitter Lake and the Great Bitter Lake, the midpoint where the northbound and the southbound caravans wait for each other before taking their turns in the one-way channels.

In the afternoon, we left the Bitter Lakes and entered the second channel. We passed palm groves, ferryboat landings, housing developments, army outposts, and the largest swing bridge in the world. It is a railway bridge that we were told opens twice a day to let the northbound and southbound canal traffic through. In the afternoon, after a morning spent doing nothing but sitting and watching, George napped on the couch in our cabin. I stayed on the verandah as long as I could before joining the ranks of the nappers, stretched out on a lounge chair on the balcony. By late afternoon, we exited the canal at Port Said. Our transit of the one-hundred-plus miles took about ten hours. We had been part of a thirty-seven ship convoy going north that day.

ISTANBUL . . . AGAIN

Exiting the Suez Canal, *Amsterdam* turned west toward Alexandria. The ship docked there for a day before turning again, this time to take an eastward path toward the Aegean Sea and the Dardanelles. Early on March 29, the ship entered the Dardanelles. By late morning, she had cruised the Sea of Marmara and was headed to Istanbul.

The sail-in to Istanbul is on my list of all-time favorites. Again both of us were on deck for our approach to the city.

> There they were!
> the minarets and dome of the Blue Mosque. . .
> then the minarets of Hagia Sophia. . .
> then the towers and facade of Topkapi Palace...
> then the minarets and dome of Suleymaniye Mosque,
> as our ship turned toward the Golden Horn.

On past stops in Istanbul, we had visited all these UNESCO World Heritage Sites. We had also visited the Grand Bazaar. But back we went to the bazaar in the afternoon of our World '08 stop. We went via the ship's shuttle. The bus dropped us just outside the bazaar in front of the Nuruosmaniye Mosque, where we saw men at a fountain washing their hands and feet as they prepared to enter the mosque for prayers. George and I meandered down the main street of the covered bazaar. And it really is a main street, with shops on each side that sell silk carpets, colorful carpet bags, leather goods, walking canes, jewelry, Turkish delight candy, evil eyes, and a variety of other more mundane things.

The most memorable event from the 2008 stop in Istanbul occurred the next night—a party in the Great Cistern that Holland America threw for its world travelers. The Great Cistern is a large open area beneath the old city that was hewn out of the underlying rock during the sixth century for use as a water reservoir. We had gone down into it on our first visit back in 1969 and thought it a big, dark, musty space.

On the evening of March 30, the cistern had been transformed into an Arabian paradise with costumed entertainers performing in niches around the edge: belly dancers, jugglers, singers, mimes, and more.

Pulsating music filled the air, tables were set up for all 1,200 of us, and waiters circulated with treats and drinks. Colored lights illuminated every corner; pennants and streamers hung from the ceiling. Passengers had dressed in whatever Middle Eastern garb we had bought along the way.

The CEO of Holland America had flown out with others from the home office in Seattle. There were speeches and presentations and a bit of mutual backslapping. Surmising that there might be lines for the buses when the event ended, George and I headed home just before the speeches concluded—home to the *Amsterdam*. We also were ready to crawl between clean sheets and sleep the sleep of the deserving. We had walked a lot that day, and our legs cried for relief.

About 11 p.m., the sound of fireworks awakened us. George and I got up to watch the reflection of the fireworks in the windows of the apartment complex opposite our verandah. Shortly, *Amsterdam* began to move. We watched the apartment buildings and old palaces on the European side of the Bosphorus pass before us. Ahead was the Ataturk Bridge, the suspension bridge connecting Asia and Europe. That night, it was bathed in changing colored lights. Slipping under the bridge, *Amsterdam* headed east into the Black Sea. Satisfied, George and I went back to bed.

BLACK SEA ADVENTURES

Amsterdam anchored in the harbor of Sochi, Russia, on April Fools Day, 2008. George and I little realized that we were foolish to do what we had chosen to do that day. We were going up into the Caucasus Mountains to see the designated site of the 2014 Winter Olympics. That sounds interesting, doesn't it? But . . .

Our bus was a dilapidated wreck of a vehicle. The seats were small, with almost no leg room. We spent two endless hours riding that disaster of a bus with just one stop to see a valley—yes, I said a valley. Eventually we got to a very small resort area where we ate a pancake— yes, one pancake with a bit of honey—and visited the restroom. Then it was back on the road to make the return two-hour trip to Sochi. The bus went at a fast clip down slippery roads. Sometimes those roads were one-way, and our bus had to wait until a traffic light changed to green to signal that it was our turn to proceed. When we passed what was to be the Olympic Village, the driver put his foot on the pedal and we sped by so fast that it was impossible to take a picture.

On the bus, the talk was about how the Russians would be able to get the roads, the vehicles, and the site ready in just six years. We know the Olympics did take place there in 2014, but the Russians had a long uphill battle to prepare it, based on what we saw.

Whereas our visit to Sochi had few redeeming qualities, our stop in Sevastopol in the Ukraine was simply wonderful. George and I had toured there on a prior cruise, choosing then to go to Yalta to see the place where Churchill, Stalin, and Roosevelt had met as the war in Europe was winding down. On the agenda for their meeting was the division of Axis lands among the victors. The Yalta Conference was a disaster because it set the stage for the Cold War and future discord.

Our 2008 Sevastopol excursion also focused on war, particularly the Crimean War. I remember our first stop as if it had happened yesterday. We visited the Panorama Museum, a structure that houses a 360° painting/diorama depicting the major battles and events of the war. The display is three-dimensional, because in front of the painting are actual tents and statue-like renderings of people, animals, and things. We could not tell where the circular mural stopped and the pieces of the diorama began.

Our guide explained about the charge of the Light Brigade as we gathered before that part of the wall painting. She pointed out the promontory in the diorama on which Lord Raglan, the British commander, had stood when he gave the order that sent nearly seven hundred men into battle and more than a hundred to their deaths. Later during the tour, we would stand on the promontory where Raglan had stood to watch the battle.

After driving across the valley of death where the battle had taken place, we traveled to Balaklava, where we visited the submarine pens the Russians had built during the early years of the Cold War. We walked through extensive tunnels cut into the rock. In these pens, the Russians had hidden submarines and kept them on alert, just in case ... It was an eerie walk, deep underground with haunting sounds piped in to give us the sense that the subs were still housed there. We stopped later to view the area from above; we could hardly believe that the submarine pens were hidden below. On the surface nothing showed.

On our drive back to Sevastopol, the bus climbed to the heights of Sapouné Ridge where Raglan had given his ill-fated command for the Light Brigade to charge the Russian forces. We were quiet as we looked down into the valley, knowing that this was a place where so many had perished. On the heights was an open-air museum with examples of tanks, guns, and trucks.

I call the tours we took on our two visits to Crimea "The Sad Tours." Great suffering came out of Yalta. Great suffering occurred in the valley of death. Yet we were glad that we had taken them because we had learned much about the history of the area and of Europe. Both tours had led us to consider the decisions leaders of the past had made that brought death and destruction to others.

In *The Charge of the Light Brigade*, Alfred, Lord Tennyson wrote:

> Not tho' the soldier knew
> Some one had blunder'd:
> Theirs not to make reply,
> Theirs not to reason why,
> Theirs but to do and die:
> Into the valley of Death
> Rode the six hundred.

Our guide told us that the charge was the result of a misunderstanding, what Tennyson called a blunder. He also explained that Tennyson had relied on poetic license when he composed his poem and wrote that six hundred British light cavalrymen had ridden out that day. Actually, more soldiers than that had taken part in the charge, over a hundred brave men were lost in the battle, and many more were wounded.

George and I wondered aloud whether the leader who directed the charge ever rued his decision and whether Churchill and Roosevelt ever regretted the so-called compromise they made with Stalin at Yalta. One of the nicest things about traveling with a trusted spouse is the ability to raise questions and to think out loud. We were fortunate to share that kind of give and take during so many years of travel.

EUROPEAN ADVENTURES

Leaving the Black Sea, the good ship *Amsterdam* headed toward European ports. Our first port of call during the European phase of our world exploration was the Greek island of Santorini—a repeat visit for George and me.

The sun shone on us as we boarded the bus for our tour of Santorini. The tour would take us to the highest point on the island, Profitis Ilias; to the largest town, Fira; and to the small village of Oia. Getting to the highest point, of course, required a drive around hairpin curves. George kept his eyes closed as the bus carried us upward. He had to agree, however, that the view from the top down into the water-filled caldera was phenomenal. The island of Santorini is actually a volcano that erupted back in the annals of time. We could see some evidence of that looking down from Profitis Ilias.

We drove across the island, with splendid views at every turn, to reach Fira and then Oia, where we stopped to explore. The buildings in the towns are white with blue domes and roofs, which against the sky produce sensational scenery. When we were there, the countryside was abloom with yellow fennel flowers. Twisted into bird's-nest patterns to protect them from the wind, grape vines dotted the landscape.

Our ship was far below in the harbor. To get back to it, we took the tram. We had ridden a donkey down in the past. The tram was a lot easier, especially on the nose. Back on *Amsterdam*, we lunched, rested, and watched the sail-away. Yes, this was a repeat visit for us, but we had had a delightful day during which we walked streets that we had not previously trod.

During the European segment of World '08, *Amsterdam* also made a stop in the famed Italian port of Venice. By now, anyone reading our story of love and travel will have realized that George and I were enamored of sail-ins and sail-aways. The entry into Venice by water is among the grandest sail-ins, and so we positioned ourselves on deck as our captain steamed right down a major canal in front of St. Mark's Square, the Bridge of Sighs, and the Doges Palace. We saw it all from the deck of our ship. There was no hassle and no walking was required. When we docked, George and I shuttled into a square from which we could conveniently walk to the major sites. Again, because we had been there before, we did not rush. We just enjoyed walking over the bridges and along the canals.

Our stay in Venice spanned two days. On the second day, we joined a tour to Padua and Vicenza, two cities we had not previously visited.

Before our visit, George and I associated the city of Padua with the Shakespearean play *The Taming of the Shrew*. Visiting Padua, we built a second association, this one with the artist Giotto, who in the early 1300s painted a series of frescoes in the Scrovegni Chapel there. The frescoes depict scenes from the life of Christ, and they are masterpieces.

Before our visit to Vicenza, we knew nothing at all about that city. Arriving there—to our delight—we found streets filled with stunning buildings designed by the great architect Andrea Palladio. Walking the streets was like visiting an outdoor museum.

On our way back to Venice, we passed an impressive Palladio-style building on a hillside. It reminded us of Jefferson's Monticello and the library on the quadrangle of the University of Virginia. It seems that Mr. Jefferson visited Vicenza, saw this building, and modeled his mansion and the library after it. Thus, we came home with a new association and some knowledge of architecture. George and I often remarked that we had learned more through our travels than through our college general education courses.

A few days later, *Amsterdam* docked in Gibraltar. Because the sea was calm, the captain had no trouble bringing us into port. George and I were happy because we had a pleasant excursion planned. On tour, we drove to Europa Point where we could see beyond the strait to Africa. Our bus took us across the airstrip, the only place in the world where a road crosses a functioning runway. From there, we could look across to Spain.

The highlight of our tour was a classic English tea with scones, jam, and clotted cream as well as finger sandwiches and cakes. We took tea at a four-star hotel that overlooks the sea. The food was good, the view fantastic. And when we arrived, there was a bonus awaiting us: We were welcomed by a Barbary ape that was sitting on the hood of a car at the entrance.

Let's talk sail-in again. We sailed up the Tagus River to dock in Lisbon, Portugal. On the way in—on our port side—we passed the Henry the Navigator Monument and the Belem Tower. We could see both from our verandah. The captain turned his ship around so it was pointed seaward, ready for the evening sail-away. In doing so, he swung the ship so we could see the statue of Christ the King high on the opposite shore. That was our view from our cabin for the entire day.

HAL supplied a shuttle to town, and so we climbed on for a walkabout. In the city, we went to the Madeira House, a store where I had purchased blouses trimmed with handmade lace on a prior visit. We did not need a map to find the store. Our first visit to Lisbon was way back in 1969, on our round-the-world-by-airplane trip; our most recent had been in 2006 when we had taken a bus up the hillside to see the fortress there. We both had good mental maps to use in navigating the city streets.

FUNCHAL, BERMUDA, AND HOME

On our way to New York, we made a stop in Funchal in Madeira and then in Bermuda. Five days after leaving Funchal, we dropped anchor in the harbor of Hamilton, capital of Bermuda.

Because George and I had stopped rather recently in Bermuda and had taken an island tour, in 2008 we opted for a morning trip on a glass-bottom boat. The boat ride itself was nice because the sun blessed us with its presence and the water was calm. However, the fish we saw were not so colorful as those we had seen in more southerly Caribbean ports— although there were some rather big ones out there.

Back on *Amsterdam*, I worked on final packing. My George, I have to admit, was a pretty lucky man! I always did the major packing. His contribution was to tape up any boxes that we had snared somewhere along the line and that I had filled with purchases. By the time I was finished, I had filled eleven pieces of luggage, nine to be shipped from the pier via FedEx and two smaller bags that we would carry home.

On the morning of April 24, lying in bed, I felt a slight change in the motion of the ship. I got up to see the lights of New Jersey on the horizon and those of the Verrazzano Bridge in the distance. The sky was clear and the moon was full, casting a ribbon of light on the darkened water. It was cold outside, but I wrapped up in a blanket and dropped a towel on the deck to protect my feet from the cold as I stepped onto the verandah. I stood there to watch as we slid under the bridge. George woke up and joined me.

There is no way I can fully describe a magical moment like this. We had had a fabulous trip and been to wonderful places, but nothing compares with the feeling that builds up inside when one enters home waters after being away for over 110 days. Although we had made the sail-in to NYC just a year before, my eyes filled with tears of contentment and happiness.

Shortly, Lady Liberty and Ellis Island came into view. The ship swung starboard, and we knew that we were turning into our berth at 59th Street. Upriver, we saw the George Washington Bridge and in the distance Fort Lee, New Jersey, high on the cliffs.

We were home.

Chapter Eighteen
SAILING THE WORLD
2009

For George and me, World '09 was different from World '07 and '08. In 2007, we were both super-excited that we were doing a world cruise. With a bit of trepidation, we wondered whether we would be content on a ship for a hundred-plus days. By 2008, we knew we would be content, but might we get bored with the same routine and with many ports we already had toured? In 2009, though we were not so excited, we were still very eager. More relaxed, we knew what to expect of ourselves and of the voyage. We knew we would never get bored.

In 2009, however, our objectives were somewhat different from the ones that had moved us in 2007 and 2008. This year we would be on a quest for the unusual, the different, and the new—even in ports we had visited before. Yes, we would look back and book some tours we had enjoyed on previous cruises, and we would walk streets we had trodden and knew well. But we would also search out unfamiliar places and streets. World '09 offered an itinerary that included areas we had never visited, such as East Africa. We really anticipated our days there. George was especially excited about seeing Komodo dragons in Indonesia. I was looking forward to riding the fast train in Shanghai.

We knew that our travels would stretch our minds. We knew, too, that our travels would stretch our bodies. We would walk, walk, and walk some more. Walking is the only way really to see things. But our bodies were getting older. George was in his eighty-seventh year. I was "only" seventy-four. Yet even then, George was always three paces ahead of me. I was forever lagging behind, moving my legs as fast as I could to keep up with his longer stride.

Looking back now, I do not know how George did it; he had out-walked me the year before at Angkor Wat, and I knew he would out-walk me as we trod the streets of the world in 2009. Right now, I am one year younger than he was in 2009. I know for sure that I could not do now what he did then.

Well, our departure day in January finally arrived, and George and I flew west to Los Angeles. World '09 started there and not in Florida, where world cruises typically begin. Our ship was the *Rotterdam VI*, sister ship to *Amsterdam* and one we knew well from prior cruises we had taken on her. On board were many friends whom we had met on our two previous world trips, including our friends Jim and Jessica.

HAWAII AND THE PACIFIC

After five days at sea, *Rotterdam* made two landings in Hawaii, the first in Hilo on the big island and the second in Honolulu on Oahu. At our first port of call, George and I took a tour called "The Best of Hilo and Welcome Lunch," offered by our travel agent. This excursion was similar to one we had enjoyed in 1969 on our airplane trip around the world. It promised to take us to Volcanoes National Park, which is home to Kilauea. Kilauea is an active volcano, but in 2009, it was spewing only steam and gases. We remembered that, when we had visited in 1969, red-hot, molten lava had been bubbling up and flames had been shooting into the air.

Sharing a table with Leta and Bill, whom we had met in 2008, we lunched at Volcano House, which overlooks the crater. After lunch, we stopped at a lava field to see ropy lava, which George called *pahoehoe,* and chunky lava, which he told me was *aa.* We stopped to trek through a rainforest area and then to walk through the Thurston Lava Tube. We

had done all of this on our 1969 trip, but—on our second time around—
we still loved every moment.

Heading back to the ship, we stopped at an orchid garden, where
George went wild videotaping the diverse varieties of orchids on display,
and then at a macadamia nut farm, where we sampled nuts and candies.
We agreed that this had been a grand outing.

The next day *Rotterdam* cruised into Honolulu. From our docking site,
George and I explored the north shore of Oahu, an area to which we
had never been. The highlight of our tour was a visit to the Byodo-In
Temple—a fine Buddhist complex on a hillside. There is a cliff behind
the temple that serves almost as a frame, highlighting the beauty of this
place of enlightenment. We had plenty of time to stroll the grounds and
for George to take his videos. From there, we hit the beaches to see huge
waves pounding in from across the Pacific and surfers pitting their skills
against nature.

As for the Pacific, *Rotterdam* spent the next week wending her way
west across the ocean. Those seven days were the longest span of sea days
on this world voyage.

George and I had a general schedule that we varied each day depending
on what was happening on the ship. Most mornings, we started in the
main dining room with raspberries, papaya, and oatmeal for breakfast,
followed by a walk around the promenade deck. George would go three-
and-a-half times around, which was a mile. I managed two laps. We
would retire to our verandah to read the ship's eight-page version of
the *New York Times,* and I would attempt the crossword puzzle, just as
at home—except that it was warm and we had the Pacific spread out
before us. Later, if the topic excited us, we would go to the showroom to
listen to the port talk or a general lecture.

At noon, we never missed trivia with Jim, Jessica, Leta, and one other
lady who joined our team. We even won from time to time. It was
uncanny though; we always excelled when there was a special prize for
the winners, such as a flashy pillow cover from India or a cuddly Holland
America stuffed moose. We still have the pillows with the covers and
the two moose to remind us of those trivia triumphs.

We generally lunched at the lido deck buffet. If we had the energy,
after our lunch had settled, we swam in the pool. Then it was time for

a siesta followed by a shower. About five o'clock, we dressed for dinner and headed up to the Ocean Bar for our one dance of the evening, a waltz. We had to ask the combo to play the waltz, for they seemed to prefer playing Latin dances.

We generally ate our evening meal in the main dining room at an assigned table for eight. There were George and I, Mel and Kelley, George and Yvonne, and another couple whose names I have forgotten. The other George and his wife had been history teachers, Mel was still working as an atomic physicist, Kelley was a shopper like no other we had ever met, the fourth gentleman had been a naval officer, and my George and I had been professors. It was a great mix, so conversation flowed freely. Typically, each night, we shared events from our day in port, and sometimes Kelley would bring one of her purchases to the table for us to admire.

After our meal in the dining room, George and I went to play a second game of trivia with our friendly team and then attended a performance in the theater. After the show, we were ready to relax in our cabin.

That's a pretty good way to spend one's retirement, isn't it? George and I agreed—especially given that on our television set, CNN reported snow in the northeast quadrant of the United States as we sat in the middle of the warm South Pacific.

LUGANVILLE AND PORT VILA, VANUATU

Rain! As George and I stepped off the ship in Luganville, a steward handed us a large umbrella. This was our first visit to Vanuatu, and regardless of the weather, our walkabout was well worth the effort, for we learned a bit about World War II as it was waged in the Pacific.

I have a sharp picture in my mind of the town. We walked off the pier and along a four-lane road that cut a swath through Luganville. Lining both sides of the road were old quonset huts but not much else, not even your typical souvenir shop, because few cruise ships dock here.

Why would there be a four-lane, paved road in the middle of this small town? Actually, Luganville had been the site of an American army

Port Vila: George is wearing his t-shirt from Africa, Dorothy her t-shirt from Vietnam.

base during the Second World War. The four-lane artery was essential for the movement of heavy equipment, and the quonset huts were also remnants of the war. The port lecturer had told us that James Michener had been based on the island during the war. It was here that he had developed ideas for his *Tales of the South Pacific*.

Port Vila, which is the capital of Vanuatu, was a more vibrant place. This time we could not just walk off the ship and into town, as we had done in Luganville; we had to take a cab. With another couple, we bargained with a driver for a ride to town and settled on ten dollars for the four of us. As soon as we rounded the bend and were out of sight of the pier, the driver stopped. He now demanded fifteen dollars, or he would take us to the police station. We said, "Take us to the police, right now!" He kept insisting on fifteen dollars, but he started the cab and got us to town. Normally we would have added a tip. Not this time. He got his ten dollars, and we got a story to share that evening at dinner.

In contrast with Luganville, Port Vila had more to explore. We strolled through a very large local produce market and looked into the windows of a few shops. We continued down the main street and found a multipurpose market selling clothing, dry goods, kitchenware, and furniture. I spied a unique wood carving—a one-of-a-kind piece probably made by a local artisan. It hangs today in one of our bathrooms. It is a visual reminder of a day that started out badly but ended with an interesting chat with the lady who sold us the carving and who spoke a little English. By the way, the cab back to the ship cost five dollars.

AUSTRALIA: SYDNEY, MELBOURNE, ADELAIDE, AND PERTH

After a stop in New Caledonia, *Rotterdam* headed to Australia and to more *rain*. George joked that the rain clouds from Luganville were following us. Under an umbrella that morning in Sydney, we walked The Rocks, the area where the first Australians settled. In the evening we took a bus supplied by Holland America across the Sydney Harbour Bridge to the heights where the zoo is located. HAL again distributed umbrellas, a very bad sign. From the overlook, we could see nothing because of low-lying rain clouds—none of the lights illuminating the bridge, the opera house, or the skyscrapers. We were completely enshrouded in the mist.

Sydney Zoo is built on a hillside overlooking the city; we were supposed to walk from one open-air animal compound to the next as we progressed down the hillside. We gave up on walking when the skies opened and dumped more rain. George and I quickly boarded a bus to take us to the restaurant at the base of the hillside where we were to dine that evening. No sense in getting wet, George figured; the smart zoo animals had probably hidden in the foliage to keep dry. We would not have seen them if we had walked.

When we went on to Melbourne the next day, the rain clouds did not follow us. The Australians in Melbourne would have applauded rain, for fierce forest fires were rampant south of the city. The fires cast a thick haze over Melbourne. We could even smell fire.

George and I took a tram from the pier into the city and then another around the perimeter. We hopped off the trolley in the square where the capital buildings of the state of Victoria are located. Because so many people had lost their lives and their property to the fires, makeshift memorials had been set up on the steps of the government buildings. Melbournians hovered around to pay their respects.

Even when we got to Adelaide, we could smell smoke from the forest fires that were plaguing the southeastern part of Australia. Now when rain was needed, there was none—just a haze from the fires. Not surprisingly, when I remember our time on the southern coast of the continent, I think first of forest fires. One guide explained that because the forests have an abundance of oily eucalyptus trees, they are more likely to go up in flames.

Fremantle was a repeat port for us; on World '08 George and I had walked the streets of the port city. On World '09, we signed up—with our friends Kelley and Mel—for a trip to Caversham Wildlife Park that would also take us on a sightseeing drive around nearby Perth. What I remember clearly about Caversham are the enclosures. The kangaroos, koalas, and emus did not roam freely as we had seen on our excursion out of Melbourne in 2008. They were in pens. My memory here is of kangaroos lethargically lying on the ground waiting to be fed.

INDONESIAN FAVORITES

World '09 made three stops in Indonesia: Lembar on Lombok Island; Komodo Island; and Semarang on Java. I have fine memories of our days there.

Our favorite stop in Lembar was at a temple complex spread out across an area that is park-like in appearance. What impressed us about this temple is that Muslims, Hindus, and Animists worship harmoniously together. There are areas within the complex for people of each faith. Some worshippers bring offerings of fruits and flowers and burn incense as part of their rituals. I kept thinking, "This is the way the world should work. People of different faiths should respect one another and even worship side by side."

My favorite memory of Komodo Island is of George, The Contented Biologist—my name for him that day—returning from his tour and showing off the ugliest T-shirt I have ever seen. George went alone to

Komodo because there was no way I would pay a hundred dollars for a tour to see a huge lizard. When George returned, he was full of stories about the dragons. He had seen two of the ugly things (my description, not his) and bought the T-shirt with a dragon on the front. In years to follow, that T-shirt went with him on most cruises we took. Bedraggled now, the shirt is still in the closet. I cannot throw it away; it holds too many precious memories.

In Semarang, George and I had an adventure that was also high on our list of Indonesian favorites. We traveled from the pier up into the highlands to board an open-air, narrow-gauge train that took us across rice paddies, through the backyards of homes in small villages, and by a lake where men fished the old-fashioned way—with poles in hand. George hung over the side of the railway car to take picture after picture. Each view was better than the one before. Indeed, the train trip was a superb excursion for picture-taking; I even snapped a few.

On our way back by coach, the driver stopped at a coffee and rubber plantation. With great volcanic peaks behind us, we sat with friends and drank coffee made from beans grown right there on the plantation. "Coffee with Friends" was a perfect ending to our Indonesian adventures.

THE MANY MARKETS OF HONG KONG

If I have added correctly, World '09 marked the seventh time that George and I had been to Hong Kong. On the first of our two days in the area, we took the roller-coaster bus ride over the mountain to Stanley Market; no visit to Hong Kong would be complete without a ramble through this popular shopping mecca and the exhilarating trip to get there.

What could we do on the second day that we had not done already? The answer was simple: the many distinctive markets that stretch from the upper reaches of Kowloon to the area down and around the Peninsula Hotel.

To start our exploration of the many markets of Hong Kong, we grabbed a cab at Ocean Terminal and asked to be taken to the bird market. We had not realized how very far away it actually is: The taxi driver kept going and going, and we just hoped he was taking us where we wanted to end up. Indeed he was. Arriving there, we saw hundreds of colorful birds waiting to join families in their homes. Along with pet birds, vendors were selling unique cages that people use for decorative purposes. Imagine—an entire market dedicated to pet birds!

Following a map we had picked up on the ship (something we always remembered to do), we walked first to the flower market and then to the fish market. This fish market did not sell edible fish, but rather fancy, colorful fish to add to a family aquarium. A shopper picked out a live fish; the vendor scooped it up and then put it into a plastic bag filled with water.

Next on our map was the ladies' market with women's outfits for sale. Having been to Stanley Market, I managed to resist. Following the route I had marked on our map, we meandered through some produce, meat, and regular fish markets. Several hours after we had started out, we found the jade market. Here I did not resist. I bought a large piece of jade in browns and creams that I could wear as a pendant. We must have looked tired, because the saleslady offered us stools to sit on as we decided on our purchase and gave us some wrapped sweets for energy.

By then we knew where we were—not far from a store where George had bought several pairs of fine wool, ready-to-wear slacks the previous year. George found another pair he liked, and we waited on a bench outside the shop while the saleslady hemmed them up. She had the job done in quick order, so that soon we were continuing down Nathan Road to the Mansions, where we remembered there were stalls selling inexpensive goods. We had Hong Kong dollars left, so we stopped in and bought a little Chinese-style jacket for me.

As the shopkeeper bagged our purchase, he told us not to loiter but to hurry back to Ocean Terminal as fast as we could. A rainstorm with strong winds was about to strike. We ran, but we did not outrun the storm. Like an angry dragon, winds swooped across Nathan Road, picking up debris and tossing it into the air to soar high among the buildings. We found the underground passageway that leads directly into Ocean Terminal, so we did not have to walk far outside. We were glad we were so close to it.

Well, that was the "something old" and "something new" we did on our seventh visit to Hong Kong. What would we do on visit number eight in another year or two?

Aboard the high-speed magnetic train in Shanghai.

SHANGHAI SIGHTS

When we opened the draperies of our cabin on Sunday morning, March 8, we saw the sun reflected off the skyscrapers of Shanghai. *Rotterdam* was docked across the Huangpu River from the Pudong New District. The view was splendid: Each skyscraper is unique with a striking design, and there are so many of them. We gaped.

After breakfast, George and I shuttled to town and did something very simple. We walked through the main park off Nanjing Road and sat on a bench to people-watch. It was a lovely Sunday morning and the beginning of spring; the trees were just bursting into leaf and early

271

flowers were blooming. Because it was a Sunday morning, many families were out walking and sitting on benches; close by was a group of senior citizens doing morning tai chi. What could be better than this? Ah, yes, we remembered—"Dancing at the Temple of Heaven on Easter Morning." Waltzing in the park in Beijing had been truly heavenly.

That evening, standing together on the verandah of our cabin, we watched the action on the Huangpu River. George and I had looked out over the river on our prior visits to Shanghai, but we loved the view even more each time we came back. Hundreds of dinner boats plied the waters of the Huangpu. The boats were lit up in reds and greens, blues and golds. The buildings of Pudong were aglow, and arcs of colored lights swept back and forth across the night sky. We both felt as if we were in fairyland—again!

The next day was one I had looked forward to from the moment we had decided to do the 2009 world cruise. This was the day we were to board the magnetic levitation train for a fantastic ride. The ride was only sixteen minutes long, but it rated a double *wow* from both of us. During our ride, the train achieved a speed of over 184 miles per hour. We felt as if we were floating on air, which we were because the train does not run on rails. It floats through some kind of magnetic action that I do not fully understand but George tried to explain to me. The ride exceeded my expectations; actually I think about it most days, because in our dining room I have a picture of the two of us on the train. We are both smiling broadly.

That same day—in under a minute—we whizzed up to the eighty-eighth floor of the Jinmao Building via a high-speed elevator. From there we looked down on Shanghai. Our guide told us that we were fortunate, because although it was smoggy, the sun was out and the views were special. He pointed out the Shanghai World Financial Center, which in 2009 was the tallest building in the city, and he identified the ironwork of a second skyscraper which was under construction and would be taller than either Jinmao or the financial center. I guess by now that building is completed. The three skyscrapers form the points of what he called "The Golden Triangle." That evening as we looked out across the river, George and I connected the dots.

FINDING FRIENDS IN NHA TRANG, VIETNAM

Having been to Nha Trang at least twice before, both George and I thought our 2009 day there might be a ho-hum one. We thought we had done much of what all tourists do, so what else was there for us? We soon found out.

George and I started the morning by hopping on the ship's shuttle to town, where we were dropped off in front of a large hotel complex. Outside the hotel gates, we saw a line of cyclo drivers waiting for customers. A cyclo is basically a bicycle that has a cab attached.

Why not? George and I each got our own cyclo, and we took off down the major boulevards of the city. The streets were filled with cyclos, because this is a major form of transportation and a way that men make a living. We showed our drivers a picture of a large Buddha that we wanted to see; they pedaled us there, and we hopped out to look more closely. I said "market," and they took us to a vast two-level produce center. George said "beach," and they pedaled us along the strand. At the beach, we climbed down, this time so George could take pictures.

As we stood looking out over the South China Sea, George whispered to me that one of our drivers was peeing right there in the street. What a city of contrasts! On one side of the boulevard were modern, high-rise hotels, on the other a beautiful beach and a man urinating. Later back on the ship, George and I talked about the diversity of customs found in different parts of the world. What would have been considered unacceptable at home was acceptable here. It is just a matter of what we are used to. In this instance, who were we to judge?

Back at the pier market, George and I wandered the stalls. From prior stops in Vietnam, I had learned that the inexpensive barrettes and blouses made in Vietnam work well for me, so I bought a couple of both. As I was paying, I heard a call, "Dorothy and George, is that you?" There were Eva and John, our beloved dinner tablemates from World '07. They pointed into the harbor where the *Queen Victoria* was anchored. They were "doing the world" with Cunard on *Victoria*. They had chosen that line for their World '09 cruise because they loved to dance and on Cunard they had many more ballroom dancing opportunities.

The four of us sat on a bench on the pier and talked. We had not seen each other in two years because John and Eva live in California, we in New Jersey. From time to time, we had chatted on the phone, but face to face was so much better. Sometimes people talk about the fates being against them. The fates were with us that morning. We had started out thinking the day would be ho-hum. Instead it was a zip-a-dee-doo-dah day.

A SINGAPORE SLING AND A SPECIAL SINGAPORE MOMENT

Rain greeted us in Singapore. Yes, more rain! We were beginning to call this the rain cruise.

George and I had booked an excursion so, regardless of the weather, we climbed on the tour bus. It dropped us at the Raffles Hotel so we could drink a Singapore Sling in the famed Long Bar—something we had never done during our many prior stops in Singapore.

Then came our special Singapore moment. We climbed into trishaws—the Singapore version of cyclos—for a spin around the city streets. By then, the rain was coming down steadily, and my trishaw driver thoughtfully wrapped a big piece of plastic over me. As the driver covered me up, he spoke to me in English. I started a conversation with him as he pedaled. After a time, he said something like this to me: "You have a new president? In January on TV, I saw your president. He is a black president? He is a dark man? Did I see right?" He asked the last question with amazement in his voice, as if he could not believe that the United States would have a president with dark skin like his.

I told him that, yes, he was right, and we all hoped that our new President Obama would do good things for both our countries. Finishing our spin-about, I thanked him with an extra tip, for he had made my day and given me a very special Singapore moment. When I cast my vote now, especially in presidential elections, I think of "my" trishaw driver and the impact my vote can have halfway around the world.

PHUKET PONDERABLES

Our day in Phuket in Thailand was a great one for George. He rode an Asian elephant and a water buffalo. He watched an elephant create a piece of modern art. He viewed monkeys climbing palm trees to pick coconuts. At first, George was not sure about all this; he was concerned about the welfare of the animals. Once assured that they were being well treated, my dear husband sat back to enjoy our adventure at an animal reserve in Phuket's Chalong Highlands.

At the animal sanctuary, George and I actually shared an elephant. We stepped up onto a platform and sat down on seats mounted on our elephant's back. The trainer checked our seatbelts (is that not a rather delightful idea—an elephant with seatbelts?) to be sure that there was no danger of our falling off. Then the elephants bearing our tour group followed one another caravan-style over paths into the hilly surroundings.

The art demonstration was a simple one: An elephant twisted its trunk around a paint brush, dunked it into a pot of watercolor paints, and then splashed color across a canvas mounted on an easel. Laughingly, George said he thought the results were better than some paintings he had seen in modern art museums. Liking weird T-shirts, George bought a black one with a picture of an artist/elephant emblazoned on the front.

Similarly, the monkey demonstration was fun to watch. The monkeys scampered up palm trees and broke off coconuts that they dropped down to the animal trainer below. This is actually the way the fruits are harvested from high up in coconut palm trees. After that, George climbed on the back of a water buffalo and held on tightly while the buffalo walked slowly around the compound and I took his picture, the one shown on the cover of this book.

Back on the ship, George and I talked about his initial concerns regarding the use of animals in situations like the ones in which we had participated that day. In Asian farming communities, water buffalo routinely work in rice fields hauling plows; we remembered having seen that in Bali. Elephants are workers, too, pulling heavy logs. I would eventually get to see that on a future trip.

Is there a difference between using elephants and buffalos as beasts of burden and using them as show animals? Is it acceptable when animals work to help mankind, but not when they are put on display for entertainment? What is the difference between riding a horse and riding an elephant or a water buffalo?

In a similar vein, I told George of feeling uncomfortable riding in a trishaw, as I had in Singapore, with a man pedaling hard to drive me around. On the other hand, as someone explained to me, people need work. Was I suggesting that it is wrong for men to pedal for their livelihood? I am still pondering that question, too.

MEMORABLE MUMBAI MOMENTS

Between our visit to Mumbai in the winter of 2008 and our visit there in the winter of 2009, something horrendous happened—the November 2008 attack in which terrorists took over the Taj Hotel and set fire to rooms there. The terrorists proceeded to Colaba Causeway, the major shopping boulevard two or three blocks behind the hotel, and let loose a barrage of bullets upon people going peacefully about their work.

On our arrival in Mumbai harbor during World '09, we saw one outcome of that vicious attack. As soon as *Rotterdam* was tied up at the pier, a patrol boat took up a position on the harbor side of the ship. For our entire stay, the boat went back and forth, day and night, alert for trouble. This had never happened on any of our three prior stops in Mumbai.

Our first morning in the city, we and another couple took a cab to Colaba. We stepped into one of the more upscale carpet shops to look around, because India is known for its handwoven rugs. The proprietor offered us chairs to sit on and tea to drink while he displayed his rugs. This was a far different shopping situation than the one we had experienced in 2008 when we were offered a seat on a mattress on the floor.

After we had purchased a small mat, we sat and chatted with the proprietor. We asked him about the attack that had occurred a few months before. Had he been affected? He was most forthcoming and told us that he lived with his family just behind the Taj Hotel. He explained that, for two days after the attack, he and his family never left their apartment; they just hunkered down, even staying clear of the windows. They feared going out. The proprietor told us that he had a friend who had been "bloodied."

When we were ready to leave, the proprietor-turned-host escorted us to the door and pointed toward a bar up the avenue. He said, "Look inside that bar. You will see bullet scars on the walls from the attack." We walked up that way; indeed, there were the scars.

So sad, and so sad also to realize the poverty of the beggars who followed us along the avenue: a young woman with a babe in arms, a man with a deformed arm, a young boy with a scarred face. That evening on the ship, George and I saw the movie *Slumdog Millionaire*, the Academy Award Best Picture winner of 2008 that was filmed in Mumbai. It tells the story of youngsters maimed and forced to beg. Having just walked the same streets and been followed by people seeking alms, we felt the powerful impact of the movie.

In Mumbai the next morning, we made a visit to the Afghan Catholic Church and happened on a scene that touched our hearts. In the square across from the church, a young lad was playing by himself. He had an elongated chunk of tile that he stood upright on the pavement. Carefully balancing it on its narrow end, he stepped back and tried to knock the tile down by throwing a stone at it. He did this over and over again. For him, this was a simple form of entertainment—simple because he probably had no money to buy a real toy.

I looked down at his bare feet; his toes were covered with a hard crust that was bloody in spots. His clothes were raggedy, his face dirty. Nevertheless, he seemed content. Perhaps he had cause to be, for he was playing, not being forced to beg as were the boys in *Slumdog Millionaire*. Since he was the only child around, I knew it was safe to give him a few rupees and a pen and pad I carried in my pocketbook. I remember the smile he gave me in return. Although we later went on to visit a temple complex where ritual bathers go to be healed, that site did not compare with "Boy Playing with Tile," which is what I titled my most memorable Mumbai moment.

DELUGES IN DUBAI AND MUSCAT, OMAN

Rain was the most remarkable thing about our days in Dubai and Muscat. We were in the desert, where the year before we had seen sun, sand, dunes, and camels. It rarely rains there; the average yearly rainfall is just a couple of inches. *But* it rained for us. After all, this was "The Rain Cruise."

In Dubai, on the evening of our first day, George and I attended a spectacular sound and light show that is based on an old Arabic tale. We had great seats in the open-air theater, and the performance began on schedule. Our eyes glued to the stage, we were completely entranced by the lights and the colors. There were singers and dancers in lovely costumes and acrobats who climbed high metal poles and swung down on wires across the stage. There was music, too: the sounds of drums and cymbals and bells.

Suddenly the lights and sounds became even more intense. Streaks of light criss-crossed the sky. Bombardments of sound crashed around us. Mesmerized, I whispered, "How are they doing this?"

George realized more quickly than I did that these sounds and lights were not part of the show. Grabbing our belongings, he said, "Let's get out of here, fast. That's thunder and lightning!" We dashed for the exit and made it to an overhang just before the rain struck. And did it rain!

Back on the bus, our guide said he had been leading groups to the sound and light show for four years. It had never rained. He had never seen anything like this. We worried about the performers, especially the young women high on those metal poles, who kept swinging across the stage with lightning flashing around them.

The rain stayed with us. Our goal the next day was to see what would be the tallest building in the world when completed later in 2009—the Burj Khalifa. Although the building had not yet been topped off when we were there, we were able to walk the lobby and the shopping areas on the ground floor. We could not see the highest floors, however. They were shrouded in rain clouds.

Yes, the rain doggedly followed us to Muscat, the capital of Oman. It rained so heavily that there was flooding in the roundabouts and some roads were closed due to the water level. Apparently, Muscat has no storm drains; they are not necessary, for it never rains (as we heard over and over again from our guide).

The main tourist market is in a wide alley that extends downward from a rise to a lower level by the harbor. The water raced down the alley like a raging river, so that we would have had to wade through it to shop. We could not even get off the bus to revisit the mosque with those beautiful wall-to-wall Iranian carpets that we had seen on World '08. The rain was too heavy. Our tour guide told us that the schools were closed for the day to allow the children to play in the rain. And this was the desert!

Leaving Muscat, our captain announced on the public address system that he was putting on extra speed and that we would arrive in the Seychelles—our next port of call—one day early. He explained that he was doing this so he would have an extra day between the Seychelles and Mombasa in Kenya. He was also changing our route to be on the safe side: When we left the Seychelles, instead of heading northwest to Kenya, he was first going to take *Rotterdam* south and approach Mombasa from that direction. Doing this, he would avoid the areas north of Kenya and around Somalia, where pirates had been striking. We had all heard about the *Alabama*, the container ship that pirates had hijacked within the past two weeks. Obviously, on our ship that evening, most conversations focused on pirates.

TORTOISES IN THE SEYCHELLES: AN INDELIBLE PICTURE

Before heading out over the mountains and into the countryside, our tour of the Seychelles took us on a quick swing through the town of Victoria to see the small replica of London's Big Ben in the square.

The Seychelles are truly a gorgeous part of the world. As we drove around the main island, our guide had the driver stop from time to time so we could take pictures and stretch our legs. At one point, we made a lengthy stop at a spice plantation. Only fifteen of us were on the bus, but just six opted for a walk to see the spice plants. Obviously, George and I were among the six. As we walked, our guide pointed out nutmeg trees, which are the source not only of nutmeg but also of mace. He showed us something he called a lipstick tree, which has large red blossoms. We crushed a blossom and coated our lips with the red liquid that oozed out.

Returning to Victoria, we stopped at the botanic gardens on the edge of town to see Coco de Mer palm trees that produce a double-lobed coconut, and to see the giant tortoises for which the Seychelles are noted. The fifteen of us clambered off the bus to get pictures. Then it was all aboard to return to the ship.

The coach was in motion when our guide shouted for the driver to stop and back up. He told us to get off the bus. "Be quick," he said. "You have to see this." What we saw were two giant tortoises in the process of mating. The male—and he was absolutely huge—was atop the female and was doing his "thing," unaware that he had an audience taking pictures of him. I guess you could say that this was the high point of the tour for our group, as well as for Mr. Tortoise.

MIGHTY ANIMALS IN MOMBASA

When we left the Seychelles, our captain figuratively put his foot on the pedal, heading slightly south before turning north to make his final approach into Mombasa. We had the speed to outrun the pirates if any were lurking. Just in case, though, he placed armed guards on the promenade deck and warned those with verandahs to lock our outside doors at night and keep our draperies closed. These were the same directions we had been given when we had sailed the coast of Nigeria on a previous cruise.

Anticipation was high as we made our speedy yet uneventful approach into Mombasa and tied up at the wharf. George and I had booked an overnight safari to two national parks, Tsavo East and Tsavo West. We were both eager to go. I was actually quivering with excitement as we climbed into our van with two other couples for the drive out to the animal sanctuaries. Our van was part of a caravan of vehicles organized by our travel agency.

Arriving in Tsavo East, at first we saw few animals, but then a family of African elephants lumbered across the road, heading toward a watering hole on the other side. African elephants are bigger than the Asian variety we had seen in Thailand, and they have longer, floppier ears. Our driver/guide opened the roof of the van so we could stand up to take photos and videos of the animals.

That morning, and later on during our afternoon game drive, we saw more elephants, zebras, giraffes, gazelles, secretary birds, lizards, dik diks, elands, and eventually lions off in the distance. Spotting animals was easy, especially with a guide to tell us where to look.

We lunched at a resort in the park, where we also stayed that evening in bungalows that overlooked a watering hole where elephants came to drink at dusk. I started this memoir with a description of the night George and I spent in our private bungalow. That night ranks near the top of our list of most marvelous travel moments.

The next morning, early, we were back in our van and headed to Tsavo West. Here we stopped at some springs to see hippos and crocodiles. About eight hippopotami were in the water, their bodies mostly submerged to keep them cool. We both were amazed to see that their skin was so pink.

We had to look carefully to see the crocodiles on the shore; they blended in well with their surroundings. If the guide had not pointed them out, we would have overlooked them completely, which might not have been the wisest thing to do.

After lunch in another luxury game resort overlooking a watering hole where monkeys were scampering about, we headed back to Mombasa. Our guide told us that we had a five-hour drive before us. The first hour was in the animal park on roads as bumpy as a washboard. The final four hours were on a two-lane highway. Whenever he could, our driver would pass slower vehicles and squeeze back in line in front of them to get ahead. We were all happy when we saw our ship in the distance.

I have a fond and lovely memory of our next afternoon in Mombasa, which we spent at the market on the pier meandering from stall to stall. Let me start by saying that before we began World '09, George had warned me about buying anything large. We were in the process of downsizing and arranging to move to a retirement community. But on the pier in Mombasa, George spied something he wanted—something he really wanted. Standing behind a stall was a four-foot-tall wood giraffe. George walked over to the vendor. Smiling, I followed, realizing that my beloved George, who very rarely bought anything for himself, had his eyes on Mr. Giraffe.

That morning, we had visited a craft center on Barack Obama Avenue, where craftsmen sat on the ground and carved exquisite animal pieces from wood. We had seen giraffes there, but they were expensive. When George spotted Mr. Giraffe on the pier and the vendor agreed to fifty dollars, George had his giraffe.

The vendor wrapped George's giraffe in a piece of burlap that was lying in the dirt; then he tied up the heavy, awkward package with a frayed piece of even dirtier twine. With a broad grin on his face, my eighty-seven-year-old husband hoisted Mr. Giraffe over his shoulder, and off we went, up the gangway and onto *Rotterdam*. That is a picture I shall never, ever forget. I just wish I had thought to take a photograph.

George had to leave his treasure with the steward at the top of the gangway to have it refrigerated for a couple of days. This was a precaution in case Mr. Giraffe was suffering from a case of termites. Once his giraffe was released from quarantine, George got a couple of big cardboard boxes from the ship's florist and fashioned a container large enough to take his prize home. Today, Mr. Giraffe stands in a place of honor in our dining room. Most mornings, I give him a loving pat and recall that afternoon on the pier in Mombasa.

A DAY IN MAPUTO, MOZAMBIQUE

On the windowsill of our dining room, near Mr. Giraffe, sits a carving of a family: a mother, a father, and a young lad. Carved from a branch about four inches across at the base with a touch of bark still clinging to the side, "The Family" has three small heads glued to necks carved upward from the main block. The head of the mother figure is covered with a small, real-cotton, printed bandana, just as we had seen so many women wearing in East Africa and also in West Africa in 2006. We bought "The Family" in Maputo, Mozambique, the next port on our World '09 itinerary. How we came by that carving is one of my favorite stories of Mozambique.

The final stop on our Highlights of Maputo tour was the cultural museum on the main square opposite the cathedral. At the museum we viewed unique sculptures made from gun parts dating from the civil war that had wracked the country until rather recently.

I recall that, as our bus was loading to leave the square, a youngster climbed on the steps of the vehicle with a wood carving in his hand and began to negotiate a price with the passenger in the front seat. I remember the passenger finally calling, "Does anyone want to buy this wood-thing I bargained for? My wife doesn't like it. The price is good, just five dollars." As soon as I had seen the boy with the family carving, I had wished I were the one negotiating, because I had never seen anything like it on any of our travels. I was quick to answer, "We do!" and I was quick to hand the youngster some dollars and claim ownership of "The Family."

I knew, too, that in this poor area across which we had driven on tour that morning, those dollars would mean a lot to this young entrepreneur. In the countryside, we had seen signs of extreme poverty: women washing laundry in a stream; small, one-room shacks made from tin and wood scraps. In the city, we had seen rows of mismatched shoes lined up on the sidewalks. These shoes had been collected by American charities and sent to Mozambique to be given away under the Clothes for Africa program. The shoes had fallen into the hands of the unscrupulous, who were selling them and profiting from American generosity. Similarly, other used goods were being sold from the sidewalks—clothing collected by American charities to be given to needy people, not to be sold to profit a few. That was the explanation our guide gave when we asked why all those shoes and goods were laid out on the sidewalks.

Our guide spoke freely to us about conditions in his country, where unemployment stood at 68 percent and HIV at 16 percent. He spoke of the deadly war that had divided his country. He spoke of the graft that still was rampant. And he spoke of the kindness of the American charities that were sending aid.

The guide also told us a little about himself. He was thirty-six years old and had worked for eleven years at the British Embassy, where he was able to hone his English skills. He emphasized that he had only one wife and three children; this was by choice, he explained. He knew three children were all he could afford, and he wanted to be able to educate them. He said that his wife came from a family of twelve, he from a family of six. Families that size were too large and a cause of poverty and unemployment. Then he offered this interesting tidbit: A prior ruler of a neighboring area had taken another wife each year and had sired over 200 children. I seldom take notes while on tour. I did write down these numbers, because I knew I wanted to remember this young man; he was such a happy person and told so many interesting stories about his country.

DURBAN, SOUTH AFRICA

From Maputo, Durban is a several-day sail down the east coast of Africa. My memories of Durban I categorize as "The Best," "Another Best," and "The Worst."

The Best: On tour, George and I stopped at the Durban Botanic Gardens. I rate the gardens an A+. They were among the most beautifully designed gardens we had ever visited. George was ecstatic as our guide walked us along shady paths. She pointed out plants native to the area and told us a little about them. The specimens were clearly marked— sausage tree, cannonball tree, fig tree, and many others. When the guide gave us free time, we explored on our own; from the signage, we knew what we were seeing. The best happened when we rounded a corner and encountered a wedding party there for a picture-taking session. Our tour group stopped and joined the professional photographer in taking pictures of this beautifully dressed wedding party, the bride adorned in flowing white.

Another Best: On tour, we stopped at what is known as the Indian Craft Market, although most of the booths were manned by Africans. The Indian Market is a shopper's paradise. Our tour guide gave us just forty-five minutes to shop. We had to bargain for each item we wanted, but in those forty-five minutes we managed to buy an elongated piece of batik with a giraffe design, a distinctive Zulu mask, three tall, thin wood statues, four little paintings, and twelve animal placemats. Loaded with packages, we were the last to climb onto the bus with just one minute to spare. The others on the bus gave us a cheer. The market got an A+ as being among the best on our world cruise.

The Worst: On our return drive to the ship, our guide warned us about walking alone in Durban. She had the bus driver take us through some upscale areas, which on the surface looked peaceful, especially the area around the beach hotels. She warned us to be careful of pickpockets and muggers if we walked around in the afternoon. She emphasized never, ever to walk the streets at night on our own. An acquaintance on the ship, who had stayed in Durban the prior year, echoed the guide's warning. Here, too, the unemployment and HIV infection rates were high. We figured that these warnings merited a rating of D for Durban. Fortunately, "the worst" did not impact George and me.

CAPE TOWN, SOUTH AFRICA

On the morning of our arrival in Cape Town, George and I rose early to watch the sail-in, one of the most glorious sail-ins because of Table Mountain in the distance. We also would be taking a full-day tour offered by our travel agent to Inverdoorn Private Game Reserve. The tour was among the poorest we have taken. George was so disturbed by it that, upon our return, he penned a critique to the agency. Here is his description of the day, in George's own words.

The Story of Our Safari in Inverdoorn Reserve
by George Hennings

When the driver first started the Land Rover, I feared we were in trouble. He "ground" quite a while to start the engine, which when started sounded like a worn sewing machine. About fifteen minutes out on safari, the engine stalled. The guide/driver ran the battery down trying to start up again. Help was called and two guys came in a pickup truck. After they worked under the hood for a time, the Land Rover started, and we were on our way. We almost stalled a number of times, and did several times. The driver ran the battery down restarting, but fortunately we didn't have to call again for assistance; he managed to get the engine started eventually. The engine belched great clouds of white choking smoke as we drove on. We had difficulty taking pictures of the animals spotted through the white exhaust cloud, and our lungs and throats were not happy either. Many times the driver had difficulty shifting gears with his shift stick. He knew from obvious past experience what to do: hammer with his fist on the base of the shift stick!

We reached the controlled, gated lion area. The Land Rover stalled as we went through the gate. Some passengers asked if it were safe to continue and risk stalling near the three lions. The driver said it was safe, but when we spotted the lions, he stopped with the vehicle in neutral for no more than two minutes. I believe he did this for fear of stalling the vehicle so close to the lions. He told us not to stand up or put our arms outside the vehicle during those two minutes. He did not want us to attract the attention of the lions. I asked him why they had not had the engine overhauled or at least tuned up. He said it was difficult to secure parts. Obviously the vehicle was unfit to offer to tourists.

So ends George's evaluation, which he sent to the agency. He forgot to say that pieces of sharp, jagged metal were hanging loose near the steps of the vehicle. One of our party cut her ankle to the bone on a piece of that metal as she climbed aboard. She had to be taken to a local hospital to be stitched up and to get a tetanus shot. Unfortunately, she was not able to leave her suite during the remainder of the voyage. On the positive side, we did see cheetahs, zebras, giraffes, and various kinds of antelopes—in addition to the lions.

The next day was better for George and me. We spent our time roaming the area around the Victoria and Alfred port. We had done that in 2006, and we did it again in 2009. The following day was good for us as well. The wind died down, and Rotterdam was able to sail out of Cape Town and head north to Luderitz, Namibia.

LUDERITZ AND WALVIS BAY, NAMIBIA

Luderitz is in a part of Africa that has fewer than three inches of rain per year. Clearly that falls within the definition of a desert. Wonder of wonders, in 2009 some of that rain fell on the day *Rotterdam* anchored off Luderitz, Namibia. We tendered in and spent the morning walking around under an umbrella. Is that not a twist of fate, the same twist that brought us rain in Dubai and Muscat?

The rain did not follow us the next day to Walvis Bay, which is north of Luderitz on the Skeleton Coast, so we had a more pleasant morning there. We walked about the area near the port. Our goal was to find more boxes in which to pack up some of our purchases. A generous lady in a stationery store came to our rescue. About to throw out two large boxes, she was happy to have us haul them away. She also gave us some bubble wrap, and we bought packing tape from her.

On our way back to our ship, we chanced on a highly polished, fat hippopotamus to add to George's growing collection of wooden animals. By the time the captain sounded *Rotterdam's* horn to signal departure, we had our new hippo and our treasures from Maputo packaged and ready for offloading in just over two weeks.

ST. HELENA, ASCENSION, AND HOMEWARD BOUND

Leaving Africa behind, *Rotterdam* steamed west toward the islands that are outcroppings of the Mid-Atlantic Ridge: St. Helena and Ascension. On May 5, the ship dropped anchor off St. Helena and the captain had the tenders lowered. This was where the seas were so rough in 2006 that I did not go ashore.

George and I got into Jamestown, the main town on St. Helena, by nine in the morning. I had my personal guide to show me the sights—husband George, who had gone into town with my cousins in 2006 despite the choppy tender ride. George took me for a walk through the gardens and then into the small church for a sit-down in a pew to catch my breath. He pointed out Jacob's Ladder, a very steep flight of stone steps up a cliff on the edge of the town. We did not even think of climbing those steps. We also passed on a cab ride to the house where Napoleon spent his final days after his defeat at Waterloo. George had been there/done that, and I preferred sitting and drinking a cup of tea in one of the small restaurants on the main square.

King Neptune was kind to us on our way to Georgetown on Ascension Island. The seas stayed calm. The next morning, though, our captain warned that there were heavy swells at Ascension. Our chances of getting tenders safely into the pier were not too great. After initial problems, however, the captain announced that the seas were quieting and it would be safe to tender. In 2006, in contrast, it had been too dangerous to make landfall.

George and I were happy travelers. During our visits in Iceland, in the Azores, and on St. Helena, we had stood at the juncture of the Eurasian and North American continental plates. Now we were at another place where the Mid-Atlantic Ridge surfaced.

In Georgetown, we had a lovely little walk to see the remains of a fort and an old palace-like building. We sat in a pew of the main church for a few quiet moments of contemplation. Then we prowled around and behind some shops in the town. Behind one shop, where waste was waiting for pickup, George made a great discovery—clean, discarded boxes in which computers had been shipped. We each grabbed one and headed back toward the tender. Other passengers who were just disembarking asked what we had bought. When they learned that our boxes were for packing, they hurried to the garbage dump to scavenge some as well. Everyone needed boxes at that point to get his or her newly acquired treasures home.

Once we left the Ascension Islands, the "feel" aboard the ship changed, even though *Rotterdam* had yet to cross the Atlantic Ocean and drop anchor at Devil's Island. The ship was also scheduled to make three stops in the Caribbean before docking in Fort Lauderdale on May 13. Nonetheless, we felt homeward bound.

The last week and a half aboard ship was a vacation cruise, not really an adventure. We simply enjoyed the shipboard amenities and the company of our large contingent of friends. Each night at supper, we reported our packing progress. On the evening before our entry into Fort Lauderdale, Mel and Kelley—the super shoppers in our dining group—reported thirty suitcases and boxes packed and labeled. Yes, that's right, thirty pieces of luggage! Other tablemates reported only twelve, but one piece was massive; they had built a container the size of a crate from at least four florist boxes and lots of tape. We reported thirteen pieces that we would be shipping via Fedex and two carry-ons.

On the morning of May 13, after 110 days of travel, *Rotterdam* sounded her horn and steamed into Fort Lauderdale. By evening, George and I looked out upon springtime in New Jersey, with trees already sprouting green leaves and flowering shrubs bursting into bloom. We slept that night in our own beds.

A few days later, I followed our friend Jim's lead and composed this haiku:

> our world cruise wound down—
> yes sad…yet glad to be home.
> What will we do now?

Chapter Nineteen
STAYING CLOSER TO HOME

What would we do now? George and I decided that, for the next year, we would stay closer to home. Our home was to be different, however, for in August 2009, we signed a contract to move into a senior citizen community as soon as the unit we wanted became available. Packing up was a huge undertaking and selling our old home was difficult, given the collapse of the housing market in 2008.

In mid-December 2009, the unit in our chosen community opened up and we moved into it. At the end of February 2010, our house in Warren sold. The day after the closing, we booked two short cruises: one to Alaska and a second to Canada. We were again free to travel and enjoy the world out there beyond New Jersey. Vacationing would be even easier, because our new community would monitor our house while we were away.

ALASKA, AGAIN

Investigating upcoming cruise possibilities, I discovered that Alaska cruises early in the season were cheaper than those that started later, when the weather was warmer. Flying into Seattle to catch an Alaska-bound ship is relatively easy, so in late May 2010, we flew west to Seattle and boarded *Amsterdam*, the same ship on which we had done World '07 and '08. We had taken this cruise several times, so not only was the ship familiar, but so were the ports. That was the beauty of the trip. We could just relax and walk the ports in a leisurely way.

The fates were with us. On the pier in the boarding area, our friends and past trivia partners, Louise and John, spotted us. We had been exchanging emails since a prior cruise with them, but had not realized we would be together on this one. We arranged with them to meet for trivia twice a day while on the ship and to lunch from time to time. They had been teachers just as we had been and are excellent trivia players. In my computer I have a picture of the four of us with another couple who joined our team. Together we made a super trivia team—absolutely unbeatable. Also, we had our friends to clap for us at the Mariners reception where we were recognized for having sailed with HAL for over 700 days.

Louise and John are from Victoria, British Columbia, and our last stop before Seattle was Victoria. Rather than sailing all the way to Seattle, Louise and John disembarked in Victoria. After they had dropped their luggage at their house, they returned to the pier with their car and drove us around their city—past the famed Empress Hotel, the stately government buildings of British Columbia, and the totem pole park. They then took us to their home for tea. What a lovely afternoon we shared with them.

George and I kept marveling at how many friends we had made through our travels. We often said that we came home with mental pictures of places we had visited and with treasures we had purchased that triggered memories. Most importantly, we came home with memories of wonderful times enjoyed with wonderful people.

A postscript to my entry on Alaska: Louise sent me this email with her account of the same cruise:

> *John and I have been looking through all of our travel photo albums over the last while—so we recently were looking at the Alaska cruise that we were on with you and George in 2010. We remember the surprise when we met you during*

*pre-boarding and what a good trivia team we had . . . I
also remember that you received your Platinum Medallions
during that cruise—on June 12th to be exact. It was the
first time HAL offered the fourteen-day Alaska cruise—
we enjoyed it so much that we have done it a number of
times since.*

CANADA AND NEW ENGLAND

On the few seven- to ten-day cruises George and I had taken, we had
seen numbers of families enjoying days at sea together. A cruise affords
family groups the opportunity for together time as well as the freedom
to tour independently in some ports to pursue individual interests.

George and I had traveled previously with his cousins and my sister.
Granted that is a small family group, but it had worked well for ship
travel and bus tours with a given itinerary that everyone knew in advance.
It probably would not work so well for a car trip that required more on-
the-spot decision-making.

In 2010, I had a small close family. I "had" my George, my sister
Barbara, and a few cousins, including John and his wife Patricia, with
whom we had taken two world cruises, and another cousin, John's sister
Evelyn. We six decided that a cousin cruise was for us.

Celebrity Cruises had begun to sail from a New York-area port. For
my sister and for George and me that meant no flying, which was an
advantage for us Jersey folks. For the cousins, that meant a relatively
easy non-stop flight into a New York airport without the need to stay in
a hotel the night before the cruise departed. Actually, until COVID-19
struck, many cruise lines offered voyages from a host of local ports to
make getting to the ship more convenient.

Although we had taken the popular Canada/New England cruise
before, the 2010 trip still was appealing. For my sister, who now had
mobility problems and used a scooter to get around, it was ideal. Barbara
could ride to the ship terminal in Bayonne, New Jersey, in a van that

could accommodate the scooter, and then once at the terminal could drive her scooter onto the ship. On our return, she could scooter off the ship and get into the van curbside. Other than Bar Harbor, which is a tender port, the ports were scooter-accessible, too.

My happiest memory of the cruise is of our evenings aboard the *Summit*, one of Celebrity's older ships. About five-thirty, we would gather for dinner in the main dining room. We had a round table for our cousin group, which was perfect for conversation; generally, we would relax and talk over dessert and coffee. Then we would go together to the showroom to enjoy the evening entertainment, with my sister scootering the length of the ship. Every year, we see more folks using scooters, especially given that ships are getting bigger and bigger and the distance from prow to stern challenges even an older person with relatively good stamina. As my sister did, some people bring their own scooters on board; others rent them through the cruise line.

I also have a memory of our getting off *Summit* in Charlottetown, Prince Edward Island, with Barbara riding her scooter down the gangway and George holding onto the back of her chair to make sure she did not zip down too fast. On the pier is an extensive market, and Barbara was able to roll her scooter from booth to booth. She could also travel through the streets adjacent to the pier to get a sense of the area. The same is true in Halifax; there are great crafts and produce markets on the pier and a nice boardwalk for scootering in front of the terminal.

Of course, some ports like Quebec are more difficult to navigate in a scooter. Barbara could handle the sidewalks of the Lower Town, but the Upper Town was off limits for her. In Quebec City, Barbara stayed back on the ship while George and I went with the cousins for a carriage ride in the Upper Town. Actually, I should say that George, I, Patricia, and Evelyn did the carriage ride. John walked, striding beside our carriage; with his long legs, he had no problem keeping ahead of the horse.

Chapter Twenty
RETURNING TO SOUTH AMERICA
WINTER 2011

Our second circumnavigation of South America began in early January 2011. The voyage was sixty days in length, and the ship was *ms Prinsendam* of the Holland America Line. *Prinsendam* carried about 800 passengers and was a perfect vehicle for a circumnavigation of South America, since it could dock in some ports that the larger *Amsterdam* and *Rotterdam* could not. It is the same ship on which George and I had sailed West Africa in 2006.

The itinerary was substantially different from our South American itinerary in 2002. The ship stopped at the Amazon ports first and then sailed down the east coast of the continent to Brazil, Uruguay, and Argentina. But after that came the exciting new element— the *really* exciting new element. *Prinsendam* sailed to Antarctica, a continent to which George and I had never traveled. After that, it sailed north, stopping in Chile, Peru, and Ecuador before transiting the Panama Canal.

FRIENDS FOREVER

The other evening, as I sat watching the *NewsHour* on public television, the phone rang. "Hi, this is Phil. I'm wondering how you are?" I was so happy to hear Phil's voice, for evenings had seemed long since COVID-19 struck and sheltering at home had become the norm. So I sat down for a chat with our friend Phil. George and I had met Phil and his wife Eileen on South America '11. Assigned to the same dining table, the four of us had bonded. It doesn't seem possible that our friendship started more than ten years ago.

George with Phil and Eileen on 'A Night Out with friends'.

We met Phil and Eileen on the first evening of the cruise. The two of them were sitting at a window table in the main dining room. We were to dine with Phil and Eileen each evening for the next two months, and in that time, they became like family. That does not always happen. There was another couple at our table, a table for six. Although we enjoyed the other couple, the bond we formed with Phil and Eileen was special.

It is hard to say why strong friendships develop, isn't it? But sometimes, everything works. We began to meet each day for lunch on the lido deck. We began to take tours together. When we got to Antarctica, we stood with them in the cold and wind to view the icy landscape. We even shared our life stories with one another. In the years to follow, we booked six cruises together. If I had to identify the best thing about our South America '11 cruise, I would say it was Phil and Eileen. We did, indeed, become friends forever.

Also aboard the ship with us were Jim and Jessica, whom we had met on World '08 and with whom we had played trivia on World '09. They live just across the border in Pennsylvania, so we had even visited with them there. On SA '11, George and I again teamed up with them for trivia, stood on deck with them in Antarctica, and partied with them in Phil and Eileen's spacious suite. Jim is the haiku poet who has encouraged me to express my feelings through poetry. Jim and Jessica, too, are our friends forever. They are avid world travelers, more so than George and I. For anyone contemplating a long cruise, my recommendation is to look for kindred spirits and once you have found them, never let them go.

HIGHLIGHTS FROM THE AMAZON REGION

Before entering the Amazon Basin, *Prinsendam* made a stop at Devil's Island, a former French penal settlement. George and I had stayed aboard the ship when *Rotterdam* had stopped there in 2009. We did a walkabout now in 2011. Although Devil's Island is a striking reminder of how cruelly people have treated others, the island has natural beauty with pounding surf, lush vegetation, and exceptional vistas. Neither George nor I, however, could imagine anyone being chained there in the awful heat and humidity. Walking about the island, we talked about that. We agreed that Devil's Island represents a contradiction between the beauty of the physical earth and the ugliness of human nature run amok.

George and I did not realize what was awaiting us when we got off the *Prinsendam* two days later in Macapa, Brazil. We were going to stand on the equator at 0° latitude, with one foot in the Northern Hemisphere, the other in the Southern.

Previously, we had stood on the Prime Meridian in Greenwich, England, with one foot in the Eastern Hemisphere and the other in the Western—at 0° longitude. We also had been aboard a ship when the captain had maneuvered his vessel to lie directly over the equator and the International Date Line, at 0° latitude and 180° longitude, or what is known to travelers as the Golden Point. Similarly, we had been aboard a ship when the captain had maneuvered his vessel to lie directly over the equator and the Prime Meridian, at 0° latitude and 0° longitude.

On the Equator.

Why was this so exciting for inveterate travelers like George and me? I really cannot explain it. After all, the concepts of latitude and longitude upon which these points and places are based are a creation of the human mind developed to aid navigation. Yet the idea is a brilliant one, with time zones dependent on those concepts.

I recently found in my files a picture of George straddling the equator at Macapa; I can see the pleasure on his face. I also found a picture of a raw egg balanced on its tip on a beam placed at the equator; the egg did not fall off. For us, our day in Macapa was a great one. We did not repeat it, because never in all our later Amazonian cruises did our ship stop to let us off. At Macapa, a ship generally pauses only to pick up and offload a local pilot who guides the vessel up and down the Amazon.

A few days later, we awoke to dancers and drummers on the wharf below our cabin. We were back in Manaus, which we both remembered from our South America '02 voyage with Regent. Because we wanted a different experience this time, we took a tour to the site of an old rubber plantation. We saw how rubber trees were "milked." We saw the house where the plantation manager and his family lived and the building where the raw rubber was formed into balls for shipment. "Good tour," George said.

Back in town, we stopped briefly for a photo op at the theater/opera house. The rubber barons were not about to leave the finer things of life behind when they claimed this area of the Amazon for rubber production. They imported the prefabricated parts of the opera house from Europe and had those reconstructed here in what essentially is the middle of the rainforest. We also saw mansions that the rubber men, after amassing their fortunes, had commissioned so they could live in splendor.

Back in town, too, we had a special treat: a Portuguese-style lunch where waiters brought out huge roasts and cut off chunks of meat to heap onto our plates. Beef, lamb, and pork roasts, whole chickens, and grilled wursts kept coming and coming. Yes, we were presented with too much food, given that there is so much hunger around the world, but we also got a taste of the Portuguese culture that can still be found today in Brazil.

George and I spent the afternoon resting and watching the action on the pier. As was true when we docked in Manaus in 2002, the scene was like a live-action film. Riverboats were tied up on the side of the pier opposite ours. On the wharf were trucks unloading their contents onto the riverboats to be carried up or down the Amazon. The mighty Amazon is more than a river; it is an important water highway that connects villages with one another. That connection is essential, because there is no motorway to carry goods and people from one village to the next.

ILHÉUS

Jorge Amado is a popular Brazilian writer. Born in Ilhéus, Amado has written more than twenty-five novels that deal with urban and rural poverty in Brazil. When we were in Ilhéus on SA '11, I sat at a table in the city square right next to Jorge Amado. I admit that he was not a flesh-and-blood Amado. He was a full-size, realistically painted, wood carving. During our walkabout in Ilhéus, George and I rated the statue of the author, who was seated at a table with one of his books before him, as the most creative and different feature of the village. I sat down at the table, which was actually part of the statue, and George snapped a picture of me.

Having taken turns sitting by Señor Amado, we went into the church on the square to rest for a moment or two. It is a lovely little structure, just right for a town of this size. We walked the streets of the town and along the oceanfront to look into the touristy

Dorothy with Señor Amado.

stalls clustered there. Of all the towns on the east coast of Brazil that we visited on SA '11, George and I deemed Ilhéus the prettiest.

RIO DE JANEIRO

While touring virtually from home in 2020, I became euphoric just thinking about Rio. On SA '11 *Prinsendam* made a couple of stops at Amazonian ports that George and I had visited on prior trips. The ship made additional stops along the upper coast of Brazil, such as in the cities of Fortaleza and Salvador and villages like Ilhéus. Just as I got excited thinking about Rio on my virtual trip, on our actual trip in 2011, I got itchier and itchier as we got nearer and nearer to Rio de Janeiro.

Our entry into Rio harbor was oddly eerie. Fog blanketed Sugarloaf and covered Corcovado, but not the very top of the mountain where Christ the Redeemer stands alone. Corcovado was our destination for the day—a good day, actually, because we found no lines for the tram to the top of the mountain. The tram took us into and through the mist. When we came out above the clouds, we saw the statue of Christ, huge with arms extended as if to bless the people of Rio, who were somewhere down there hidden in the mist. Whether a believer or not, one cannot help being touched by Christ the Redeemer. Everyone needs somebody who looks out for him or her—who extends arms of comfort. In a way, the statue is symbolic of that human need. I know that I descended the mountain with a heightened sense of inner peace.

Have you heard the expression, "Going from the sublime to the ridiculous"? Both George and I felt we had done that when we climbed on a tour bus that evening with Phil and Eileen to attend a samba show. Buxom young women with minimal clothing—almost nothing covering their bosoms or their bums—gyrated to the accompaniment of raucous music. We had attended a samba show in 2002, but the amount of shaking of bare butts did not compare with what we saw that night. I do not think anyone in the audience could have fallen asleep during the show.

BUENOS AIRES AND MONTEVIDEO

Whereas the samba is associated with Brazil and Carnival, the tango is the dance of Argentina. On our first evening in Buenos Aires, George and I went with Eileen and Phil to the same tango venue that we had visited back in 2002. It was wonderful and so different from the raucous samba performance we had been to in Rio. The tango is a precision dance when performed by professionals. It is an unbelievable dance: We kept wondering how the two performers did not trip one another as they twisted their legs in, around, and under—quickly! Most in the audience were Argentinians who knew the couples and clapped especially hard for an older pair who had been performing for years. George and I probably had seen them in 2002.

Earlier that same day, our tour took us into areas of Buenos Aires that we recognized and into other areas that were new to us. We stopped in the central square again and stood below the balcony where Eva Peron had greeted her people. Again, too, we visited the big cathedral on the same square.

But there was more in store for us. Our guide led us to the subway station on the main plaza and down to the tracks. We hopped aboard a subway car for a ride that took us to a lovely little coffee shop. There we sat at tables alongside locals who were out for a Sunday morning coffee. That was a highlight of our day.

Our visit to the colorful Italian section was memorable as well. The houses in the Italian section are painted in bright yellows, blues, and pinks. We meandered the streets of the area and took pictures of the houses. We watched a couple dancing the tango on a street corner and found a black leather jacket for me in one of the stores.

Montevideo is just downriver and across the Rio de la Plata from Buenos Aires. George and I had had a lovely day there in 2002; we had followed the directions of a man, who had approached us in the main square, to a leather shop where we had bought jackets. So, we visited Montevideo nine years later with memories already in place. We shuttled to the square, walked under the archways that line it, and took more pictures of the statue of the horseman in the middle. I kept looking for the little man who had talked to us on our first visit, but he was nowhere to be seen. Eventually, after walking down the avenue to revisit the cathedral, George and I found a bench and sat in the sunshine. What a simple memory of a day well spent.

THE FALKLANDS

Looking back, I could remember nothing—absolutely nothing—about *Prinsendam's* stop in the Falklands. The islands were on the itinerary, but what had George and I done? I found two photos marked "Falklands"; what these photos showed was a coastline in the distance. Friends Jessica and Jim came to my rescue. They sent this series of two emails:

> YES! We did stop at the Falklands on Feb 10. Jessica and
> I took a Jeep to visit the penguins.

For a couple of hours, I stewed. What had George and I done? Then came Jim's update:

In my notes it states that those passengers who were planning to leave the ship later in the morning were unable to do so because of sudden sea swells. Those of us who got off early had to wait until late afternoon to return and we happened to be on the very last tender back.

We, who love to travel, are certainly unique beings. I got upset when I could not recall a day from our travels. Jessica and Jim were intrigued and spent considerable time investigating. Of course, this was COVID-19 stay-at-home time, and everyone was happy to find something interesting to do.

ICY ANTARCTICA

It was cold, icy cold. I had on my puffy winter coat with its faux fur-lined hood pulled up over my head and my woolen Icelandic hat beneath the hood. George wore his new, bulky, down coat that we had bought for these cold days. Holland America Line had given us special gloves with fingers that slipped off for picture-taking. George had on his; I just kept my hands dug deeply in my pockets. We both wore woolen scarves wrapped around our necks.

That day, I composed a verse to express my elation:

> We are in Antarctica!
> We are surrounded by icy waters,
> icebergs,
> hanging glaciers,
> snow covered mountains,
> dark colored crags.
>
> We are in Antarctica!
> it is beautiful, glorious, magnificent beyond belief.
>
> We are in Antarctica!

With our trusty Kean bag in icy Antarctica.

George and I had recently been to Glacier Bay in Alaska, but the bays and inlets of the icy continent in which we were sailing were ten times, fifteen times, maybe twenty times more striking than any other glacial area we had visited.

Prinsendam cruised Antarctic Sound, the waters surrounding the South Shetland Islands, and Wilhelm Archipelago for three days. We passed flat-topped icebergs and pointed ones, small floes and huge ones. The first day was misty, eerie, and bleak, but then the sun came out and the world around us glistened. At times, the distant mountains glowed golden as they reflected the rays of the sun.

Even then it was cold and windy on the decks of *Prinsendam*. The winds were so powerful that our petite friend Eileen had to shelter in the corner of her verandah; they gusted so violently that she feared the blasts would lift her off her feet. George and I could remain on deck for no longer than an hour at a time before having to go inside to warm up with a cup of hot pea soup. Serving pea soup to passengers on sightseeing-at-sea days is a tradition on Holland America ships.

But we saw no emperor penguins, no penguins at all. The only evidence we saw of them was snow off in the distance, stained pink from penguin poop. I told George that we would have to come back another time to see the penguins. I was not kidding.

A high point in our Antarctic adventure was when young researchers from the Palmer Station came aboard while *Prinsendam* idled off the coast near the American research center. These dedicated young people explained their research and the effect of global warming on Antarctica— on the pack ice and on the animals who inhabit this remote part of earth. We were impressed with their sincere concern for the environment and their love of what they were doing.

The evening of the third night of our Antarctic adventure, *Prinsendam* chugged northward and away from Antarctica. Our captain announced that it seemed likely he could maneuver the ship so we could see Cape Horn, which is surrounded by such rough seas that many early explorers lost their lives attempting to go around it. The next day, he gave us a thumbs-up. There would be fog and the sea would be choppy, but we would be close enough to take pictures.

We sailed away from Cape Horn to spend an afternoon riding a bus along the inlets and amid the mountains of the Tierra del Fuego archipelago near Ushuaia in Argentina. We found the scenery in this area of the world to be absolutely breathtaking, with a more beautiful vista appearing at each bend of the road.

As we relaxed on our bus, George put his arm around me and said, "A few years ago, I would never have dreamed that I would get to all seven continents and I would visit Tierra del Fuego." In my mind, I agreed with him, remembering friends back home who have no interest in seeing the wonders of our earth and who have never gone beyond the borders of their own country. They have missed out on so much that is wonderful!

Just think, this was the second time we had seen Cape Horn, the second time we had been so close to the bottom of the world. Who would ever have believed . . .

CHILEAN MOMENTS

Working our way north up the west coast of South America, we sailed the waters of Chile for the next week. My favorite port along that coast is Punta Arenas; I love the unique market in the central park there. The entire area is lined with quaint wooden carts, each with colorful markings. Each sells Chilean goods, especially finely made baby-alpaca sweaters that come in lovely designs and hues. I remember that park each time I wear one of the sweaters I bought there.

Puerto Montt is another favorite port along the Chilean coast. I have a single, sharply focused picture in my mind that is tied to this town. It is a picture of a volcanic peak, snow-tipped and reflected in the blue of the lake below. I "took" this mental picture as we toured the countryside that is just east of Puerto Montt. On tour, we stopped at a restaurant with windows that looked out across the lake to the volcanic peak. As we enjoyed lunch there, a local folkloric group performed. I recall that shops in this region sell lapis lazuli jewelry, for that blue gemstone is mined nearby.

Arriving at Isla Robinson Crusoe, we walked the area around the port, which was under repair. It had been ravaged by a rather recent earthquake and tsunami. We looked up from there to the caves on the hillside where Alexander Selkirk had lived. Selkirk was the castaway after whom Daniel Defoe modeled his character, Robinson Crusoe. George and I had our picture taken beneath the sign "Isla Robinson Crusoe." I have that picture mounted on my photo board in our dining room. I often look at it when I give Mr. Giraffe his morning pat.

I call my memory associated with Valparaiso, which is a major city on the Chilean coast, "A Night Out with Friends." While *Prinsendam* was docked in Valparaiso, Phil, Eileen, George, and I attended an evening event at a hacienda/ranch/vineyard in the nearby countryside. Music, dancing, food, vineyards, alpacas, and gauchos—we enjoyed all of these together during this lovely Chilean evening. Travel is not only cathedrals and monuments; the best travel moments are often ones shared with friends in a beautiful country setting.

The next day, the four of us toured Santiago, the large capital city of

Chile. Sitting on the bus together as we returned to the ship, however, we decided unanimously that we had preferred our evening party at the hacienda to the hustle and bustle of the city.

On the negative side—in travel, as in life, there is generally a negative component—our sail among the Chilean fjords was a mist-out. We knew from our visit in 2002 that there was beauty out there somewhere, but we did not see it. Perhaps another year?

PERUVIAN MOMENTS

We did not have to worry about rain in the coastal region of Peru when we docked in Pisco. The northern part of Chile and the southern area along the coast of Peru are desert. It almost never rains there.

We crossed desert terrain to get from Pisco, where the *Prinsendam* had docked, to the ruins of Tambo Colorado. Here is what the tour brochure said about Tambo Colorado:

> *This well-preserved adobe and stone structure, in all likelihood built atop an ancient fortress of the pre-Inca culture of Chincha, was adapted and transformed into a grain depository, administrative, and military center by the Inca Pachacutec in the 15th century. This ancient complex continues to be the most interesting artifact of the Inca culture on the Peruvian coast. There is evidence that the site was used to worship the sun, as well as study astronomy and everything related to agriculture.*

At the site there was no vegetation at all, just hot sun and sand. We clambered among the ruins and got hotter by the minute. What a contrast in temperature to what we had experienced less than a week before in icy Antarctica.

Our guide explained about the successive civilizations that had built upon this land—civilizations that were powerful and then sank into oblivion to be replaced by others that also disappeared. "The Rise and Fall of Empires" could well be a phrase to sum up what we saw. Surely a

lesson can be learned here, if humankind can learn from the past.
As per the brochure, this is what we did next:

> From Tambo Colorado you'll continue on to a private
> hacienda (farm) where you will enjoy a delicious set-menu
> lunch after a brief tour of the family's property. Many
> crops are grown here, including asparagus, tangelo, and
> macadamia. You'll see the various plantations and hear about
> the Benavides Family. Textiles are produced to help the local
> Ayacucho native families. Lunch will be accompanied by
> local musicians playing for you.

George and I enjoyed all of that and then some. Sitting at a lunch table, we felt we had won the lottery. A gentleman joined our table. He was a Benavides and the owner of the hacienda; he also was a minister in the Peruvian government. George figured out that, by opening his home to visitors and running it as a tourist site, Señor Benavides was making more money than on the sales of his asparagus, tangelos, and macadamia nuts combined. He was a charming gentleman and an excellent host who regaled us with stories about life on the hacienda.

My purpose in quoting from the brochure is to emphasize how important it is to read these descriptions carefully and ask questions of the staff at the shore excursions desk before opting for a tour. Those men and women can even tell you how long the stops will be at each location and how much walking will be involved. It also helps when comparing tours in different ports.

Because we enjoyed our visit to the ruins of Tambo Colorado, when George and I got to Lima, the capital of Peru, we opted for a similar tour that combined a walk through ancient ruins with lunch on a ranch. The ruins we visited were those of Pachacamac City, dating from 700 CE. The ruins are cut from and into sandstone and are surrounded by dry desert landscape. The civilization of which they were a part flourished until the Incas arrived.

Our guide explained that Pachacamac City was named for the creator god known as the Earth Maker or Pacha Kamaq. He pointed out a pyramid-type structure that once was a temple to the sun. Thinking of what the guide had said, George and I later talked of how universal is the search for meaning in life, the search for understanding of the origins of the earth and of living organisms. We talked of the importance of the sun in so many civilizations and the reverence of the earliest people toward their sun god. My George was a free-thinking Unitarian, a questioner with an inquiring mind; that characteristic made him a great travel companion.

Lunch was at an Andean-style ranch. We sat on a patio to watch a horse show that was a delight. While we watched, we ate small potatoes served on picks so that we could dip them in a mustard sauce. For lunch, we moved under an arbor and sat together at long tables. Later we went into the gardens to see rows and rows of lettuce under cultivation, aided by irrigation. I do not remember what they served us for lunch or what other crops were being grown, but I do remember those potatoes—golden, white, and purple in color. Perhaps Peruvian potatoes, native to South America, are a metaphor for something fundamental in life: diversity.

> diverse potatoes
> add pleasure to our dining:
> purple, gold, and white
>
> different people
> add pleasure to our living:
> American mix
>
> different countries
> add pleasure to our travels:
> one world united

PANAMA BRIDGES

Arriving in Panama City, Phil, Eileen, George, and I took a tour northward into the highlands of Panama. On our bus, we passed first through the lush green growth of the rainforest and then climbed up into the mountains.

The great Continental Divide of the Americas—which starts in Alaska and ends at the tip of Argentina in Tierra del Fuego—runs down across Central America. That was what we were seeing.

We stopped for a hike through rather wild, verdant parkland. Streams flowing down from the Continental Divide added to the beauty. Using walking sticks that were distributed to help us navigate the uneven trail, we crossed the streams by bridges—narrow, swaying bridges that had a wood-slat walking surface with only ropes forming the side supports and handrails.

Faced with the first of those daunting challenges, George stopped and then built up his courage. Carefully and slowly, he concentrated on putting one foot ahead of the other. I have a photograph that I took of George crossing the first bridge. As I think I have said before, George did not appreciate heights; my photo of him forcing himself to cross the swaying bridge shows that. His face reflects determination. "I can do this," he must have been saying to himself.

I have a wonderful photo, too, of Phil and Eileen crossing the same bridge. Their smiling faces are alight with the pleasure of our Panamanian adventure.

On our return trip to Panama City, we drove back over the great Bridge of the Americas. The Bridge of the Americas links the North American segment of the Pan-American Highway to the South American segment and spans the entrance to the Panama Canal. As we crossed it, we could see our ship anchored in the harbor, as well as other vessels waiting their turn to transit the canal. This was an easy bridge for all of us to cross.

Bridges! Are bridges a metaphor, too—a metaphor that highlights the importance of making connections between and among people who come from different backgrounds but share common needs? People face the bridges they must cross in different ways at different times. They face some bridges with trepidation, some with determination, and others with pleasure. Perhaps travel teaches us that; perhaps it teaches us to recognize how easy it is for us to cross some bridges in our lives and how difficult it is to cross others.

THE CANAL AND HOME

The next morning, *Prinsendam* pulled up anchor and sailed under the Bridge of the Americas. We progressed through the western series of locks into the Culebra Cut. The cut is where the canal passes through the Continental Divide, which we had just seen the day before in the highlands of Panama. Later, after crossing the artificial Gatun Lake, we made our descent into the Caribbean by the eastern series of locks.

From the prow of our ship, Phil, Eileen, George, and I watched as the water level went down in a lock, the giant doors opened, and we moved into the next lower lock. It was a clear day that we enjoyed together, and our talk was of the future. Phil said that they might want to repeat the circumnavigation of South America in the winter of 2013. Might we do that together? Yes, a good idea; let us plan on that. And we did. We began to plan . . .

A few days later we disembarked *Prinsendam* in Fort Lauderdale. Parting on the pier, the four of us agreed that we had had a wonderful trip. We had seen so much—from the hot rainforest of the Amazon to the ice of Antarctica. But the best was finding each other. That friendship continues to this day. I email Phil some mornings when I need someone to talk to. He calls from time to time. Perhaps sometime in the future, we will be able to talk face to face.

Chapter Twenty-One
RETURNING TO SOUTH AMERICA AGAIN
WINTER 2012

B ack home in Jersey, George and I booked the *Prinsendam* for its circumnavigation of South America in the winter of 2013. We would do that with Phil and Eileen.

We also booked the Regent ship *Mariner* for its sail around South America in the winter of 2012, one of two cruises we would take that year. These South American cruises would get us out of Jersey during the cold and snowy months. We chose Regent for 2012 to experience different shipboard activities from those offered by Holland America. We also would be offered different tours, all of which are now included in the upfront price of a Regent cruise. Both cruises started from Lauderdale, went through the canal, sailed the west coast of South America and then cruised the east coast of the continent to do the Amazon on the way home.

GOOD BEGINNINGS

On the first day of South America '12, George and I met Beverly and Richard, who would become close friends and the mainstay of our dinner group. We also met Jane and Graham from Australia, who would also be at our table each evening. At the first trivia session, we sat with Michael, Noel, and Tom, with whom we would team during the entire voyage. George and I were ready—ready for a wonderful cruise. As we had learned on South America '11 when we had met Phil and Eileen, good friends make a great cruise.

Good tours also make a great cruise, and our first tour was better than good. We stopped in Cartagena, Colombia, where George and I booked an afternoon excursion. The tour took us to the top of the hillside above the city to look down on the bay and to visit the ornate La Popa Monastery. We stopped at the fortress in town for a photo op, popped into the shops nestled within the city walls, and climbed into a horse-driven carriage for a ride around Cartagena. When we first stepped into our carriage, the sun was still shining, but toward the end of our ride, the lights of the city flickered on to create a totally different picture of Cartagena—a more romantic one. But the best was still ahead. We stopped at a waterside restaurant for dinner, where we could look out on the bay. Lots of ships were moored there, and we could see their lights reflected in the water. The sky was aglitter with stars, and the moon cast a glow across the water. It was an absolutely beautiful night.

A VISIT TO QUITO

Regent offered all guests doing the circumnavigation an overnight trip to Quito, the capital of Ecuador. The cost, including air and hotel, was part of the cruise fare. For George and me, doing an overnight with touring on the days before and after was a stretch. My George had begun to have arthritic pain in his lower back. To ease the pain, he used a cane, yet even then he could not walk so far and so fast as he had done in prior years. But, as he said, we had never been to Quito, and we could go there for "free." So we went for it.

Actually, George did very well. We had bought a three-legged seat cane on an internet site, so that whenever a guide stopped and talked about what we were seeing, George could sit down and rest his aching joints.

Regent had chartered a plane to take us from Manta, on the coast of Ecuador, to Quito, which is inland. The descent into Quito is something to remember, for the city is surrounded by mountains. Think of a bowl, Quito deep in the center of it. To fly in, the pilot must make a steep dive, or so it felt to us. I kept telling George, as we nose-dived onto the runway, that the pilot probably did this every day and could manage it with ease. The pilot did just that, getting us into Quito early so we could tour the city in the afternoon.

On tour, we stood in the vast central plaza in front of the impressive San Francisco Monastery, with its two bell towers and broad stairway leading up from the square into the church. Seeing us, vendors came running. One vendor—a young Ecuadorian artist— carried a stack of his oil paintings. I took a photo of him and bought one of his canvasses—a primitive of a snow-capped volcano looming above a village filled with Ecuadorians, a super-huge condor hovering in the sky. I also took a photo of a woman in traditional dress, with her black hair in a long, thick braid down her back and a black, wool, fedora-type hat on her head. To us, she was the epitome of an Andean woman.

We explored other lovely plazas, one the site of the Quito cathedral. The cathedral was beautiful, its interior adorned in 22-karat gold. We could not recall ever seeing another cathedral so ornately decorated. We sat in a pew and just gawked at the gold.

Later, we returned to the San Francisco Monastery for a tour of the church, a cocktail hour in the cloister galleries, and dinner in the refectory. The cloister was where the brothers had walked while they contemplated and prayed; the refectory was where they had eaten when the monastery was fully operational. That evening—trodding where the brothers had trod and dining where they had dined—we felt we had been transported back to another age, to the seventeenth and eighteenth centuries. It was an awesome experience, one few travelers have the opportunity to enjoy.

George with an artist in Quito.

The following morning, we made two equator stops. The first stop was in a pretty park with a stone monument that is topped with a globe. George and I stood on the equator line painted on the pavement in front of the monument and had our pictures taken. This spot was identified before the days of GPS and, as it turns out, is not exactly on the equator. We went next to a nearby garden that was more recently identified with GPS as being at 0° latitude. We again had our pictures taken. George and I were still excited to straddle the equator, even though we had stood at 0° latitude when we visited Macapa in Brazil on South America '11.

The plane ride out of Quito was as exciting as the ride in. The pilot lifted the nose of his plane almost straight up to avoid the mountains that were practically at the end of the runway. That is an exaggeration, of course, but that is how it felt to us.

Mariner had sailed on to Guayaquil, Ecuador, while we were in Quito. It was a short flight to Guayaquil from Quito and a short bus ride to the ship. As is the Regent custom, the ship's staff and crew were lined up on the pier to welcome us "home."

SALAVERRY AND LIMA IN PERU

Our record so far was two tours taken and two tours rated an A. Despite our prior qualms about the overnight in Quito, George had managed all the walking, flying, and busing. From our next stop in Salaverry, Peru, we joined a tour to Chan Chan to see the ruins of a civilization—the Chimu—important from 900 to 1470 A.D. What we saw were acres and acres of ruins of a mud village that was still being excavated.

I think we must have walked miles in the hot sun—another exaggeration to be sure, but it did feel like that. George carried his seat cane, sitting whenever the guide stopped to deliver her commentary; we plodded along at the back of the group. Previously, we had always been at the front on tours, but things do change, just as civilizations rise and fall. Still, it was a good tour: a knowledgeable guide, thoughtful fellow passengers who kept track of us when we lagged behind, and an interesting place to be. Another A on our scorecard of tours.

Our tour the next day in Lima also rated an A. It was perfect for us. The high point was a repeat visit to the National University of San Marcos, which is said to be the oldest university in South America. The grounds are lovely, as are the lecture halls. In one of them, I stood at the podium as if I were lecturing, and George took my picture. That was pure fun. We had good stops at a convent, two mansions, and the central square, where we watched the changing of the guard at the Presidential Palace. We had driven by the palace in the past but never had seen the changing of the guard.

Back on the ship, I canceled the tour we had booked for our second day in Lima. That tour was to take us to more convents and monasteries. Of course, we would have been walking throughout.

As I noted before, tours are now included in the base price on Regent. Knowing this, I had pre-booked a tour for each day we were in port. After a couple of days of steady touring and walking, we realized that a person can have too much of a good thing. Instead, we stayed aboard *Mariner* on our second day in Lima and popped off just for an hour to walk around the shops on the pier. Clearly, we still had energy to shop for leather belts and alpaca sweaters.

PISCO, MATARANI, AND ANTOFAGASTA IN CHILE

George and I began to keep a report card on which we graded tours in Chile.

Pisco: another A. The tour we took was again just right for us. It was a drive across desert terrain to Paracas National Reserve. We stood on a high point in the desert and looked out on the Pacific Ocean. Best of all, we did not have to walk far. We learned that shorter, easier tours were better for us at this stage of our travel life. One's physical stamina is something all travelers must take into account in selecting tours.

Matarani: not even a gentleman's C. We had chosen a drive to an area of lagoons to see birds. As for the drive, the bus traveled over winding roads that snaked high above the coast. We saw crosses by the roadside in memory of those who had been killed in auto accidents right there. Yes, not one cross, but many!

As for the lagoon and the birds, we were supposed to see lots of wildlife. We saw six turkey vultures, a few ordinary ducks, and one flamingo. George counted them. His final rating for the tour: a D minus. Yet we were fortunate. Our tour got back in the afternoon so we did not have to ride the coastal road after dark. Others who had taken lengthier trips came back with hair-raising accounts of riding that dangerous road at night.

Antofagasta: another A for a tour that worked for us. We made a number of stops, but the one that stood out was the morning fish market where local fishermen were bringing in their daily catch. The market overlooks the port, where small fishing boats are moored. At that early hour, Chileans were out and about, buying fish for supper.

We also visited an old silver refinery with a museum on site. Toward the end of the tour, our excellent guide gave us the opportunity to walk the streets of Antofagasta and visit a museum on the square or to stroll slowly to the bus. We chose the latter. We were learning that it was best not to push ourselves too hard. Traveling is supposed to be a pleasure, not a forced march.

LAGUNA SAN RAFAEL, THE INSIDE PASSAGE, AND THE BEAGLE CHANNEL

George and I had boarded *Mariner* just a month before, on January 5. Now here we were on February 5, anchored in a large bay in the Inside Passage of Chile. Local catamarans came right to our ship, and we climbed on one for a ride up a channel that was too small for *Mariner* to enter. Our destination was the San Valentin Glacier.

The lounge of the catamaran where we sat to look out at the glacier was heated. For picture-taking, we could pop up to a top deck and then come back inside to warm up. The glacial scenery was breathtaking. George remarked on how unbelievably blue the face of the glacier was. Another A+ tour rating, possibly an A++.

The next day, *Mariner* sailed into another fjord where we glacier-watched. One glacier we saw had the same spectacularly blue-colored ice as the San Valentin Glacier. It was gorgeous. The following day, we cruised into still another bay. From our verandah, we were able to take pictures of a glacier that dropped directly down into the bay where *Mariner* was anchored. This was A+ cruising, with scenery brought right to us. It was perfect for George, who was still bothered by arthritic pain in his hip and his leg.

Later, during our last day in the Beagle Channel, the captain set a course south and into the Drake Passage toward Cape Horn. When we left the Beagle Channel and entered the open seas, we really rocked and rolled. The sea was angry gray, and the swells were something to see and feel. I was amazed that my head and stomach held steady; I did not even pop a seasick pill. Mostly, we stayed in our suite and watched the sea from our window. We did not dare even to go out on our verandah. Finally, walking with great care, we rode the elevator to one of the upper decks to take pictures of Cape Horn. We could not imagine how the early explorers in their small vessels, which were not much larger than two of our life boats combined, could have handled seas like this.

ON THE RIO DE LA PLATA

Mariner made a stop in Ushuaia, Argentina, before setting a northward course. After a few other stops, we entered the Rio de la Plata and docked in Montevideo, Uruguay. On prior trips, George and I had loved walking about Independence Square in Montevideo, but since we had never gone beyond the central square and avenue, we decided to take a short tour to see more of the city.

The most striking features of the tour were the life-sized metal sculptures depicting the early movement of European settlers into Uruguay. We saw three of these sculptures chronicling the beginnings of the country, and we were impressed. To us, the sculptures could just as easily have been telling the story of the migration of settlers westward across the plains of North America. We saw renderings of a mule-drawn covered wagon, of oppressed Indian populations, and of a horse-drawn supply wagon mired in mud. We had not fully realized that the settling of North America by European immigrants was paralleled with a similar settling of European populations in South America. But most certainly, this was so. Our schools unfortunately do not include much South American history in the curriculum.

Earlier in the cruise, as we had steamed northward up the eastern coast of South America, we had visited an Argentinian community settled by the Welsh and then later a Brazilian community settled by the Germans. Again we were getting an important history lesson in European immigration into South America.

Aboard *Mariner*, Terry Breen, a historian and authority on South America, was the port lecturer. As part of her many presentations, she talked about European settlements in what was to become Portuguese-speaking Brazil and in what were to become Spanish-speaking areas—literally the rest of South and Central America. She explained about Pope Alexander VI, who in 1493 had issued the papal bull that divided the known world between Spain and Portugal. In retrospect, does it not seem hugely presumptuous that the property rights of the peoples already living in Africa, Asia, and North and South America could be considered irrelevant while Europeans just staked their claims to these parts of the world?

On Rio de la Plata near Montevideo is a resort community, Punta del Este, where we stopped after leaving Montevideo. Our expectations were low when we got off the ship on the morning of our visit. We returned so happy that we had chosen to go to an art museum there. In the central garden of the Museo Ralli was an exquisite collection of metal sculptures of children engaged in various forms of play. Just delightful! For anyone considering a stop in Punta del Este, it is something to investigate.

Upriver from Montevideo is Buenos Aires. What does one do when one has made two stops there already? We opted for a short boat ride along the canals that lie to the north of the main city. It proved to be a good choice. On our bus ride to the boat dock, we passed through a residential part of Buenos Aires that we had not seen before. Later, from the boat, we saw upscale neighborhoods that line the shores of the canals. Terry Breen had explained that some North Americans retire there, as well as in Uruguay. A retiree can buy a nice residence in a good area for under a hundred thousand American dollars. In fact, she had bought property there in anticipation of her own retirement.

RIO DE JANEIRO, BRAZIL, AND NORTHWARD

During our 2002 stop in Rio, George and I had opted for the cable car tour up Sugarloaf. In 2011, we had chosen the tram tour to see Christ the Redeemer on Corcovado. Because we believed that nothing could beat those two adventures, our expectations were low as we boarded a four-wheel-drive vehicle that would take us to the Tijuca Forest. This would be a ho-hum day, we thought. We were wrong.

Our driver/guide gave us an exciting ride through morning traffic as he navigated the streets out of the city. The ride up through the forest itself was even more thrilling, for the driver kept his foot on the accelerator as he spun us around curve after curve.

The view from an outlook in the Tijuca Forest, where we made a stop, was unbelievable: We could see Sugarloaf and also Corcovado, with Christ the Redeemer standing atop it. Below were the beaches—Copacabana and Ipanema. The whole of Rio was spread before us. It was a wonderfully clear day, the sun was bright, and any early morning mist had been blown away. We were "blown away," too.

In the evening, George and I went with Regent to the same samba show at the Plataforma that we had attended in 2011—a show that we had not particularly enjoyed. We repeated it because it was fun to drive out at night to see Rio aglow with lights. It was also good fun to be out with our friends Bev and Rich, who had never seen the show. Our reaction remained the same: too loud; more a Las Vegas-type revue than a professional samba performance. Again we contrasted this with the Argentinian tango show in Buenos Aires. If anyone is choosing between the two, the tango show with the intricate footwork and precision steps is the one to pick.

Our sail-away from Rio the next afternoon was wonderful, simply wonderful. The weather cooperated as we bid farewell to one of the most beautiful harbors in the world. *Mariner* sailed north, taking us to a number of beach resorts and to Salvador and Fortaleza. We canceled many of the tours we had pre-booked when at home and opted for walkabouts, especially in cities we had visited before. We had learned that, just because a tour was "free," we did not have to take each and every one.

UP THE MIGHTY RIVER, AGAIN

Before dawn on March 4, *Mariner* crossed the bar and entered the mighty Amazon. The bar is a raised portion of seabed caused by the deposition of silt flowing out of the Amazon. Opening our draperies in the early morning at an hour when the sun was just appearing on the horizon, we looked out upon cocoa-colored water, brown from all the silt the river was carrying. We could see land—not the riverbank but large islands that sit in the delta. "Sunrise on the Amazon" is the name I gave the simple watercolor drawing I painted that day in art class.

Mariner made the usual port stops as we cruised the Amazon. George and I took excursions in two of those ports. Both excursions were on riverboats. Both were lots of fun, made even nicer because Beverly and Richard were with us.

The first of the two was from Manaus on a riverboat that carried about fifty passengers. It took us upriver to a docking site where we transferred to a smaller motorized craft. In it, we chugged deeper into the rainforest. We were literally surrounded by jungle, branches and vines at times hanging out over the channel we were navigating.

And then: *supreme happiness for a biologist!* Right in front of our little boat—so close we could almost reach out and touch them—were giant Victoria water lilies. George and I had seen these unique and lovely green plants in botanical gardens, but never in their natural habitat. Here we were literally engulfed by them. I kept repeating, "Oh, George! Oh, George! Finally! Finally!"

The Victoria water lily has large, very fragile, flat, green, pie plate-like leaves with slightly crinkled edges. When a lily first blossoms, the flower is white, but by the second night it turns a lovely pinkish color. Yes, yes, yes—we saw both white and pink flowers, and we brought home lots of pictures to prove it. For George, this was a minor miracle, because we had taken this excursion twice before. This trip was the one and only time we saw the lilies. And to think, we even saw them in bloom.

According to a reference book George later checked, the scientific name for the lilies is *Victoria Amazonica*. The name highlights the fact that these plants were named for Queen Victoria, who was a young queen of England when European explorers first came upon them, and for the Amazon, which is their natural habitat.

Transferring back to our riverboat, we set off to see the Meeting of Waters—the place where the dark Rio Negro flows into the lighter-colored Amazon. Because the waters differ in color, we could see clearly the line where the two flow side by side for miles. Our riverboat cut right across the line, something we had not done on our prior trips up the Amazon.

Two days later, when our ship docked in Santarem, we climbed onto another small rivercraft and motored into one of the adjacent lake areas. From the boat, we saw sloths, lots of different birds, and iguanas. We also saw houses built on pilings as protection against rising river levels. The rivercraft stopped far up in the lake, and the crew passed out drop lines so we could fish for piranha. One crew member snared a piranha; seeing that, we all crowded around to get a picture.

I could feel little nibbles on my drop line. I felt proud when I pulled in my fishing line with a small—very small—piranha attached. Before I could secure it, my piranha dropped off. This is not a fish story. George actually saw my catch, but the fish fell from my line before he could take a picture to record my moment in the spotlight. No other passenger on the boat managed to bring a fish to the surface, as I had done.

MARVELOUS MEMORIES

Yes, *Mariner* made the obligatory stop at Devil's Island, and yes, this time George and I tendered in to walk around the lower level. It was too hot and humid for us to climb to the top to explore the cells. The ship also made stops at a couple of Caribbean Islands. One was Barbados where we took a short tour with our now old friends Bev and Rich. The best part of that tour was a stop for refreshments on the Atlantic side of the island, the wild side where the Atlantic Ocean crashes onto a rocky shore. The four of us sat at a window table to drink a toast to our lasting friendship. The friendship has lasted, even though we did not cruise together again. Email is a great way to maintain contact.

On March 15, Bev and Rich reserved a table for dinner for "our" gang of nine—three players from our trivia team plus George and me, Bev and Rich, and Jane and Graham from Australia. It was my birthday, and this party made it one of the nicest I have ever celebrated. Our great dining stewards brought me a cake and everyone sang the birthday song.

Since our trivia team was there, two of the chaps had prepared a special fifteen-question quiz that I had to answer. Many were geography questions because we were travelers, after all. I did get most of the answers right. I remember I did not know who was the only prime minister of Great Britain to be assassinated while in office—a question written by Michael, the strongest member of our team. Although I goofed a bit, my friends awarded me a prize, a gleaming necklace made of Murano glass from Italy.

Two days later, George and I were home in Jersey. It had been a good cruise, despite George's arthritic pain that had been rather severe at

Dorothy holding her necklace gift and wearing her elephant dress from Bangkok.

times. The cruise had been especially memorable because we had made new friends, Bev and Rich, whose residence in Massachusetts made them close enough to visit on land.

A postscript for all trivia buffs: The only prime minister of the United Kingdom to be assassinated while in office was Spencer Perceval, a member of the Tory party who became PM in 1809—this according to Michael, who won many trivia games for our team.

Chapter Twenty-Two
REPEATING ASIA/PACIFIC
FALL 2012

One of the loveliest scenes in the world: dinner boats decked out in blue, gold, red, violet, and green lights, passing our verandah hour after hour, their colors reflected in the waters of the river below. George and I saw that scene again in Shanghai on this voyage of new discoveries and revisits to places we knew well in Asia and along the Pacific Rim. This view seemed to get better each time we were in Shanghai.

We had not thought that we would ever get back to Shanghai or visit the idyllic water town of Zhujiajiao, which is a short distance from Shanghai and is billed as "The Old China." Just eight months before, during South America '12, George had been slowed down by arthritic pain. He had suffered when he walked, and could not walk too long before needing to sit down. Fortunately, we had found an excellent doctor. She had given George a shot of something in his spine. Slowly, slowly, the inflammation decreased to the point that now, pain-free at age ninety, George was eager to go and we were off, eastward bound on the good ship *Amsterdam*.

REMEMBERING HAKODATE, YOKOHAMA, OSAKA, AND NAGASAKI

After ten days at sea, *Amsterdam* docked in Hakodate on the northern island of Japan. Fish—yes fish—are what I remember about Hakodate. George and I went to the morning market where locals were out shopping for dried and fresh fish, crab and other shellfish, fresh fruits and vegetables, and even bouquets of flowers. There were tables in the market where family groups were enjoying delicacies of the sea. They waved. We waved. They smiled. We smiled.

On our way back to the ship, I composed a simple haiku:

> in the market street
> cod, crab, roe, scallops, and more . . .
> WE ARE IN JAPAN!

Yes, we were in Japan. On our ride from the pier to the market, we had noticed the closeness of the small houses, snuggled one against the next. Japan is a small country where land is scarce and valuable.

Yokohama was our second port of call in Japan. I particularly remember our morning entrance into the harbor. Passing under a new suspension bridge, we looked ahead toward rows of skyscrapers constructed after World War II. The glass windows of the buildings reflected the rising sun of Japan, creating a glistening wall of silvery gold that welcomed us. It had rained earlier that morning, and so to make the scene even more ethereal, a rainbow arched over the buildings, surely a good omen for our day to come and for our entire seventy-five-day trip.

I remember, too, the Great Buddha in Kamakura that we visited on a short morning tour the same day. Set in a pocket park, the Kamakura Buddha is made of metal—bronze, I believe, for that is what it looked like to me. The Buddha is huge! Many schoolchildren were on field trips to this important religious site the morning we visited. It was fun to watch them scampering about and enjoying their day out. We took pictures of them and of the Great Buddha, pictures which I looked at this morning as I took my virtual tour of Japan.

We also visited a Shinto Hachimangu shrine on our tour that day. The shrine is an active temple where believers still worship. They wash ceremonially before entering the sacred space, and they post wishes on wood cutouts when they leave. One prayer we saw hanging amid others read, "I wish I pass my exams at Kyoto University." As professors, we thought that the young scholar who left this wish might do better to study for his exams.

But the reason both George and I recalled this shrine so well was that, to get there, we had to climb sixty-five steps. We knew how many because George had counted them on his way up—a climb that brought him no pain.

A day later, the ship docked in Kobe. Our destination for the day was Osaka, a half-hour ride from Kobe. In Osaka, George and I wandered the buildings and grounds of a Shinto shrine dedicated to three sea goddesses. We walked down a lane lined with stone lanterns, and we passed by a reflecting pond over which there is an arched bridge painted bright orange. The temple was simply lovely. Worshippers were bowing, clapping, and ringing the temple gong. Some were bringing their beautiful young children to be named and blessed.

Our final stop in Japan was Nagasaki. George and I had visited the Peace Park in 2002 during our first Asia/Pacific cruise. Rather than repeating the visit, we went with our evening dining partners on a tram ride around the city. They had researched the combination of trams between major points of interest and plotted out stops in small neighborhoods and local shopping areas. From our morning adventure, we brought back two significant memories.

When we boarded a tram after a stop in an upscale neighborhood, all the seats were taken. The trolley car was filled with teenagers on their way to school; most had smartphones in hand and were texting and/or talking the way American teenagers do. As soon as these young people saw the four of us, they hopped up and gestured for us to take their seats. George wondered aloud, "Would American teens have done the same?"

Our friends had heard of a Confucian Shrine, Koshi-byo, conveniently located near the pier. A trolley made a stop on a corner just half a block from the shrine, so on our way back to the ship, we hopped off for a quick look.

We were amazed. The complex was stunning, and the word *stunning* is not an exaggeration. In the main courtyard were rows and rows of carved marble statues of wise men, each at least five feet tall. The inner temple was filled with gold- and red-adorned gods and goddesses and altars and wall hangings. The four of us were the only ones at the shrine, so we could wander at will in a place that was serene and beautiful—a place I think I will remember forever.

Late in the afternoon, *Amsterdam* cast off from the pier and continued through the Seto Inland Sea. We could look back to see in the distance one of the longest suspension bridges in the world, a bridge spanning the Inland Sea. Ahead was the South China Sea, which we would cross to get to Jeju Island, South Korea.

JEJU, SOUTH KOREA

Anyone stopping in Jeju must get out of the city. Jeju has little to commend it. That is in contrast to the wonderful places beyond the city limits, where we toured on our day there. "Oh, what a beautiful morning" we had; "Oh, what a beautiful day."

The beauty began with a visit to a botanical garden which is housed in a huge, conical-shaped structure with a glass roof. Inside the cone, we explored a cactus garden, a tropical garden, a flowering-plant garden— all meticulously tended. An elevator took us to the top of the cone to look down upon the surrounding countryside.

Near the gardens is a waterfall we were also to visit. When George and I learned that we would have to walk down 120 steps to get to the falls and walk up the same number on our return, we decided we did not need to see that particular waterfall. Instead, we sat comfortably at a small refreshment stand to wait for our group.

What an excellent decision this turned out to be. A class of eight- and nine-year-old children were enjoying snacks at the refreshment stand. Seeing us, their teacher struck up a conversation. He was a young man, fluent in English and very eager to talk. The happy, grinning youngsters gathered around. They wanted to have their pictures taken with us. We spent a delightful half hour with those children.

When our tour group returned from their walkathon, they looked exhausted. Jim, our friend and trivia partner, reported that the actual number of steps was 200 each way. Patting ourselves on the back, we decided we had done far better snacking with the children than struggling to climb those steps.

Lunch was interesting, and I do mean *interesting*. We lunched in an upscale hotel dining room. The table decor was simply lovely, with little dishes of sauces and condiments at each place setting. The first course was abalone porridge, not bad but rather tasteless. The second was seaweed soup, too fishy for me. We were also served a bowl of rice to add to a larger bowl of vegetables and meat; we could not determine what kind of meat it was, but it was tasty. The *piece de resistance* was a dense mass of intertwined, silvery fish with beady eyes that stared up at us. No thank you.

But an unexpected treat was still ahead. We drove to a coastal area known for its igneous rock formations. These hexagonal structures are a result of a lava flow that cooled at just the right rate to form columnar joints. George and I had learned about columnar joints in our study of geology, and we had seen similar jointing along the Palisades across the Hudson River from New York City. These in South Korea were more perfectly formed than those on the Palisades.

We had always wished that we had gone to the Giant's Causeway in Northern Ireland, also known for columnar joints. Years later, on my own, I eventually got to the Giant's Causeway. The Korean outcroppings are so much more striking because the tall, hexagonal columns rise up out of the ocean. Standing on a cliff by the sea, we looked down upon the rock outcroppings. We had never seen such perfectly formed columnar joints anywhere else in the world. And with the sea crashing below . . . sheer perfection.

Oh, what a beautiful morning! Oh yes, what a beautiful day!

SINGAPORE, A CITY STATE

Before our stop in Singapore in October of 2012, I knew nothing of what had happened there during World War II. The Japanese—I learned on tour that day—had crossed the Strait of Johor, invading from a direction unanticipated by the United Kingdom forces encamped there. The outcome had been a complete rout of the UK troops and thousands killed.

This resounding defeat was brought home to George and me when we visited the World War II cemetery where over 7,000 bodies of members of the Australian, New Zealand, and British armed forces are interred. The cemetery is a somber place, beautifully maintained with flowers and memorial stones and a wall of names of men and women lost.

George and I stood before the grave of a young lieutenant who had died at age twenty. We figured that this young man must have graduated from university and received his commission before he was sent to Singapore, which at that point was a British colony. Since my George was about twenty at that time and was sent to Europe to serve in the United States Army, we both were moved when we saw this boy's stone, as well as thousands of other gravestones that recognize the sacrifice these young men and women made.

On tour, we also stopped at a World War II POW camp, which now is the site of the Changi Museum. There we visited memorial chapels and studied displays telling about the cruelty the Japanese showered on the local populace and the military personnel they captured.

On our way back to the ship, we made a stop at a vast monastery complex, the Bright Hill Temple, which is famed as a place for ancestor worship. It is gorgeous, but it stands in stark contrast to the POW camp and cemetery we had seen. During our travels, we had visited all manner of shrines, cathedrals, churches, chapels, synagogues, and temples like Bright Hill. Despite these diverse places of worship all over the world, humankind persists in making war, continuing to pick cruelty over kindness. We learned that in a striking way on our Singapore tour.

Singapore was the halfway mark on our Asia/Pacific '12 cruise. I am proud to report that our trivia team—Jim and Jessica, George and I, Don

329

and Mitzie—had the highest cumulative score of all the teams that played for the first thirty-five days.

In trivia, teams assign a name to their group. Our name was Friends Forever. That remains an appropriate name, for at least once a week, we still email one another. Jim Smith is a fine writer—a true "Word Smith"—and his emails are a delight to read. Mitzie has become one of my dearest friends. She and I have gone on other cruises together after we both lost our husbands, and are planning future cruises that we hope to take. We may have won at trivia, but we won something far more precious: lasting friendship. In retrospect, I know how trivial a trivia win is, given the sadness and reminders of war we saw on October 26 in Singapore.

SEMARANG, INDONESIA

Places on the itinerary of a cruise are important, of course. As years go by, however, I become more certain that the people on a trip make or break it. People with whom we dine each night and play trivia on a daily basis, people next to whom we sit during watercolor class and at crafts, people with whom we travel on tours are at the core of our cruise experience.

George and I were fortunate on Asia/Pacific '12, for besides the friends-forever folks on our trivia team, we enjoyed the company of a host of others. We enjoyed, too, our interaction with our cabin and dining-room stewards. Our stewards became our family away from home, and we became theirs during the seventy-five days we were with them.

Because we had been to Semarang in Indonesia on prior trips, George and I did not book a tour there in 2012. We stayed on the *Amsterdam*, and what a wonderful day we had. In Semarang, the families of our Indonesian stewards came aboard ship to be with them. Our cabin steward, knowing that we would be on the ship, asked if he could introduce his family to us. We met in the library. Smiling broadly, he introduced his wife and his son, his mother and his father, his brothers and sisters. Oh, how proud he was of his beautiful family and how proud he was of George and me, his shipboard family. His Indonesian family lined up so we could take their pictures. We posed, too, so they could take ours.

It is amazing how warmly we felt toward these fine men—our dining and cabin stewards. My favorite on this cruise was a tall, slim twenty-two-year-old, who served us breakfast in the main dining room. Putu quickly learned that I love papaya. At my place each morning, he had a plate of papaya waiting. When he saw me coming, he would rush to pull out my chair, and he always greeted me with, "Here comes Papaya Lady." Later in the cruise when we were returning from a walkabout at the Bay of Islands in New Zealand, George and I went to the Crow's Nest for afternoon tea. There was Putu. When he saw us coming, he glowed. He welcomed me with "Here comes Papaya Lady." I responded, as I had begun to do at breakfast, with "Hello, First Grandson." In Indonesia first sons are named Putu.

LEMBAR, LOMBOK ISLAND, INDONESIA

Rather than staying "home" when we reached Lembar in Indonesia, we opted for an island tour that was rather similar to one we had taken on a prior visit to Lombok Island. We loved the scenic beauty of the Indonesian countryside and figured we would sit back on the bus and simply savor that beauty.

Lady Luck smiled on us again. Arriving at a museum we remembered from before, I spied an adjacent room with pairs of little shoes lined up neatly on the steps outside. We poked our heads in and discovered that it was an elementary school classroom. When the teacher saw us, she stopped her lesson and waved us in. She had all the young and smiling children greet us—in English. They wore uniforms, as most Indonesian school children do, and they were sitting on the floor. The girls had their heads covered with identical scarfs, but their faces were not covered. George and I smiled broadly at them and gestured with our hands. A moment to remember!

Another magical moment was still ahead. Our tour had advertised a visit to Banyumulek Village, which is known for its pottery; it was a place to which we had not gone before. Although our expectations were low, our visit turned out to be great fun. We traveled through Banyumulek in a four-person, horse-drawn cart adorned with bells that jingle jangled as we rode along the lanes of the village. At one point, the cart stopped. We climbed down to walk the village and to watch women who were working at pottery wheels. Many smiling children wanted their pictures taken with us, and vendors followed us. What a lovely place. We brought home some souvenir remembrances, too—a couple of masks that are on display in our kitchen.

Sitting here today at my computer, I wonder whether life in Banyumulek goes on the same way now as it did then. I wonder if there are still horse-drawn carts with bells that jingle jangle and women potters who sit on the ground and spin their wheels. I wonder if things have changed—modernized—and whether, if change has happened, the people are any happier.

EDEN

Amsterdam circled the northern coast of Australia, stopped in Darwin in the Northern Territory, and sailed the Torres Strait between New Guinea and Australia. She made an unanticipated stop at Hamilton Island, where George and I swam in the Coral Sea. Ah, imagine: *We swam in the Coral Sea!*

Our ship went on to make scheduled stops in Brisbane and Sydney, ports that George and I knew well. *Amsterdam* then sailed south to Eden, a small town between Sydney and Melbourne where we would spend a day. Eden is in a part of Australia that enjoys a temperate climate. We saw hardwood forests and evidence of logging activity. We saw evidence, too, of a whaling industry that had been active sometime in the past. We would hardly have thought we were in Australia until our bus pulled off the road by a trailer community. Lounging in front of the trailers was a mob of kangaroos. When the kangaroos saw us, they hopped away on their strong rear legs, providing us with a great photo op. Our guide told us that roos cannot hop backward, a fact that neither of us had known.

We took morning tea at the lovely Seahorse Inn, which dates from 1843 and which overlooks a bay that is an arm of the Tasman Sea. It was a help-yourself tea with scones and sandwiches. Some folks complained because they had anticipated a high tea with white-glove service. George and I were simply happy to be there. After all, here we were in New South Wales with a beautiful beach spread at our feet, drinking tea with friends in an inn that was close to 170 years old.

Leaving the bayside, our bus took us through small villages to see an Australia that most folks do not visualize when thinking of the southern continent. We passed farms and drove through forested areas. This was not the dry, red terrain that is to be seen in the central outback. George said that, if he had not known better, he would have thought we were in the state of Maine.

Later in the morning, we stopped at Wheelers Oyster Farm, where the owner showed us how oysters are raised today in Australia, contrasted with the ways employed in the past. We sat down on a deck that looked out on lush countryside to nibble oyster snacks. Our allotment was four per person. Not an oyster enthusiast, I tried one and gave my other three to George.

How can I summarize our day? George and I were in Eden, not the Biblical garden of religious lore, but a unique part of Australia. In Eden, we expanded our understanding of this small continent, this great country, this diverse island. I guess I have to say that people are never too old to learn more about their planet; with every trip we took, we came home richer in understanding. Folks talk about saving the earth for future generations. Places like Eden are what they are talking about, especially if we consider Eden a metaphor for Planet Earth.

SUNRISE, SUNSET ON THE PACIFIC

New Zealand's Bay of Islands
and then Auckland . . .
Fiji
and then Samoa . . .
the vast Pacific ahead

George and I were now on a grand vacation aboard a floating hotel. We enjoyed days filled with watercolor and trivia, music and stage shows, walks on the open deck and dinners with friends. We would often stand at the stern and watch the pattern of the ship's wake in the water behind us. We would sit in the Crow's Nest and watch the bow rise and fall as *Amsterdam* steamed eastward.

Sunrise, sunset, the days flew by, until one morning we woke to see Honolulu on the horizon—our country welcoming us back. Strange to say, we felt more secure being in Medicare country.

In Honolulu, George and I changed hats, becoming not vacationers but travelers in search of firsthand knowledge of a past gone crazy. It was a radical change in perspective, because we were going that day to the *Arizona* Memorial to view the remains of what Franklin Delano Roosevelt called "a date which will live in infamy"—December 7, 1941.

We stopped first at a serene but terribly sad spot, the Punchbowl, high above Honolulu. Here, in a volcanic crater, is a war cemetery, with thousands of granite memorials set in the ground, each the burial place of a man or woman who served his or her country. Overhead flew the American flag, a symbol of survival and endurance and freedom. It flies there today, too, attesting to the strength of our democratic way of life.

At the Pearl Harbor Visitor Center, we viewed a movie recounting the hour-by-hour events of December 7, 1941, and we viewed the posters and displays exhibited there.

I do not remember December 7, for I was too young. George remembered. He had often told me how he and his friend Fred— the Frederick Arnold who was George's college and army buddy and had later taught biology for many years at Kean—had stood in the auditorium of Montclair State College the following day and listened

334

to FDR address the nation over the radio. He had told me he knew at that moment that his and Fred's future had changed. I have written previously about that moment, but it bears repeating to remind us how so many people's lives can be impacted by a single, horrendous event.

George and I boarded the harbor craft that carries visitors across the channel to the *Arizona* Memorial. We passed the Battleship *Missouri* anchored nearby and pulled into the site where the remains of the *Arizona* lie beneath the waters of the harbor. Silently, gravely, we walked through the impressive white marble structure to stand below the wall bearing the names of the brave men and women who lost their lives when, in the words of FDR, "the United States of America was suddenly and deliberately attacked by naval and air forces of the Empire of Japan."

The sky the day of our visit was bright blue. Old Glory was flying overhead. Quiet reigned aboard the harbor craft taking us back to the visitor center. We had just made a trip into the past, into American history; we had been reminded again that a nation must stay alert to keep democracy alive and well.

In a way, our visit to the *Arizona* Memorial was a fitting close to our Asia/Pacific 2012 voyage of discovery. On that voyage, we had realized over and over again how fortunate we were to go places that taught us important lessons about the earth and its diverse peoples, about events of the past that changed the future, about the interconnectedness of humankind.

Leaving Honolulu the next day, *Amsterdam* made stops on Maui and on the Big Island, where we got off to stretch our legs before we headed east to the mainland.

> five sunrises
> five sunsets
> five days later we were home in New Jersey

Chapter Twenty-Three
SEEING SOUTH AMERICA–AGAIN
WINTER 2013

Our South America '13 cruise with Holland America started with disaster, and it was a disaster that we never could have anticipated. George and I had begun planning SA '13 while we were on South America '11 with our friends, Phil and Eileen. Actually, the first few days of 2013 went as planned. We met the Hoffmans in a Fort Lauderdale motel the night before the cruise and dined together in a restaurant they had chosen. By noon the next day, we were on the lido of *Prinsendam* lunching together. It was a smooth beginning that quickly went south.

TO AND THROUGH THE PANAMA CANAL

The first tour we had pre-planned together was to the highlands of Costa Rica during our stop in Puerto Limon. On the morning of the tour, we were surprised when Phil appeared alone. Eileen was suffering from the norovirus, he reported, probably from something she had eaten the evening before we boarded. She had been dizzy and had fallen, her dizziness caused perhaps by dehydration. She was feeling a bit better, but she felt she should stay back and rest.

We were disappointed that Eileen had to miss the tour. Riding through the countryside, we passed lush fields where bananas, sugar cane, macadamia nuts, and coffee were growing. There were stunning views of far-off mountains. Our lunch venue was an open porch from which we could look out over mountains and valleys.

"Eileen would have enjoyed this," I remarked as we lunched. "Such a shame!"

A day later, *Prinsendam* started her transit through the Panama Canal. It was 6:30 a.m. and George and I went out on our verandah to watch. We saw the lights of other ships that were waiting in the queue for their turn to enter the canal. We could see lights from the canal flickering up ahead.

Then our phone rang. "Who would be calling at this early hour?" George wondered.

It was Phil. Eileen had fallen for the second time on the cruise and had struck her head; she had spent the night in the ship's infirmary. The ship's doctor was concerned and had decided Eileen needed more care than he could render on the ship. Phil said that they were being put off the *Prinsendam*, and Eileen was going to the hospital in Panama City.

Phil was distraught, and so were we.

We got a second phone call to tell us that Eileen would be pushed off the ship as *Prinsendam* was transiting the second set of locks. George and I would be allowed down on the lower deck at the hour when they were scheduled to leave. When we got to that deck at the assigned time, the staff captain was already there. Phil had a travel bag over his shoulder. Eileen was in a wheelchair, crying, "We planned this trip for two years, for two years! This can't be happening!"

When the top surface of the lock and the floor of the deck where we were standing were even, the staff captain gave the order, "Now!" A crew member dropped the gangway, another wheeled Eileen off with Phil running after her, the crew member ran back onto the ship, and the officer in charge ordered the gangway up. The maneuver took just a minute or two. What was so unbelievable was that *Prinsendam* never stopped the entire time. She just kept inching downward. I doubt that anyone else on the ship realized what had happened. This was probably our ninth or tenth transit of the Panama Canal. It is the one we both remembered most clearly.

The best news is that, a week later, Phil and Eileen had arrived home safely, and she had stabilized. Another piece of good news is that they had bought travel insurance. The insurance paid for her hospital stay, her doctors' bills, Phil's hotel accommodations, and their return flight to Chicago. It reimbursed them for the amount they had paid for the unused days of the cruise.

Their story is a lesson about cruising. Trip insurance is not cheap, especially for senior citizens; but when one needs it, insurance certainly comes in handy. After that, George and I always bought a top-of-the-line policy. Translated, *top of the line* means expensive.

PERUVIAN PLEASURES

> window table, please
> one that looks upon the seas
> dine and watch with ease

This is exactly what George and I did each evening as we sailed south along the Peruvian coast toward Lima: We dined and watched with ease. One evening, from our table, we saw schools of tuna; the fish literally surrounded us. They came—on and on endlessly—performing, putting on a dinner show, flying, almost dancing to the undulating rhythm of the Pacific. It was as though nature knew we missed our friends and was filling the void.

The morning we pulled into Callao, which is the port for Lima, George and I rode the shuttle into Miraflores, a nearby resort. Once the bus left the dangerous port area, the drive was special. From the cliffside road, we could look down on white, sandy beaches and on waves rolling slowly in from across the Pacific. On the cliffs, we saw well-kept hotels and gardens.

Having been to Callao before and having used the shuttle then, we knew that the round-trip ride was perfect for us that day. We were not in the right frame of mind for a bus tour with lengthy commentaries by guides. Still disturbed after seeing Eileen wheeled off the ship in

Panama, we wanted simply to walk the cliffside paths at our drop-off spot. We wanted to drink in the beauty of Planet Earth.

We did take an excursion when we got to Pisco—a speedboat trip to the Ballestas. The Ballestas are islands off the coast and are sometimes called "Peru's Galapagos." Mother Nature was on our side that morning. Arriving at the islands, we saw lots and lots of animals: colonies of sea lions, Peruvian boobies, pelicans, and even waddles of penguins. Incidentally, we had learned through trivia that the present-day collective noun for penguins is *waddle.*

On the Ballestas, we also saw natural bridges that the sea had carved into the cliffs—cliffs upon which sea lions rested and sea birds roosted. Our speed boat roared under the natural bridges, of course at top speed.

On the way back, our little boat slowed for a photo op at The Candelabra, a huge cutting in the sand cliffs high above the ocean. The origin of The Candelabra is unknown, but the design cut into the cliffs does resemble two giant candle holders towering over the dry desert landscape.

"A good excursion and a good morning," George remarked when we got back to the ship. George and I were beginning to feel a little better about our trip without our friends.

CHILEAN DELIGHTS

Two days later, when we arrived in Arica, Chile, George and I were back into bus-tour mode. Our guide told us that Arica is the driest city in the world. To emphasize the point, he explained that his young children had never seen rain; there had been none in about thirteen years. The land certainly was dry as we crossed starkly beautiful desert areas. Even the mountains were barren. We spotted a few cacti, but not really many of them, for the cacti were surviving only on morning mist.

We saw almost no signs of human occupation until we arrived in a small village where men, women, and children welcomed us with singing and dancing. A medicine man blessed us. We knew that his blessing was important, because the switchback roads we had traversed to get here were a nightmare. And yes, we had to travel those roads on our return trip.

Going back, we stopped to see something unexpected—two very tall statues, one of a woman and one of a man, standing alone out in the desert, impressionistic in style and designed by a local artist. Why the artist had placed these pieces way out there where few people would see them we never learned. We had a hypothesis: Perhaps the woman and man were telling us to stand tall, to stand strong no matter the conditions surrounding us.

In Coquimbo, our next Chilean port of call, George and I thought back to our stop in that area in 2002 and decided just to stay near the pier. We remembered that there is little to see in Coquimbo, a desperately poor port city. We also remembered standing at a bus stop waiting for a local bus to take us to La Serena, a prettier and more interesting town nearby. George had had his camera slung carelessly over his shoulder. We both had gone into high alert when a police car had pulled up to the curb. An officer inside had rolled down a window, pointed to the camera, and gestured for George to hold it more securely.

Chile is a narrow country that extends across more than forty degrees of latitude. It took a few days for us to get to the tip of South America. Sailing south, *Prinsendam* made stops at cities and towns we had visited before. We generally just wandered about.

On February 1, *Prinsendam* sailed through the Strait of Magellan, heading to Ushuaia. We had a great sail down Glacier Alley, passing one glacier after another on our port side. During a wonderfully scenic day, George and I sat on our verandah and watched the "show" with no effort required on our part. Even on a third time through, we felt our sail-by was awesome.

The wind was vicious when we docked in Ushuaia. George and I headed out for a walk, but we did not last long. Afraid of being blown off our feet, we hurried back to the ship. *Prinsendam* was scheduled to leave port that evening, but our captain decided to wait for the winds to abate. He announced that we had a problem with one of the fire detection systems and a technician was flying in to join the crew. The winds were delaying airplane traffic. We finally sailed, but we had been delayed by a day. As our captain explained, there is no guarantee of gentle winds and smooth seas.

The winds and the seas cooperated the next day. Leaving Ushuaia via the Beagle Channel and entering the open sea, we were able to circle Cape Horn. We rocked. We bounced. We swayed. We rolled. But everyone got to see the Horn. That day we sailed the Drake Passage, heading to Antarctica—the second time for us.

George in his Icelandic hat.

ANTARCTIC SPLENDORS

I described the grandeur of Antarctica when I talked about our 2011 circumnavigation; 2013 was even better. We saw penguins and penguins and more penguins—no emperors but lots of the smaller varieties.

On SA '13, we also encountered a snowstorm. The Indonesian crew members were on deck playing in the snow and having snowball fights. Some had never seen snow falling from the sky. George and I went out on deck to scoop up some Antarctic snow, which obviously looked like New Jersey snow.

The second morning, researchers from the Palmer Station came aboard just as they had in 2011, and we went again to hear them explain the work they were doing. Later, the captain took us on a sightseeing sail among the glaciers and pack ice. Not only did we see penguins, but we saw whales, sea lions, and flocks of birds. We so wished that Phil and Eileen were with us to see them, too.

By noon, we were still cruising up some of the most magnificent ice-filled channels one can imagine. We snagged a window table for two in the dining room for lunch. As we ate, a large flat-topped iceberg floated by the window. On the iceberg stood four penguins. Yes, *four* penguins and right by our dining-room window! George forgot lunch, grabbed his camera, and—coatless—hit the outside deck to get a photo. During dessert, we saw whales breaching. George was off again, running to take another picture or two.

At supper time, we sat at our window table to see more ice. Some of the icebergs were the size of a car, some the size of a large house. Our ship was totally surrounded by sparkling slush. The port lecturer came on the PA system to explain that this ice was newly calved from surrounding glaciers. He explained that it actually was very old ice that had formed high up on the ridges in past centuries. It only now was reaching the sea, pushed down by ice that had built up behind.

Although I cannot travel as I write this—due to COVID-19—I feel so thankful that George and I had this simply splendid day. I sit here and marvel at what we saw. Just thinking about that day sends chills up my spine, not from cold but from excitement.

FINALLY THE FALKLANDS

Finally we had made it! Our captain was able to drop anchor and tender us into the Falklands. We had booked a penguin tour, and we were super delighted to be on our way. I guess you could say that 2013 was the year of the penguins, because we had seen penguins already in Antarctica and in Chile. Now we were off to see more.

The excursion had two parts. We started in a sixteen-passenger van that took us on an unpaved, bumpy road. We made one stop outbound—a photo op to snap a picture of a sign that read, "Mined area." The mines were remnants of the war between Argentina and the United Kingdom that had occurred in 1982—the Falkland War.

After a half hour, we switched to a four-wheel-drive van, four of us to a vehicle. Then the fun began. The driver left the unpaved road and took off over rutted meadows to Bluff Cove, a nesting place for king and gentoo penguins. At Bluff Cove, we saw four stately adult kings with a couple of chicks cuddled close and hundreds of the smaller gentoos. The noise was deafening, the smell was powerful, but the picture before us was perfect. Photographers in our midst, and that included my George, had struck gold.

Having walked for a time among the penguins (watching carefully where we placed our feet), George and I hiked along a path overlooking the ocean. The wind coming off the Atlantic was powerful, so we clung to each other as we made our way to a quaint little restaurant by the seaside. We sat at a window table and looked out on the beach while we drank hot chocolate and munched cookies and brownies that local ladies had baked. At the restaurant, we were able to buy a small drawing of a pair of king penguins, which we would use as a model in watercolor class.

Back on *Prinsendam*, we took afternoon tea in the main dining room with others from the tour. We all deemed our day in the Falklands a high point of the voyage so far.

NOW NORTHWARD

None of the stops to come—as we sailed northward—could compete with our fabulous Falkland day. George and I had been to each of those ports before and so they blended together in our minds, especially the stops in beach locations. Even the great cities of Montevideo, Buenos Aires, Rio, Salvador, Fortaleza, and Manaus did not make our hearts beat faster, because we knew them so well from prior trips. They had become ordinary places to us. In those cities, we walked around and enjoyed the feel of trodding familiar avenues.

There was one exception—Punta del Este, Uruguay. Having taken a neat little tour in this seaside resort the year before, George and I opted to stroll the streets. Not really knowing where we were going, we stumbled on a unique sculpture rising out of the sand on the beach. We walked closer to investigate. Called *La Mano* or in English *The Hand*, the large modern art piece is literally five massive stone fingers extending skyward, the palm buried in the sand. George and I walked among the fingers and over the palm, contemplating what the sculptor was saying to us.

In Arica, we had seen the modern rendering of a woman and a man together in their own bubble. It was far, far out in the desert. The couple seemed to tell us to stand strong, a message especially important today. Looking back now on *La Mano*, I sense a related message: Open your hands. Reach your fingers heavenward. Do not give up hope. Grasp the future.

ANOTHER ENDING

South America '13 had had a depressing beginning. Heading up the Amazon and then toward home, we decided that despite the unfortunate and premature departure of our friends from the ship, we had had some marvelous moments. We had seen penguins and sea lions, viewed icebergs and the driest of deserts, crossed the equator and the Tropic of Cancer, sailed the Atlantic and the Pacific. Many people only dream of being in places we had been and of seeing things we had seen. Today, on the first day of spring in 2021, as I work on my memoir and look back on a year without traveling somewhere wonderful, I realize how great my opportunities have been. Sometimes we do not fully appreciate the things and the loved ones we have had until we lose them.

Chapter Twenty-Four
GOING BACK TO ASIA AND THE PACIFIC
FALL 2013

We called our 2013 Asia Pacific cruise "The World War II Cruise to the Pacific." When Holland America announced this itinerary, George and I decided that it was a "must do" for us. First, the itinerary included places made famous, or perhaps infamous, because of military action during World War II. Second, it included places we had never visited. Third, two sets of trivia friends were booking and Kelley and Mel, our dining companions from World '09, were booking the cruise as well. This definitely was a trip for us.

Here are a few people, places, and things that were high points and low points of our Asia Pacific Adventure in 2013.

MAJURO, MARSHALL ISLANDS

When I wear my flowery frock on warm summer evenings, friends ask, "Where did you get your pretty dress?"

I reply, "Majuro."

Often they ask, "Where in the world is Majuro?" Few people know where it is. Even fewer have been there.

Majuro was the first new port for George and me on Asia/Pacific '13. It is an atoll in the Pacific and is the capital of the Marshall Islands. Majuro is so small that the ship offered no excursions and the port lecturer's recommendation was to stroll the village lanes.

The evening before our landfall in Majuro, it had rained heavily. As a result, when we walked off *Amsterdam*, the roads were muddy. Nevertheless, because it was a Saturday morning, the locals had come out en masse to look us over. We enjoyed that. George and I found a bench not far from the ship, and we sat and looked at the locals looking at us. A couple who could speak English sat down to talk. Chatting with them made for a fun morning.

What was not fun was seeing an ambulance pull away from *Amsterdam*. A passenger had taken ill and was being put off the ship to go to the hospital. George took note of the ambulance—old, rusty, decrepit. He wondered what the hospital was like and whether the person going there would be as fortunate as our friend Eileen and get home safely.

We wandered around looking for shops, but to no avail. Kelley, our dining companion on World '09 and now again on Asia Pacific '13, is a shopper beyond compare. That night at supper, she showed us her purchases—flowery dresses of lightweight fabric, the kind that the ladies of Majuro wear every day. I said *dresses*. Kelley had bought a dress for each of the women at the table, including one for herself. The following night, we ladies wore our new, island frocks to supper, and the men wore flowered shirts. Thanks to Kelley, we enjoyed a delightful South Pacific evening aboard the ship.

GUAM AND SAIPAN

Until the World War II historian on board *Amsterdam* talked about Guam and what happened there in the 1940s, I had not known that the Japanese had bombed Guam and had captured it only a short time after their attack on Pearl Harbor. I had known that the Japanese controlled the island until the Second Battle of Guam in 1944, when American forces recaptured it. Our intent was to visit the war memorial park when *Amsterdam* docked in Guam.

We were in for a huge disappointment. As *Amsterdam* sailed toward Guam, the United States government was shut down over a budget dispute. Who runs the park? The American government, so the memorial park in Guam was closed, too. Instead of a visit to the memorial, our excursion took us to a shopping market. The World War II vets on board were aghast. Even the shoppers on board were unhappy. We all wondered what would happen in Saipan, our next World War II-related stop.

The news was not good. No budget agreement had yet come out of Washington. When we climbed aboard our bus in Saipan, the guide told us that, because of the American government shutdown, the World War II museum was shuttered. The American Memorial was off limits, too, but she said she might be able to sneak us in. We would have to wait and hope.

As we waited, we headed to Banzai Cliff, known also as Suicide Cliff. While we sat on the bus beneath the cliff, our guide told a heartbreaking story. In July 1944, the American forces won a decisive victory in Saipan. Many Japanese civilians were living on the island at the time. The Emperor of Japan had told them that if the Americans gained control of the island, the invaders would rape, torture, and kill. He ordered the Japanese to commit suicide. Believing their esteemed emperor, they did what he had commanded: They jumped to their deaths off Banzai Cliff. Mercifully, one teenager was spared. Caught in bushes as he jumped, he survived. Recently he had come back from Japan, where he had gone to live. He had returned to see the plaques erected beneath the cliff. By then, he was an older gentleman who, through a stroke of luck, had lived a full and productive life.

The guide talked about how easily people can believe in and follow a national leader like Hitler or the cult leader James Warren Jones. She left us with much to consider.

Then she gave us a thumbs-up. The war museum was definitely closed, but she knew a back road into the memorial. She had just received a text message that this road was open. She would see if we could slip in that way. Her persistence paid off. Our group got onto the grounds where we climbed off the bus—quietly and reverently. We saw the American flag flying beside the flags of the U.S. Army, Navy, Marine Corps, and Army Air Corps. We saw the monument that commemorates the Americans and Chamorros who died in the Battle of Saipan and the thousands who fought there. As a World War II veteran, George felt blessed to stand at the memorial and pay his respects to those who had died during the Battle of Saipan.

What a superb guide we had had. We learned later that we were the only ones from our ship to visit the American Memorial Park that day.

TYPHOON TO NAGASAKI

After a stop in Kobe, Japan, where George and I did our customary walkabout, *Amsterdam* was scheduled to go to Okinawa. Mother Nature put a hex on those plans. Our captain reported that he was monitoring a typhoon headed toward our intended route. He had charted a safer route for us. He would scoot into the sheltered Inland Sea to dock in Nagasaki. We were skipping Okinawa.

First it was the United States government that had thwarted us, now Mother Nature!

Saddened that we would not get into Okinawa to see the war memorial there, the two of us made plans with our trivia-playing friends—Mitzie and Don—for a Nagasaki tour that would take us into the countryside. Outward bound, we drove through really lush and beautiful farmlands under cultivation with a variety of crops in all shades of yellows and greens. The farm fields were in river valleys, the waters channeled for irrigation. Darker green hills provided a backdrop for the lighter colors of the lowlands. Our frowns at missing Okinawa were turning into smiles.

The major stop on our tour was at a six-tiered pagoda. The lowest level was of stone, the upper tiers of stunning white wood. Young people welcomed us at the entrance; they were dressed in traditional garb and posed with us for pictures. Inside were displays of life in old Japan; it was really a mini-museum.

Leaving the pagoda, we drove through villages to see homes and alleys with lovely garden areas. In one village we stopped for lunch at a traditional restaurant with lots of local dishes. I remember the delicious soup!

The ride back to Nagasaki was as captivating as the ride out. Our guide, who was from Okinawa and had flown in for the day when our stop there had been canceled, told us that what we had seen on our tour was far more beautiful than what we would have seen in Okinawa. She may have been trying to placate us, but we all agreed that our day had surpassed our expectations.

That evening at our dinner table, we all shared what we had seen and done in Nagasaki and in the preceding ports. We had not dined together for a while; we had all been so busy.

We ladies had another lovely surprise waiting for us that evening. Our friend Kelley had arrived early to place a package by each of our plates. In Kobe, she had found a shop selling second-hand happi coats. She had bought one for each of us. The next evening we four ladies came to the table attired "happily." My green and cream happi coat still hangs in my closet to be worn on special occasions.

SHANGHAI, HONG KONG, SINGAPORE, AND NHA TRANG IN VIETNAM

I went through the booklet that described tours in Shanghai, Hong Kong, Singapore, and Nha Trang in Vietnam before we arrived in these ports in 2013. I put a check next to each tour in the four locations—a check that meant we had done that already. I ended up with checks next to all of the interesting tours.

Because these cities were old friends, on this revisit, we often walked the streets on our own. In Shanghai, we did repeat a tour to the fabulous Jade Buddha but then walked the Bund. In Hong Kong, we strolled our favorite area around Nathan Road and then sat on a bench in the quiet park nearby to watch older Chinese joining together for tai chi.

In Singapore, we visited for the first time the famed orchid gardens and re-walked the streets of Chinatown. In Nha Trang, we re-did the pier markets and took another trishaw ride.

Were we not fortunate to be able to return and return again to such fabulous places? To anyone who is reading this and who has traveled rather extensively, I say, "You can go back again! It is fun to walk familiar streets and feel you belong there." And to anyone thinking of traveling for the first time, I say, "Being in a new environment and seeing new things expand the way you think. Travel is a most wonderful way to learn!"

REPEATS: BRUNEI, KOTA KINABALU, AND MANILA

George and I never forgot the Brunei hotel where we stayed in 1974. We often retold the story of how water had to be carried to our room to flush the toilets. Neither did we ever forget our trip in 1974 upriver from Kota Kinabalu to see the longhouses deep in the jungle nor the boat that took us there.

Nonetheless, we loved our repeat stops in 2013. We even repeated for the third time our tour in Brunei to the water village to see an entire community suspended on pilings above the river. In Kota Kinabalu, we took a city highlights tour hoping to catch sight of Johnny's Hotel, for we remembered it so clearly. But that was not to be. Probably our 1974 hotel had been torn down to make way for more impressive hotels which do not have the homey feel that Johnny's did. Of course, change is inevitable, whether we are talking about Borneo, New Jersey, or our aging bodies.

Our stop in Manila was also a repeat visit. There, George and I saw General Douglas MacArthur in Rizal Park. He was sitting on a bench contemplating the disastrous retreat of the American and Filipino forces at Corregidor during World War II. Of course, the MacArthur we saw was a life-sized bronze rendering. Also in the park were life-sized bronzes of monks and friars who were among the first Europeans to come to the Philippines; they brought Christianity to the islands. On our morning tour of old Manila, we walked Rizal Park with our friends Don and Mitzie, together enjoying the quiet of this lovely place and thinking about the historical significance of the bronze pieces we had seen.

We also walked the grounds of the old Spanish fort, visited the cathedral, and entered a reconstructed mansion circa 1800s. The grand finale was a performance by a lively group that sang and danced in the street. Noisy, yes, but fun! With my little camera, I captured a great picture of the street performers and also of us with our dear traveling companions, Don and Mitzie.

It was an A+ morning all around. A+ for people—Don and Mitzie; A+ for places—the lovely Rizal Park; A+ for things—the bronze statue of MacArthur that brought to our minds the Battle of Corregidor and General MacArthur's "I shall return."

RABAUL, PAPUA NEW GUINEA

We enjoyed one unbelievably interesting day after another. Our morning excursion in Manila far exceeded our expectations, but the day George and I spent in Rabaul, Papua New Guinea was even more spectacular. In my mind, our day in Rabaul rates among the top days of sights, culture, and shopping we ever experienced in our travels.

Awakening early for sail-in, George and I saw something totally unexpected; ahead was a steaming volcanic cone with a cloud of gases hovering over an asymmetrical crater rim. The rim was really lopsided with one side lower than the other. Yes, this was a gently active volcano: no lava, no ash, just a gaseous cloud. At breakfast, we chose a window table where we could look out on the steaming cone while eating our papaya, raspberries, and for a change, French toast with maple syrup.

Our breakfast-with-a-view delayed us. We did not start down the gangway until well after nine. Walking toward us across the open square in front of our ship was our dining mate, the greatest shopper of all time, Kelley. As was to be expected, she was toting several large bags of things she had already purchased.

"Dorothy and George," she called out. "Come! Come! Around the corner! I found vendors selling masks. Follow me." Excited, Kelley practically ran, with us close behind her. We bought first a mask of birch bark cloth, which Kelley said we had to have because there was no right side up. Next we bought two bulky masks and a huge, dark one, then a small one with an exquisite sheen, then a really different one with little pieces of cord tied around the sides—six masks in all—until George called a halt. We even had trouble carrying all of them back to the ship.

On *Amsterdam*, we stowed our purchases and set out again. We were headed to the people's market a few blocks from the ship. The port lecturer had told us that this was where the locals shopped. We found the area. It had two parallel rows of stalls selling produce of every kind. We explored slowly, enjoying the ambiance of the place.

At the last stall on the left—I can picture the spot exactly—was a man who looked old enough to remember what took place on Rabaul Island during the war. He had only one arm; perhaps he had lost the other in battle.

We approached his stall, smiled at him, and took a chance that he might know a little English. He did. He said he had been part of the local forces during the battle that took place on Rabaul during the Second World War. George pointed at himself and said that he had served in Germany during World War II and that he, too, remembered those times.

By then a crowd had gathered around the man to watch and listen. I will never forget what the man asked next. Touching his own face, he asked, "Is it true that your American president is dark like me?" We told him that it was true. We told him that our president was Barack Obama and that President Obama had a beautiful wife and two daughters, yes, with dark faces like his.

Our new friend's face glowed. He translated to those gathered around, and they smiled also. Both George and I recalled the same question asked by the trishaw driver in Singapore about a year before. We never forgot those two men and their question. The question made us realize that the world still watches what America does.

GUADALCANAL IN THE SOLOMON ISLANDS

Standing atop Bloody Ridge on Guadalcanal, we could not conceive of the horror that young men—Americans and Japanese alike—endured here. It must have been a living hell.

Our guide described the World War II battle that raged for three days on Edson's Ridge, more familiarly known as Bloody Ridge. Located above Henderson airfield, the ridge was a strategically significant point on Guadalcanal, one that was important to both the Americans and the Japanese. The Americans held the ridge, then the Japanese captured it, and then the Americans again ... Back and forth the battle raged, with more young men killed or wounded each day.

On the morning in 2013 when we stood atop the ridge, we looked down upon beautiful countryside, spread out in all directions before us. All was a vibrant green. All was serene. The surrounding area looked like a little piece of paradise, made even more idyllic when families with young children and beautiful babies in their arms came up the ridge to say hello.

In contrast, on those days in September 1942, the area was filled with the ear-shattering and deadly sounds of battle. I silently said a prayer of thanks that my George did not have to endure those terrible days.

We stood before the American Memorial, a series of polished granite pieces that tell the story of the Battle of Guadalcanal. It honors all the Americans who died and suffered on Bloody Ridge during the three-day battle. We went on to stand before the Japanese Memorial, four pieces of geometrically shaped white stone that honor the Japanese who fell in service to their country. Both memorials are stark reminders of the heavy cost of war.

With our tablemates that night at dinner, we talked about what we had seen on Bloody Ridge. That night also, lovely Kelley gave us a mask she had found for us in a local market. We had asked her to look for one; since our tour focused on the war, it made no stops for shopping. The mask Kelley found is very different from those we bought in Papua New Guinea. It is finely carved with a very high sheen. Mother of pearl highlights its eyes, eyebrows, and cheeks. Actually, this mask resembles one of our Kenyan masks more than any of our New Guinea masks; the highlighting on the cheeks is similar to the way the street dancers we had seen in the Philippines paint their faces.

Masks are an art form with considerable significance in diverse cultures around the world. We have found them in Southeast Asia and the Pacific Islands, in South America and Central America, in China and Africa. They are at times used during ritual dances and religious observances. Our collection of more than seventy-five masks includes three with noses that are really handles to hold in front of the face during dance performances and four from New Guinea that have cowrie-shell eyes. In our collection, also, there are two from East Africa with braids made from cord and several with elongated earlobes that come from different areas of the world. Some of our masks are rather small; others are very heavy and large. We learned that anthropologists use similarities and differences among masks as a means of investigating human migration patterns. For George and me, collecting them was another way of thinking about how interrelated the cultures of the world really are.

The three largest masks in the middle are from Rabaul. Note the cowrie eyes.

THE ISLANDS OF THE SOUTH PACIFIC

George and I agreed we had had enough of serious war tours that made me weepy. We decided that we would lighten up our lives in the remaining days of our Grand Pacific and Asian Voyage. Rather than taking a tour to see war relics in Luganville, Vanuatu, we hopped a bus to a lagoon for a swim. The scenery there and back was exceptionally beautiful. We drove through lush, green jungle. The color of the lagoon was a lovely aqua blue.

And we did swim! Others who were on the bus with us grabbed hold of a long rope, swung out over the lagoon, and then dropped down into the water. We did not do that. Holding hands so we would not fall, we waded—carefully, step by step—into the lagoon. And then we swam; we swam together in a blue lagoon deep in the jungle of a South Pacific island. It sounds surreal, doesn't it?

On our return back through town, our minivan took us down the same four-lane road on which we had walked in the rain on our prior trip to Luganville. The road was one the American forces had built to ensure rapid deployment of equipment on an island that housed the second largest American military base in the Pacific, smaller only than the one in Hawaii.

We swam again at Matira Beach when we got to Bora Bora. I think I have said that Matira Beach was our favorite beach in the world, with a gentle gradient that makes it easy to wade far out into the lagoon. There are no strong waves or currents, and there is a gorgeous island view from the water. George and I had truly shifted into vacation mode. It was time for rest and relaxation.

I must say that I never thought I would swim with the stingrays. I have always been squeamish around animals. I admit that I have a strong aversion to snakes and spiders, but my aversions are broader than these common fears. That is the reason we never went to the Galapagos. I had no interest in walking among vicious-looking lizards. Recall that I did not get off the ship with George to see the Komodo dragons. So it was a leap of faith in myself and in him when I allowed George to coax me into swimming with the stingrays on the Polynesian island of Moorea.

Heading out to an area where stingrays live, our motorboat crossed the lagoon that surrounds Moorea and went past upscale hotel cabins suspended on stilts above the water. From the boat we could look up at the sharp peaks of Moorea. The vistas were so beautiful that they did not look real; rather they looked like someone had painted them on a canvas in oils.

The motorboat eventually anchored off a little islet where the water was clear and we could see the sea bottom. The guide enticed the stingrays to come near our boat by throwing food for them into the water; the rays actually surrounded the boat. Many of our fellow passengers jumped right in. Of course, George was in the first group to jump into the water with the animals and to play with them. I figured this was my one and only opportunity. With help from the guide, I climbed in and tentatively put out my hand to pet a ray. The skin was not icky at all, just smooth and warm. I put out my hands—both hands this time—and petted "my" ray some more. I could hardly believe that I was frolicking with the stingrays and enjoying it.

Here is my cinquain, a five-line verse with a 2/4/6/8/2 syllable pattern, to celebrate my accomplishment:

> Stingray—
> I face my fear
> reach out to touch her skin
> make friends where once was groundless fear
> success!

Later, after a picnic on a nearby beach and before a return boat ride to *Amsterdam*, we took a relaxing swim. We had had a splendid day in the sun. I had done something I never thought I would have the courage to do. Perhaps that is what travel is all about—stretching ourselves beyond what we thought we could do.

Soon, very soon, too soon, George and I arrived home, back in the real world.

Chapter Twenty-Five
FINDING FRIENDS AND GOOD PEOPLE
2014–2016

Typically, travelers pick cruises based on itinerary. That is what George and I generally had done over the years. As we grew older and had been to so many places, the people with whom we traveled began to take precedence.

BIRTHDAYS WITH GOOD FRIENDS

You might recall that our friend Eileen had been wheeled off the *Prinsendam* when the ship was transiting the Panama Canal in the winter of 2013. By June of 2014, Eileen had recovered and was ready to sail again. In June, I wanted to do something special to celebrate George's ninety-second birthday. Why not take an easy cruise up to Canada's Maritime Provinces and New England? Phil and Eileen agreed; the four of us booked a round-trip, Boston-to-Boston cruise. We would not only celebrate George's birthday on June 16, but our wedding anniversary on June 15. Thus began a yearly ritual that continued for three years.

On board *Maasdam*, the four of us chose a dining table together and planned our activities in the ports of call. Part of our yearly tradition was lunch in a restaurant in Bar Harbor. We would climb the hill from the dock to get to Testa's, arrive early enough to snag a table that overlooked the harbor, and order lobster rolls. Each year the walk up to town from the port became tougher to do. Fortunately, there was a low wall halfway up the hill where we could sit before attempting our final approach. I have wonderful photos of the four of us sitting on that wall and then at our Bar Harbor table—photos taken in June of 2014, 2015, and 2016.

Each year when we reached Quebec, we always did the same thing. We walked the Lower Town together and then rode the elevator to the Upper Town. At the top, we would simply sit on a bench and look out over the St. Lawrence River. We might walk a little, especially when it was warm and sunny, but sitting on a bench and talking worked well for us. After all, that's what friends are for.

In other ports, we would vary our routine. One year when we were in Sydney, Nova Scotia, we took a ship's tour to Baddeck on Cape Breton Island to see the Alexander Graham Bell house and museum, which we found to be a lovely place to visit. Another year, we hired a car and driver to take us over the nearby mountain to admire the view and visit a school that taught Cape Breton young people the arts and crafts that are part of their heritage. Another year, we took the Big Pink Bus around the town of Sydney.

2016: George at age Ninety-four!

Each June 15, the four of us would go to the ship's specialty restaurant to celebrate George's and my anniversary. On June 16, I would order a birthday cake to be delivered to our assigned table in the dining room; the dining stewards would gather around the table and sing the Indonesian birthday song to George and then we would all sing *Happy Birthday*. We did that for the last time in 2016, when George turned ninety-four and we celebrated our forty-eighth anniversary.

I have a wonderful picture of a smiling George, dressed in his navy blue jacket, ready to dig into a piece of birthday cake. I took the photograph on June 16, 2016. I also have a picture from the same June cruise of a handsome and relaxed George sitting in the ship's lounge. That photograph today is on a plaque by the side of office 128 in George Hennings Hall at Kean University. The plaque announces that "From 1960 to 1987, George Hennings was a faculty member in the sciences. 128 Hennings Hall was his office for many of those years."

Before we disembarked in 2014, 2015, and 2016, we booked the same cruise for the following year. The cruise was a way to be together, for our friends are from Chicago and we from New Jersey. As I've mentioned, this cross-country friendship continues even today. Almost every month, Phil and I email one another.

MAKING FRIENDS THROUGH THE INTERNET

More and more cruisers are joining internet roll calls in anticipation of cruises they are going to take. I still do that at Cruisecritic.com by going to the section called "boards" and then clicking on the ship and cruise I am planning to take.

For example, when George and I booked an Atlantic Adventure Cruise in the fall of 2014, I posted our names on the roll call for that *MS Maasdam* cruise. By then, we were avid trivia players, so I advertised for teammates. I got four acceptances, which meant we had a team and potential friends before we had even boarded the ship. The six of us began to exchange emails and eventually sent pictures so we would recognize one another at the first trivia.

Sitting in a lounge aboard the ship on the first evening of the cruise, I spied a couple on their way to the dining room. "There are Ralph and Jean," I told George. Based on the photo they had emailed, I was certain it was the Reeds. I called out. They turned. And thus began our friendship.

This story of friendship on the high seas gets even better because Ralph and Jean are exceptional trivia players. With the help of the other two whom I found on the CC boards, we won the first cumulative trivia competition on the Atlantic Adventure Cruise. Our team was so good at trivia that the cruise director would not let us play as contestants on the second half of the cruise. "You have to give others a chance," Mark said. That was six years ago. Since then, I have taken other cruises with Jean and Ralph.

From the Atlantic Adventure Cruise, I have another marvelous memory—perhaps one of the best ever. Arriving in Arrecife in the Canary Islands, Jean, Ralph, George, and I booked a tour with a volcanic-activity theme. Called "The Island of Fire Mountain and Camel Ride," it was an

Camel ride. Photograph by Ralph Reed.

excursion made for us. The tour bus took us across landforms created through volcanic action less than 300 years ago; we saw weird, reddish rock outcroppings in every direction.

Eventually, our bus stopped beside a line of camels. They were "our" camels, and they were waiting for us. George and I shared a camel that had a sling-like contraption on its back that supported a little seat on each side. Jean and Ralph were ahead of us, sharing a camel as well. From their position, they could take a picture of George and me on our camel. It is one of my most cherished photographs taken on our travels.

When the camel drivers gave the word, the line of camels started up over the side of a volcanic cone from whence we could look out upon the unique landforms that blanketed the area. I recall that the camels wore muzzles. I figured that the metal cages they wore over their mouths prevented them from spitting at us, as camels are known to do, or even biting. I recall, too, that to my side of our camel, the camel driver tied a bag of rocks as a counterbalance to George's greater weight.

The camel ride was the part of our excursion that was the most fun. We did, however, stop at a place where hot volcanic matter is so close to the surface that the tour guide could throw potatoes into a pit in the earth and then later take them out roasted. We even saw vents where hot steam was billowing up from deep within the earth.

Returning to the ship, George and I recalled our excursion in Walvis Bay in Namibia in 2006, when we went to an area described as a moonscape. We agreed that our visit to Timanfaya National Park in the Canary Islands was even more exotic than the one to the moonscape. After all, in Namibia we did not ride a camel.

Recall that this all happened in 2014, a number of years ago. As I write this memoir, I am planning a cruise with Ralph and Jean for the end of 2021, if the virus abates. Isn't it amazing—to find friends at an internet chat site and for that friendship to last and last?

A BLACK SEA/ADRIATIC SEA CRUISE WITH FRIENDS

In the fall of 2015, George and I cruised the Adriatic Sea and returned also to the Black Sea for the third time. We were sailing with longtime friends Jim and Jessica and newer friends Mitzie and Don on a familiar ship: the *Prinsendam*. Captain Roberts was at the helm. There were some new ports on our itinerary, but not that many. We had chosen this cruise to be with friends. Here are highlights from four of our stops.

Albania—One Good Man: George and I wanted to go to Tirana, the capital of Albania, which is inland from the Adriatic port of Durres where *Prinsendam* made a stop on this voyage. It was a place we had not been before. A ship's excursion was the most secure option, because Tirana is rather far from the coast.

Both of us were impressed by what we saw on tour. On our way to Tirana, the bus drove us through small villages and pretty countryside. We saw no signs of the poverty that we had expected, given recent discord in the region.

Arriving in Tirana, we found a city with much more character and beauty than we had anticipated. An attractive main avenue has a broad, grassy, park-like center strip separating the traffic going each way. On the green is the obligatory statue of a national hero on horseback. At the top end is a modern-looking museum building; other attractive buildings line the avenue. We saw no clutter or rubbish as we had observed in other cities of the world.

Our guide led us through the National Historical Museum, where artifacts were attractively displayed, and then gave us time to wander. She told us we were going to walk to an art museum down along the avenue. George and I decided to start out ahead so we could walk there slowly. With directions from the guide as to where and when we were to meet, we started out. This is something we had learned to do, given that George was now, at ninety-three, on the far right of the curve age-wise.

We reached the art museum where we were to meet our group. We saw no benches, but near the museum was a small mosque. Wondering if we might find a place inside to sit and wait, George and I entered. "No. No," we heard. A man was calling to us and vigorously shaking his

362

head. He was wearing a flowing black robe; he was obviously someone in charge. "Closed. No enter," he repeated.

"Just to sit. Tired," I said pointing at both of us and pantomiming the act of sitting. That good man looked at us, understood, and took action. He set out two chairs from a stack in a corner, gestured for us to sit, and then turned on all the lights in the mosque. With lights aglow, the mosque was exquisite; it was a perfect little gem. We sat, looked around, and said our own prayer of thanksgiving. This was a beautiful moment to be treasured—the high point of our day in Tirana—all because of the thoughtful act of *one good man*.

Kusadasi—Another Good Man: Shopping is great fun in Kusadasi, a major tourist center on the Adriatic. When we stopped there in 2015, however, we encountered a problem. The *Prinsendam* was assigned a docking space that was the farthest from the terminal. Leaving the terminal, we had an even longer walk to the bazaar.

George and I took it slow and easy. Once in the bazaar, we sat on one of the couches conveniently located in the area between the shops. We bought some nice things—a few long-sleeved dress shirts and a pair of Prada shoes for George, a pair of gold hoop earrings for me. Slowly, we trudged back to the ship, stopping for a soda and for internet connection at a cafe that looks out on the statue of Ataturk high up on the hillside. Then we trudged among the many shops lining the way to the terminal. I saw the door that we had used to exit the terminal earlier. As I opened it, a uniformed official on the other side pointed and said, "No, you must walk up there and around and then around to get in." Up there seemed miles away.

"Oh my, George," I said, for at that point George was leaning heavily on his cane. Beseechingly, I looked the official in the eyes. "My husband is ninety-three," I pleaded, "He is exhausted. Can you please let us in this way? Please? Please?"

Here was another good man whose heart was filled with compassion and kindness. Checking the IDs around our necks, he waved us in. There were seats on the other side. We sat down to rest before making the final trek to *Prinsendam*.

Sochi—And a Good Couple: Entering the Black Sea, the *Prinsendam* took us back to Sochi, a Russian port near the site of the 2014 winter

Olympics. When we had passed the Olympic site in 2009, we had wondered how Russia could ever get the area up and running in just five years. We wanted to find out, and so George and I chose a tour that would take us back into the Caucasus Mountains.

We found that the roads were very much improved; the one-way roads controlled by a traffic signal were a thing of the past. We discovered, however, that we had misread the tour description. The tour took us not to the Olympic Village but to a nature reserve and a riverside village. Fortunately, the scenery was spectacular and the village picturesque.

When we had booked the tour, we had inquired if we could stay on the bus during the stop in the village rather than walking along the riverside to get to the restaurant for tea. The staff at the ship's tour desk had assured us that would not be a problem. Better yet, we had been told, the bus would take us right to the front door of the restaurant where we were to have tea.

Wrong! The driver insisted that we had to get off the bus and walk—there and back. George and I were game, and so we started off with our group. We lagged farther and farther behind, catching up only when the guide stopped to explain something en route. One of our fellow travelers saw that we were struggling. He and his wife walked along with us, chose a table in the restaurant with us, and even walked back to the bus with us. At our tea table, the man explained that he had been an industrial arts teacher; his wife had been a teacher, too. They were such friendly people, newly retired and beginning to see the world. We told them that we had been teachers and had been traveling the world together since 1969. Our disaster had turned into delight.

What good and observant people they were! Talking at supper that night with our friends, Mitzie and Don, we shared the events of our day. We all agreed that, in our travels, we had stumbled on some really compassionate people—Good Samaritans willing to go out of their way to help others.

Batumi, Georgia—with Good Friends: Was there a stunning high point in our cruise of the Black Sea? Absolutely so. Although we visited a number of interesting cities and towns along the north coast of Turkey, the best stop on the entire cruise was in Batumi, a seaside resort in the country of Georgia. There we wanted to try something different—something cultural—and so, with our friends, we attended an afternoon performance of the state dance company. We had been told that this was a "must see." It was. The costuming was splendid. The music was splendid. The dancing was splendid. The performance also provided background into the traditions of this country that we had never thought we would visit.

From our dining table that evening, George and I, Mitzie and Don looked out upon the promenade of Batumi where we had strolled in the morning before attending the dance performance. By nightfall, glittering lights along the shore had turned the seaside resort into a perfect paradise. We saw the ferris wheel illuminated in the far distance. Nearby, we saw the lighted windows of the hotels where wealthy Russians of the past had stayed when they had come to Georgia to catch some sunshine in the wintertime. I have a wonderful picture of the four of us at our dining table. We four friends—Friends Forever, as we called ourselves—are smiling, healthy, and happy to be together in this unforgettable Black Sea country so far away from home.

And now a thought about friends, Good Samaritans, and cruising:

> ah, the sites of the world are splendid to see
> and the things we bring back keep memories free
> but it's the dear friends, good people we meet
> who beckon us back, back "home" to the sea

friends forever.

Chapter Twenty-Six
RIDING INTO THE GREAT BEYOND
2016

In January 2016, George and I took an Amazon cruise with friends Mitzie and Don. My fondest memory from that warm-weather voyage is of George, Mitzie, and me on a small motorized canoe chugging up a tributary of the Amazon. Although he loved being deep in the world's largest rainforest, George was nervous. He worried about how safe our craft was.

In June 2016, we joined our friends Phil and Eileen for our annual New England/Canada cruise, adding a seven-day Bermuda extension. From that add-on, I remember George's climbing up a steep set of stairs to a lighthouse lookout, which was also the rest stop; the stairs were too much for me to attempt.

Both of us had always wondered when Holland America would again offer a trip departing from New York City. Such a voyage would be ideal for us. A limo would take us directly to the pier, and we would be in our cabin by noon—no flying and no pre-cruise, overnight stay in a hotel.

Arriving home after our June 2016 cruise, we discovered the trip we were looking for. On September 7, the *Zuiderdam* was leaving from NYC to go to Quebec and just twenty days later was to return. In retrospect, it was an extravagant expenditure; after all, we had recently come back from our annual New England/Canada birthday cruise, but then again, why not? Sea air, fine food, good care. And so we booked.

BOARDING *ZUIDERDAM*

Rob, our driver, picked us up early on September 7. He loaded our luggage into the trunk of his limo, along with the motorized scooter that George had bought in preparation for this cruise and future ones we had booked. There is generally a lot of walking on a cruise if one takes advantage of all the sightseeing opportunities available. We had become more keenly aware of that on our fall 2015 Black Sea adventure when George had begun to have trouble walking long distances.

Searching the internet, we had learned of a unique, lithium battery-powered scooter that folded into a small, compact unit. It weighed under sixty pounds so that a strong man could lift it into a car. George had been practicing driving his scooter around our house and opening and closing it with the key fob that came with it. More manufacturers are producing this kind of vehicle today than back in 2016; now, numbers of disabled and older people are using them on cruises.

Rob offloaded George's scooter onto the sidewalk in front of the 59th Street pier in New York City. George opened it with the fob, and off he drove into the terminal. Checking in was easy; after we had shown our passports and tickets, an agent escorted us to the VIP lounge, where we waited. We were given the VIP treatment because we had amassed so many sailing days with Holland America Line—by then, well over a thousand days, or about three years in total for each of us.

What happened next made that day very special. Sitting in the lounge, George looked up and on the wall saw a huge painting of the old *Queen Elizabeth*. He pointed and exclaimed, "That's my ship, Sweetheart! Take my picture."

The painting really was of George's ship, the *Queen* on which he had sailed to Europe during the Second World War. I did what George wanted: I took his picture.

Someone seated near us offered to snap another one of both of us in front of the painting. I love those photographs. George looked so nifty in what had become his cruising outfit: an orange baseball cap with the HAL logo and a jacket with an embroidery of the Taj Mahal on the front. While we waited to board, George told the kind man who had just taken our picture about his "first cruise"—to war on the *Queen*.

Dorothy and George with "The Queen".

ON THE SHIP NORTH

Once on the *Zuiderdam,* we settled in: We unpacked and then went to the shore excursion desk to book tickets to an extravaganza—a stage show we would attend and enjoy at our stop in Saguenay, Canada. Getting used to driving his scooter, George zipped along the decks from one end of the ship to the other. We had a large table for the two of us in the dining room; we could sit side by side looking out across the Atlantic as we sailed north. In the evenings on *Zuiderdam,* we saw some great shows. Fortunately, we ran into some old trivia partners with whom we teamed. From time to time, we actually won.

Because Bar Harbor is a tender port, when we arrived there, George and I stayed on the ship, went swimming in the main pool, and relaxed on our verandah. In Halifax, George drove his scooter down the ramp into the terminal and then out onto the boardwalk. Once outside, I told him to ride toward me as I videotaped him driving his scooter. He was really having a ball "playing" with his new toy: When he got near me, he smiled his warmest smile, waved, and scootered in the direction from which he had come. He was performing for the camera.

On the pier in Sydney, Nova Scotia, we wandered the aisles of the craft market, George on his fun scooter and I on my feet. We did the same in the ports to follow. We both felt that we had won the jackpot because the scooter was accomplishing what we had hoped it would: George could get around without a problem.

Toward the end of the first segment, as is customary on Holland America cruises, the ship scheduled the Mariner reception where those who had cruised many days with HAL were recognized. George and I stood up to have our picture taken with the captain and the hotel director; we had the greatest number of travel days with HAL of any passengers on the voyage. We found a copy of that photograph on our bed the next night. It is such a good picture that I have it mounted on my photo board in the dining room with my other favorite travel photos.

Arriving at the turnaround point in the cruise—the halfway mark—we chose to stay on the ship. Quebec is a big city with curbs to navigate and lots of traffic. Safer to stay on board, we thought. What we did was go to the enclosed hot pool and relax. Steam was wafting gently from the pool, no one else was there, and we rather enjoyed floating peacefully in it, especially since we were using a free coupon for entry rather than paying a surcharge.

ON THE SHIP SOUTH

Two nights later, I awoke to hear George coughing. His cough had a strange, raspy sound. I called the medical emergency number and shortly a nurse arrived. She took George's temperature and reported that it was a little elevated. She gave George some Tylenol and told us to see the doctor in the morning. "Nothing to worry about," she said. In the morning the doctor set up a drip with an antibiotic; after the intravenous infusion was finished, the doctor sent us back to our cabin. George was quarantined until the next morning when we returned to the medical center. His temperature down, George was released from quarantine just in time for us to zip into the main dining room for breakfast.

That morning, *Zuiderdam* had docked again in Sydney. My George was feeling so much better that, just before noon, I ran off the ship to download email on the pier. I warned him, before I left, not to get out of his chair while I was gone.

But disaster struck while I was away; George had tried to stand up, but his legs had collapsed from weakness. I found him on the floor. Because he could not get up on his own, I called the cabin stewards, who helped him into the chair in front of the window, where he could regain his strength and watch the action on the pier.

A little after three in the afternoon, George said he was going to the bathroom. Fearful he might again fall from weakness, I held tightly onto him. But once in the bathroom, he went limp in my arms; even more frighteningly, he did not respond when I spoke to him.

Oh, no! What was wrong with him? I just held onto my sweetheart for dear life. Fortunately, we had a handicapped cabin with an emergency alert chain in the bathroom. I pulled and pulled. Our phone rang in response, but there was no way that I could go to answer it. I just held onto George and kept pulling the alert cord. I knew someone would come, because I heard the announcement—code blue, code blue, code blue, and then our cabin number—over the PA. *Code blue* meant help was needed immediately in our cabin.

An emergency team responded. They lifted George onto the bed. By then, the ship's doctor and a nurse had come. The doctor decided George must go to the hospital, where he could get more intensive treatment than on the ship. The emergency team took him in a wheelchair to the medical center and got him ready to leave. Five crew members came to our cabin to help me gather our things. Within twenty minutes, I was all packed up.

I started down the corridor, followed by stewards carrying our luggage. Then I stopped short. I had forgotten George's scooter. I ran back, hopped on it, and drove it to the gangway and down—even though I had never driven it before. On the pier was an ambulance with lights flashing. Crewmen loaded our luggage into the ambulance while I stood nervously on the pier and waited for my sweetheart. And then he was there—on a stretcher. Thankfully, he was awake; he even smiled his dear smile at me. The crewmen put George in the back, I rode up front, and

In Halifax, going north, September 17.

then we were off—with sirens blaring. All this happened quickly, for the ship had to sail at four o'clock because of the tides.

OFF THE SHIP

It is difficult for me to think back to the nearly seven days we spent together in the emergency ward of the hospital. Because no intensive care rooms were available, we had to stay in a cubicle separated from the central nurses' section by only a curtain. The first night we were there, a really thoughtful nurse introduced me to a young woman whose mother was in a cubicle across from ours. The young woman, Karen, was coming each night to stay with Ella, her sick mom. Now, Karen also came to keep me company. Actually, I met Ella and her entire family: Ella's husband Mike, her three sisters, and a few others, too. They became my support group. Thank goodness we were in English-speaking Canada. Thank goodness for Karen and Mike.

When George had arrived at the hospital, he had been lucid and had been able to answer the questions that the admitting nurse had asked him. The diagnosis on his chart from the ship was pneumonia. I immediately began to make arrangements for private medical transport to get us home, also calling our doctor in New Jersey to secure a room in a local hospital upon our arrival.

But within two days, George was no longer alert: On oxygen, he just lay there, unable to talk to me at all. He seemed to be getting weaker and weaker. And I kept getting more and more frightened and distraught. I sat by his side and told him over and over, "Get better, Sweetheart. Get better for me."

The first doctor who treated George rarely came to check on him. He never had time to talk to me. By the sixth day, I gave up on him and demanded that another doctor be assigned to us. The new doctor came immediately, checked George, and then began to explain what was happening: George's original pneumonia had led to sepsis, and his body was shutting down as the powerful infection ran through his entire system. The doctor told me that George's brain was functioning at only 20 percent capacity; the same was true of his other vital organs. No, my sweetheart would not get better.

I was absolutely devastated. Weeping, but knowing that there was nothing else I could do and that George had already signed a similar directive at home, I completed the no-resuscitation papers required in Canada, and we moved together into palliative care.

Surrounded by our luggage, heartbroken, in shock, I felt so alone and so far away from home. As I sat by George's bedside—with my hand touching and rubbing the warm skin of his arm—my new young friend Karen walked into our room. She wrote her telephone number on a chalkboard on the wall and told me to call if I needed help.

That night, lying next to George in the king-sized bed in our darkened, palliative-care room, I felt his body jerk. Then, he lay perfectly still. When I pushed the call button, the nurses came running and confirmed my worst fear. My dearest, dearest sweetheart was gone—gone on his final journey into the great beyond.

Realizing I needed someone, the nurses saw Karen's telephone number on the chalkboard and phoned her at her father's home where she was staying while her mom was in the hospital.

She came. Yes, Karen came in the middle of the night. I will always remember the cold of her coat against my cheek as she hugged me close. She spoke to the nurses, named the funeral home to which George should be taken, and piled me and all of our luggage into her car. Then she drove me to her father's house.

At Mike's home, Karen gave me a cup of tea and put me in her bed; she herself bunked on the living room couch. The next morning, Mike drove me to the funeral home. He literally took over and made the arrangements. We could pick up George's ashes in two days. Could life get any worse than this?

I had to downsize our luggage, because I was flying home. Providentially, George's three pairs of shoes—one the Prada we had just purchased in Turkey—fit Mike. So did George's two pairs of trousers from Hong Kong, each with its leather belt that we had bought in an exotic, far-off land. And so did George's jeans and black jacket with the Taj Mahal embroidery. I gave them all to this dear, compassionate man who had left his wife's side at the hospital to help me. These wonderful people would not let me go to a hotel. They said I must stay with them while I waited for word from the funeral home.

Two days later, dressed in George's Taj Mahal jacket, his jeans, and his shoes, Mike drove me to the Sydney airport. Karen helped me check in and then took me to security. I rode George's scooter through the checkpoint and then onto the tarmac. There I closed the scooter, removed its battery, and saw it stowed beneath the plane. How I did this I do not know.

Before she left me, Karen gave me a last hug. A devout Catholic who puts her faith into action every day, she said, "You'll be OK. You have an angel up in heaven now, taking care of you."

With tears running down my cheeks, I answered, "Karen, I have had two angels right here on earth looking after me." Even now, years later, Karen and her father continue to email me to see how I am making out on my own. In 2019, Mike emailed me to let me know that he had lost his Ella, too.

I love these two dear Cape Bretoners; they held me together at the lowest point of my life.

GOING HOME

I had to change planes in Halifax, and of course, when I was aching to be home, my plane to Newark was delayed by four hours. Waiting in an airport restaurant, I ordered a Coke to keep me going. As I sat at a table alone, I opened an email from James Gurland of the Kean Foundation. He had sent me a eulogy about George that was being circulated among the faculty at the university, the school where we had taught and where George always said he had found me. The eulogy was so truly beautiful that I burst into tears, right there in the airport restaurant. A waitress hurried over. I explained that I had just lost my husband. When eventually my flight was called, I gestured to the waitress for the check. She came over, patted me on the back, and said that there was no charge for the soda; it was a gift. She told me to get home safely.

I managed to scooter to my plane, pop the lithium battery out of the vehicle, and give the scooter to the steward to stow in the cargo hold. The plane ride home was interminable. Then after landing, I had to wait while someone retrieved George's scooter. I drove it up the ramp at Newark Liberty, heading toward the baggage claim.

I could not believe it. There at the top of the ramp was a good man, Spencer Scott, a family friend. He had been waiting for me for four hours. Near collapse, I hugged him, so thankful to be with someone I knew.

All I can say is something I have said already: The world is full of good, compassionate people who put others' needs often ahead of their own. These people are the angels of the earth. I have been fortunate to have found them in my times of need.

RECOVERING

On the plane homeward bound, I had closed my eyes and pleaded with George in my head: "I will never go on a ship again. I will never go on a plane again. Just help me get home, George. Just help me get there."

At home, I began to look back upon the wonderful life that George and I had enjoyed *together*, the wonderful people we had met *together*, the wonderful places we had visited *together*. . . I resolved to meet the challenges that life would continue to throw at me; I resolved to keep traveling. That is what my George would have wanted me to do.

On my iPad, I have a beautiful video of my sweetheart riding his scooter on the boardwalk in Halifax two weeks before he passed. Watching it again and again, I see George come toward me, smile, wave, and then, figuratively speaking, "ride away into the sunset." He was splendidly happy that day in Halifax. He was doing what he most enjoyed—wandering the world with me.

Top photo: 1970, bottom photo: 2000.

ACKNOWLEDGEMENTS

I often think how very fortunate I was to have had a husband who loved to explore the world and who traveled with his eyes wide open to the beauty of Planet Earth and the wonders that humankind has created. If we had not married, I would not have memories of so many years of travel. Without him as my constant companion on land and sea, there would have been far fewer wanderings for me, especially to faraway places. And, of course, there would have been no book, *Wandering the World with George.* Thank you, dear one, for opening windows to the world with me. As the song says, "Thanks for the memories."

When George died, my friend Elizabeth Frair shared with me a verse from the book of *Proverbs*—"The memory of a good man will be a blessing." I surely have been blessed.

I have also been favored with friends who encouraged me to travel with them after my loss.

I thank Phil and his wife Eileen. With these dear people, I dared to "journey on when hope was gone." With them I took a round-trip transit through the Panama Canal in January 2017. On that first, terribly tough, tear-filled trip without George, the Hoffmans insisted that I dine and tour with them. I mourned with Phil when, in 2019, he lost his beloved Eileen.

I thank my dear travel companion Mitzie, with whom I cruised in March 2017. She had lost her Darling Don (that was her name for him) just three months after I lost my George. And so we consoled each other as we sailed together across the Pacific to revisit the islands of Polynesia, reminiscing about cruises the four of us had enjoyed. Since then, she and I have sailed along the west coast of Mexico to Peru and twice have taken the Voyage-of-the-Vikings cruise. Thank you, Mitzie, for being my friend forever.

I thank my friends, the Smiths—Jim and Jessica. I sailed with them on a round-the-world cruise and on a series of back-to-backs in Europe in 2018. Jim's emails have brought me a bit of joy as I adjusted to my life alone. Often the emails have included haikus—and they still do.

Following his model, I learned to express my thoughts and feelings in poetry—a great form of release during the days of the "dastardly demon," an expression Jim coined as he wrote about COVID-19.

I thank also my many other travel companions:

- my cousin Evelyn and her daughter Jan Ellen, with whom I sailed to Alaska in 2017.
- the Krteks, who—starting in 2017— kept showing up on my cruises without telling me they were sailing: "Surprise, surprise!" Angela would say, "We have come to be with you."
- Marcia and Terry, with whom I dined for 128 days on World '18: I shall never forget Terry Saunders running ahead to secure seats for all of us in the theater for the evening show—what a dear man.
- the Johnsons, who invited me to dine with their family on a fourteen-day cruise of Europe in 2018, after we had been together on World '18.
- my neighbor Beverly, who stepped in at the last moment in 2018 to take a trip with me when she knew I would have been alone.
- the Reeds, who were companions on one of the VOV cruises I took with Mitzie, who included me on tours they were booking independently, who teamed with me for trivia in 2019, and with whom I now exchange emails almost daily.

All of these friends helped me look forward with hope, so that I could look back upon my travels and write *Wandering the World with George*.

I also want to thank those at home who helped me cope with my loss and, in doing so, brought me to the point where I could write my travel memoir.

First is my faithful friend Jenny Yu. During the time of the dastardly demon, we would often talk on the phone in the evenings. She would share her thoughts and listen to my ramblings. And several times a week, when outside dining was permitted in the community where we both live, she and I would eat together—often bundled up in our woolies as a protection against the cold. Thank you, dear friend.

My cousin Evelyn maintained contact, telephoning every weekend from her home in Minnesota, checking that all was well with me, especially after my sister's death in 2019 and the onset of COVID-19 in 2020. Recently, she taught me the advantages of Zoom so we could see one another. As she says at the end of her weekly calls, "Love you, cousin!"

Bill and Sandra Stevens have been a constant support, starting from the time Bill drove me to the county courthouse to probate George's will. When I call with questions, he always provides thoughtful counsel. A heartfelt thank you.

James Gurland of the Kean development office helped me through the worst of the isolation dictated by COVID-19. His nightly telephone calls brought me cheer when I most needed it. His support when my sister died is something I will never forget. Thank you, James; you are a good friend when things get tough.

And then there is the rest of the team at Kean University, where George and I taught together for so many years:

- Dr. Dawood Farahi, past president of Kean University: It was he who made the suggestion to name a science research facility at Kean in honor of my husband. If still alive, George would join me in saying a heartfelt thank you.

- Dr. Lamont Repollet, president of Kean University: It was he who decided that a university of Kean's stature should field a press that has, as its mission, the publication of books and treatises by writers who are associated with the school in some way or who share its vision. It was he who decided that my book would be the first major publication of the Kean University Press. Thank you, Dr. Repollet.

- Karen Smith, vice president of University Relations at Kean: It was she who led the production effort. Efficiently, she shepherded *Wandering the World with George* from manuscript to book format. Many thanks.

- Joseph Moran, creative director at Kean University: Joey developed the final design for *Wandering the World with George*. It was he who laid out the pages so that the text flowed smoothly from page to page and from chapter to chapter. It was he who integrated the photographs into the text so that the words and pictures melded together. Joey was so willing to work with me to arrive at a final design that made me happy. You are a pro, Joey. You made a difference. Bravo!

- Beth Fand Incollingo, copy editor: Beth was the perfect person to work on my manuscript. Whereas I am a bit sloppy with detail, she is a researcher to her very core. Beth looked up every date, name, and fact for accuracy. She double checked my questionable spellings, and she added the necessary commas I had failed to insert. She helped me find the precise word needed in a sentence, and she pushed me to rewrite and explain more fully. Beth, I thank you so very much. My book is much stronger as a result of your skill and dedication.

Marcel Proust tells us, "The real voyage of discovery consists not in seeking new landscapes, but in having new eyes." Writing my travel memoir has been my voyage of discovery; rethinking the trips I took with George forced me to look at Planet Earth with new eyes. I truly hope that my book does the same for readers, encouraging them to explore the earth around them to the fullest and to view the world with eyes wide open.

DOROTHY GRANT HENNINGS

Dorothy Grant Hennings, Distinguished Professor Emerita, Kean University, taught language arts in the Department of Instruction, Curriculum, and Administration until her retirement in 2002. Throughout her career, Dr. Hennings authored fifty textbooks for teachers and children with prominent publishers such as Houghton Mifflin, Prentice Hall, Harper Row, and Scholastic Press. She was s sought-after speaker and over the years spoke to audiences in twenty-five states. She received the Outstanding Teacher Educator in Reading Award from the International Reading Association in 1992 and the Distinguished Service Award from the New Jersey Reading Association in 1993. Over the years, she was listed in *Who's Who in America* as well as in *Who's Who in Education* and *Who's Who of American Women*.

After receiving degrees from Barnard College, the University of Virginia, and Columbia University, and after teaching science and English in New Jersey public schools, Dorothy Hennings arrived at Kean as a professor in the School of Education in 1964. She met George Hennings in his laboratory when she stopped by to borrow some lab equipment. The two were married in 1968, linked by a love of education, a dedication to the development of skilled teachers, and a love of travel.

Dr. Dorothy Hennings served on the Kean University Foundation Board from 2005 to 2015. In 2010 she received an Honorary Doctorate in Humane Letters from Kean. In 2013, she and her husband were honorees at the Kean University Gala, where they were awarded the first William Livingston Award for excellence in education and philanthropy. Today, the building at Kean that is home to the College of Education is named Dorothy Grant Hennings Hall and the College of Science, Mathematics and Technology is named for Dorothy and George Hennings.

The author in Bali, 2018.

George and Dorothy in Kusadasi, 1975.